T0094147

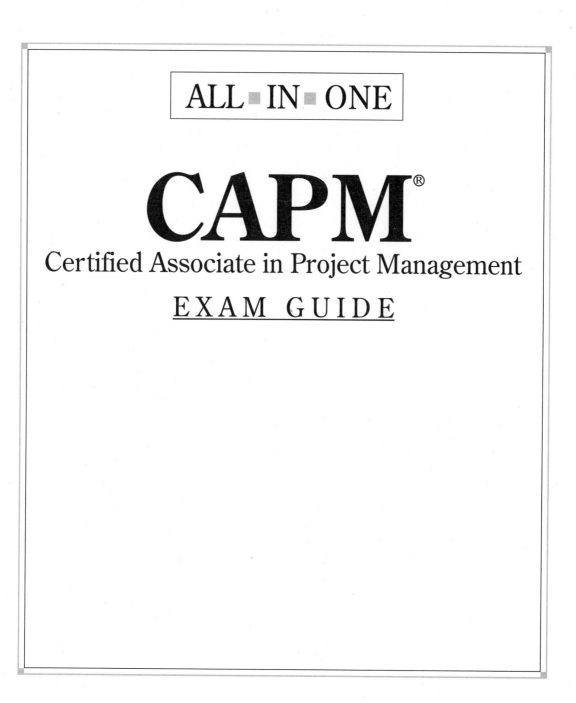

ALL·IN·ONE

CAPM®

Certified Associate in Project Management

EXAM GUIDE

ALL·IN·ONE

CAPM®
Certified Associate in Project Management
EXAM GUIDE

James Lee Haner

New York   Chicago   San Francisco
Athens   London   Madrid   Mexico City
Milan   New Delhi   Singapore   Sydney   Toronto

McGraw Hill books are available at special quantity discounts to use as premiums and sales promotions, or for use in corporate training programs. To contact a representative, please visit the Contact Us pages at www.mhprofessional.com.

CAPM® Certified Associate in Project Management All-in-One Exam Guide

1 2 3 4 5 6 7 8 9   LCR   28 27 26 25 24 23

Library of Congress Control Number: 2023940665

ISBN: Book p/n 978-1-260-46757-4 and insert p/n 978-1-260-46758-1
of set 978-1-260-46759-8

MHID: Book p/n 1-260-46757-0 and insert p/n 1-260-46758-9
of set 1-260-46759-7

Sponsoring Editor
Wendy Rinaldi

Project Manager
Nitesh Sharma,
    KnowledgeWorks Global Ltd.

Acquisitions Coordinator
Caitlin Cromley-Linn

Technical Editor
Daral Woerle

Proofreader
Lisa McCoy

Indexer
Claire Splan

Production Supervisor
Thomas Somers

Composition
KnowledgeWorks Global Ltd.

Illustration
KnowledgeWorks Global Ltd.

Art Director, Cover
Jeff Weeks

*To Colleen McAllister, my lovely wife. I promise,
"I will write no more books—forever."
My "hobby" is DoR and DoD . . . ready and done.*

*And to Cate McCoy, colleague and comrade.
Even while battling a serious illness,
you were always there to inspire me
and make me a better writer.*

ABOUT THE AUTHOR

Dr. James Lee Haner is the CEO of UBR Consulting, specializing in "Building Better Businesses." James's certifications include

- PMI: CAPM, PMP, PgMP, PMI-ACP, PMI-RMP, PMI-SP
- IIBA: CBAP, CCBA, ECBA
- ScrumAlliance: CSM, CSPO

Dr. Haner's management and leadership roles have included establishing a corporate web presence, creating a successful organization-wide employee development plan, and developing the IT infrastructure for a start-up company. With a PhD in adult education, James brings more than three decades of dynamic experience as a distinguished college professor; award-winning author of books, articles, and blogs; and successful management and leadership consultant to each learning experience.

As an author, James has written *CAPM Certified Associate Project Manager All-in-One Exam Guide, PMP Project Management Professional Practice Exams*, and *Your Golden Ticket to the 2021 PMP Exam: Complete Coverage of the Newest Exam Content Outline and the New Question Types*, and is co-author of *CAPM Certified Associate in Project Management Practice Exams*. In addition, he is a contributing author to *140 Project Management Tips in 140 Words or Less; Making Sense of Sustainability Project Management; PMP: Practice Makes Perfect; Program Management: A Life Cycle Approach*; and *Sample Exam Questions: PMI Project Management Professional (PMP), Fifth Edition*; and was technical editor of *PMI-ACP Agile Certified Practitioner All-in-One Exam Guide*.

He is a member of the Project Management Institute (PMI) and the International Institute for Business Analysis (IIBA). James has won the Dale Carnegie Course "Highest Achievement Award." He earned the Vietnam Service Medal while serving in the U.S. Air Force.

About the Technical Editor

Daral A. Woerle, Esquire, PMP, is a graduate of Pennsylvania State University. He served on active duty in the U.S. Army for eight years before obtaining a law degree. He has been providing leadership and consulting services for over 35 years. Currently, Daral serves as the president of PinnaclePM, a management consulting company focusing on providing project management, process improvement, and training services to a broad range of organizations, government entities, and businesses, from small startups to Fortune 100 companies.

Daral's experience comprises working with all levels of management and technical staff, from senior leadership to support and functional teams. Some of his projects have included establishing project management offices for numerous clients, developing the requirements for a contract management system to oversee the implementation of a $50-million-a-year Navy fighter aircraft training program, creating a business-process-improvement framework for the United Nations' Capacity Development Operational Training Service (CDOTS), and the implementation of a matter-management system for the United Nations' Office of Legal Affairs (OLA), which comprises over 125 practicing attorneys from around the world.

Daral has earned both the PMI Project Management Professional (PMP) certification and Prince2 Practitioner certification and is an authorized PMP prep course instructor, with experience teaching this topic to both in-person and remote students. As an instructor for Learning Tree International for over 17 years, he has taught dozens of courses to thousands of students both here and abroad. In addition, he has developed and taught numerous courses on a variety of topics for companies, government entities, and educational institutions. Some of these courses are part of Penn State's Project Management Certification program.

CONTENTS AT A GLANCE

CONTENTS

Part II CAPM Testing Areas

FOREWORD

What's so special about this book? The meticulous mapping of the CAPM Examination Content Outline (2023 Exam Update) and the multiple books on the Reference List (RL), that's what!

All the major sections in Chapters 3 through 6 begin with a cross-reference to the corresponding domain, task, and, where applicable, enabler in the ECO.

Every chapter provides thorough coverage of the chapter, section, and/or figure references as specified in all the RL books. The *CAPM All-in-One* team has done all the navigation work for you! Now, you can focus your study time because you know exactly where the questions on the CAPM exam will come from. And likely some of the answers, too.

This book is a comprehensive study guide for the CAPM exam. It clearly and concisely covers all the topics you'll encounter on the exam. The book also includes practice questions, flash cards, word puzzles, and a bonus "50 Confusing Terms on the CAPM Exam" appendix to help you assess your understanding of the material.

This book is a must-have if you are serious about passing the CAPM exam. It will provide you with the knowledge you need for exam success, and it serves as an essential on-the-job reference in your project management career.

James is passionate about helping others learn about project management and is committed to providing you with the best possible preparation for the CAPM exam.

If you have any questions about this book's material, don't hesitate to contact the author. He is happy to help you in any way he can.

I wish you all the best in your CAPM certification journey!

Joseph Philips, PMP, PMI-ACP, ITIL, Project+, CTT+
Director of Education for Instructing.com, LLC

ACKNOWLEDGMENTS

At McGraw Hill, I thank Wendy Rinaldi, PMP, who has now "put up with me" for three books. You've always listened to my "great" ideas and have never been afraid to tell me, "No, stick to the format." Also at McGraw Hill, I thank Caitlin Cromley-Linn, who patiently helped me to get the numbering for the figures and tables and the page formatting right—chapter by chapter. And at KGL, thanks to Nitesh Sharma, the PM, who "strongly" encouraged me to meet all the due dates . . . every time, on time.

And I owe thanks to my T-E-A-M. I relied on your collaboration and support. Your recommendations and conversations helped to guide my writing process and make this book informative and engaging for the readers. Your real-world examples and encouraging feedback improved my work. In particular, I thank you for the following contributions: Cate McCoy, CAPM, PMP, PMI-PBA, for your honest appraisal of all the words and ideas in this book: "It's beautiful, leave it in. It's corny, take it out." Cindy Woolston, (CAPM, 2023), for the herculean effort of developing the flash cards. Dan Cohen, PMP, for being a relentless consistency checker and making this book a "teacher's book" by creating diagrams, word puzzles, and a memory card. Daral Woerle, PMP, the technical editor (as well as a lawyer and former Army officer), for ensuring all the words mean what they are supposed to mean and keeping me focused on *semper procedo* during our seven-month mission. Gabor Stramb, PMP, for laboriously mapping the CAPM ECO to the reference books. Greta Blash, PgMP, PMP, PMI-PBA, PMI-ACP, and Steve Blash, PMP, PMI-ACP, DASSM, for selflessly, tirelessly, and respectfully reviewing and contributing to the detailed content and definitions. John Newton Moore, PMP, PRINCE2, ICP-APM, A-CSD—who else could I go to for the British perspective? You are truly, predictively, adaptively agile. Lee R. Lambert, PMP, "A Founder of the PMP," for your personal guidance on this book. Oliver F. Lehmann, MSc, ACE, PMP, author-practitioner, for your advice and insight into Project Business. Peter Dillon-Parkin, BCS-CPBA, ISTQB-CT, "Mr. BA"—the figures and diagrams in Chapter 6 are alive and meaningful because of you.

Thank you to the thousands of folks who have attended my PMI boot camps over the last 19 years. Your questions, comments, and critiques have helped me author a better book.

INTRODUCTION

This book is intended not only to help aspiring candidates pass the Certified Associate in Project Management (CAPM) exam but also to help working project managers apply the latest project management best practices to their projects.

If you're looking for a definitive book on how to pass your CAPM certification exam, this is the book for you. It will clearly, quickly, and fully explain how to pass your certification exam the first time. Then you can get back to your life. PMI exams aren't fun, and I'm certain you have more important things to do than spend more time than necessary to pass an exam.

Here's what this book will do for you as a CAPM candidate:

- Clarify the CAPM exam objectives in detail.
- Help you to focus your efforts only on exam objectives.
- Advise you how to pass the CAPM exam—not just take the exam.
- Offer you "roadmaps" for each chapter's content.
- Give you more than 450 practice questions in the book and in the TotalTester test engine.

With three major sections, Part I provides a broad overview of project management and how it pertains to the CAPM exam.

- Chapter 1, "Working as a Project Manager," discusses the complete role of the project manager and how the project manager leads and manages the project team and stakeholders. It's a meaty chapter.
- Chapter 2, "Managing a Project in Different Environments," discusses the environment where projects happen. The project life cycle describes the phases a project moves through from start to completion.

Part II contains Chapters 3 through 6, which correspond to the CAPM Examination Content Outline (2023 Exam Update). Chapter 7 covers the PMI Code of Ethics and Professional Conduct.

- Chapter 3, "Project Management Fundamentals and Core Concepts," covers project management fundamentals in both predictive and adaptive methodologies. These fundamentals provide the foundation of managing a project. This chapter prepares you to be tested on project life cycles and processes, project planning, and your understanding of project roles and responsibilities.

- Chapter 4, "Predictive, Plan-Based Methodologies," is a deeper dive into the predictive and adaptive approaches to project management. It'll help you to understand how each approach is used and when. It explores setting up controls to monitor the project as well as working with project schedules.

- Chapter 5, "Agile Frameworks/Methodologies," introduces agile and other adaptive development approaches (e.g., Scrum, Extreme Programming [XP], and others). You'll need to know how to plan project iterations, document project controls, and prioritize tasks, and this chapter will prepare you well.

- Chapter 6, "Business Analysis Frameworks," explores what a business analyst does and how they recommend appropriate communication channels and elicit and validate requirements.

- Chapter 7, "Understanding the Code of Ethics and Professional Conduct," doesn't correspond directly to the *PMBOK Guide*, but it correlates to the PMI Code of Ethics and Professional Conduct. I'll explain how you can answer ethics-related questions directly and accurately for your exam. Keep in mind that agreement to abide by the PMI Code of Ethics and Professional Conduct is required for CAPM candidates, and you could see several exam questions on ethics and on adhering to PMI's professional code.

Part III includes two appendixes and a glossary:

- Appendix A, "50 Confusing Terms on the CAPM Exam," defines these "confusers" and will be your guide on the CAPM exam when you encounter terminology that is potentially confusing or unclear. All terms are consistent with the CAPM Examination Content Outline (2023 Exam Update) and the books from the Reference List. See capm-references.pdf (pmi.org).

- Appendix B, "About the Online Content," discusses all of the online resources available for this book, including how to access the TotalTester practice exams, as well as all the downloadable files that will help you study for the exam.

- The glossary includes definitions of all the key terms that are covered in the chapters, and you should attempt to memorize and understand all of them.

How to Use This Book

This book contains all the information you need to to pass the CAPM exam, as well as some extra information about the profession of project management. Here is a guide to all the extra bits and pieces in the book:

- **Exam Tips** These elements give you direct tips for the exam.
- **In the Real World** These sidebars provide examples of the theory in action from my own experience. They are intended to add to your understanding of the concept being explained and to share with you some of the lessons I have learned throughout my career.

- **Notes**   These elements provide slightly more information about the topic being discussed.
- **CAPM ECO Mapping**   All the major sections in Chapters 3–6 begin with a cross-reference to the corresponding task and, where applicable, enabler in the ECO.
- **Review Questions and Answers**   At the end of each chapter, there are 20 multiple-choice questions that test your knowledge and understanding of the topics just covered, followed by an answers section with explanations.

Preparing for the CAPM Examination

If you are just beginning your CAPM quest, you should read Part I immediately, as it will help you build a solid foundation for your exam. If you already have a solid foundation in project management and need specific information on the domains, tasks, and enablers in the CAPM ECO, then move on to Part II. You'll find that Chapters 3 through 6 in this part each correspond structurally to the specific ECO exam domain that it covers, which will help you—gulp—pass the CAPM exam.

The book is designed so that you can read the chapters in any order you like. However, if you examine the *CAPM Reference List*, you'll notice that the order of information presented there is the same as the order of information in this book. In other words, you can refer to the *CAPM Reference List* and then read a more detailed explanation in this book. This book is a guide to the *PMBOK Guide, Seventh Edition* and the other reference books for the CAPM exam.

The CAPM exam will test you on your experience and knowledge in four domains, as Table 1 shows. Each domain task includes enablers; enablers are examples, not specific requirements, of how a project manager might accomplish the domain tasks.

 NOTE   The domain specifics and their related exam percentages are correct as of this writing. I strongly encourage you to double-check these specifics at www.pmi.org (look for the latest "CAPM Examination Content Outline" document). It's possible they've changed since this writing.

Domain 1	Project Management Fundamentals and Core Concepts – 36%
Task 1	Demonstrate an understanding of the various project life cycles and processes.

- Distinguish between a project, program, and a portfolio.
- Distinguish between a project and operations.
- Distinguish between predictive and adaptive approaches.
- Distinguish between issues, risks, assumptions, and constraints.
- Review/critique project scope.
- Apply the project management code of ethics to scenarios (refer to *PMI Code of Ethics and Professional Conduct*).
- Explain how a project can be a vehicle for change.

Table 1   Objectives for the CAPM Examination (2023 Exam Update) (*continued*)

Task 2	**Demonstrate an understanding of project management planning.**

- Describe the purpose and importance of cost, quality, risk, schedule, etc.
- Distinguish between the different deliverables of a project management plan versus product management plan.
- Distinguish differences between a milestone and a task duration.
- Determine the number and type of resources in a project.
- Use a risk register in a given situation.
- Use a stakeholder register in a given situation.
- Explain project closure and transitions.

Task 3	**Demonstrate an understanding of project roles and responsibilities.**

- Compare and contrast the roles and responsibilities of project managers and project sponsors.
- Compare and contrast the roles and responsibilities of the project team and the project sponsor.
- Explain the importance of the role the project manager plays (e.g., initiator, negotiator, listener, coach, working member, and facilitator).
- Explain the differences between leadership and management.
- Explain emotional intelligence (EQ) and its impact on project management.

Task 4	**Determine how to follow and execute planned strategies or frameworks (e.g., communication, risks, etc.).**

- Give examples of how it is appropriate to respond to a planned strategy or framework (e.g., communication, risk, etc.).
- Explain project initiation and benefit planning.

Task 5	**Demonstrate an understanding of common problem-solving tools and techniques.**

- Evaluate the effectiveness of a meeting.
- Explain the purpose of focus groups, standup meetings, brainstorming, etc.

Domain 2	**Predictive, Plan-Based Methodologies – 17%**
Task 1	**Explain when it is appropriate to use a predictive, plan-based approach.**

- Identify the suitability of a predictive, plan-based approach for the organizational structure (e.g., virtual, colocation, matrix structure, hierarchical, etc.).
- Determine the activities within each process.
- Give examples of typical activities within each process.
- Distinguish the differences between various project components.

Task 2	**Demonstrate an understanding of a project management plan schedule.**

- Apply critical path methods.
- Calculate schedule variance.
- Explain work breakdown structures (WBS).
- Explain work packages.
- Apply a quality management plan.
- Apply an integration management plan.

Table 1 Objectives for the CAPM Examination (2023 Exam Update)

Task 3	**Determine how to document project controls of predictive, plan- based projects.**

- Identify artifacts that are used in predictive, plan-based projects.
- Calculate cost and schedule variances.

Domain 3	**Agile Frameworks/Methodologies – 20%**
Task 1	**Explain when it is appropriate to use an adaptive approach.**

- Compare the pros and cons of adaptive and predictive, plan-based projects.
- Identify the suitability of adaptive approaches for the organizational structure (e.g., virtual, colocation, matrix structure, hierarchical, etc.).
- Identify organizational process assets and environmental factors that facilitate the use of adaptive approaches.

Task 2	**Determine how to plan project iterations.**

- Distinguish the logical units of iterations.
- Interpret the pros and cons of the iteration.
- Translate this WBS to an adaptive iteration.
- Determine inputs for scope.
- Explain the importance of adaptive project tracking versus predictive, plan-based tracking.

Task 3	**Determine how to document project controls for an adaptive project.**

- Identify artifacts that are used in adaptive projects.

Task 4	**Explain the components of an adaptive plan.**

- Distinguish between the components of different adaptive methodologies (e.g., Scrum, Extreme Programming (XP), Scaled Adaptive Framework (SAFe®), Kanban, etc.).

Task 5	**Determine how to prepare and execute task management steps.**

- Interpret success criteria of an adaptive project management task.
- Prioritize tasks in adaptive project management.

Domain 4	**Business Analysis Frameworks – 27%**
Task 1	**Demonstrate an understanding of business analysis (BA) roles and responsibilities.**

- Distinguish between stakeholder roles (e.g., process owner, process manager, product manager, product owner, etc.).
- Outline the need for roles and responsibilities (Why do you need to identify stakeholders in the first place?).
- Differentiate between internal and external roles.

Task 2	**Determine how to conduct stakeholder communication.**

- Recommend the most appropriate communication channel/tool (e.g., reporting, presentation, etc.).
- Demonstrate why communication is important for a business analyst between various teams (features, requirements, etc.).

Table 1 Objectives for the CAPM Examination (2023 Exam Update) (*continued*)

Task 3	**Determine how to gather requirements.**
	• Match tools to scenarios (e.g., user stories, use cases, etc.).
	• Identify the requirements gathering approach for a situation (e.g., conduct stakeholder interviews, surveys, workshops, lessons learned, etc.).
	• Explain a requirements traceability matrix/product backlog.
Task 4	**Demonstrate an understanding of product roadmaps.**
	• Explain the application of a product roadmap.
	• Determine which components go to which releases.
Task 5	**Determine how project methodologies influence business analysis processes.**
	• Determine the role of a business analyst in adaptive and/or predictive, plan-based approaches.
Task 6	**Validate requirements through product delivery.**
	• Define acceptance criteria (the action of defining changes based on the situation).
	• Determine if a project/product is ready for delivery based on a requirements traceability matrix/product backlog.

Table 1   Objectives for the CAPM Examination (2023 Exam Update)

 EXAM TIP   Domain 2, "Predictive, Plan-Based Methodologies" and Domain 3, "Agile Frameworks/Methodologies" questions will be mingled across the four domains and not limited to any domain or task in the CAPM ECO.

About the CAPM Exam

PMI provides to you, for free, the *PMI Certifications Handbook* through its website, https://www.pmi.org/-/media/pmi/documents/public/pdf/certifications/project-management-professional-handbook.pdf?rev=14b861fa3f614fd8869bb55f65bd7077. I highly recommend that you download and read this short book as you prepare to pass the CAPM exam. This is the source for all things related to the exam: costs, application requirements, exam content, and policies.

New Question Types

The CAPM exam consists of 150 questions, which are a mix of multiple-choice, drag-and-drop, and animation/comic strip format. The exam may also include point-and-click (hot spot/hot area) questions. Have a look at the CAPM ECO, available at https://www.pmi.org/-/media/pmi/documents/public/pdf/certifications/capm20ecofinal.pdf, for examples and details about the new question types.

Passing the CAPM Exam

This is a pass-fail exam, and PMI does not reveal the passing score. The scoring model for the test is based on four categories: Needs Improvement, Below Target, Target, and

Above Target. At the end of your exam, you'll see where you land on this scale for the entire exam and a breakdown of your proficiency in each exam domain. Strive to be on Target or Above Target to pass the test.

I know, that's not much information to go on when it comes to preparing or quantifying an exam score, but that's all that PMI tells us. In my classes, and now in this book, my advice is to aim to score 80 percent or better for your practice exams and quizzes. In my experience, people who consistently score at an 80 percent mark or better are 90 percent sure to pass the CAPM exam.

CAUTION   CAPM candidates are limited to three exam attempts within one year. If you fail three times within one year, you'll have to wait one year after the third exam attempt before resubmitting your exam application again. Focus on passing your exam the first time.

Let's face the facts: Studying to pass the CAPM exam is arduous work. In the CAPM Reference List, PMI lists several of its own publications as references that candidates may find helpful to review: *A Guide to the Project Management Body of Knowledge, Seventh Edition* (commonly called the *PMBOK Guide*), *Agile Practice Guide*, *Business Analysis for Practitioners: A Practice Guide*, *The PMI Guide to Business Analysis*, *PMIstandards+*, and *Process Groups: A Practice Guide*.

The January 2023 Reference List also lists two non-PMI books: *Effective Project Management: Traditional, Agile, Extreme, Hybrid* by Robert K. Wysocki and *Project Management Answer Book, Second Edition* by Jeff Furman. Both books are written from a "practitioner" point of view and will help you pass your CAPM exam.

NOTE   The *PMBOK Guide* and the other PMI books are exceptional reference books, and it's what your CAPM exam is based on. Those books are written, edited, and reviewed by hundreds of volunteer project managers. These are good people who've invested their time and experience into the books. Thank you to them for their hard work and contribution to the project management community. Having said that, know they are tough books to sit and read. Use them as reference points for your exam prep.

PMI has a formal way of naming things: processes, process groups, knowledge areas, enterprise environmental factors (EEFs), organizational process assets (OPAs), and project documents. Know the PMI terms. There may be other industry-specific terms used in projects where you work. In this book, I use these terms in both formal and informal ways. For example, collecting requirements (informal) in PMI-speak means elicitation (formal): an iterative process of alternating the steps of eliciting—capturing, gathering—information and analyzing the information obtained. As another example, I might call initiation a phase (informal) where PMI means (formal) the Initiating Process Group: Develop Project Charter and Identify Stakeholders.

The struggle is real. You don't want this journey to last any longer than necessary, and your goal should be—it better be—to pass your certification exam on your first . . . and only. . . attempt. So don't simply think of "taking the exam." Instead, focus on "passing your exam," so you can get back to your real life.

Just as your projects have plans, you need a plan for how to study, how to prepare, and then how to pass the exam. You can relax on this part—I've done most of the work for you. See Table 2: A Sample Study Strategy, later in this Introduction.

Use This Book to Score a Triple Play

Back in the day when I was a college professor, I learned a fascinating fact about how adults learn best and I developed a related theory called the Triple Play, which uses Bloom's Taxonomy (a hierarchical framework that categorizes educational goals into six levels of complexity, from lower-order thinking skills to higher-order thinking skills). The Triple Play for learning says that if I give you the opportunity to learn something at least three times, you'll know it, know when to use it, and be able to apply it.

Passing the CAPM exam is difficult, and you need to experience the content three times before you can expect to remember it, know when to use it, and how to apply it. *I hear, I forget. I see, I remember. I do, I understand.*

1. Deface this book. Have a roll-up-your-sleeves-and-get-messy experience with the content.

   - Use a pen or pencil for annotating, highlighting, and commenting. Underline, circle, or highlight key words and phrases—this can be helpful if you need to do something with your hands to help you stay focused.

   - Annotate margins with symbols, abbreviations, or summaries of the text.

   - Write notes in your own words instead of copying down information from the book.

   Physical activity while studying increases learning. The more deeply you force your brain to think, the better chance you'll have of learning and remembering.

2. Download the flash cards from the online content and study them every single day. Every day buzz through as many terms as you can. If you know the terms, you'll be able to better answer the questions. Yes, it's time consuming and painful, but so is taking the exam twice, and it costs money. The idea is that you'll "flash" through these every day as you plow through this book—it'll help you keep the chapter contents fresh in your mind as you happily move toward the end of this fine piece of literature. Look at the name of the term and define the term aloud; flip the card over and make certain you're correct. This is a wonderful time to use collaborative-learning strategies. Analyze the words by categorizing them according to similarities. Expand your knowledge by reading the back of the flash card and naming the term on the other side.

3. Answer the end-of-chapter and online sample exam questions (described in the following section). What did you get right? Wrong? Why or why not? Passing the CAPM exam is difficult, and you need to experience the content three times before you can expect to remember it, use it, and apply it. *I hear, I forget. I see, I remember. I do, I understand.*

CAPM Practice Exam Questions

At the end of each chapter, you'll also find 20 practice exam questions. These questions test your comprehension of the chapter. I've written these questions to be as tough as what you'll likely encounter on the live exam. My logic is that if you can answer my questions, you can answer PMI's questions, too. In the digital content, you'll find a Microsoft Excel spreadsheet titled "Exam Scores." Enter your chapter scores in the spreadsheet, and you can track which chapters you need more work on and focus your study time accordingly. Maintaining the data about your performance and tracking your progress will help you to identify the areas of improvement, and working on those areas progressively will enable you to control and ensure steady progress.

In addition to the end-of-chapter exams, the TotalTester Premium test engine that comes with this book contains hundreds of practice exam questions. The questions in this pool emulate those you'll find on the actual CAPM exam. The practice questions are mapped to the style and frequency of question types you will see. The questions are a terrific way to dive deep into the project management, agile, and business analysis content on your exam.

You can customize your practice exams by domain or by chapter, and you can even select how many questions you want included in each exam and how much time you have to complete it. If you choose to take a CAPM practice exam, it will pull 150 questions from the pool, weighted with the same balance you'll find on the actual CAPM exam, and you'll have three hours to complete it. Check out Appendix B for more information about how the TotalTester Premium test engine works.

I recommend that you complete these exams after you've completed reading and taking the end-of-chapter exams in this book. Keep taking each exam over and over until you can answer every question correctly. As I love to say in my CAPM Boot Camps, repetition is the mother of learning. Repetition is the mother of learning. Repetition is... (you get the idea).

Create a Strategy to Pass Your CAPM Certification Exam

I've outlined quick references for how you should study and then pass your exam. You may be slightly ahead of other readers in your exam preparations, so I've intentionally left dates and time lines to your discretion. I think a couple of chapters a week is realistic—but I wouldn't do more than that. Take some time and create a schedule of when you'll study, and then take measures to make certain you can keep the schedule you create.

Table 2 provides a sample strategy that you can modify as you see fit. Your schedule may take more or less time—this is just a sample strategy.

CAPM Certified Associate in Project Management All-in-One Exam Guide

Days	Chapter	Activities
1–2	Introduction in the frontmatter	Set up TotalTester. Download and review flash cards. Study the laminated Memory Card included with the book (also included as a download).
3–4	1	Read Chapter 1 and answer questions at end of chapter. Answer Chapter 1 word puzzle. Answer two matching questions for Chapter 1. Review flash cards.
5–6	2	Read Chapter 2 and answer questions at end of chapter. Review flash cards. Answer Chapter 2 word puzzle. Answer two matching questions for Chapter 2.
7–8		Review Introduction and Chapters 1 and 2. Study Appendix A, "50 Confusing Terms on the CAPM Exam."
9–10		Take a sample exam in TotalTester. Study Appendix A, "50 Confusing Terms on the CAPM Exam."
11–12	3	Read Chapter 3 and answer questions at end of chapter. Review flash cards. Answer Chapter 3 word puzzle. Answer two matching questions for Chapter 3.
13–14	4	Read Chapter 4 and answer questions at end of chapter. Review flash cards. Answer Chapter 4 word puzzle. Answer two matching questions for Chapter 4.
15–16	5	Read Chapter 5 and answer questions at end of chapter. Review flash cards. Answer Chapter 5 word puzzle. Answer two matching questions for Chapter 5. Study the laminated Memory Card included with the book (also included as a download).
17–18		Review Chapters 1 through 5. Review chapter exams to date. Review flash cards. Study matching questions for Chapters 1–5.
19–20	6	Read Chapter 6 and answer questions at end of chapter. Review flash cards. Answer Chapter 6 word puzzle. Answer two matching questions for Chapter 6.

Table 2   A Sample Study Strategy

Days	Chapter	Activities
21–22		Review chapter exams to date.
		Review flash cards.
		Practice your brain dump: a technique of quickly jotting down key information, concepts, and formulas on a scratch paper before the start of the exam to aid in memory retention and time management during the exam.
23–24	7	Read Chapter 7 and answer questions at end of chapter.
		Review flash cards.
		Answer Chapter 7 word puzzle.
		Answer two matching questions for Chapter 7.
25–26		Take your first 150-question exam in the TotalTester.
		Review your answers.
27–28		Review Introduction and Chapters 1 through 7.
		Review flash cards.
		Review seven word puzzles.
		Review 14 matching questions.
29–30		Review chapter exams to date.
		Study Appendix A, "50 Confusing Terms on the CAPM Exam."
		Review flash cards.
31–32		Take your second 150-question exam in the TotalTester.
		Review your answers.
33–34		Practice your brain dump.
		Review flash cards.
		Review seven word puzzles.
35–36		Take your third 150-question exam in the TotalTester.
		Review your answers.
		Review the laminated Memory Card included with the book (also included as a download).
37–38		Pass CAPM exam.
		Send e-mail to James@JamesLeeHaner.com with comments on this book and how it helped you pass your exam.

Table 2   A Sample Study Strategy (*continued*)

 CAUTION   Once you've achieved CAPM certification, it is valid for three years. At the end of the three years, you can renew your CAPM certification or let it lapse. Ideally, you'll have accrued enough project management experience to sit for the PMP exam.

Tips to Pass the Exam

Obviously, you want to pass your Certified Associate in Project Management (CAPM) exam on the first . . . and only . . . attempt. Why bother sitting for an exam if you know you're not prepared? In this section, you'll find the details you must know to pass the exam. These facts won't be everything you need to know to pass the CAPM exam, but you can bet you won't pass the exam if you don't know the critical information contained in this section.

For starters, don't think of this process as "preparing to *take* an exam"—think of it as "preparing to *pass* an exam." Anyone can prepare to take an exam: just show up. Preparing to pass the CAPM exam requires a mindset shift, diligence, and a commitment to study.

Focus on the Most Important Exam Domains

Adjust your study strategy to spend more time on the more valuable domains than on the less valuable domains, per the weighting assigned by PMI in the CAPM ECO. The domains are presented next in order from highest to lowest percentage of items on the exam.

Domain 1: Project Management Fundamentals and Core Concepts, 36 percent (approximately 54 questions)   This domain requires you to understand the different project life cycles and processes and the basics of project management, such as how to plan projects, execute planned strategies or frameworks, solve problems, and identify roles and responsibilities.

Domain 4: Business Analysis Frameworks, 27 percent (approximately 41 questions)   This domain tests your understanding of business analysis roles and responsibilities, stakeholder communication, requirements gathering (aka requirements elicitation), product roadmaps, and validating requirements through product delivery (which is about traceability).

Domain 4 also tests your knowledge of how project methodologies influence business analysis processes, which basically is about how the role of the business analyst differs depending on whether the project is a predictive, plan-based project or an agile/adaptive project.

Domain 3: Agile Frameworks/Methodologies, 20 percent (approximately 30 questions)   This domain requires you to understand when it's appropriate to use an adaptive approach, how to plan project iterations, and how to differentiate various agile methodologies. The domain also covers document control and artifact creation as well as how to prepare and execute task management steps (i.e., do the work).

Domain 2: Predictive, Plan-Based Methodologies, 17 percent (approximately 26 questions)   This domain requires you to recognize when using a predictive, plan-based approach is appropriate and to understand common scheduling and planning techniques like using the critical path method and creating a work breakdown structure. It also covers project controls.

Learning to Learn

When I study to pass a PMI exam, I have an exam learning headquarters. It's quiet, with no distractions, and it's only for exam studying. You should do the same. Time your study sessions. Don't overdo your study sessions—long, crash-study sessions aren't that profitable.

In addition, attempt to study at the same time every day, at the time your exam is scheduled. Use this study time to seriously immerse yourself in the content and prepare to pass.

Take the test during your high energy time of the day. Peak times are when your energy and concentration levels are at their highest. That might sound funny, I know, but we all have our peak times during the day and then our slow times when these levels are lower. Never schedule an exam for your slow times! It's during your peak times that you can tackle difficult tasks, well, like a CAPM exam. My peak time during the day is 8 A.M., after two cups of coffee. Discover what your peak time is during the day. Only schedule your exam for that time. Otherwise, you are cutting against the grain. (P.S. Most Pearson VUE test centers schedule CAPM exams from 8 A.M. until 5 P.M. . . . ending at 8 P.M.)

Quizzes in This Book

As I mentioned earlier, you'll find an end-of-chapter quiz in each chapter that'll test your comprehension of what's been covered in that chapter. Take these quizzes over and over until you can answer the questions perfectly every time. If you miss a question, do the research to understand why you missed the question. To repeat myself, repetition is the mother of learning.

Enlist Others

Ask someone to listen to you explain a difficult concept in your own words. If you can't explain it, you probably don't understand it. Form study groups with other candidates and learn from each other.Another option to consider is joining a PMI chapter, where you can connect with mentors who can offer valuable advice on passing the exam, gain insights from members' real-world experience, and have your CAPM queries answered by professionals in the project management field.

Ask for patience from workmates, family, and friends as you focus on your studies. Preparing for the CAPM exam does require effort, and you may strain some of your relationships if you don't communicate why you need to spend time studying.

Create Your Own Brain Dump

If you could take one page of notes into the exam, what information would you include on this one-page document? Of course, you absolutely cannot take any notes or reference materials into the exam area. However, you can create one sheet of notes of anything you have trouble remembering. You absolutely may re-create this once the exam has officially started.

Here is PMI's policy on this matter and what will be enforced at Pearson VUE test centers:

- Testing candidates can start to utilize their scratch paper/note boards once the exam has officially started.
- Doing a "brain dump" during the 15-minute tutorial period or prior is not allowed.
- All scratch paper/note boards will be collected at the end of the testing session.

Practice creating a brain dump so you can immediately, and legally, re-create this document once your exam has begun. Once your exam process begins, re-create your reference sheet. The following are key pieces of information you'd be wise to include on your reference sheet. You'll find all this key information in the laminated Memory Card included with the book (also included as a download).

- Motivation models
- The Scrum life cycle
- Risk strategies: positive and negative
- Emotional intelligence matrix
- Frequently used business analysis terms
- Requirements traceability matrix
- Earned value management formulas
- Key leadership behaviors
- PDCA cycle
- Organizational structures and their influence on project managers
- RACI chart
- Conflict style grid
- Development approaches
- Requirement types

NOTE When I took my CAPM exam, I went in knowing I couldn't do a brain dump before I started the exam. So, I spent 5 minutes going through the tutorial, started my exam, and did the brain dump as soon as I started the exam. If you go into the exam treating it as a 2-hour and 50-minute exam instead of a 3-hour exam, then you can take the time to do your brain dump, and just pace yourself slightly faster to complete the rest of it. I was given my paper when I was seated and told that I wouldn't be able to write anything until I clicked the Start button.

Prepare Before the Exam

In the days leading up to your scheduled exam, follow these tips to prepare yourself for success:

- *Get some moderate exercise.* Get out of your house. Find time to go for a jog, lift weights, take a swim, or do whatever workout routine works best for you.
- *Eat smart and healthy.* If you eat healthy food, you'll feel good and feel better about yourself. Be certain to drink plenty of water. Hydration increases cognitive function. Drink caffeine in moderation (to avoid caffeine-withdrawal headache).
- *Get your sleep.* A well-rested brain is a sharp brain. You don't want to sit for your exam feeling tired, sluggish, and worn out.
- *Overcome test anxiety.* Use positive affirmations: "I am, I can, I will." Breathe deeply. Put on your "happy face."
- *Don't study the day or night before you're scheduled to take your exam.* Take the day off work. **Treat this day mostly as a day to relax.** Your brain needs time to assimilate, integrate, and reach the right level of calm.

 NOTE   A healthy brain is the best study tool to help you rise to your challenge . . . pass the CAPM exam!

What to Expect on Testing Day

The CAPM exam is a computer-based test hosted at Pearson VUE test centers. Once your application has been accepted, PMI will provide you with directions on how to schedule your test at a Pearson VUE test center. PMI will send an e-mail with a testing code, a URL for scheduling the exam, and specific directions on how to complete the exam registration process.

 NOTE   Visit the Pearson VUE test center before the day you have booked the exam so that you know where it is and where you will park (or how you will get there from the nearest public transportation stop).

On your testing day, you should arrive at the Pearson VUE test center about 30 minutes before your exam time. Be early—allow yourself enough time to relax. The receptionist will check you in and confirm that your valid, government-issued ID matches the PMI application. Be smart and use the exact same name on your application and training certificate as appears on your government-issued ID. Note that your government-issued ID must have a photograph, or else you'll need a secondary ID with your name and photo. Social Security cards and library cards are not accepted.

After the Pearson VUE test center receptionist checks you in, you'll be assigned a locker for your belongings. You cannot take anything into the testing room with you. All phones, purses, wallets, and items you've brought with you must go into the locker until the exam is over. Take some water and some easy-to-eat food. Ask the receptionist if you are allowed to access the locker for snacks or drinks.

The testing administrator will ask you turn out your pockets and roll up your shirt-sleeves. Next, they'll wave a magnetic wand over you to confirm you're not trying to smuggle anything into the test center. You cannot take anything into the center other than the clothes you're wearing—and those must stay on for the duration of the exam. You can't shed sweaters or jackets (and certainly not your pants) during the test, so dress comfortably.

You'll be seated at a computer workstation and given either six sheets of paper and two pencils, electronic whiteboard, or a laminated sheet of paper—legal size and a marker. You don't get to choose which; the testing center decides. The proctor will log you into the software and get you started. You'll have a 15-minute tutorial, if you choose to complete it, on how to use the exam software. You are not allowed to write anything down during this tutorial. Once the tutorial is done, your exam timer begins, and you can now jot down your brain dump and then start answering test questions. The exam software will allow you to move backward and forward in the questions, mark questions for review, highlight key words, and even strike out answers you don't want to choose. The software interface includes a built-in calculator that is easily accessible from all pages of the exam. You cannot pause the timer, but you are required to take a ten-minute break after you've answered 75 questions; the timer will NOT stop while you are taking the break.

Are you easily distracted? The exam room is a busy place. Test takers are wandering in and out. The proctor may be walking around to check for cheating (or seated outside the exam room watching through monitors, with window visibility to the room). Most Pearson VUE test centers also provide ear plugs or headphones if you want complete silence. Talking or disturbing other test takers is not tolerated, so behave. You can't eat or drink in the testing room. You can't cheat, of course. You can't tamper with the computer. You must be on your best, professional behavior or you'll be booted from the test center, and you'll fail the exam. After you take a break, you'll have to turn out your pockets and have the magnetic-wand treatment again before you go back into the testing room. So, be prepared.

Check your progress throughout the exam—aim to answer 75 questions by the 80- to 90-minute mark and all 150 questions by the 3-hour mark. After you've answered all the test questions in each 75-question part of the exam, you'll have an opportunity to review any questions that you've marked for review.

NOTE You will not be able to go back to the prior section once you click Submit and take the break.

After you're done reviewing the second 75-question part of the exam, the testing software will make you confirm that you're done to end the test. Before you get to see your score, you'll have to complete an irritating, but necessary, survey of the testing experience. Then, after that survey, your pass/fail results will be displayed. You'll exit the testing room, and the testing administrator will give you a signed score report. Get your stuff out of the locker and go celebrate!

Online vs. Test Center?

The decision to take the CAPM exam online or at a test center ultimately depends on your personal preference and circumstances. Here are some factors to consider:

Online Exam:

- Requires a reliable and stable Internet connection.
- May have technical requirements for your computer or testing environment.
- May have additional rules and requirements to follow during the exam.

Test Center Exam:

- Provides a quiet and distraction-free testing environment.
- Offers a standardized testing experience with professional proctors and equipment.
- Allows for easy access to scratch paper, pencils, and other testing materials.

In the end, the choice of whether to take the CAPM exam online or at a test center relies on your personal preferences and specific circumstances. It is important to weigh the pros and cons of each option before deciding.

Testing Tips

The questions on the CAPM exam aren't always direct and easy, and the answer choices may offer a few red herrings. However, there are some practical, exam-passing tips. For starters, you may face questions that state, "All of the following are correct options except for which one?" The question wants you to find the incorrect option, or the option that would not be appropriate for the scenario in the question content. Be sure to understand what the question is asking for. It's easy to focus on the scenario presented in a question and then see a suitable option for that scenario in the answer. However, if the question is asking you to identify an option that is not suitable, then you just missed the question. Carefully read the question to understand what is expected for an answer.

Here's a tip that can work with many of the questions: Identify what the question wants for an answer, and then look for an option that doesn't logically belong with the other possible answers. In other words, find the answer that doesn't fit with the other three options. Find the "odd one out." Here's an example:

EVM is used during the _____.

A. Controlling activities of the project

B. Executing activities of the project

C. Closing activities of the project

D. Entire project

Notice how options A, B, and C are exclusive? If you choose A, the controlling phase, it implies that earned value management (EVM) is not used anywhere else in the project. The odd one out here is D, the entire project; it's considered the "odd" choice because, by itself, it is not an actual process group. Of course, this tip won't work with every question—but it's handy to keep in mind.

Usually, you will find at least one answer that is "more wrong" than the others. Get rid of that choice immediately. Cross it out. Now, you only have three answers to look at . . . not four. You just improved your chances of getting the right answer from 25 percent to 33 percent.

Watch out for answers that are completely new to you. After you have studied this book and answered all the TotalTester questions, there will be no answers on the exam that you've not "heard of" before. The exam is designed to evaluate your project management knowledge, based on the PMI way, not to trick you. If you see an answer that sounds like some good "lingo" and is entirely new to you, it is likely a wrong answer.

For some answer choices, it may seem like two of the four options are both possible correct answers. However, because you may choose only one answer, you must discern which answer is the best choice. Sometimes, the question itself provides some hint describing the progress of the project, the requirements of the stakeholders, or some other clue that can help you determine which answer is the best one for the question.

 EXAM TIP Read all the answers carefully before you look at the question. This will improve your chances of getting the best answer. Even better, read the answers in reverse order (D, C, B, and then A). Changing how you read the answers tells your brain to think differently and you might notice something you missed the first read through.

Answer Every Question—Once
As stated in the CAPM ECO:

> The CAPM examination is comprised of 150 multiple-choice questions. Of the 150 questions, 15 are considered pretest questions. Pretest questions do not affect the score and are used in examinations as an effective and legitimate way to test the validity of future examination questions. All questions are placed throughout the examination randomly.

Assume every question on your exam counts. Don't think about which questions count and which are pretest. As indicated in the ECO, the questions will appear in random order on your exam. The exam questions are not grouped by domains, tasks, or enablers from the ECO.

All we know is that there is a 10 percent (15/150) probability that any exam question could be a pretest question. If a particular question is confusing, there is a 10 percent chance that it could be a pretest question. Answer all the exam questions with the same degree of focus and attention and move on. Always forward! Do not leave any question blank, even if you don't know the answer to the question. A blank answer is a wrong answer.

EXAM TIP   NO! NO! NO! NEVER leave a question unanswered. NEVER!

As you move through the exam and encounter questions that stump you, use the "mark for review" option in the exam software, choose an answer you suspect may be correct, and then move on to the next question. When you have answered all the questions, you are given the option to review your marked answers in each half of the exam . . . first 75 questions and second 75 questions.

Subsequent questions in the exam may prompt your memory to produce answers to questions you have marked for review. However, resist the temptation to review questions that you've already answered with confidence and haven't marked. Also, don't overanalyze the situation. Most often, your first instinct is the correct choice. When you complete the exams at the end of each chapter, use this same advice.

Use the Process of Elimination

When you're stumped on a question, use the process of elimination. For each question, there'll be four choices. On your scratch paper, whiteboard, or laminated sheet, write down "ABCD." If you can safely rule out "A," cross it off your paper. Now focus on which of the other answers won't work. If you determine that "C" won't work, cross it off your list. Now you've got a 50–50 chance of finding the correct choice. PMI has added the option to "strike out" answers in the exam testing software, so use that tool as well.

If you cannot determine which answer is best, "B" or "D" in this instance, here's the best approach:

1. Choose an answer (no blank answers!).

2. Mark the question in the exam software for later review.

3. Circle the "ABCD" on your scratch paper, whiteboard, or laminated sheet, jot any relevant notes, and then write the question number next to the notes.

4. During the review, or from a later question, you may realize which choice is the better of the two answers. Return to the question and confirm that the best answer is selected.

Watch Out for Absolutes and Negatives

Look at the structure of the question and identify words like "not," "except," "only," and "always," as those can change the meaning of a question or answer choice. Choose carefully if you pick an answer containing words like "always" or "never" or "not" or "except." There are very few absolutes in project management. Responses with these restrictive terms are often the incorrect answers. If the answer, or the question, is in the form of a double negative, rephrase the sentence as a positive statement and see if that makes it easier to solve. For example, "The stakeholders are not unfamiliar with the project" can be rephrased as, "The stakeholders are familiar with the project."

EXAM TIP   The CAPM exam does not use formatting for critical words used in the questions. For example, you will not see a word in capital letters, bold, or italics on the exam.

Take Three Practice Exams

When using the TotalTester software, I recommend this strategy:

1. Take your first 150-question exam with no time limit. Open book, open mind. Take all the time you need.

2. Take your second 150-question exam—open book, open mind. This time set a timer and practice answering each of the questions in 72 seconds or less. Attempt to answer 150 questions in three hours.

3. Take your third 150-question exam as if it were exam day—closed book, open mind. "See" yourself in the testing room. Practice your brain dump. Answer 75 questions, take a ten-minute break, and go on to the second half of 75 questions. Answer all questions as accurately as possible.

Now, your mind is ready to manage the rigor of a three-hour exam under stressful conditions.

Use all the three hours. It is more important to pass the exam than it is to go home early. If it will help, write this statement "I AM A CAPM!" at the top of your scratch paper or whiteboard so you can remind yourself of this ideal. In a three-hour exam, it is possible to get tired and just want to get it over with. Stay focused. You have the energy to succeed.

Summary

- Read each question carefully and patiently. Getting the right answer can be easier when you fully comprehend what the question is asking.

- Reread the question! Seriously, a lot of mistakes are made because people don't read the questions fully.

- Read all four answers before deciding on which one is correct. Sometimes the first one looks good, and you may be tempted to mark that one as correct when a better one is further along.

- Eliminate any obviously wrong answers.

- Place the answers on a spectrum of most right to most wrong and choose the most right one.

- Guess! Leave no question unanswered.

Everything You Need to Know

As promised, this section covers all the information you need to know going into the CAPM exam. It's highly recommended that you create a method to recall this information.

Enter a check mark for each task only after you are confident that the corresponding statement is a fact. Here goes.

Quick Facts: Project Management Fundamentals and Core Concepts

☐ Task 1: I understand the various project life cycles and processes.

☐ Task 2: I understand project management planning.

☐ Task 3: I understand project roles and responsibilities.

☐ Task 4: I know how to follow and execute planned strategies or frameworks (e.g., communication, risks, etc.).

☐ Task 5: I understand common problem-solving tools and techniques.

Quick Facts: Predictive Plan-Based Methodologies

☐ Task 1: I can explain when it is appropriate to use a predictive, plan-based approach.

☐ Task 2: I understand a project management plan schedule.

☐ Task 3: I know how to document project controls of predictive, plan-based projects.

Quick Facts: Agile Frameworks/Methodologies

☐ Task 1: I can explain when it is appropriate to use an adaptive approach.

☐ Task 2: I know how to plan project iterations.

☐ Task 3: I know how to document project controls for an adaptive project.

☐ Task 4: I can explain the components of an adaptive plan.

☐ Task 5: I know how to prepare and execute task management steps.

Quick Facts: Business Analysis Frameworks

☐ Task 1: I understand business analysis (BA) roles and responsibilities.

☐ Task 2: I know how to conduct stakeholder communication.

☐ Task 3: I know how to gather requirements.

☐ Task 4: I understand product roadmaps.

☐ Task 5: I know how project methodologies influence business analysis processes.

☐ Task 6: I can validate requirements through product delivery.

A Letter to You

My goal for you is to pass your CAPM exam on the first . . . and only . . . attempt. As I teach my PMI Exam Prep Workshops for different organizations around the globe, I'm struck by one similarity among the most excited course participants: these people want to pass their exam. Sure, project management is not the most exciting topic, but these individuals are excited about passing their exam. I hope you feel the same way. I believe that your odds of passing the CAPM exam are like most things in life; you're going to get out of it only what you put into it. I challenge you to become excited, happy, and eager to pass the exam.

From my grandson, Hudson: "How do you communicate with a fish? Drop him a line!" If you're stumped on something I've written about in this book, or if you'd like to share your CAPM success story, drop me a line at James@JamesLeeHaner.com. Finally, I won't wish you good luck on your CAPM exam—luck is for the ill prepared. If you follow the strategies I've outlined in this book and apply yourself, I am certain you'll pass the exam.

Be the BE$T,
Dr. James Lee Haner
PMI: CAPM, PMP, PgMP, PMI-ACP, PMI-RMP, PMI-SP
IIBA: CBAP, CCBA, ECBA
ScrumAlliance: CSM and CSPO
Website: JamesLHaner.com
Phone: 986-777-0999

PART I

Project Management Foundation

Working as a Project Manager

In this chapter, you will

- Explore the project manager role
- Understand the project manager's influence
- Learn project management competencies
- Learn to manage and lead a successful project
- Study project integration

Are you managing projects but don't have the project manager title? Are you a new project manager? Are you working toward becoming a project manager? CAPM candidates typically have job titles like project team lead, associate project coordinator, project analyst, project coordinator, and project staff lead. Job roles matter as well, and any role that requires you to manage yourself and others to achieve project goals and create deliverables can benefit from the knowledge required to earn the CAPM certification. The CAPM exam will test your knowledge of the typical roles and responsibilities of a project manager.

You'll need to be familiar with the most common types of activities and characteristics of a project manager. Be aware that this means you'll need to recognize the roles and responsibilities for both predictive environments and adaptive (agile) environments, even if you don't work with an organization that uses one of those approaches. I'll address both environments in this chapter and what you can expect in either.

Where you work or will work as a project manager is likely different from where other readers of this book work or will work as a project manager. Just as every project is unique, so, too, is the environment in which a project exists. Consider software development projects, construction projects, IT infrastructure projects, learning and development projects, and as many different types of projects as you can imagine. Each of these different projects operates in a distinct environment. The environment is a factor of influence in these projects and in your projects. Remember for the CAPM exam that there is no blanket approach that fits every scenario; how you best operate as a project manager in your organization depends on the environment.

Exploring the Project Manager Role

Project management is about getting things done. Projects are temporary endeavors that don't last forever. Project management is about getting the project started as quickly and as effectively as possible and then leading the project team to completion: getting it done. Projects often have no business value until they are complete. Consider a construction project: Generally, no one can use the new building until the construction project is done. The project has no value until the completed building begins to earn a return on investment. The longer a project takes to complete, the greater the exposure to risk, the more expensive the project is likely to be, and the more frustrated stakeholders will be because the project is still in progress. Project managers get it done.

Adaptive projects often have a series of releases, usually about every three to six months. Adaptive projects can realize and use benefits as soon as it makes good sense to do so. For example, a project may have multiple releases of software planned: Version 1, 1.1, 1.2, and so on. Each release, or increment, of the completed product enables the organization to realize business value—which is not something we can always do in a predictive project.

You can't just charge in and start firing off assignments and putting people to work. Project management requires a structured approach. For starters, project managers are often involved in the project design before the project is even initiated. A project manager may meet with the portfolio or program review board, customers, and management to offer input before a project is selected, funded, initiated, and staffed. Project managers may work with business analysts (or take on the role of a business analyst) to elicit business requirements, create high-level estimates, and develop business cases and feasibility studies—all work that precedes project initiation.

The project manager has roles and responsibilities, but so do people on the project team. Roles are assigned to determine who does what on the project: developer, app tester, plumber, or technical writer, for example. In many projects, project team members, like the project manager, play multiple roles on a project. While the project manager is responsible for leading and managing the project team, the project team is responsible for completing their work assignments. Scrum projects, for example, call for the development team to be self-organizing and to determine who'll complete what work in each iteration.

During planning, which is both an *iterative* activity (as critical information changes, project plans need to be adjusted accordingly) and an *interactive* activity (planners meet with users and validate the plan), the project manager and the project team will plan the work; next, they'll execute the project work. As the project manager leads and manages the project team, they will rely on the project team's expertise, experience, skills, and technical abilities to complete assignments. It's unrealistic for the project manager to have the skills and depth of knowledge of each project team member. The project manager should rely on the expertise of the project team when it comes to planning, and then the project team members must complete their assignments as promised.

In the Real World

During my career as a project manager, I have made repeated and frequent use of experts with knowledge greater than my own. Doing so not only assists with a better output but also is a great way to learn. Don't hesitate to gather around you experts who can help you with any aspect of project management. Additionally, don't discount your own experience when it comes to providing an expert opinion.

Defining the Adaptive Project Manager

To define the project management role in an adaptive project is tricky, because there are so many different adaptive approaches available. The flavor of adaptive project management will directly influence the project manager's roles and responsibilities in the approach. You'll need to recognize the project management roles and responsibilities for the most common adaptive approaches. For the most part, however, the principles of project management are similar in either adaptive or predictive approaches: follow the rules and get stuff done.

Throughout this book, I'll reference the roles, principles, and attributes of project management as if they apply to all project management approaches, unless there's a significant difference between the project management roles in a predictive versus adaptive environment.

Here are the project management definitions for the most common adaptive (agile) project management approaches:

- **Scrum** There is no project manager. Instead, the project management role is divided among the three roles: the scrum master, the product owner, and the development team. The scrum master, the closest role to a predictive project manager role, serves as a coach, protects the development team from interruptions, gets the development team what they need, and makes certain all roles are following the Scrum rules. The easiest way to learn about Scrum is to walk through the flow of events, shown in Figure 1-1. We will go into detail about Scrum in Chapter 5.

- **Kanban** In Kanban, the role of the project manager is to facilitate the flow of work and ensure that the team is following the Kanban principles and practices. The project manager does not have a traditional role of assigning tasks and deadlines to team members, as these are self-organized by the team itself. This means they'll ensure that defects aren't moving through the Kanban system, make sure that requirements are being completed, manage the work in progress (WIP), maintain the Kanban board, and help stabilize the processes in the project. The primary characteristic of Kanban is the Kanban board, shown in Figure 1-2; that's where its name comes from—Kanban means visual signal.

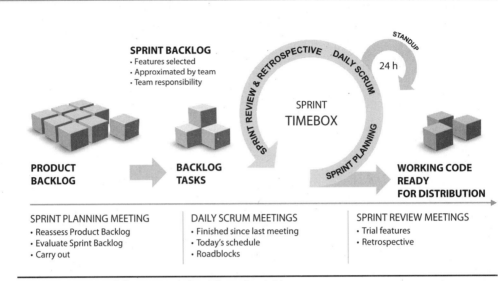

Figure 1-1 Scrum follows a predefined flow of activities.

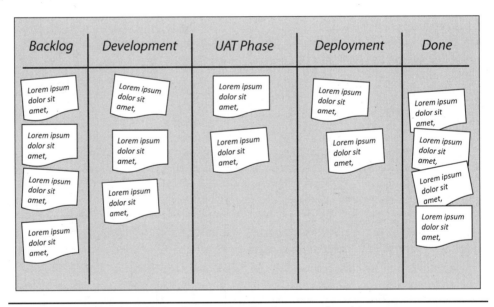

Figure 1-2 A Kanban board helps the team visualize the status of work items.

- **Lean** The project manager in a Lean environment also has many of the traditional project management responsibilities, but they also must work with the team to promote efficiency, accuracy, and reduce waste. The Lean project manager will aim to identify bottlenecks, perform root cause analysis (RCA), and then take steps to improve bottleneck issues. Lean project management begins with defining the value the project creates and then planning with the team how to achieve that value by eliminating waste, improving the process, and serving the project team.

- **Extreme Programming (XP)**   There is no project manager. XP has two project management roles, manager and coach, which are typically fulfilled by different people who take on project management activities. The manager role tracks performance, ensures that everyone is following the rules, and leads the continual planning processes. The coach role coaches the team on the XP rules, remains calm even when others are panicking, helps the team become self-reliant, and intervenes only when there's a problem that the team is overlooking.

In the Real World

I remember being new to the profession of project management and thinking it was better just to get on with the job and that planning was a negative outcome in a cost-benefit analysis. It was with the wisdom gained with experience (and mistakes) that I learned that proper planning precedes execution, resulting in a much greater chance of project success.

Leading the Project Team

It's been said that project managers manage things and lead people. Project management is about doing whatever it takes to achieve the desired results. Leadership is all about motivating and inspiring individuals to work toward those expected results. Management and leadership go together in project management, and you'll need both to be an effective project manager.

Most of us have worked for a project manager who hasn't been all that motivating. A good project manager, like you, motivates and inspires people to see the vision and helps the project team realize how their work contributes to business value for the organization. The project manager needs to inspire the project team to overcome obstacles to get the work done. Motivation is a constant process, and the project manager must be able to motivate the team to move toward completion—instilling passion and providing inspiration for completing the work. Finally, motivation and inspiration must be real; the project manager must have a personal relationship with the project team members to help them achieve their goals.

 NOTE   Leadership can also come from project team members, not just from the project manager. A leader doesn't always have to be a single person; leadership can come from multiple sources.

Communicating Project Information

Communication is all important in project management. You will build a communication plan that shows who needs what information, when the information is needed, what's the best modality to deliver the message, and who should have access to the information. As a project manager, you may spend most of your time communicating, maybe as much as 90 percent: talking with the project team, meeting with stakeholders, e-mailing management, coordinating with vendors, and more and more. If you're a good communicator, you can be a great project manager.

Communication is a two-way street that requires a sender and a receiver. *Active listening* is needed in important conversations. Active listening happens when the receiver of the message paraphrases what the sender has said and reflects on the feeling in the message to clarify and confirm the message. For example, if a project team member tells you, with a frown, that they hope an assignment will be done in seven days, you'd paraphrase that the work package will be done a week from today. This gives the project team member the opportunity to clarify that the work package will actually be done nine days from today because of the upcoming weekend—they'll need seven working days to complete the assignment. Then, you can ask about the emotion in the message, "It seems you are worried about meeting the due date."

There are several communication avenues:

- Listening and speaking
- Written (either physical or electronic) and spoken (either face-to-face or remote)
- Internal, focusing on stakeholders within the project and within the organization, such as project team member to team member
- External, focusing on customers, vendors, other projects, organizations, government, the public, and environmental advocates
- Formal, as in project reviews, stakeholder briefings, product demos, progress reports, project documents, or presentations
- Informal, such as conversations, e-mails, instant messaging/texting, websites, social media, and "bump into" meetings
- Vertical, which follows the organizational flowchart
- Horizontal, such as peers of the project manager or team

Communication management includes variables and elements unique to the flow of communication. Here are some key facts to know:

- **Sender-receiver model**   Communication requires a sender and a receiver. Within the sender-receiver model may be multiple avenues to complete the flow of communication, and barriers to effective communication may be present as well. Other variables within this model include recipient feedback, surveys, checklists, and confirmation of the sent message.

  As you can see in Figure 1-3, the model demonstrates how communication moves from one person to another. I like to think of each portion of the model as a fax machine to visualize all the components. Take a look.

  Sender   This is the person who will send the message. Let's say I want to fax you a contract.

  Encoder   This is the device that encodes the message to be sent. My fax machine is the encoder.

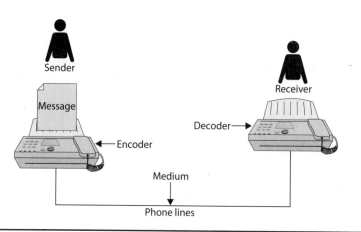

Figure 1-3   The communications model demonstrates the flow of communications.

Medium   This is the device or technology that transports the message. The telephone line is the medium between our fax machines.

Decoder   This is the device that decodes the message as it is being received. Your fax machine is the decoder.

Receiver   This is the person who receives the message.

Noise   This can be anything that interferes with or disrupts the message. It's possible that static on the phone line may distort the fax message between the two fax machines.

Acknowledgment   Some fax machines can print an acknowledgment of receipt. In a conversation, the receiver can offer nonverbal clues of acknowledgment. Acknowledgment means receipt of the message, but not necessarily agreement with the message.

Feedback/response   You receive my fax, jot down a note to me, and then send it back through your fax machine to mine. When you send your message to me, the communications model is reversed.

EXAM TIP   You'll likely see how communication moves from one person to another on your CAPM exam.

- **Media selection**   There are multiple choices of media for conveying information. Which medium is appropriate? Based on the audience and the information being sent, the medium should be in alignment. In other words, a "bump into" hallway meeting is probably not the best communication avenue to explain a large variance in the project schedule.

- **Style**   The tone, structure, and formality of the message being sent should be in alignment with the audience and the content of the message.

- **Presentation**   When it comes to formal presentations, the presenter's choice of words, voice tone and inflection, body language, visual aids, and handouts all influence the message being delivered.

- **Meeting management**   Meetings are forms of communication. How the meeting is led, managed, and controlled all influence the message being delivered. Agendas, minutes, time boundaries, rules of order, and recording the meeting are mandatory for effective communications within a meeting.

Negotiating Project Terms and Conditions

You don't always get what you want, and as a project manager, you'll really know that's true. Project managers must negotiate for the good of the project. In any project, the project manager, the project sponsor, and the project team will have to negotiate with stakeholders, vendors, and customers to reach a level of agreement acceptable to all parties involved in the negotiation process. Negotiation is about more than give-and-take and compromise; negotiating is about determining what's most fair for everyone, deciding what's best for the project, and respecting all parties in the process.

In some instances, typically in less-than-pleasant circumstances, negotiations may have to proceed with alternative dispute resolution (ADR) techniques, ways of resolving negotiations other than traditional court processes or litigation. Specific examples of ADR techniques include mediation and arbitration. Negotiations typically center on the following:

- **Priorities**   Many projects experience delays or unexpected changes in priorities that cause the project to come in behind schedule and over budget. When it comes to the tough decision-making around what to do when the priorities change (or how to manage changing priorities in the first place), it's the project manager's job to know what all stakeholders want and negotiate how to get them there as reasonably as possible.

- **Development approach**   There's a wide variety of projects and organizational structures, so there's no one-size-fits-all development approach to project management. For project management to be effective, the development approach must be tailored to your organization's project types, human resource capabilities, and company culture. Three development approaches are available: traditional (predictive; plan driven), hybrid (customized; tools, templates, and processes driven), and adaptive (agile; change driven).

- **Project scope (functions and features)**   As a project manager, it is your duty to protect your team from unrealistic project expectations, which means negotiating with that stakeholder (be it the sponsor, your boss, or a client) to figure out what is and isn't workable.

- **Schedule**   Project work needs to keep up with schedule requirements. Coordination between all parties is vital to maintain progress and meet due dates. Project managers must be able to bring a project to a timely conclusion, despite stress, surprises, and delays by stakeholders.

- **Cost**   "Show me the money!" Many problems arise on projects due to money. Subcontractors want more money, vendors increase prices, and resources sometimes don't deliver as promised. You must mitigate these situations when they happen, particularly in the face of changes, obstacles, and disputes.

- **Changes to the project scope, schedule, or budget**   Projects often experience some kind of delay: your task estimates were wrong, there wasn't enough staff accounted for, a team member has to take a week off due to illness, or a stakeholder wants to change the requirements. No matter the cause of the delay, it's up to you to negotiate with all affected stakeholders how the project should move forward with its timeline.

- **Vendor terms and conditions**   When negotiating with suppliers and vendors, you are at a disadvantage if you don't know the terms of your contract. So, it is imperative that you understand supplier and vendor contract terminology.

- **Project team member assignments and schedules**   Project team members can be divided not only based on their functionality and area of expertise but also on whether they are shared resources. When you have a dedicated resource, that person is working on only your project. You get to allocate all of their project time. The shared resource person is not just yours. Other projects have claims on this resource, too. Therefore, when and where this person's hours will be available must be negotiated.

- **Resource constraints, such as facilities, travel issues, and team members with highly specialized skills**   A core part of a project manager's job is negotiating just how much each team member has to contribute to a project each week. You need to balance the team's needs—training, vacation time, and competing projects—with the project's needs. One way to achieve this is by using a resource calendar for each team member, which shows the working days each specific resource is available enabling you to plan work while you negotiate competing priorities with the relevant team members.

Have you seen this before? The sponsor wants a brand new project that can do everything—send out invoices, balance a budget, keep customers happy, and monitor all the security cameras in 12 locations. This dreamer wants the project done in three months and with a team of four people.

NOTE   The purpose of negotiations is to reach a fair agreement among all parties. Be respectful of all involved; you may have to work with them throughout the project and beyond.

Active Problem-Solving

Projects can be cumbersome and tedious, can have competing objectives, and can have constraints that seem to box in the project manager. Project management demands problem-solving. Problem-solving is the ability to understand the problem, identify a viable solution, and then implement a solution. Though you want to be accurate in your decision, you don't want to take too long to act. This is why many project managers will say it's better to fail fast—try your best option, and if it doesn't work, adapt. In any project, countless problems require viable solutions. And like any good puzzle, the solution to one portion of the problem may create more problems elsewhere.

Active problem-solving is what the development team does in adaptive projects. They'll examine the work, determine how much work they can feasibly complete in the next iteration, and then be self-organizing to determine who'll do what work. Knowledge work, such as software development, is full of problem-solving. The XP framework, for example, takes problem-solving head-on by using paired programming to code, check, and partner on developing solid, quality code that works and that passes predefined tests.

Problem-solving requires a clear understanding of what the problem is—this means first defining the problem. A viable solution focuses on more than just the problem. In defining the problem, you must discern between its causes and effects. This requires root cause analysis to identify the effects, which include the problem plus all the possible causes and combinations of causes. A cause-and-effect diagram, also known as a fishbone, Ishikawa, or why-why diagram, can help you determine causal factors for a problem you'd like to solve.

Cause-and-effect diagrams show the relationship between the variables within a process and how those relationships may contribute to inadequate quality. They can help organize both the process and team opinions, as well as generate discussion on finding a solution to ensure quality. Figure 1-4 shows an example of a cause-and-effect diagram.

If a project manager treats only the symptoms of a problem rather than the cause of the problem, the symptoms will perpetuate and continue throughout the project's life. Root cause analysis looks beyond the immediate symptoms to the cause of the symptoms—which then affords opportunities for solutions.

Root cause analysis doesn't solve the problem, however; you'll still need to implement your solution. Solutions based on expert judgment can be presented from vendors, the

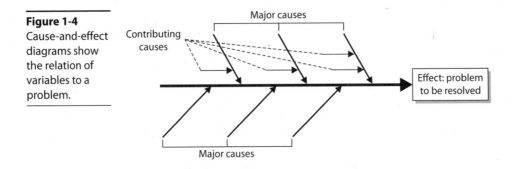

Figure 1-4 Cause-and-effect diagrams show the relation of variables to a problem.

project team, the project manager, or various stakeholders. In addition, a timely decision is needed, or the window of opportunity may pass and then a new decision will be needed to address the problem. As in most cases, the worst thing you can do is nothing.

Identifying the Project Manager Influence

Project managers have a wide sphere of influence. The projects we manage can affect end users, customers, vendors, and the public, and people can still be affected even long after the project manager has retired. Projects can also be influenced by many different groups of people: end users, managers, vendors, the project team, and more. The influence you have as a project manager will often depend on your experience, your maturity within the organization, and the size of the project you're managing.

Influence isn't something we often think about as project managers, but it's a factor that you should consider when planning and executing the project, and certainly when you're communicating with stakeholders. Not that you must play politics, but a project manager must consider the implications of the project's success, the communications between the project manager and project team, and the perceptions of the stakeholders regarding the project and its leadership. Over time and with experience in your organization, you'll find it easier to understand the undercurrent of politics and the hidden messages in questions and comments, and you'll have a broader, wiser view into what's happening in the organization and how your project (and you) affects the environment. Figure 1-5 shows the levels of influence between stakeholders and project managers.

Figure 1-5
Stakeholder and project manager influence are connected.

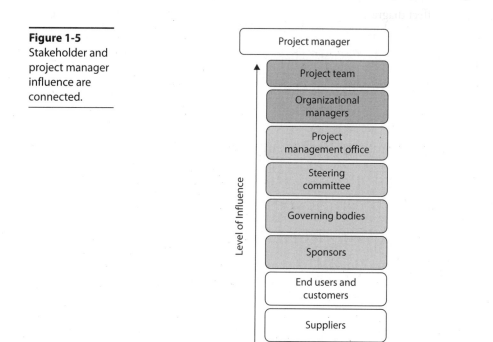

For your CAPM exam, consider the different levels of influence the project manager has on the following stakeholders:

- **Project team**   The project manager leads and directs the team to reach the project's objectives.

- **Organizational managers**   The project manager will likely need to work with managers to have access to people, processes, and resources.

- **Project management office**   The project manager will work with the project management office, if one exists, to manage the project and provide assets, directions, and support.

- **Steering committee**   The project manager may have to report to the steering committee on the project status and progress.

- **Governing bodies**   The project manager may have to report to internal project governance or to government agencies regarding how the project is adhering to laws and regulations.

- **Sponsors**   The project sponsor will want information on the project status and decisions the project manager has made to keep the project moving forward toward its objectives.

- **End users and customers**   The project manager is responsible to these people for what the project is creating, how the project may interfere with their lives as the project is in progress, and how the project will contribute to their lives once it is done.

- **Suppliers**   Suppliers need to be informed of when resources and services are needed, and they are influenced by the project manager's planning and the procurement policies of the organization.

- **Stakeholders**   All the people and groups that are affected by the project and can affect the project are stakeholders that the project manager can influence for the betterment of the project.

These are stakeholders. One of the first processes you'll need to complete in a project is stakeholder identification. The sooner you correctly identify all the stakeholders and build a stakeholder register (contains identification information, assessment information, and stakeholder classification), the better your project will perform. People don't like to be overlooked, especially when your endeavor is going to affect them. My motto is "When in doubt, don't leave them out!" Stakeholders are linked to the project manager and influenced by the project manager. The better the project manager coordinates, plans, and communicates within each of these stakeholder spheres, the better the project manager can influence these groups for continued project support, improved synergy, and sustainability of the project within the organization.

Influencing the Project

No one sets out to fail on purpose, but it's not unusual for projects to fail, miss their key performance objectives, or scrape across the finish line with a blown budget and late delivery. The success, or failure, of a project is indicative of how well the project manager led the project team, balanced the constraints, executed the project plan, and monitored the project progress. The person with the greatest influence over a project is the project manager, and the project's outcome is largely based on the project manager's ability to influence the project to reach its objectives. Sure, some projects are doomed from the start because of lack of finances and qualified resources, an unrealistic schedule, or other problems, but these are the exceptions, not the rule. Besides, a proficient project manager will address these issues and risks with management and stakeholders to find solutions.

Communication and a positive attitude can do wonders for the success of a project. Communication is paramount in project management; project managers must communicate with stakeholders through a variety of methods: verbal, written, and nonverbal. Messages must be direct and appropriate for the audience, and the communication style should be tailored based on what's being communicated to whom. Show me a project manager who is a bad communicator and I'll show a project manager who's leading a bad project.

Project managers must communicate good and bad news, project status, and other project information throughout the life of the project. Communication isn't one-way, however. The project manager needs to work with the team, clients, vendors, and other stakeholders to get these individuals to contribute to the conversation. This means asking questions, listening to stakeholder concerns, following up on ideas and promises, and keeping the project stakeholders involved, excited, and motivated to continue the project.

A positive attitude is also a key component of project success. Although it's tough to quantify what constitutes a positive attitude, it's easy to agree that those with bad attitudes may be unhappy in their lives, in their jobs, and with their organization. Unhappiness is demonstrated in the way an unhappy person manages projects; this attitude affects the project team and the stakeholders, and it can create a hostile work environment—or, at a minimum, a project that is no fun to work on. Negative project managers are incapable of inspiring others, leading the project team, and motivating people to do good work. A bad attitude or a good attitude is infectious; how you behave as a project manager will reflect on how your team will also behave.

Influencing the Organization

You know that no two projects are alike, and this also holds true for organizations. Every organization is unique in its policies, modes of operations, and underlying culture. There are particular political alliances, differing motivations, conflicting interests, and unique power struggles within every organization. So where does project management fit into this rowdy scheme? Right smack in the middle. You need to know your organizational structure, the governance, the politics, and how things get done where you work.

A project manager must understand the unspoken influences at work within an organization—as well as the formal channels that exist. An understanding of how to balance the implied and the explicit will enable the project manager to take the project from launch to completion. We all reference politics in organizations with disdain. However, politics aren't always a bad thing. Politics can be used as leverage to align and direct people to accomplish activities—with motivation and purpose.

EXAM TIP   Don't read too much into the questions as far as political aspirations and influences go. Take each question at face value and assume that all the information given in the question is correct.

As a project manager, you'll also interact with other project managers within the organization. You'll discuss projects, competition for resources, priorities, project funding, and alignment of project goals with organizational goals. Such networking among project managers isn't gossip; the transfer of information helps each project manager see how projects are faring and how decisions and events in the organization can affect projects and decisions, and it helps ensure their projects' viability and quality. This informal network of project managers can influence how things get done in the organization.

Considering Social, Economic, and Environmental Project Influences

Large projects have more influences than smaller projects. In a larger project, you'll likely have to deal with social, economic, and environmental influences—variables that can cause your project to falter, stall, or fail. You must take time to become aware of influences outside of traditional management practices. The acknowledgment of such influences, from internal or external sources, enables the project manager and the project team to plan how to react to these influences to help the project succeed.

Consider a construction project that will reduce traffic flow to one lane over a bridge. Obviously, stakeholders in this instance are the commuters who travel over the bridge. *Social influences* are the people who are frustrated by the construction project, the people who live near the project, and perhaps individuals or groups that believe their need for road repairs is more pressing than the need to repair the bridge. These issues must all be addressed, on some level, for the project team to complete the project work quickly and efficiently.

The *economic influences* in any organization are always present. The cost of a project must be weighed against the project's benefits and perceived worth. Projects may succumb to budget cuts, project priority, or their own failure based on the performance to date. Economic factors inside the organization may also hinder a project from moving forward. In other words, if the company sponsoring the project is not making money, projects may get axed to curb costs.

Finally, *environmental influence* on, and created by, the project must be considered. Let's revisit the construction project on the bridge. The project must consider the river under the bridge and how construction may affect the water and wildlife. You must consider not only the short-term effects that arise during the bridge's construction but also long-term effects that the construction may have on the environment.

In most projects, the social, economic, and environmental concerns must be evaluated, documented, and addressed within the project plan. Project managers cannot have a come-what-may approach to these issues and expect to be successful.

Considering International Influences

For your CAPM exam, consider the effects of a project that takes place in more than one country. In these large projects, how will the project manager effectively manage and lead the project team? How will teams in Boise, Idaho, communicate with teams in Luanda, Angola? What about the language barriers, time zone differences, currency differences, regulations, laws, and social influences? These concerns, which can become risks, must be considered early in the project. International influences can include online meeting platforms (Zoom, Teams, WebEx, etc.), travel, and face-to-face meetings.

As companies and projects span the globe to offer goods and services, the completion of those projects will rely more and more on individuals from varying educational backgrounds, social influences, and personal values. The project manager must create a communications management plan that takes these issues into account.

Considering Cultural and Industry Influences

When you sign up for your CAPM exam, you'll have the option of joining the Project Management Institute (PMI), and I hope you take the opportunity! PMI will provide news and opportunities for learning, and it offers a great way to stay current on project management trends.

Successful project managers stay abreast of what's happening in the project management community. They subscribe to newsgroups, read magazine articles, and take training to become more proficient in their role as a project manager. By staying current on what's happening in project management trends, you can identify opportunities, learn about new standards, and share best practices. In addition, you can monitor what's happening in your application field: healthcare, construction, or information technology, for example. This will help you, as a project manager, identify potential projects that your organization may need to undertake to meet market demand, organizational needs, customer requests, technological advances, legal requirements, ecological impacts, or social needs.

After you earn your CAPM, you'll likely take continuing education to earn professional development units (PDUs) to maintain your CAPM certification. Don't view this education as a chore, but as an opportunity to continue to advance your career and the project management profession.

Building Project Management Skills

Earning the CAPM certification takes time and dedication, but the reward of doing so is that it demonstrates you have the requisite level of project management knowledge. As I've mentioned, once you're a CAPM, you'll need to maintain your certification with continuing education by earning PDUs. Your CAPM certification is a three-year cycle, in which time you'll need to earn 15 PDUs to maintain your CAPM. If you fail to earn the 15 PDUs, you'll lose your CAPM status and must start the entire journey over—not a wise decision.

It's not terribly difficult to earn PDUs. You can earn them by serving as a project manager, by volunteering for PMI events, by writing books and articles, and by participating in many other activities. On PMI's website (www.pmi.org), hover your mouse pointer over the Certifications tab and click the Maintain Your Certification link to find complete rules and opportunities to earn PDUs. Not all your professional development activities can come through volunteering and events, however. As of this writing, CAPMs will have to earn a minimum of nine education PDUs and are allowed a maximum of six "giving back" PDUs for volunteering or contributing to the project management community.

Enhancing Skills and Competencies

Give thought to maintaining your CAPM. If one of your goals with the CAPM is to be marketable, then look for educational opportunities that'll give you PDUs and help you earn new certifications. To earn PDUs to maintain your certification, you'll attend online or in-person training. It's a good idea to take stock of what you know, or don't know, and choose your training accordingly. Consider your career goals, areas of your project management expertise that may be lacking, or what's interesting to you. Take training that will benefit you—don't just trudge through training because you must. Be strategic! Choose training and education that will make you a better person and project manager, plus help you keep your CAPM.

In practice, competencies are what project managers are good at: knowledge, skills, abilities, expertise, capacity, qualification, experience, and know-how. Successful project managers exhibit the following participative competencies:

- **Communicating collaboratively** Your job is to become more analytical about planning communication and more objective about how it is likely to be received. You must be an honest broker of information. Project managers provide the information that team members need to hear. You need to explain the challenges the team faces.

- **Making effective decisions** Decisions must be made with a commitment to seeing them through. Effective decisions can be made by fixing attention on a few major decisions rather than a lot of little ones, along with focusing on making "right" decisions. You need to explain the decisions you make and the potential consequences associated with those decisions. You must also be willing to remind the team of decisions they have already made and help them deal with the consequences.

- **Applying emotional intelligence** Emotional intelligence (EI)—a subcategory of social intelligence—is a strong indicator of an individual's ability to lead successfully. The key to strong EI is having a balanced and appropriate approach to feelings and emotions. For project managers, especially when under stress, taking a moment to consider EI can be helpful and even essential. To this end, project managers should adapt their emotions to facilitate better communication with team members and colleagues. Understanding how emotions impact communication—and then managing that impact—can eliminate unnecessary or unproductive responses.

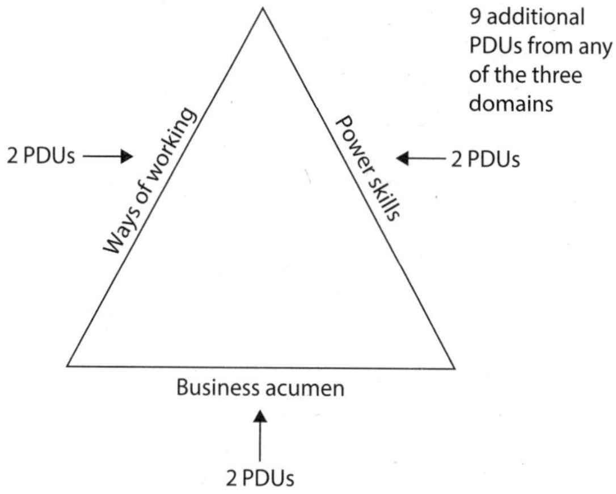

Figure 1-6
The PMI Talent
Triangle

9 additional
PDUs from any
of the three
domains

2 PDUs →   ← 2 PDUs

Ways of working   *Power skills*

Business acumen

↑
2 PDUs

Introducing the PMI Talent Triangle

The PMI Talent Triangle has recently undergone some changes, and now has three new skillsets, which are shown in Figure 1-6. As a CAPM, you'll need 15 minimum PDUs distributed across these three domains:

- Ways of Working (formerly Technical Project Management)
- Power Skills (formerly Leadership)
- Business Acumen (formerly Strategic and Business Management)

By focusing on these three components, project managers can build a strong foundation for success in their careers and ensure the success of their projects. The PMI Talent Triangle is used as a framework for professional development, as well as a benchmark for evaluating the competence of project management professionals.

Ways of Working (How To Do Your Job)

This component recognizes the importance of agile and adaptive approaches to project management, as well as the need for project managers to be able to work effectively in cross-functional and virtual teams. It includes the knowledge and skills required to apply agile and adaptive practices, as well as the ability to lead and participate in collaborative and dynamic project environments.

Power Skills (How To Help Others Achieve Their Goals)

Power skills refer to a set of essential skills that are critical to the success of a project manager. Some of the most important power skills in project management include the following:

- **Leadership** This includes the ability to effectively communicate and collaborate with project stakeholders, as well as the capacity to motivate and inspire a team to achieve project goals.

- **Communication**   This involves the ability to clearly and effectively communicate project information to stakeholders, as well as the capacity to listen to and understand the needs and concerns of project partners.

- **Stakeholder engagement**   This involves building and maintaining positive relationships with key stakeholders, as well as the ability to effectively manage stakeholder expectations and resolve conflicts.

- **Problem-solving and decision-making**   This involves the ability to analyze complex situations, identify and evaluate options, and make informed decisions that align with project goals and objectives.

- **Adaptability and flexibility**   This involves the ability to quickly adapt to changing project requirements and conditions, as well as the capacity to be flexible and open-minded in response to challenges and obstacles.

- **Emotional intelligence**   This involves the ability to understand and manage one's own emotions, as well as the ability to effectively interact with and influence others.

By developing and refining these power skills, project managers can be more effective in their roles and ensure the success of their projects.

Business Acumen (How To Be Better at Your Job)

Business acumen refers to the understanding of the business context in which projects are delivered and the ability to make informed decisions that align with the organization's goals and objectives. A project manager with strong business acumen is able to understand and apply financial management principles, as well as assess and understand the market conditions and industry trends that impact project delivery. Some of the key aspects of business acumen in project management include the following:

- **Financial management**   This involves understanding and applying financial management principles, such as cost estimating, budgeting, and cost control, to ensure that projects are delivered within budget and on time.

- **Market awareness**   This involves understanding the market conditions and industry trends that impact project delivery, as well as the ability to assess the impact of external factors, such as economic conditions, on project outcomes.

- **Strategic alignment**   This involves the ability to understand the organization's goals and objectives and make decisions that align with the organization's strategic direction. It also includes the ability to assess the trade-offs between project goals and organizational objectives.

- **Risk management**   This involves the ability to identify, assess, and manage risks that could impact project outcomes, as well as the ability to make informed decisions in response to project risks.

By developing business acumen, project managers can better understand the business context in which projects are delivered and make informed decisions that align with the organization's goals and objectives. This helps to ensure that projects are delivered in a manner that supports the organization's strategic direction and adds value to the business.

Managing Politics in Projects

Yes, you'll have to deal with office politics in project management. Stakeholders almost always have a political agenda, and they can try to leverage the project manager to get their way. Unfortunately, project managers often get mired in stakeholders' competing objectives and succumb to office politics that can affect the project for the worse. Politics are really a way of describing how organizations operate—the undocumented, but present, undercurrent of how decisions are made within the organization. Project managers must understand how organizations work, who wields authority, and how to navigate through the politics, good or bad, to keep the project moving toward a successful conclusion.

Though the project manager may hope to avoid politics, it's nearly impossible to do; politics can begin with the perception of the project manager and the power they have. Perception of power refers to how other people—from the project team, to management, to stakeholders—view not just the project but also the project manager. The project manager does have some power over the project and how they are perceived by others.

Although every scenario is different, you should be familiar with several types of power that affect your role as a project manager and for your CAPM exam:

Personal Powers

- **Referent power**   The project manager is respected or admired because of the team's past experiences with the PM. This power is a result of your own personality and whether or not you are liked and respected by other people. This is about the project manager's believability in the organization. When you have been working as a project manager for a long time and earned some credibility, you have this power.

- **Information power**   The project manager has control over data gathering and distribution of information. As the saying goes, well-informed means well-armed. Information is the key to success for any project. If you are responsible for processing or possessing some information, you have a greater chance of completing the project successfully.

- **Expert power**   The project manager has deep skills and experience in a discipline (for example, years of working in IT helps an IT project manager better manage IT projects). Expert power is a positive power that influences others to follow your lead. If you do not possess expert knowledge, it is difficult for you to gain respect from team members.

Positional Powers

- **Legitimate power**   The project manager's power is a result of the position they have as the project manager. This is also known as formal, authoritative, and positional power. Team members will obey your orders because they know you have the authority. People may respect you initially because of the fact that you are the manager, but your subsequent actions could cause this form of power to become invalid; therefore, it is not the best form of power to use. This type of power is found in project-oriented and strong-matrix organizations. However, this power does not exist in a functional organization or a weak-matrix organization. You will have to use your soft skills to get the job done in those cases.

- **Reward power** The project manager can reward the project team. Reward power is positional power; you can have it if you work in a project-oriented or strong-matrix organization. Although you can have reward power in a functional or a weak-matrix organization, here, you can offer your team members only non-monetary benefits.

- **Coercive (punitive) power** The project manager can punish the project team. Coercive power is also known as punishment power. This type of power is associated with a strong-matrix organization. Usually, you will use this power when a member is not performing well or is creating problems.

Notice that I've framed these types of power from the project manager's point of view, but the reality is that any stakeholder, from a customer to the project sponsor, can hold these powers. This is all part of the political side of organizations; being able to recognize the power being implemented can help you as project manager better manage a project and its outcomes.

PMI favors expert and reward power and discourages coercive power. An effective project manager knows when it is appropriate to use each type of power.

Serving as a Leader and Manager

Leadership and management are not the same things: Leadership is more about emotional intelligence and inspiring people to work together to achieve great things. Management is about getting things done. Management is concerned with the results and the work required to achieve those results. For your CAPM exam, you'll need to discern between leadership and management. Understand that management focuses on getting the project done, while leadership is about inspiring and motivating people. There are opportunities to do both on every project.

As a successful project manager, you'll serve as both a leader and a manager. You'll lead the team by showing them opportunities that help them accomplish the project, create something new, and complete the project work with an eye toward how the project contributes to business value for the organization. As a manager, you'll keep the team organized and the work authorization moving, and you'll address the core subject matter of project management. You'll be accountable and hold the team accountable for the scope, costs, quality, risk management, and other facets of project management.

Effective leadership promotes project success and contributes to positive project outcomes.

Learning Leadership Styles

Think about all of people you've worked for—specifically the managers you've admired. Think of how that individual led their team. Managers' characteristics, such as their temperaments and values, made you admire them. Employees often look to their managers to determine what is acceptable behavior—how they treat others, their energy about the project, and their ethics. A project manager's characteristics inform how their team members behave. Leadership styles are the methods you and others employ to offer leadership within the project. Effective leaders flex their style to the situation. That's an important concept, because it's not just the project manager who can offer leadership: the team, stakeholders, and even vendors can offer leadership at different times throughout the project.

Many leadership styles are used within organizations, and you should recognize these for the CAPM exam:

- **Visionary leadership**   Visionary leaders have a clear idea of what they want to do and how they plan to accomplish it, along with the strength to pursue it.

- **Change agent leadership**   A change agent is a leader who is able to set a direction for change and lead change. This leader is aware of the psychology of people and how to engage stakeholders and staff in order to gain buy-in and overall momentum toward significant change.

- **Authentic leadership**   Authentic leaders know who they are, what they believe in, what their values are, and what their priorities are. They lead accordingly and ensure that their words align with their actions in order to build trust.

- **Servant leadership**   The leader puts others first and focuses on the needs of the people they serve. Servant leaders provide opportunity for growth, education, autonomy within the project, and the well-being of others. The primary focus of servant leadership is service to others.

- **Transactional leadership**   The leader emphasizes the goals of the project and offers rewards and disincentives for the project team. This is sometimes called management by exception, because it's the exception that is rewarded or punished.

- **Laissez-faire leadership**   The leader takes a hands-off approach to the project. This means the project team makes decisions, takes initiative in the actions, and creates goals. Although this approach can provide autonomy, it can make the leader appear absent when it comes to project decisions.

- **Transformational leadership**   The leader inspires and motivates the project team to achieve the project goals. Transformational leaders aim to empower the project team to act, be innovative in the project work, and accomplish through ambition.

- **Charismatic leadership**   The leader is motivating, has high energy, and inspires the team through strong convictions about what's possible and what the team can achieve. Positive thinking and a can-do mentality are characteristics of a charismatic leader.

- **Interactional leadership**   The leader is a hybrid of transactional, transformational, and charismatic leadership. The interactional leader wants the team to take action, is excited and inspired about the project work, yet still holds the team accountable for their results.

- **Adaptive leadership**   Adaptive leaders are able to adjust their approach to match the needs of their environment. Such leaders challenge people, pushing them out of their comfort zones, letting people feel external pressure and conflict in order to effect change.

- **Affiliative leadership**   Affiliative leaders focus on building strong relationships and leveraging those relationships to get things done. They tend to be very high in social skills and very good at building networks across the organization.

- **Dispersed leadership**   Successful leadership in an organization cannot reside solely in the top of the organization. Today's world is a complex, fluid, dynamic environment. Organizations need leaders at every level of the organization, from the bottom to the top. It's imperative that leadership is embraced by everyone in the organization.

- **Soul-based leadership**   Soul-based leadership is based on the old concept of every living being on board a ship or a plane being considered a soul rather than an inanimate object. Every soul is important and treated with value. As a leadership style, this requires the incorporation of concepts like inclusiveness, equality, and autonomy. Everyone that works for you is a unique individual with something of value to offer. In the current state of the smart machine age, this also differentiates people from machines.

- **Situational leadership**   Situational leadership suggests that effective leaders are able to assess the development level of the people they are leading and then adapt their leadership style to match the situation. This allows them to provide the right level of direction, support, and guidance to help people develop their skills and reach their full potential.

- **Autocratic leadership**   The autocratic leader retains most of the authority, gives orders to subordinates, and expects that subordinates should give complete obedience to the orders issued. In this type of leadership, the decisions are taken by the leader without consulting others.

- **Democratic leadership**   Also called "shared leadership" or "participative leadership," democratic leadership encourages each team member to participate in decision-making by sharing their opinions. A democratic leader encourages open conversation, helps their project team members to set goals and evaluate their own performance, and motivates them to grow.

- **Directive leadership**   Under directive leadership, managers must guide the team's work goals and establish the path by which they can achieve those goals. Directive leadership sets clearly defined objectives and rules for team members.

- **Assertive leadership**   Assertive leaders are active, direct, specific, and honest. They respect themselves, require respect from others, and respect everyone they work with at all levels.

- **Supportive leadership**   In supportive leadership, the project manager does not simply delegate tasks and receive results but instead supports a team member until the task's completion. A major upside to supportive leadership is that the manager will work with the employee until they are empowered and skilled enough to handle tasks with minimal supervision in the future.

- **Consensus leadership**   A consensus leader makes a decision only after consulting the group members. A decision is not made final until all the members agree to support the decision.

Creating a Leadership Persona

You need to define what it means to be a leader and how you'll improve upon those leadership qualities as a project manager. When you think of a leader, you likely think of a personality of someone who's excited, inspiring, and leads by doing. Or maybe you think of a football coach giving a great half-time speech about overcoming the odds and winning the game. Or perhaps it's some combination of leadership characteristics that motivate, inspire, and prove admirable. All of these traits are centered on the personality of a good leader.

For your CAPM exam, you'll need to recognize some personality traits that directly affect your ability to serve as a leader for your project team. These personality traits stem from experience, maturity, patterns of thinking, feelings, and repeated behavior. Recognize these personality traits:

- **Authentic**   Show concern for others and accept who they are.
- **Courteous**   Be polite and behave respectfully toward others.
- **Creative**   Create, think through problems, and seek solutions through creativity.
- **Cultural**   Be sensitive to cultural norms and beliefs.
- **Emotional**   Show empathy, understand others' emotions, and manage personal emotions.
- **Empathetic**   Show that you care for the project team and stakeholders.
- **Ethical**   Be right in the moral sense—honest, responsible, respectful, and fair.
- **Fail fast/learn quickly mindset**   Acknowledge mistakes and put key learnings into action.
- **Honest**   Be bold in telling the truth.
- **Integrity**   Adhere to the PMI Code of Ethics and Professional Conduct and be truthful and honest enough to do what is right.
- **Intellectual**   Demonstrate intelligence and respect the intelligence of others.
- **Managerial**   Have management aptitude in all aspects of the project.
- **Political**   Understand the politics at play within an organization.
- **Service-oriented**   Provide for others what they need to be successful.
- **Social**   Be friendly, approachable, and understand the needs and wants of the project team and stakeholders.
- **Systemic**   Understand existing frameworks and systems and build project systems to get things done in an orderly fashion.
- **Transparent**   Keep team members in the loop, share the good and the bad (while not oversharing), and welcome honest feedback from the members of your team.

A project manager with a flexible leadership style and positive personality traits can build a project environment that prioritizes vision, creativity, motivation, enthusiasm, encouragement, and empathy.

Performing Project Integration

Project integration management addresses how the project is integrated with the goals, tactics, and vision of the organization. Integration at this level means that you're working with the project sponsor to ensure that the goals and objectives of the project mesh with the goals and objectives of the organization. A project must support the broader vision and purpose of the organization, or the project likely isn't contributing to business value and may have challenges garnering support within the organization.

Within the project level, the project manager continues integration by leading and managing the project team. The people who have the greatest effect on project success are the project team members. Project teams can include contractors, channel partners, and internal staff. The integration challenge is to create one project team from a diverse collection of contributors to optimize team performance and realize project benefits. The project manager can't do everything, of course, and the project team will execute the project plan. When the project team executes the project plan, their work needs to support the goals of the project, which in turn must support the goals of the organization. If those two things are not in sync, the project will no doubt face challenges, issues, and unrest.

Integrating Processes

Project managers must consider three other factors that contribute to the project's complexity:

- **Uncertainty in projects**   Projects by definition have some level of uncertainty. Not everything can be known before a project begins. Risk management and change control processes focus on understanding and controlling uncertainty.

- **Human behavior**   Perhaps the most complex aspect of project management is human behavior. People don't always get along, and this can cause problems within the project that stem from behavior outside of the project.

- **System behavior**   How your organization works is entirely different from how other organizations work. You'll need to understand the business framework of what it takes to interact with employees, departments, and systems to manage the project.

Building Your Cognitive-Level Integration

When we first begin as project managers, we're often assigned projects that are low priority, with easily achievable objectives. As we become more mature in the role of a project manager and gain experience and insight into project management, we're assigned more complex projects. It's the experience that gives us the wisdom to manage the more complex projects.

The idea of integration at the cognitive level means that we not only rely on our experience—an excellent teacher—but we also learn from others. We take classes, read books, attend PMI chapter meetings; we make a deliberate effort to learn more so that we can manage projects more effectively. Cognitive-level integration is the act of learning on purpose, not just by doing, to ensure that we're well-rounded in all knowledge areas of project management, even those areas we don't touch frequently. That's why your CAPM exam will cover the whole breadth of project management, even if you have little experience in Agile methodologies and business analysis frameworks.

Examining Context-Level Integration

Context-level integration is the management of a project in consideration of how the project environment has changed, and is changing, in organizations today. Consider a project 20 or 30 years ago: social networking, texting, and virtual teams weren't a reality back then, but these variables are certainly in play in most organizations today. As project managers, we need insight into how our projects will take advantage of these and other evolving project landscapes and how these elements can create benefits, or disruptions, to the project.

Your organization may allow texting and virtual teams in a project, while another organization may prohibit the use of those elements. Neither approach is better than the other; they're just different. Each facet of the context level brings benefits but also costs that can affect how a project moves forward. The project manager needs to understand what's allowed to be used, what's not allowed, what's being ignored, and why.

Chapter Summary

This chapter focused on the foundations of what it means to be a project manager. I wouldn't be surprised if you already recognize most of the information in this chapter if you're currently serving as a project manager and working toward your CAPM certification. However, don't shrug off these elements, because you'll likely see the information on your exam.

One of the most important parts of this chapter is recognizing the difference between project management and leadership. Management is about getting things done. Leadership is about aligning, motivating, and inspiring people. Be familiar with both aspects of project management, not just the mechanics of getting things done.

Management utilizes positional power to do the following:

- Maintain the project
- Administrate duties
- Focus on project systems
- Control the project work

- Focus on the next project achievements
- Question how and when things will happen
- Control and administer finances
- Keep the status quo
- Do the right things at the right time
- Address issues and problem-solve

Leadership influences and inspires people to do the following:

- Develop personality and skills
- Perform their work with innovation
- Build relationships
- Trust one another
- Examine the long-range vision of the project
- Question why and what will happen
- Challenge the status quo
- Do the right things at the right time
- Align with the organization's vision with motivation and inspiration

Some overlap exists between management and leadership, but the difference is in the attitude, the desire to do things well, and a positive mindset focused on serving others and serving the good of the stakeholders, team, and organization.

The role of the project manager is to manage the project work, lead the project team, and get things done. The project manager works with the project team to achieve the project objectives, contribute to business value, and coordinate the activities, communications, and events that happen within a project. Project managers facilitate processes to reach predefined results and then usher the project through initiating, planning, executing, monitoring and controlling, and ultimately into project closing.

Through experience and training, the project manager's competency increases. The project manager should ascertain their level of skill in management and leadership areas; identify strengths, weaknesses, opportunities, and threats; and then decide to improve upon management prowess. The PMI Talent Triangle aims to address the three common areas of education for project managers, which PMI labels Ways of Working, Power Skills, and Business Acumen.

The role of the project manager isn't just about managing project work and resources but also includes leadership. Leadership is the ability to align, motivate, and inspire people to want to do the project work, succeed in their lives, and focus on the long-range vision of the project. Leadership styles are the methods a project manager can utilize to help the project team members be inspired and motivated and to perform well within the project.

Questions

1. Project leadership and project management are not the same thing, but they are connected. Leaders and managers rely on communications within a project to help motivate, manage, and ensure that the project is moving forward toward its objectives. In communicating, the receiver restates what the sender has said to clarify the message and to enable the sender to offer more clarity if needed. What is this communication component called?

   A. Active listening

   B. Sender-receiver model

   C. Communications planning

   D. Leader listening

2. You are the project manager for your organization and you're working with a new client to start a project at the client's site. You and the client are negotiating the price, schedule, and other concerns for a contract for the new project. In the negotiating, you and the client should be negotiating for what result?

   A. Best price for the contracted work

   B. Fair agreement for both the client and the vendor

   C. Most profit for the contracted work

   D. Risk distribution between the two parties

3. You are the project manager of the Systems Upgrade Project for your organization. As a project manager, you want to influence the organization and the project team for the better. What two key aspects are most helpful in influencing your organization as a project manager?

   A. Management and leadership

   B. Communication skills and a positive attitude

   C. Experience and knowledge

   D. Experience and willingness to learn

4. Wendy is a new project manager for her company, and she's working with her project team to develop the project management plan. Wendy knows that she must rely on several different skills to make her first project successful. Of the following management skills, which will a project manager use most?

   A. Leading

   B. Communicating

   C. Influencing the organization

   D. Negotiating

5. Caitlin is the project manager for her department. She has been working with her manager to examine her skills and her career. Her manager believes that Caitlin should take more training in power skills to make her a better project manager in her organization. The power skills of a leader include the ability to manage relationships and conflict. Which activity best represents this power skill?

   A. Choosing the best team

   B. Building trust

   C. Creating a give-and-take relationship with the project sponsor

   D. Establishing two-way communication with the project sponsor

6. As a CAPM candidate you should be familiar with the PMI Talent Triangle. You'll be earning professional development units to maintain your CAPM certification status once you've passed the exam. Of the following choices, which are not primary sides of the PMI Talent Triangle? (Choose two.)

   A. Power Skills

   B. Ways of Working

   C. Continuing Education

   D. Business Acumen

   E. Communication Skills

7. While management is about getting things done, leadership is about motivating people. You know that leadership is a desirable trait for a project manager and is heavily referenced throughout the *PMBOK Guide*. Which of the following characteristics are attributes of leadership? (Choose three.)

   A. Fiscal responsibility

   B. Respect for others

   C. Problem-solving ability

   D. Desire to learn and improve

8. Greta is a junior project manager and new to her organization. Her current project has more than 100 stakeholders. Some of the stakeholders have competing objectives and are getting in Greta's way to get things done. To influence her stakeholders Greta needs which of the following?

   A. An understanding of the organizational budget

   B. To research and document proven business cases

   C. An understanding of formal and informal organizational systems

   D. Positional power

9. Markael is a new project manager in his company. Before joining this company, Markael worked as a project manager for more than 20 years at an IT service provider. Markael has a deep understanding of electronics, software development, and data warehouse technology and is highly skilled in his field. What type of power does Markael have in this scenario?

   A. Expert

   B. Positional

   C. Referent

   D. Information

10. What type of power does a project manager have when the team admires the project manager because they've worked with them before the current project or they know of their reputation as a project manager?

    A. Situational

    B. Referent

    C. Positional

    D. Expert

11. Nika is the project manager for her company, and her team likes working for her. Nika has a good attitude, is easy to work with, and is a good planner. The project team views Nika as a member of management who can give them a good review and possibly affect a bonus payment if the project is completed on time. What type of power does this project manager have?

    A. Punitive

    B. Situational

    C. Reward

    D. Guilt-based

12. There are several different tactics and leadership styles you can adopt in a project. Which one of the following is the best description of being a servant leader?

    A. The leader emphasizes the goals of the project and offers rewards and disincentives for the project team.

    B. The leader puts others first and focuses on the needs of the people the leader serves.

    C. The leader takes a hands-off approach to the project.

    D. The leader inspires and motivates the project team to achieve the project goals.

13. You are the project manager for your department. As a project manager, you will have to use some positional power to keep the project moving forward. You'll also need to develop leadership skills to align, motivate, and inspire people. Of the following choices, which one is most likely associated with management skills?

A. Focus on the next project achievements

B. Build relationships

C. Support the project team

D. Challenge the status quo

14. You are the project manager for your organization. In your current project, you're coaching Mary on project integration management. Mary has questions about project integration management at the context level. Which one of the following is the best example of project integration management at the context level?

A. Using social networking, texting, and virtual teams can help project managers to stay connected with their team members.

B. A robust communication management plan is dependent on the number of stakeholders involved in the project.

C. Larger projects require more detail than smaller projects.

D. Planning is an iterative activity that will happen throughout the project.

15. You are the project manager of a project. The project team is experiencing some trouble with a new material that the project will utilize. You gather the team to lead an active problem-solving session. Which one of the following is the best definition of active problem-solving?

A. Define the problem and the desired solution.

B. Discern the cause and the effect of the problem.

C. Document the problem and its characteristics to see the whole effect.

D. Test the materials to identify the solution.

16. Rajesh is a functional manager who regularly attends your retrospective meetings to check up on "his people" from the real estate division who are on the project. Rajesh likes to "play PM" and attracts attention to the fact that he is well liked by the project sponsor. Rajesh is seen as heroic and inspiring because he orchestrated the launch of the mobile home loan application last year. What form of power is Rajesh using?

A. Position/legitimate

B. Personal/referent

C. Authoritative/formal

D. Situational/substantial

17. A project manager is meeting with the project team. In this meeting, the top 10 percent of project team members are openly praised for their hard work. The bottom 10 percent of the project team members are disciplined and somewhat berated in the meeting. The balance of the project team is not addressed. What type of leadership is happening in this scenario?

   A. Transactional leadership

   B. Laissez-faire leadership

   C. Interactional leadership

   D. Pressure-based power

18. Andre is the project manager for his organization, and he has seven people on his project team. Who is responsible for executing the project plan and creating the project deliverables?

   A. Project lead

   B. Project manager and the project team

   C. Project manager

   D. Project team

19. As a project manager, you need both leadership and management skills. Which one of the following statements best describes the difference between leadership and management in a project?

   A. Management is the process of getting the results that are expected in the project. Leadership is the ability to motivate and inspire individuals.

   B. Management is the process of getting the results that are expected by the project stakeholders. Leadership is the ability to motivate and inspire individuals to work toward those expected results.

   C. Leadership is about creating excitement to be managed. Management is the coordination and administration of tasks to achieve a goal.

   D. Leadership is the process of getting the project team excited to create results that are expected by project stakeholders. Management is the ability to keep track of the project results.

20. Communication is paramount in project management and can best be summarized as follows: who needs what information, when do they need it, and who or what's the best _____ to deliver the message?

   A. person

   B. resource

   C. format

   D. modality

Answers

1. A. Active listening is the participatory component of a conversation that confirms what was said and enables the sender to offer clarity, if needed. B is incorrect because the sender-receiver model shows how communication moves between two people. C is incorrect because communications planning is a project management process plan for who needs what information, when the information is needed, and in what modality. D is incorrect because leader listening is not a valid project management term.

2. B. The purpose of negotiations is to reach a fair agreement for all parties involved. A and C are incorrect because these two choices are mutually exclusive and not concerned with the other party in the contract. D is incorrect because the fair agreement between the parties would address the risk distribution.

3. B. The two key aspects that are most helpful in influencing an organization are communication skills and a positive attitude. A is incorrect because, although management and leadership are values for a project manager, they aren't the most helpful aspects of influence. C is incorrect because experience and knowledge are self-contained skills and don't do much to influence, inspire, and motivate others. D is incorrect because, although experience and a willingness to learn are good attributes and are intrinsic for a good project manager, they will not influence the organization.

4. B. Communication is the key general management skill a project manager will use the most. A, C, and D are incorrect because, although leading, influencing the organization, and negotiating are necessary management skills, communication accounts for the majority of a project manager's time.

5. B. Building trust is an underlying aspect of managing relationships and conflict. Other aspects are satisfying concerns; seeking consensus; balancing competing and opposing goals; using persuasion, compromise, and conflict resolution skills; developing and nurturing personal and professional networks; taking a long-term view; and continuously developing and applying political acumen. A, C, and D are incorrect. A is incorrect because not all managers choose a team—some inherit a team, and they still have to be able manage relationships and conflict. C is incorrect because managing conflicts and relationships happens between the project managers and stakeholders other than the project sponsor. D is incorrect because leadership is not focused on just the relationship with the project sponsor.

6. C, E. Continuing Education and Communication Skills are not among the three sides of the PMI Talent Triangle. A, B, and D are incorrect because the three sides of the PMI Talent Triangle are Power Skills, Ways of Working, and Business Acumen.

7. B, C, D. Leadership skills include respect for others, problem-solving ability, and a desire to learn and improve. A is incorrect because fiscal responsibility is an example of a management skill. Fiscal responsibility is also a desirable trait for project managers, but it's a management skill rather than a leadership skill.

8. **C.** To influence an organization (to get things done), a project manager must understand the explicit (formal) and implied (informal) organizational system within an organization. A is incorrect because the project manager may not even have access to an organizational budget. B is incorrect because a proven business case may not map to every scenario when influencing an organization. D is incorrect because positional power may relate only to a small portion of an organization, not to multiple facets of influence.

9. **A.** Markael has expert power in this scenario because he's highly skilled in this technology. B is incorrect because positional power is also known as formal, authoritative, and legitimate power. C is incorrect because referent power is a result of your own personality and whether or not you are liked and respected by other people. D is incorrect because information power means the individual has control of the data gathering and distribution of information.

10. **B.** Of all the choices presented, referent power is the best answer. The project manager is respected or admired because the project team has knowledge of past experiences with the project manager. This is about the project manager's credibility in the organization. A is incorrect because situational power means the project manager has power because of certain situations in the organization. C is incorrect because with positional power, the project manager has legitimate, formal, hierarchy power. D is incorrect because expert power means the project manager has deep skills and experience in a discipline.

11. **C.** When the project team sees the project manager as someone who can reward them, the project manager has reward power. A is incorrect because punitive power means the team thinks the project manager can punish them. A is incorrect because situational power is a distractor. D is incorrect because guilt-based power is a distractor.

12. **B.** A servant leader puts others first and focuses on the needs of the people the leader serves. Servant leaders provide opportunity for growth, education, autonomy within the project, and the well-being of others. The primary focus of servant leadership is service to others. A is incorrect because this answer describes transactional leadership. C is incorrect because this answer describes a laissez-faire leadership approach. D is incorrect because this answer describes the transformational leadership style.

13. **A.** Management focuses on the next project achievements. B, C, and D are incorrect because these three choices are attributes of leadership. Leaders do build relationships, support the project team, and challenge the status quo. This isn't to say that managers don't do these things, but it's the attribute of management versus the attribute of leadership in this question.

14. **A.** Of all the choices presented, this answer is the best example of project integration management at the context level. B, C, and D are incorrect examples of project integration management at the context level.

15. **A.** Active problem-solving begins with problem definition. Problem definition is the ability to discern between the cause and effect of the problem. Root cause analysis looks beyond the immediate symptoms to the cause of the symptoms—which then affords opportunities for solutions. B, C, and D are incorrect choices because these approaches don't first define the effect and the causes, which is crucial to active problem-solving.

16. **B.** This type of power is based on charm and attraction. A is incorrect because positional/legitimate power is the formal position granted in the organization or team. C is incorrect because authoritative or formal power is the formal position granted in the organization or team. D is incorrect because situational/substantial power is a distracter.

17. **A.** Transactional leadership means the leader emphasizes the goals of the project and offers rewards and disincentives for the project team. This is sometimes called management by exception, because it's the exception that is rewarded or punished. B is incorrect because laissez-faire leadership means the leader takes a hands-off approach to the project. C and D are incorrect because the leader is a hybrid of transactional, transformational, and charismatic leaders. The interactional leader wants the team to act, is excited and inspired about the project work, yet still holds the team accountable for their results. Pressure-based power is not a leadership type, but rather a type of power where the project manager can restrict choices to get the project team to perform the project work.

18. **D.** The project team members are responsible for executing the project plan and creating the project deliverables. A is incorrect because the project lead isn't the only role responsible for executing the plan. B is tempting, but it is incorrect because the project team is responsible for executing the plan—that is, doing the work to create the project deliverables. C is incorrect because, although the project manager may be accountable for the project, it's the project team that builds the project deliverables.

19. **B.** Of all the choices, this answer best describes the difference between leadership and management in a project. Management is the process of getting the results that are expected by project stakeholders. Leadership is the ability to motivate and inspire individuals to work toward those expected results. A, C, and D are incorrect because these statements do not reflect the difference between management and leadership in a project.

20. **D.** Project communication can be summed up as follows: who needs what information, when do they need it, and what's the best modality to deliver the message. A, B, and C are not valid choices. Although these are tempting choices, they aren't the best answers to the question.

References

- *PMBOK® Guide* (2021)
- *The PMI Guide to Business Analysis* (2017)

Managing a Project in Different Environments

In this chapter, you will

- Explore Agile methodologies for project management
- Learn how a project utilizes enterprise environmental factors
- Discover how to work with organizational process assets
- Understand how different organizations operate
- Learn the types of organizational structures and their characteristics

You have lots of work to do as a project manager: meetings, planning, coordination, leading the project team, and ensuring that the project work is done according to the project plan. You're with the project all the way, from the get-go to the final lessons learned report. You work with business analysts to elicit requirements from stakeholders. You keep stakeholders informed of changes and manage their contribution to the project. It's an ongoing job that ends just after the project work does.

Within your organization, several factors affect how you manage the project. You and the project team must follow organizational rules for managing and doing the project work. In your role as a project manager, you're expected to complete forms, use specific software, templates, and perform other duties that are unique to your organization. Regulations and laws may also affect how you and the team do the project work. If you're using an Agile approach to project management, you must enforce and follow specific rules. In addition to these items, you may leverage and adapt past project files, records, and information databases to make the current project management experience more successful.

These enterprise environmental factors, organizational process assets, and organizational systems all affect your success as a project manager. Enterprise environmental factors and organizational process assets are referenced over and over in the *PMBOK Guide,* the *PMI Guide to Business Analysis,* and in this book because they have a direct influence on the processes you'll utilize in your projects. For the CAPM exam, you will need to recognize these organization-specific considerations that affect projects and business analysis work.

EXAM TIP Remember that the CAPM exam tests a lot of elements, including your understanding of PMI terminology and concepts. You may come across questions that have one answer option that is a term you would use on the job and another answer option that is the equivalent PMI term. In this instance, always answer according to the PMI terminology. For example, PMI uses the term "activity" to mean "a distinct, scheduled portion of work performed during the course of a project." You probably use the term "task," which is what software programs call it.

Exploring Agile Methodologies for Project Management

Adaptive, Agile, Scrum: you've likely heard agile project management go by lots of different names. Agile project management, regardless of the specific approach, has one central theme: change is expected and welcome. The truth is, there are lots of different types of agile project management, and it's a growing philosophy to project management that's now 20 percent of your CAPM exam. That's right; you'll need to know a good deal about agile project management for your CAPM exam. This is a big shift from CAPM exams in the past, but don't worry if you're not experienced in Agile. In this section, I'll walk you through the big picture of agile project management, and I'll continue to address agile frameworks/methodologies in Chapter 5.

Let's nail down the two big camps of project management right away: predictive and Agile. *Predictive* is the traditional project management approach, where everything is predicted up front in the project. The project team and stakeholders work together to define the requirements and create a plan, and then they resist any changes to the project scope, because any change in scope can skew the entire project. *Agile* project management is flexible: changes are welcome in the project. Agile projects prioritize requirements throughout the project, and changes can enter the project but have to be prioritized, so some initial items may get bumped down the requirements list to make room for more important items that the stakeholders decide they really want.

When you begin a project to build a house, you can define everything that's going to happen in the construction project, all the way down to a single cabinet in the kitchen. When developing software, however, you don't always know exactly what's needed in that software. You and your customer may have identified a lot of the requirements, but those may change over time. In a predictive project, such as a construction project, it's difficult to change after the project is in motion. Agile welcomes change and expects change.

As of this writing, 20 percent of your CAPM exam will be on agile project management. That's approximately 30 questions (depending on the makeup of the 15 pretest questions). Although that is a big slice of the exam, consider that many of the exam questions are either obviously related to predictive projects or obviously related to Agile [agile] projects. You'll need to know some general rules of Agile, recognize the different Agile flavors, and always choose the best answer for business value. In that mix of 30 Agile-related questions, you'll also be tested on hybrid approaches to Agile—something that's really tough to define clearly because hybrid means an organization uses both predictive and agile methodologies in one project.

Scrum

When people think of agile projects, they almost always default to the most popular approach: Scrum. I'll admit that I'm biased toward Scrum; I'm certified in Scrum, and I love the Scrum approach to project management. Scrum has evolved since the 1990s, and the Agile Manifesto created a framework, a general structure, of how a Scrum project for developing software should operate. Scrum offers characteristics of product management—not just project management—because your goal is to create working software, or, for your exam, create value for the customer. Scrum is covered in detail in Chapter 5.

Kanban Method

The Kanban method is an evolution of the Japanese lean-manufacturing approach used in knowledge work projects in the early 2000s. Getting started with Kanban is pretty easy, because its main idea is to start where you are. The primary characteristic of Kanban is the Kanban board; that's where its name comes from—*Kanban* means visual signal. From Chapter 1, you'll remember the Kanban board shows the flow of work through the system so that you can visualize where the team is in the process, how the team delivers work, what work exists, and any limits to the work in progress (WIP).

Lean Principles

From manufacturing, Lean principles have been adapted into agile software production environments. IT teams work in a three-phase cycle of building, measuring, and learning. This approach creates a partnership mentality between the development team and the customers to ensure that the work being done is in constant alignment with the business value goals of the customers. Like all agile approaches, Lean prioritizes work based on feedback from the customer, but it adds the principles of reducing waste and keeping things simple. Simple, of course, doesn't mean that it's easy; it means that it's the *minimum viable product (MVP)*. MVP asserts that what's created is just enough to satisfy the project customers, while enabling the customers to offer feedback for improvements.

The Lean approach is deceptively simple. For Lean to be successful, the team and stakeholders need open communication, defined processes, and transparency throughout the project. Lean means constant improvement, constant growth, and the willingness to realize that increments of improvements—even small improvements—over time will result in increased business value.

Extreme Programming

Extreme Programming, or XP, is an agile framework that aims for quality software and a quality of life for the development team. XP can contribute to the quality of life for the development team by fostering a positive work environment, reducing individual pressure and stress, and providing opportunities for personal and professional growth.

XP promotes pair programming, in which all code is developed by a pair of programmers sitting together at the same machine. One person writes code while the other person does continuous code review. This can reduce the likelihood of working long hours to fix problems or meet deadlines, which can contribute to a better work-life balance.

Hybrid Agile Approaches

Agile project management approaches are evolving all the time. No laws dictate which approach an organization must use or how an organization chooses to utilize Agile. You're free to choose the best parts of several different approaches and meld together a new homegrown version of Agile that works for you. These homegrown approaches, called *hybrid approaches*, enable an organization to build a customized approach to project management. Hybrid can include traditional methodologies, such as planning in detail up front, and can then implement Scrum, Kanban, Lean, or XP practices thereafter.

EXAM TIP PMI promises that you'll see some questions about hybrid on your exam—nothing to be worried about. Recognize the main themes of these agile approaches and the predictive approach used in traditional environments.

Disciplined Agile

Disciplined Agile (DA) is an agile methodology that provides a flexible and pragmatic approach to software development that can be tailored to fit the unique needs of a team or organization. DA combines Agile and Lean principles and practices with other proven frameworks, such as Scrum, Kanban, and SAFe, to provide a comprehensive approach to software development.

The core principles of DA are customer focus, simplicity, pragmatism, and continuous improvement. DA recognizes that different teams and organizations have unique needs and constraints and provides a flexible framework that can be tailored to fit those needs. DA also emphasizes the importance of adopting a continuous improvement mindset, which involves regularly assessing and improving processes and practices to ensure that they are effective and efficient.

One of the key features of DA is its process goal-driven approach. DA defines a set of process goals that *teams can work toward,* such as "improve quality" or "reduce time-to-market." Each goal has a set of practices and techniques associated with it, which teams can use to achieve the goal. This approach allows teams to focus on the outcomes they want to achieve, rather than being overly prescriptive about the practices they use to get there.

Another important aspect of DA is its focus on scaling Agile to the enterprise level. DA provides guidance and tools for teams to work together in larger organizations, and it emphasizes the importance of coordination and collaboration between teams to achieve common goals.

In the Real World

Many different types of project management methodologies exist. They range from the highly iterative Agile methodologies used in IT projects to the more predictive methodologies (also known as traditional methodologies) that have a clear linear progression from project startup through to closure. In developing an appropriate project management methodology for an organization, consideration must be given to the type of projects, the size of projects, the organizational culture, the time frame for project delivery, and the maturity of the organization. The development of a project management methodology is not a one-size-fits-all proposition. In fact, a good methodology will always be flexible enough to accommodate different projects.

Working with Enterprise Environmental Factors

Enterprise environmental factors are conditions that the project manager must live with—they are outside of the project manager's control. Even if you don't like existing enterprise environmental factors, there's nothing much you can do about them; you've got to deal with them. Enterprise environmental factors will affect your project, influence your decisions, and even direct how you're allowed to do the project work. These factors can come from within your organization, such as a policy, or they can come from outside of the organization, such as a law or regulation.

Many project managers like to say that enterprise environmental factors are negative because they constrain the project manager's choices, but that's not always the case. Though some enterprise environmental factors can limit the project manager's options, some can make the project manager's job easier and help the project be more successful.

For example, one enterprise environmental factor in an organization could require that all the scheduling be managed by a person in a scheduler role. That's a fantastic constraint that frees the project manager's time from the tedious task of scheduling tasks.

Working with Internal Enterprise Environmental Factors

Internal enterprise environmental factors are conditions that your organization has created for the project manager. You don't always know why these factors exist—they may result from a policy, a department requirement, or a tradition. It's not always necessary to understand why you're required to do something; often it's just easier to accept it, do the work as it's been requested, and move on. Sometimes, however, an enterprise environmental factor can be outdated, and it doesn't hurt to understand why it's required, especially if the factor is getting in the way of progress.

For your exam, you'll probably be required to accept any existing internal enterprise environmental factors and work accordingly to answer exam questions.

Internal enterprise environmental factors include the following:

- **Organizational culture, structure, and governance** Your organization's mission, belief, culture, leadership, organizational hierarchy, and authority relationships are all examples of internal enterprise environmental factors that are part of your organization.

- **Geographic distribution of facilities and resources** Where your resources are located will affect how you manage the project, access resources, and schedule work. Resources are more than just people and also include physical resources. These factors can also address virtual teams and cloud computing—certainly elements that are now common and will affect the project.

- **Infrastructure** The facilities, equipment, IT hardware and software, and capabilities of the infrastructure are enterprise environmental factors that can limit, or propel, a project.

- **Resource availability** The time at which resources are available for your project will affect when your project can be completed. Resources include people, equipment, facilities, and materials.

- **Employee capability** Consider the expertise of your project team members. Their skills and knowledge can directly affect the project work. If the project centers on a new technology, team members' learning curves or skills gaps can affect the project duration and approach to the work.

- **Information technology software** Examples include scheduling software, mobile app development, network configuration, software implementation, hardware installation, database management, and IT emergency recovery.

Considering External Enterprise Environmental Factors

While internal environment influences are created by the organization, external environment influences exist outside of the organization. Influences external to the organization can enhance, constrain, or have a neutral influence on project outcomes. External environment influences, like internal influences, can affect the project for better or worse. Here are some of the most common external environment influences you should be able to recognize:

- **Marketplace conditions** The marketplace describes the climate your business operates within. Consider your organization's competitors, market share, brand recognition, technology trends, trademarks, and other factors that can affect how you manage your project.

- **Social and cultural influences** The political climate, ethics, regional customs and traditions, public holidays and events, codes of conduct, ethics, and perceptions about your business or trade can affect how you manage the project.

- **Legal restrictions** Some of the most common external environment influences are national and regional laws and regulations that directly affect your project, how your organization conducts business, employment, licensing, procurement practices, and how you protect data.

- **Commercial databases** Many industries, such as manufacturing and construction, utilize commercial databases to help predict duration of tasks, costs, risks, and what-if scenarios. If your organization uses such database types, it's using an external enterprise environmental factor.

- **Academic research** Publications, benchmarking, and industry studies that affect project decisions are enterprise environmental factors to consider. This information doesn't have to come from a university but could include information from trade associations or groups to which your organization belongs.

- **Industry standards**   Your organization may be required to adhere to government or industry standards regarding your project's production, quality of work, or products your organization creates.

- **Financial considerations**   These external enterprise environmental factors include international projects and currency exchange rates, interest rates, inflation rates for long-term projects, and other financial considerations that can influence project decisions.

- **Physical environment elements**   Where the project work will take place introduces external environment influences that can affect project decisions. The weather, access to job sites, and other constraints are all external enterprise environmental factors.

 EXAM TIP   For your exam, you'll probably be required to accept any existing internal and external environment influences and work accordingly to answer exam questions.

Leveraging Organizational Process Assets

Unlike enterprise environmental factors, organizational process assets (OPAs) are always internal to the organization. OPAs include organizational processes, policies, procedures, and items from a corporate knowledge base. OPAs are things that can be utilized to help business analysts do their job better. A common example of OPAs are documents from completed similar projects that can be adapted to the current project work to save time. Rather than create a project management plan from scratch with each project, the project manager can adapt a previous project to the current project and be on their way—that's one benefit of an OPA.

OPAs include anything from within the organization that you can use to manage business analysis better, including retrospective sessions, knowledge transfer, risk management templates, traceability tools, and even lessons learned from past projects. Organizational process assets are grouped into two categories:

- **Processes, policies, and procedures**   These OPAs are created outside of the project, such as from a project management office, and aren't updated or changed by the business analysis effort. Should a business analyst want to change or deviate from a process, policy, or procedure, they'd need good reason to do so and would need to follow the organization's approach to changing the policy.

- **Organizational knowledge repositories**   These OPAs are updated throughout the project. As you add information, such as cost and time, actual experiences, lessons learned, and performance metrics, you'll update the associated organizational process assets forms accordingly.

See the difference in these OPA categories? If it's a policy or process, you abide by it. If it's a form or template, you update, edit, and store it.

NOTE A general rule of thumb for remembering the difference between organizational process assets and enterprise environmental factors is that, generally speaking, OPAs can be used to assist a project, whereas EEFs will often constrain a project. Additionally, as the name suggests, organizational process assets must be owned by the organization, which is not true of EEFs.

In the Real World

The most common form of organizational process asset that most project managers encounter is the project management methodology that an organization has. A project management methodology itself can mean many things. It can be as simple as a range of blank templates available to the project manager, or at the other end of the spectrum, it can be a fully defined set of processes, procedures, templates, and databases that must be used for all projects.

Adhering to Processes, Policies, and Procedures

Let's examine some OPAs that your organization may have in place that affect how you manage a project. Remember that these OPAs are unique to your organization; they are not universal to all organizations. Processes, policies, and procedures are not part of the 49 project management processes, but are unique organizational processes that determine how you get things done in your organization. The rules of your project management methodology will help dictate who's required to do what in the project, how the team interacts, and what the expectations of the stakeholders are.

Utilizing Initiating and Planning Processes, Policies, and Procedures

When a project is first launched, the project manager and possibly other stakeholders may pause to examine the big picture of the project. This examination takes place early in the project to determine the project's overall magnitude. The size and scope of the project can determine what OPAs are needed: Are you building a skyscraper, developing software, or replacing laptops? What processes are needed to complete the project, based on the size and scope of the project?

If you aren't going to be purchasing anything for your current project, there's no need to deal with the procurement processes. And if you are purchasing items, you may be required to use a preapproved vendor list to obtain these items, which is an OPA. Your organization may have created such process assets to help you select which project management processes are needed and which are not, based on the project's goals.

Other OPAs to consider at the launch of the project are human resource policies, management approaches, estimating techniques, checklists, and improvement goals for your project. Your organization may also require that templates be used for project plans and forms be used for resource assignments, and other assets may have been created for you to help assist the launch and planning of your project. Of course, all of these project management processes can be tailored to what works in your organization. The project management processes are not prescriptions, and not all processes are needed to the same depth on all projects.

Recognizing Executing, Monitoring, and Controlling Processes, Policies, and Procedures

As your project moves into executing the project plan, you'll also be working with monitoring and controlling activities. In both of these project management process groups, OPAs may have been created by your organization to use within portions of your project. One of the most common OPAs for any company is a process for how changes to the project are managed. Your organization can utilize forms, a web site, or special software to enter, track, and control changes—these are OPAs.

Tracking activities, requirements, costs, issues, and defects is also a part of OPAs. Though tracking such items is a typical requirement of project management, how you do this within your organization may be unique to your organization and entirely different from how a project manager tracks these items in another organization. The concept is the same, but the application of the OPAs is specific to each organization.

Several other OPAs are utilized in executing, monitoring, and controlling processes, policies, and procedures:

- Communications requirements and approaches to communicating
- Prioritizing, approving, and tracking work authorization
- Templates and forms (consider the change log, risk register, and issue log)
- Organizational standards for work, proposal evaluation for vendors, and performance measurement

Reviewing Closing Processes, Policies, and Procedures

Closing is a project management activity that can happen at the end of each project phase and at the end of the project. Your organization may have a particular approach to how you'll close a project or phase. Consider final project audits, evaluations, signoffs for deliverable acceptance, contract closure, release of project resources, and knowledge transfer. The final activities prescribed by your organization for a project are all part of its OPAs.

EXAM TIP Remember that in Scrum, you close out each sprint with a retrospective to improve upon the next sprint of the project.

Leveraging Organizational Knowledge Repositories

Organizational knowledge repositories include the databases, files, and historical information that you can use to help plan and manage your projects. These organizational process assets are created internally to your organization through the ongoing work of operations and other projects. A knowledge repository should be organized, searchable, easy to access, and part of all project managers' go-to resources—though that may not be the case in every organization. Having worked as a consultant with big and small companies, I have seen organizational knowledge repositories stuffed in a hallway closet, including reports and project plans—basically a jumbled mess, and hardly an ideal situation.

For your CAPM exam, go with the idea that an organizational knowledge repository is an electronic set of databases that you can access quickly to find the information you need. Here are some examples of organizational knowledge repositories:

- Repositories of historical information from past projects
- Data repositories for metrics
- Issue and defect management data repositories
- Business knowledge repositories
- Repositories of configuration management knowledge from past projects
- Lessons learned repositories

Working Within an Organizational System

Of course, where you manage a project will be entirely different from where I manage a project. The environment in which we both work, the expectations of our organizations, the reporting structures, and the rules we follow are unique to each organization. The structure of the organization and the governance framework create constraints that affect how the project manager makes decisions within the project. The organizational system directly affects how the project manager utilizes their power, influence, leadership, and even political capital to get things done in the environment.

For your CAPM exam, you'll need to recognize that the organizational system can be a type of constraint, because the organizational system will affect how the project manager acts within that system. Stakeholders with more power, influence, and political capabilities than the project manager can also directly affect how the project is managed, the goals of the project, and other stakeholder interests in the project. Though you won't need to know all the characteristics of organizational development, you will need to know some key facts about how projects may operate in different organizations.

Working in a System

Organizations are, to some extent, a system. A system uses multiple components to create things that the individual components could not create if they worked alone. For example, consider the system involved when purchasing something on the Internet: web client, service provider, web host, payment gateway, payment processor, credit card company, and likely more components, depending on the transaction and individuals involved. All these different components are needed to make the purchase happen. It's a system that creates a result for the customer and the retailer.

Regarding project management, *systems* describe the components your organization deals with to reach the desired result. Systems are dynamic and can be optimized for better performance. The individual components within a system can also be optimized independently of the system. The interaction of these components creates the organizational culture and capabilities. The organizational systems determine the power, influence, interest, competencies, and political sense of the people within the systems.

Project managers typically don't manage a system—that's the responsibility of an organization's management—but the project manager may see opportunities for improvement within the system and make recommendations accordingly. Projects operate within the system that the organization has created, and just because a system exists doesn't mean that the system was planned or that it is effective.

Operating Within a Governance Framework

The governance framework includes the rules, policies, and procedures that people within an organization agree to abide by. It's the structure that everyone agrees to operate within as part of the organization. Governance frameworks operate within systems, but frameworks are more about creating boundaries, providing directions, and establishing the roles and responsibilities of the people and groups within the organization. Governance frameworks define how the objectives of the organization are created, how risks are assessed and tracked, and how organizational performance can be optimized.

For your CAPM exam, you'll need to recognize that a *governance framework* addresses the organization, but it also addresses projects. Regarding projects, a governance framework needs to address four key factors:

- Alignment with organizational mission
- Risk management and distribution of positive and negative risks
- Performance on time, costs, and technical objectives
- Communications with the correct stakeholders at the correct time

A governance framework is a top-down approach to control within the organization. Though the leadership and management of the organization may have created a governance framework, the governance of each project and program will be more specific to the particular program and project. For your exam, know that *project governance* includes defining the authority to approve changes and make other business decisions related to the project. The project governance can be created by the project manager, or the governance framework can be established by the project management office, the department the project is operating within, or the organization itself.

Identifying the Organizational Influences

Projects happen within organizations, and in most instances, the organization is larger than the project. This means that you, as a project manager, must answer to someone, some department, or even a customer of the organization. As much as I'd like to call all the shots on all the projects I manage, and I'm sure you wish the same, we both know we must answer to someone within our organization. The people that project managers answer to are the *organizational influences*.

How a project is influenced is largely based on the type of organization that the project is occurring within. Project-centric organizations fall under two big umbrellas:

- **Organizations that exist primarily to perform projects for others**   Think of architects, IT consulting firms, engineering firms, design consultants, and just about any other agency that completes work for others on a contract basis. (This is what I do as a writer and corporate educator, for example.)

- **Organizations that use management by projects to manage their business**
These organizations manage their work through their project management system. An IT department, for example, may treat an upgrade of all their network servers as a project. A manufacturer may treat the creation of a customer's product as a project. In the traditional sense, these activities are part of the organization's operations, but because there's a definite beginning and ending to that specific work, the organizations are taking advantage of project management systems they've adapted or created.

You also must consider the maturity of the organization in which the project is being hosted. A large internal organization that's been established for years will likely have a more detailed project management system than a startup entrepreneurial company. Organizational standards, regulations, culture, and procedures influence how the project should be managed, how the project manager will lead and discipline the project team, the reporting relationships, and the flow of communications that will take place.

It's also important for the project manager to know the organization's *cultural norms* and to operate accordingly. Consider the following cultural components within an organization:

- Defined values, beliefs, and expectations of the project work
- Policies and procedures, both within the organization and external to the organization (consider the policies that govern the banking industry, for example)
- Defined authority for the project manager and over the project manager
- Defined working hours and work ethics of the project team, project manager, and management

NOTE *Cultural norms* describe the culture and the styles of an organization. Cultural norms such as work ethic, work hours, views of authority, and shared values can affect how a project is managed.

Completing Projects in Different Organizational Structures

In addition to the organizational system and the governance framework, project managers must also consider the organizational structure they are operating within. The organizational structure is more than just the hierarchy of the organization, reporting structures, and authority over resources; it also defines how the authority, resources, roles, and functions are distributed throughout the organization. For example, a company could divide the organization according to departments and have departments "hire" teams from other departments to complete assignments. Or the organization could be structured by roles and responsibilities, where resources are freely used among the different departments and lines of business. Or there could be hundreds of other structures, rules, and configurations regarding how an organization structures its lines of business, departments, and resources.

For your CAPM exam, however, you'll need to recognize only the most common types of organizational structures and how each structure will influence the project manager's power over project decisions, the budget, and project team members. Which structure you're operating within will determine how much authority you have in the organization and in the project. For your exam, you'll need to recognize the organizational structure and then answer questions based on the structure presented in the question. You may see several very similar questions, and the only thing that changes in the question is the organizational structure—which would, of course, change the answer entirely. Knowing these structures will help you tremendously on the CAPM exam.

Recognizing Organizational Structures

Organizations are structured into one of several models that will affect some aspect(s) of the project. The organizational structure will set the level of authority, the level of autonomy, and the reporting structure that the project manager can expect to have within the project.

Organizational structures include the following:

- Functional (centralized)
- Weak matrix
- Balanced matrix
- Strong matrix
- Project-oriented
- Virtual
- Hybrid

 NOTE Understanding the type of organizational structure you're working in will help you be a better project manager.

Functional Structure

Functional organizations, sometimes called *centralized organizations*, are entities that have clear divisions regarding business units and their associated responsibilities. For example, a functional organization may have an accounting department, a manufacturing department, a research and development department, a marketing department, and so on. Each department works as a separate entity within the organization, and each employee works within a department unique to their area of expertise. In these centralized organizations, there is a clear relationship between an employee and a specific functional manager.

Projects in a functionalized structure may find general resistance to collaboration across its organization. Functional organizations do complete projects, but these projects are specific to the function of the department that the project falls into. For example, the IT department could implement new software for the finance department. The role of the IT department is separate from that of the finance department, but the need for coordination between the two would be evident. Communications between departments flow through functional managers down to the project team.

Project managers in functional organizations have the following attributes and resources:

- Little power
- Little autonomy
- Report directly to a functional manager
- May be known as a project coordinator, project expeditor, project administrator, or team leader (or project scapegoat)
- Project role is part-time
- Project team is part-time
- Little or no administrative staff to expedite the project management activities

Matrix Structures

Matrix structures are organizations that blend departmental duties and employees together on a common project. These structures allow for project team members from multiple departments to work together toward the project completion. In these instances, the project team members have more than one boss. Depending on the number of projects a team member is participating in, they may have to report to multiple project managers as well as to their functional manager.

Weak Matrix Structure   Weak matrix structures map closely to functional structures. The project team may come from different departments, but the project manager reports directly to a specific functional manager.

Project managers in weak matrix organizations have the following attributes and resources:

- Limited authority
- Management of a part-time project team
- Part-time project role
- May be known as a project coordinator, project expeditor, project administrator, or team leader
- May have part-time administrative staff to help expedite the project

Balanced Matrix Structure   A balanced matrix structure has many of the same attributes as a weak matrix, but the project manager has more time requirements and power regarding the project. A balanced matrix structure includes time-accountability issues for all the project team members, because their functional managers will want reports on their time spent within the project.

Project managers in a balanced matrix have the following attributes and resources:

- Reasonable authority
- May manage a part-time project team
- A full-time role as a project manager
- May have part-time administrative staff to help expedite the project

Strong Matrix Structure

A strong matrix equates to a strong project manager. In this type of organization, many of the same attributes for the project team exist, but the project manager gains power when it comes to project work. The project team may also have more time available for the project, even though the members may come from multiple departments within the organization.

Project managers in a strong matrix have the following attributes and resources:

- A higher level of power
- Management of a part-time to nearly full-time project team
- A full-time role as a project manager
- A full-time administrative staff to help expedite the project

Project-Oriented Structure

The project-oriented structure is at the pinnacle of project management structures. This organizational type groups employees, colocated or not, by activities on a project. The project manager in a project-oriented structure may have complete, or very close to complete, power over the project team. Project managers enjoy a high level of autonomy over their projects, but they also have higher levels of responsibility regarding the project's success.

Project managers in a project-oriented structure have the following attributes and resources:

- High to complete level of authority over the project team
- Work full-time on the project with a team (though there may be some slight variation)
- A full-time administrative staff to help expedite the project
- Manage the budget
- Support of a strong PMO

Virtual Structure

A virtual organization uses a network structure to communicate and interact with other groups and departments. A point of contact exists for each department, and these people receive and send all messages for the department. As you might assume, communications can sometimes be challenging in this structure because all messages are filtered through the department's point of contact.

Virtual organizations can be structured based on departments, but also on groups of stakeholders in a larger project. The project manager in a virtual organization has low authority over the project team and shares authority over the project budget with the functional manager. Depending on the project size, the project manager could be full-time, but the project team is likely part-time. In this structure, the project manager could have part-time or even full-time administrative staff to help with the project management.

Hybrid Structure

Truth is, few companies map to only one of these structures all the time. For example, a company using the functional model may create a special project consisting of talent from many different departments. Such project teams report directly to a project manager and will work on a high-priority project for its duration. These entities are sometimes called *composite* organizations because they may be a blend of multiple organizational types.

Table 2-1 summarizes the most common organizational structures and their attributes.

 EXAM TIP The CAPM exam usually does not identify the organizational structure being discussed. When the question does not specify a form, assume matrix.

	Project Manager Authority	Project Manager Role	Resources on Project	Budget Control	Project Administrative Staff
Functional (centralized)	Low	Part time	Little	Functional manager	Part time
Strong matrix	Moderate to high	Full time	Moderate to high	Project manager	Full time
Weak matrix	Low	Part time	Low	Functional manager	Part time
Balanced matrix	Low to moderate	Part time	Low to moderate	Project manager and functional manager	Part time
Project-oriented	High to almost total	Full time	High to total	Project manager	Full time
Virtual	Low to moderate	Full or part time	Low to moderate	Mixed	Full or part time
Hybrid	Mixed	Mixed	Mixed	Mixed	Mixed

Table 2-1 Organizational Structures and Their Influence on Project Managers

Managing Project Teams

The type of organizational structure you're operating within will also determine the type of project team you're managing. As outlined in the previous section, in a project-oriented structure, you'll have a full-time project team, sometimes called a *dedicated* project team. In a functional or matrix environment, you'll likely have a part-time team. When you're working with project team members that float from project to project, as in a matrix environment, you'll have to coordinate with other project managers, functional managers, and the project team members about your project plans and need for resources.

Project teams in a functional, matrix, or project-oriented organizational structure often use contract-based workers to help achieve the project scope. These contractors are individuals who are represented by third parties or consulting agencies. When you're working with companies that have been hired to help and become part of the project team, you've created a partnership between your company and the vendor's company. This partnership is ruled by the contract and may conflict with the project manager's approach, style, and project governance. You can alleviate much of the strain in a partnership by clearly communicating expectations of the entire project team and determining as early as possible whether the contractors have issues with the way the project team will be managed.

In today's electronic-based world, it's more and more common to work with virtual teams. Virtual teams use web-collaboration software to enable employees to work remotely, to host meetings, and to share electronic workspaces. This, of course, saves on travel expenses, enables utilization of talented workers from all areas of an organization, and permits easier communications than telephone conversations and e-mail. Virtual teams do face additional problems that need to be addressed, such as time zone differences, language barriers, technology reliability, and cultural differences.

Working with a Project Management Office

A *project management office (PMO)* represents a management structure that standardizes project-related governance processes and facilitates the sharing of resources, tools, methodologies, and techniques. A PMO coordinates the activities of all the project managers by providing improved project management in terms of scope, schedule, cost, quality, risk, and other factors. Its primary goal is to create a uniform approach to how projects operate within the organization.

PMOs can exist in any structure, but most are used in matrix structures and in project-oriented environments. Organizations establish a PMO for a variety of reasons: aligning work with strategic goals, engaging and collaborating with stakeholders, developing talent, and realizing value from investments in projects. The character and function of a PMO vary between organizations, and even within the same organization.

The role of a PMO is typically to support the project manager in the form of providing templates, project management software, training, and leadership, and even granting authority for the project's existence. Often, the PMO provides the administrative support a project manager can expect in a project-oriented environment.

Here's the big caveat with PMOs: Project team members in a PMO-oriented environment are traditionally working on one project at a time. A PMO, however, may elect to share project team members among projects if this best serves the organization. So, basically, there's no hard-and-fast rule for the assignment of project team members to an individual project if they are reporting to the PMO rather than directly to the project manager.

EXAM TIP   For your CAPM exam, keep this in mind: The project manager reports to the PMO, and the PMO may exercise its authority over the project manager's control of the project team.

There are several types of PMOs in organizations. Exploring how each type varies in the degree of support, control, and direction, as well as assigned roles and responsibilities, reveals the range of benefits PMOs can deliver. Here are some common PMO types you should recognize for your CAPM exam:

- **Supportive**   The PMO plays a consultative role, providing templates, training, historical information, and best practices.
- **Controlling**   The PMO controls the project through specific project management methodologies the project manager is required to use, such as frameworks, tools, forms and templates, and governance frameworks.
- **Directive**   The PMO manages the project directly. The project manager is part of the PMO and is assigned to projects through the PMO only.

Case Study: Managing Projects from Start to Completion

This case study examines the project process and the phases a project moves through to reach its conclusion. The Riverside Community Park Project was an endeavor to create a 140-acre community recreation park alongside the White River. The project, led by Thomas Stanford and assisted by Jan Steinberg, offered many deliverables for the community, including the following:

- A walkway along the river, connecting restaurants and neighborhoods
- Hiking trails
- Baseball and soccer fields
- Water access points
- Picnic areas
- Children's playgrounds
- An indoor swimming facility
- Parking areas

Examining the Project Deliverables

The first phase of the project was in-depth planning and development. The project scope was broken down into four major categories:

- River-related deliverables, such as docks and fishing areas
- Structural-related deliverables, such as the indoor swimming facility
- Environment-related deliverables, such as the hiking trails
- Common areas, such as the picnic and parking areas

Each of these deliverables was broken down into components that could, in turn, be broken down into exact deliverables for the project. For example, the indoor swimming facility included the excavation of the grounds for the building, the construction of the building, and the construction of the indoor swimming pool.

Each deliverable was broken down to ensure that all the required components were included in the project plan. Each category of deliverables went through a similar process to ensure that all the deliverables were accounted for and that the project plans were complete. Stanford and Steinberg worked with a large project team that specialized in different disciplines within the project work.

For example, Holly Johnson of EQHN Engineering served as team lead for the river-related deliverables. Johnson had years of experience in construction projects dealing with lakes, rivers, and manufactured waterways. Her expert judgment contributed to the development of the plan and the work breakdown.

Don Streeping of RHD Architecture and Construction helped Stanford develop the requirements, features, and components of the indoor swimming facility. RHD architects designed the building and swimming facilities for the project and helped map out the timeline for a feasible completion and successful opening day.

Grey Jansen with the Department of Natural Resources and Marci Koening with the Department of Urban Planning worked with Stanford to create several different hiking trails and a pedway along the riverfront. The elaborate trail system offered trails ranging from challenging hikes to pleasant strolls. In addition, the pedway allowed visitors to walk through more than 50 acres along the river and to visit restaurants, shopping centers, and other commercial ventures within the park. Without Jansen's and Koening's expertise, the project would not have been a success.

Finally, John Anderson led the team responsible for the common areas. The children's playgrounds were topnotch, with ample parking and access to the park. In addition, Anderson's team created soccer fields and two Little League baseball diamonds.

Examining the Project Phases

When the project was launched, the 140-acre tract was a marshy, brush-filled plot of land that was mostly inaccessible to the public. For this undertaking to be successful, the project had to move through several phases. Many of the deliverables, such as the parking areas and maintenance roads, had to be created first to allow the equipment and workers to access the sites throughout the park.

Phase One

The first phase of the project was in-depth planning. Stanford and Steinberg worked with each of the team leaders and other experts to coordinate the activities to create the deliverables in a timely fashion. To maximize the return on investment, the project's plan called for immediate deliverables for the public.

The planning phase of the project resulted in the following:

- The project plan and subsidiary plans, such as cost, risk, and scope management plans
- Design specifications for each of the major deliverables
- A schedule that enabled the project team and stakeholders to work together to create the project deliverable
- The creation of a work authorization system
- Continued community buy-in for the project

Phase Two

Once the project's plan and coordination between teams was realized, John Anderson's crew went to work on Phase Two of the project: creating accessibility. This phase of the project became known as the "rough-in" phase because roads, parking, and preparation of the park were needed immediately. This phase resulted in the following:

- Access roads throughout the park
- Entry roads to the park at several points throughout the city
- Junction roads that allowed easy access for construction equipment to be stored on site for the project's duration
- Right-of-way for access to public land

Phase Three

In Phase Three of the project, each team began working independently, each with an eye toward common delivery dates. For example, Johnson and Jansen had expertise in separate deliverables: the water access points and the trails throughout the park. The project plan called for trails along the river and through the woods, which would be built by Johnson's crew. In tandem with creating the hiking trails, Johnson's team went to work on the river pedway. At several points along the river pedway, trails from the woods would connect to the paved surface. These two deliverables were timed so that both teams would work together on connecting the nature trails with the river pedway. In addition, preservation of the environment in the woods and in the water was an important consideration.

Streeping's primary responsibility was the creation of the indoor swimming facility. This deliverable required excavation, construction of the indoor swimming pool, and construction of the facility to house the indoor swimming pool. Streeping had to coordinate the construction with Anderson, as the swimming pool required the largest parking area in the compound. Stanford and Steinberg worked with each team leader to facilitate a common schedule for each of the deliverables.

This phase saw its first completed deliverable for the project: a children's playground was opened near the park entrance that the public could begin using immediately. The playground could host up to 75 children at once with parking for up to 50 cars. In addition, a picnic shelter was opened adjacent to the playground. Because of the proximity of the park and playground to nearby shops and restaurants, this deliverable was well received by the community, and the public began enjoying the facilities immediately.

Other deliverables in the phase included the following:

- Restroom facilities installed at several points throughout the park
- Excavation of several water access points
- Excavation for the swimming facility
- Clearing and leveling for the soccer and baseball fields

Phase Four

Phase Four of the project focused on creating more usable deliverables for the public. The focus was on the hiking trails throughout the park and on partial completion of the river pedway. The hiking trails required brush to be removed, some trees to be removed, and the land to be graded for passable hiking. The pedway was initially formed as a concrete path that would be blacktopped once it was connected throughout the park. Like the hiking trails, the pedway required the removal of brush and trees while considering the environmental preservation of the river.

Jansen's and Anderson's teams worked together to clear the pedway, remove the brush along the riverbank, and preserve the older trees to create a stunning walk along the river. To create maximum deliverables, the pedway was implemented at opposite ends of the 50-acre trail, with plans to be connected at acre 25. This allowed the public to enjoy the deliverables in increments from either end of the park.

This phase created these deliverables:

- Seven of the ten hiking trails in the system were cleared and opened for public usage.
- A total of 30 acres of the river pedway were completed (15 acres on both ends of the pedway).
- The swimming pool was excavated and the concrete body of the pool was installed.

Phase Five

Phase Five of the project was perhaps the most exciting, as it completed several deliverables:

- The remaining three hiking trails were completed. These trails included bridges over small creeks that feed into the White River.
- The remaining 20 acres of the river pedway were excavated and completed with the concrete pour. People could then walk or ride their bikes the entire 50-acre length alongside the river.

- The soccer and baseball facilities were installed, which included restrooms, concession stands, bleachers, fences, and dugouts. The fields were also seeded and fertilized, with expectations to be officially open for public use the following spring when the grass was healthy.

Phase Six

Phase Six of the project was the longest, but most satisfying, phase. This phase focused on the completion of the indoor swimming facility. The structure included two Olympic-size swimming pools, diving boards, locker rooms, sauna and steam facilities, and a restaurant. The building was situated on a hill that overlooked the river pedway—it was the crown jewel of the park. The facility was completed as planned and was opened to the public.

This phase also included the following:

- Completion of blacktopping the 50-acre pedway along the river
- Closing and sodding of the temporary construction equipment corral
- Installation of the remaining playgrounds and picnic areas throughout the park
- Opening of the water access points, including a commercial dock for fishers and boaters
- Official opening of the soccer and baseball fields

Controlling Project Changes

Throughout the project, the public had many requests for changes to the project scope. The project scope was quite large, and the project budget had limited room for additional changes without requesting additional funds.

When changes were proposed, such as the addition of tennis courts to the common areas, they were considered for validity, cost, risk, and the impact on the project scope. A change control board, which Stanford initiated, considered the proposed changes and then approved or declined the changes based on predetermined metrics such as time, cost, and overall change to the original project scope.

When the project was initiated, a public meeting was held to gather input from the community on the deliverables they would most like to see in the park. At this point of the project, the stakeholders—the community at large—had a great opportunity to voice their opinions on what the park should and should not include. Once a consensus was created for the park deliverables and a scope was created, it became challenging for anyone to add to it.

Some changes, however, proved valuable and were added to project deliverables. For example, the commercial fishing and boating dock within the park was a viable opportunity for a local businessperson to provide a service for boaters and the community at no cost to the project. Keening and Johnson worked with the business to ensure that it met the city codes and safety regulations and fit within the scheme and overall effect of the project.

Other changes, such as the tennis courts, were declined. Though there were many tennis players in the community, this request was denied for several reasons:

- The city already supported many tennis courts in the community.
- A private tennis club near the park protested the addition of the tennis courts, because this would be an economic blow to their business.
- No tennis players had requested the courts at any of the public meetings discussing the creation of the park.

Changes, especially in a project of this size, had to be tracked and documented. Any changes that were approved or declined were cataloged as part of the change log for reference against future change requests that may have entered the project.

Chapter Summary

Agile project management will make up 20 percent of your CAPM exam, and you'll be tested on pure agile terminology and hybrid approaches to project management. You'll need to recognize the attributes of the most common Agile approaches even if you personally don't work with Agile. Your exam will certainly test you on the popular approaches to Agile, which include Scrum, Kanban, Lean, and XP. Scrum is the most popular approach and uses the idea of a product backlog, typically four-week sprints, daily scrums, sprint reviews, and retrospectives. Kanban breaks down the work but moves items through the system and illustrates the WIP in the Kanban board. Lean aims to reduce waste, empower the team, and build quality into the project. XP relies on paired programming, continuous integration, and test-first programming. Disciplined Agile provides a flexible and pragmatic approach to software development, with a focus on customer value, simplicity, pragmatism, and continuous improvement. It emphasizes a process goal-driven approach, as well as scaling Agile to the enterprise level.

Projects exist and operate within internal and external environments that have varying degrees of influence on the project. Internal and external environments can influence planning and other project activities. These influences can yield a favorable, unfavorable, or neutral impact on project outcomes, stakeholders, or project teams.

Two important concepts, from a business analysis point of view, were covered in this chapter: enterprise environmental factors and organizational process assets. EEFs describe the conditions that will affect your business analysis effort, influence your decisions, and even direct how you're allowed to do the business analysis work. EEFs can come from within your organization, such as a policy, or from outside of the organization, such as a law or regulation.

Organizational process assets are created only internally to the organization. OPAs include organizational processes, policies, and procedures and items from a corporate knowledge base. OPAs are things that can be utilized to help the business analyst. They are grouped into two categories: processes, policies, and procedures and organizational knowledge bases. Processes, policies, and procedures are created outside of the project, such as from a project management office, and aren't updated or changed by the project.

An organizational knowledge base is the treasure trove of information collected from past projects, databases, and knowledge repositories that you can access to help manage your business analysis activities.

This chapter also discussed governance frameworks. A governance framework describes the rules, policies, and procedures that people within an organization abide by. It's the structure that everyone agrees to operate within as part of the organization. Governance frameworks operate within the organizational system, but frameworks are more about creating boundaries, providing directions, and establishing the roles and responsibilities of the people and groups within the organization. Governance frameworks define how the objectives of the organization are created, how risks are assessed and tracked, and how organizational performance can be optimized.

The organizational structure can help the project team identify the stakeholders, and it also identifies the project manager's authority. There are seven organizational structures you should recognize for your CAPM exam: functional (centralized), weak matrix, strong matrix, balanced matrix, project-oriented, virtual, and hybrid.

There are several types of PMOs in organizations. Exploring how each type varies in the degree of control, support, and direction, as well as assigned roles and responsibilities, reveals the range of benefits PMOs can deliver. Here are some common PMO types you should recognize for your CAPM exam: supportive, controlling, and directive.

Questions

1. You are working with your project team, business analysts, and stakeholders to plan out the project work. Some of the resources are in Chicago and other resources are in London, UK. The distribution of resources, such as in your project, is also known as what?

   A. Enterprise environmental factor

   B. Organizational process asset

   C. Virtual team

   D. Constraint

2. Understanding enterprise environmental factors is an important part of your role as a project manager or business analyst. Which of the following choices is an enterprise environmental factor? (Choose three.)

   A. Employee capability

   B. Infrastructure

   C. Templates

   D. Organizational culture

   E. Policy manual

3. In your industry, your products must adhere to a government regulation. This government regulation will affect how you manage your project. The government regulation in this scenario is best described as which one of the following?

   A. Organizational process asset

   B. External enterprise environmental factor

   C. Constraint

   D. External constraint

4. As the project manager, you must work with your project team to identify the project phases within the project schedule. To help with this identification, you are using the project plan and project documents from a completed and similar project. These project files are commonly known as what term?

   A. Enterprise environmental factors

   B. Lessons learned

   C. Organizational process assets

   D. Supportive PMO

5. A governance framework is important for the success of the project, programs, and portfolios within an organization. A governance framework addresses all the following items except for which one?

   A. Alignment with the organizational mission

   B. Change control procedures

   C. Performance on time, cost, and scope

   D. Communications with stakeholders

6. Khalid is the owner of a large manufacturing company. In his company, organizational resources are pooled into one project team, but the functional managers have less project power than the project manager. What type of structure is Khalid operating in?

   A. Simple

   B. Weak matrix

   C. Project-oriented

   D. Strong matrix

7. Project team members are most likely to work full time on a project in which of the following organizational structures?

   A. Functional

   B. Weak matrix

   C. Strong matrix

   D. Project-oriented

8. Marcy is the project manager of the GQD Project for her organization. She is working with Stan, the project sponsor, and they are identifying the most likely phases for this type of project work. Why would an organization divide a project into phases?

   A. To provide better management and control of the project

   B. To identify the work that will likely happen within a phase of the project

   C. To identify the resources necessary to complete a phase of the project

   D. To define the cash-flow requirements within each phase of the project

9. You are the project manager for your organization. Lei, a new project team member, is working on multiple projects at once. He approaches you, worried about who he reports to. In addition, Lei has a functional manager who is assigning him work. What type of structure are you and Lei operating in?

   A. Functional

   B. Weak matrix

   C. Program office

   D. Project-oriented

10. You are the project manager of a new project. When is the likelihood of failing to achieve the objectives the highest within your project?

    A. There is not enough information provided to know for certain.

    B. At the start of the project.

    C. At the end of the project.

    D. During the intermediate phases of the project.

11. You are the project manager for your organization, and you're working with the project team to explain the approach of the project life cycle and how you'll be managing proposed changes to the project scope. Your company is a project-oriented company; who will make decisions on change control?

    A. Project manager

    B. Project team

    C. Functional manager

    D. PMO

12. You are the project manager for your organization, and you're working with your company's project management office. The PMO has provided you with forms, templates, software, and some advice on how best to manage the project. What type of project management does your company have?

    A. Consultative

    B. Supporting

C. Controlling

D. Directive

13. You are a project manager acting in a functional organization. The functional manager and you disagree about several deliverables the project will be creating. The functional manager insists that you begin the project work now. What must you do?

A. Begin work.

B. Resolve all the issues with the functional manager before you begin working.

C. Continue planning because you are the project manager.

D. Begin work if the issues don't affect the project deliverables.

14. You are a project manager working under a PMO. Your project resources are shared among several projects. To whom will the project team members report?

A. The project manager of each project they're assigned to

B. The functional managers

C. The PMO

D. The product manager of their primary project

15. An organization is implementing a new agile project management approach for their software development projects. In this approach, they've decided that one person will program and a second programmer will evaluate the code being written to ensure accuracy. Which agile project management approach is being implemented?

A. Scrum

B. Kanban

C. XP

D. Lean

16. You are the project manager for your organization, and you're working with the project team to explain the approach of the project life cycle and how you'll be managing proposed changes to the project scope. Your company is a weak matrix company; who will make decisions on change control?

A. Project manager

B. Project team

C. Functional manager

D. PMO

17. Geraldine is a project manager for the NHG Corporation. She has identified several positive stakeholders for her construction project and a few negative stakeholders. Geraldine and the project team have been meeting regularly with the positive stakeholders but have not met with the negative stakeholders. Ibrahim, the chief project officer from the PMO, tells Geraldine she needs to meet with the negative stakeholders as quickly as possible. What type of PMO is Geraldine working with?

   A. Consultative

   B. Directive

   C. Controlling

   D. Supportive

18. Siju is the project manager for his organization. In his next project, his team will comprise local workers and workers from Scotland, India, and Belgium. Siju knows that he needs to consider the working hours, culture, and expectations of this virtual team to manage it successfully. Which of the following are cultural attributes of an organization? (Choose three.)

   A. Policies and procedures

   B. Work ethics

   C. View of authority relationships

   D. Experience of the project management team

19. Joey is a new project manager for your organization. Management has asked him to begin creating a project management plan with his project team based on a recently initiated project. What can Joey do to get a head start on writing the project management plan?

   A. Go look for an organizational process asset from a previous project.

   B. Go look for an enterprise environmental factor from a previous project.

   C. Assemble the project team and start writing a new and unique project management plan.

   D. Hire a contracting agency to provide a "Technical Writing" class.

20. You are the project manager in your organization. Unlike your last job, which used a weak matrix structure, this organization is using a project-oriented structure. Who has full authority over project funding in a project-oriented structure?

   A. The project manager

   B. The functional manager

   C. The PMO

   D. The project sponsor

Answers

1. **A.** The distribution of resources is an enterprise environmental factor. The location of the resources can affect how the project operates and communicates with resources and stakeholders. B is incorrect because the distribution of project resources is not an organizational process asset. C is incorrect because, although resources located in different parts of the world could be a virtual team, the better choice is EEF. D is incorrect because, although the project manager may see the distribution of resources as a constraint, the question doesn't state if this is a positive or negative factor for the project.

2. **A, B, D.** Employee capability, infrastructure, and organizational culture are all enterprise environmental factors. C and E are incorrect because templates and a policy manual are not enterprise environmental factors.

3. **B.** A government regulation is an external enterprise environmental factor that has been created outside of your organization. You must adhere to the regulation, so it is an EEF. A is incorrect because an organizational process asset is created internally to help the project. C and D are incorrect because, while the regulation may be seen as a constraint, the best choice is that a regulation is an EEF.

4. **C.** Project files and documents from a past similar project are organizational process assets. A is incorrect because enterprise environmental factors direct how the work is to be completed, rather than serving as input for planning and decisions, as do project files from a completed and similar project. B is incorrect because lessons learned is one type of organizational process asset, not the term for the collective project files from a completed and similar project. D is incorrect because PMO stands for project management office.

5. **A, C, D.** A governance framework address alignment with the organizational mission, performance issues, and stakeholder communications. B is incorrect because a governance framework does not address the change control procedures.

6. **D.** This is an example of a strong matrix organizational structure. Organizational resources are pooled into one project team, but the functional managers have less project power than the project manager. A, B, and C are incorrect choices because this is not a simple, weak matrix, or project-oriented structure.

7. **D.** Organizations with project-oriented structures often have project team members assigned to the project on a full-time basis. A, B, and C are incorrect because these structures have part-time project teams.

8. **A.** Organizations often divide projects into phases to make the management and control of the project easier and more productive. B and C are incorrect because these statements identify an attribute of a phase, not the reason to create all phases. D is incorrect because this statement is not true for all projects. In addition, cash-flow forecasting is part of planning and is not universal to all project phases.

9. **B.** The best choice is that you and Lei are operating in a weak matrix structure. This is the best choice because Lei is working on multiple projects and he is also receiving work assignments from his functional manager—something that isn't likely to happen in a functional or project-oriented structure, making A and D incorrect. C is incorrect because a program office isn't a specific organizational structure.

10. **B.** Projects are most likely to fail at the start of the project. As the project moves closer to the project completion, its odds of finishing successfully increase. A is incorrect because it is not an accurate statement. C is incorrect because the project is more likely to finish successfully at the end of the project. D is incorrect because the intermediate phases show progress toward project completion. The further the project moves away from its start and the closer toward completion, the higher the odds of success.

11. **C.** A centralized structure is also known as a functional structure. In this environment, the functional manager is in charge of the project budget. A, B, and D are incorrect because the comptroller, project manager, and project sponsor are not in charge of the project budget in a centralized structure.

12. **B.** A supporting type PMO will provide support, such as forms, templates, software, and advice on the project. A is incorrect because this isn't a valid PMO type. C is incorrect because this type of PMO is more concerned with compliance than supporting the project manager role. D is incorrect because a directive PMO manages the project directly.

13. **A.** Because you are working within a functional organization, you have little to no power, and the functional manager has all the power. You must obey the functional manager and get to work. B, C, and D are all incorrect choices for the project manager in a functional structure.

14. **A.** When resources are shared and a project management office exists, the project resources report to the PMO for staff assignments, but they'll report to the project manager of each project they're assigned to. B is incorrect because resources are not shared among several projects in a functional structure. In addition, a functional structure does require the project manager to report to the functional manager. C is incorrect because the PMO may be responsible for staff alignment and assignment, but the project team does not report to the PMO. D is incorrect because the project team members would not report to a product manager.

15. **C.** In this scenario, the organization is implementing XP, or Extreme Programming. XP readily uses pair programming, where one programmer is writing the code and a second programmer evaluates the code for quality control and accuracy. A, B, and D are incorrect because Scrum, Kanban, and Lean do not utilize pair programming as XP does.

16. **C.** In a weak matrix, the functional manager has more authority than the project manager and will likely make project decisions. In general, decisions on scope changes would be in accordance with change control procedures. That might

authorize the functional manager to make the decision or require it to go to the project sponsor. This is the best answer since the scenario does not give any further details on change control. A, B, and D are incorrect because the project manager, the project team, and the PMO will not likely have change control authority in a weak matrix.

17. **C.** Geraldine cannot simply ignore the negative stakeholders. Their influence on the project may cause the project to fail. Geraldine must work with the negative stakeholders to squelch their protests, or consider their demands to ensure compliance or agreement with their issues. The controlling type of PMO often exists in organizations with independent or diverse business units that want support with delivery while maintaining more direct control over their projects. B and D are incorrect because Ibrahim is giving Geraldine an assignment, something that wouldn't happen with a directive or supportive type of PMO. A is incorrect because there is not a PMO structure called consultative.

18. **A, B, C.** The policies and procedures, the work ethics, and the view of authority relationships are all classic examples of an organization's culture. D is incorrect because the project management team's experience is not a cultural attribute of an organization.

19. **A.** An organizational process asset from a previous project can be used to help a project manager do his job better. B is incorrect because a project management plan is not an enterprise environmental factor. C is incorrect because a common practice is to use completed documents from similar projects and adapt them to the current project. Technically, the staffing management plan is part of the overall project management plan, but B is the best answer presented. D is incorrect because hiring a contracting agency to provide a "Technical Writing" class won't help.

20. **A.** In a project-oriented structure, the project manager has the power over the project funding, not the functional manager. Project managers in a project-oriented structure manage the budget. B, C, and D are all incorrect statements because they do not have full authority over project funding in a project-oriented structure.

References

- *Agile Practice Guide* (2017)
- *CAPM Certified Associate in Project Management Practice Exams* (2019), Haner and McCoy
- *Effective Project Management, Eighth Edition* (2019), Wysocki
- *PMBOK Guide* (2021)
- *Process Groups: A Practice Guide* (2022)
- *The Project Management Answer Book* (2015), Furman

PART II

CAPM Testing Areas

Project Management Fundamentals and Core Concepts

This chapter covers the tasks in Domain 1:

- Demonstrate an understanding of the various project life cycles and processes
- Demonstrate an understanding of project management planning
- Demonstrate an understanding of project roles and responsibilities
- Determine how to follow and execute planned strategies or frameworks
- Demonstrate an understanding of common problem-solving tools and techniques

This domain represents approximately 36 percent of the CAPM examination.

Demonstrate an Understanding of the Various Project Life Cycles and Processes

Task 1

The project life cycle and the product life cycle are different; they are not synonyms. Project life cycle and product life cycle are two distinct concepts in project and product management. A product is created by a project. You should know the difference between these two concepts to align your business objectives with your project objectives.

A project life cycle refers to the series of stages that a project goes through from its initiation to its closure. It provides a structured approach to managing projects, ensuring that all necessary steps are followed for successful completion.

Projects are born, they live, and then they die. That simple metaphor of being born, living, and dying is exactly what PMI calls the duration of a project: the project life cycle. A project life cycle is the project, from start to finish. Every project in the world has its own life cycle. Consider any project you've ever worked on, whether it was in construction, manufacturing, or information technology. Every project was born (initiated), lived (planned, executed, monitored, and controlled), and then died (closed). That's the project life cycle.

If we were to visit a technology company and check out its projects, we'd see that those projects have life cycles different from those of a construction company's projects. Every project life cycle is unique to the nature of the work being completed.

 EXAM TIP Because every project has its own life cycle, regardless of the application area, it's tough for PMI to ask specific questions on this subject. You'll likely encounter questions about what a project life cycle is, and maybe encounter questions about the activities that would take place in a project's life cycle.

A product life cycle refers to the whole "life" that a product goes through from its conception to its discontinuation in the market. If your company had a brilliant idea to create a new piece of software, initiated and managed a project to create the software, and then implemented the software, that would be most of the product life cycle. The remainder of the product life cycle is the usage and support of the software until some day, sadly, when the software is determined to be out-of-date and retired from your organization. The product life cycle is the whole gosh-darn span of time, from concept to usage to retirement.

 EXAM TIP Take care to read any questions about life cycles to determine whether they are referring to the project life cycle or the product life cycle. The project life cycle refers to the project from initiation to closure. The product life cycle refers to the design, manufacturing, use, and obsolescence of the product. The product life cycle can be many years longer than the project life cycle.

Examining a Project Life Cycle

Before choosing a project life cycle, there is pre-work to do. Pre-work activities refer to the tasks and processes undertaken before a project is formally initiated. These activities help to ensure that the project is well-planned, feasible, and aligned with the organization's goals and objectives. These activities are crucial to the success of the project and help ensure that the project is properly planned, resourced, and executed. A business case, a feasibility study, and a statement of work (SOW) are common pre-work activities that are conducted before the start of a project.

- **Business case** A business case is a document that provides a detailed analysis of the costs, benefits, and risks associated with a project. It is used to justify the project to stakeholders, including executives and funders, by demonstrating the potential return on investment (ROI) and the impact that the project will have on the organization.

- **Feasibility study** A feasibility study is an evaluation of whether a project is technically, financially, and economically feasible. It assesses the potential risks and benefits of a project and determines whether the project is worth pursuing based on the available resources, market conditions, and other relevant factors.

- **Statement of work (SOW)** The SOW is a document that outlines the scope and objectives of the project, as well as the work that will be performed to achieve those objectives. It defines the work that needs to be done, who will do it, how it will be done, and when it will be done.

A project life cycle describes the sequence of stages a project goes through from initiation to closure. The exact stages, and their names, vary depending on the methodology used.

A project is an uncertain venture, and the larger the project, the more uncertainty that is involved. For this reason, among others, projects are broken down into smaller, more manageable phases. Project phases enable a project manager to see the project as a whole and yet still focus on completing the project one phase at a time.

Every project moves through phases, and phases compose the project life cycle. Phases are logical approaches to segmenting the work, but they primarily allow management, an organization, or a project manager to have better control over the work done in each phase. Each phase within a project determines the following:

- The work that will happen in that phase
- The deliverables that will be created as a result of that phase
- How the phase deliverables will be reviewed, approved, and validated
- The needed resources for that phase
- How that phase will be approved to allow successor phases to launch

You can most often identify a project life cycle by the phases that exist within the project. A construction project may, for example, move through these phases: research, preconstruction, site work, foundation, framing, rough-in, interior finishes, exterior finishes, landscaping.

The end result of a phase generally creates a project deliverable and enables the project to move toward its completion. Check out the preceding example. Just because a phase has been completed does not necessarily mean that the next phase can automatically begin. A *phase-end review* is needed to determine whether the phase deliverable has met all its obligations and, if it has, to authorize the initiation of the subsequent phase. A phase-end review is also known as a phase exit, phase gate, or a go/no-go point.

NOTE A phase-end review is also known as a phase exit, phase gate, decision gate, stage gate, kill point, or go/no-go point.

Imagine a construction project to build a new sports complex for your city. The foundation of the entire sports complex may not need to be 100 percent complete for the framing of the building to begin. The framing could begin as long as the risk associated with starting this phase of the project is acceptable. The practice of overlapping phases is called *fast tracking* (we'll see this term again in the Chapter 4 discussion of predictive, plan-based methodologies). Though fast tracking does save project time, it can increase project risk in several ways: insufficient planning, overlapping tasks, and increased resource constraints.

In most organizations, regardless of the project manager's experience, management wants to see proof of progress, evidence of work completed, and good news about how well the project is moving. Phases are an ideal method of keeping management informed of the project progression. The following illustration depicts a project moving from conception to completion. At the end of each phase is some deliverable that the project manager can show to management and customers.

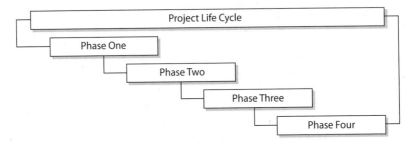

A wide range of companies still use the multiple phases approach in various industries. According to a study by PMI, 56 percent of projects used traditional methods in 2022.

Because every project in the world is unique, it's impossible to say exactly what must happen in every phase of a project life cycle. There are, however, characteristics of every project life cycle that are universal:

- Phases in a predictive, plan-based life cycle are typically sequential, and the completion of a phase enables subsequent phases to begin.
- Project costs and staffing requirements are generally low at the project beginning phases, while costs and resources are highest in the project intermediate phases. As the project moves toward completion, the cost and resource requirements generally wane.
- The likelihood of the project's success is always lowest during the early phases of the project. As the project moves toward completion, the likelihood of the project's success increases.

Working with Project Management Processes

Projects are chockablock with processes. A *process* is a set of actions and activities to achieve a product, result, or service. It's the work of project management to move the work of the project toward the deliverable the project aims to create. The goal of these processes is to have a successful project, but a project's success is based on more than just leveraging these processes. A successful project depends on five main things:

- Using the appropriate processes at the appropriate times. A project manager must recognize situations within the project that call for different processes and then determine which process or combination of processes is most needed to meet the project objectives.

- Following a defined project management approach for execution and project control.

- Developing and implementing a solid project management plan that addresses all areas of the project.

- Conforming the project and the project management approach to the customer requirements and expectations.

- Balancing the project scope, schedule, cost, quality, resources, and risks while meeting the project objectives.

Sure, all of this seems so easy on paper, doesn't it? But project management is not an easy task, and the goal of a certified project manager is to recognize the situations, react to the problems or opportunities, and move the project work toward achieving the customer's requirements. Project management processes are the actions that help any project manager do just that.

Exploring the Project Management Processes

Process Groups: A Practice Guide is a PMI publication that provides an overview of the five process groups, which are used to organize and manage the various processes involved in a project. The guide uses a popular Process Groups model that will help you with:

- **Initiating**   Management and/or your customer is authorizing the project or a project phase to begin.

- **Planning**   You and the key stakeholders are defining and refining the project goals and objectives. Once the project objectives have been defined, you and the key stakeholders will plan on how to reach those objectives.

- **Executing**   Now that you have a project plan, it's time to put the plan into action. You've heard the saying, "Plan your work and now work your plan"? This is the "working your plan" part.

- **Monitoring and Controlling**   Your project team is doing the work, but it's up to you to measure and correct things to ensure that the project team is doing the work as it was planned. The results of your measurements—primarily in cost, schedule, scope, and quality—will show discrepancies between what was planned and what was experienced. These discrepancies are your project variances.

- **Closing**   There's nothing more fun, usually, than closing a project. This process group focuses on formal acceptance of the project's final deliverable. Note that technically the approval of the deliverable is the result of the Validate Scope process, in the Monitoring and Controlling process group. The Close Project or Phase process makes that acceptance formal with a project sign-off. The Closing process group also focuses on bringing the project or project phase to a tidy ending.

Before you get too deep into studying to pass the CAPM exam, learn this: You do not have to do every single project management process on every single project. The project manager and the project team must determine which project management processes are most appropriate for each project. Once they have identified the necessary processes, they must also determine to what extent the processes are needed. The processes are tailored to their project. Larger, high-risk, high-profile projects require more detail than smaller ones.

Tailoring is a common theme throughout the *PMBOK Guide*. It's an important concept for project managers because you'll need to tailor the project management process to every project you're managing. Every project is different, and not every project needs the same processes, to the same depth, and with the same approach. Tailoring is what project managers do on every project, though larger projects, as a rule, will require more detail and more processes than smaller projects.

The project management processes have been recognized as good practices for most projects, but they are not a mandate for good practices on all projects. For your CAPM examination, however, you'll be tested on some to all of the project management processes. Yep. Although you might not use all of the project management processes in the real world, the exam could test you on all of the processes. Why? Because there is, no doubt, more than one way to manage a project. PMI isn't stubborn enough to say it's our way or no way—that'd be unreasonable.

 EXAM TIP The CAPM exam will ask you questions about the process groups and the specific processes within each group covered in *Process Groups: A Practice Guide*.

The approach that PMI does take, however, is based somewhat on W. Edwards Deming's *plan-do-check-act (PDCA) cycle*, as Figure 3-1 demonstrates. In Deming's model, adapted by the American Society for Quality (ASQ), the end of one process launches the start of another. For example, the end of the planning process enables the launch of the doing process. Once the work has been completed, you check it. If the work checks out, you move right into the acting process.

Figure 3-1
The standard project model is based on Deming's PDCA model.

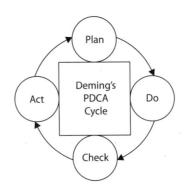

Distinguish Between a Project, Program, and a Portfolio

Task 1, Enabler 1

Project, program, and portfolio management are separate yet interrelated elements of the profession of project management. The combination of the project management, program management, and portfolio management disciplines is seen as integral and necessary to deliver the organizational strategy and, therefore, any action undertaken in any of the three elements should always align with the organization's strategy.

Projects typically fall under some umbrella within an organization: project portfolio management, project offices, or programs. The project management context describes all the different scenarios where a project may reside. A project can be a stand-alone project, a project within a program, or a project within a portfolio. I'll discuss all of these scenarios in this section.

Your real-life organization may have one, all, or even none of these descriptions—don't sweat it. For your exam, however, you'll need to be familiar with these different organizational situations and how each one affects the project and the project manager.

A project can be part of a program and part of a portfolio. Figure 3-2 shows that all programs are part of a portfolio, but that projects can either be directly part of a portfolio or part of a program.

What Is a Portfolio?

The project portfolio defines the rules for selecting, maintaining, and even funding the projects within an organization. We all know that a company usually has only so much money to invest in the projects it selects. Project portfolio management defines the projects that should be selected based on need, risk and reward, return on investment, and practically any other issues an organization identifies. Portfolio management focuses

Figure 3-2
The relationship between portfolios, programs, and projects within an organization

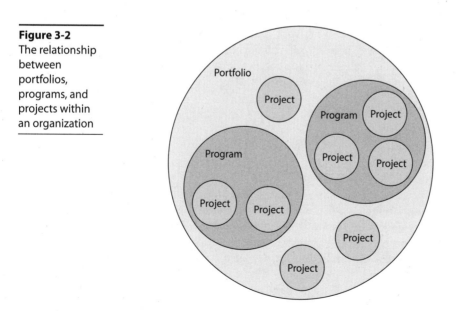

on the selection and initiation of the best programs and projects that the organization should invest in. Portfolio management is not overly concerned with how the programs and projects should be managed—that's project and program management.

Unfortunately—or fortunately, depending on how you look at it—project managers aren't usually directly involved in project portfolio management. This activity is generally reserved for senior management because they decide which projects best propel an organization's mission, purpose, and strategy. Portfolio managers manage the portfolio management processes—selecting projects, distributing risk exposure, and ensuring that the projects and programs are aligned with the organization's strategies and business objectives. Program managers and project managers inherit upper management's vision and then manage the programs and projects they've been assigned.

Project portfolio management is the selection, management, and collection of projects within an organization. Unlike a program (described in the next section), the projects in a portfolio may not be directly related, but they contribute to the organization's overall strategic plan. For example, a construction company may have a portfolio of projects, some of which are high-profile projects that could change a city skyline, while other projects are minor, such as the construction of a small garage or home.

What Is a Program?

A *program* is a collection of related projects organized to gain benefits from the projects that wouldn't be realized if the projects were managed independently. A program is not just a large project; it's a collection of projects. Consider a program of building a skyscraper. There could be lots of projects within the skyscraper program: structure, elevators, electrical, plumbing, and tons more.

If each project were managed independently, a lot of work would have to be duplicated within the construction of the new skyscraper. But by creating a program, you can save time and effort by managing projects collectively. For example, the electrician, the telephone installer, and the network engineer can pool their resources to pull the electrical cables, telephone cables, and network cables all at once.

The point to take away from this discussion on programs is that projects are usually contributing one major deliverable and can work together to save time, effort, and dollars. Program managers manage programs. And yes, there are project managers within each project within the program.

What Is a Project?

You probably have a good idea of what a project is already. The *PMBOK Guide* defines a project as "a temporary endeavor undertaken to create a unique product, service, or result." Projects can stand alone or be part of a program or portfolio.

Projects, like good stories, have a definite beginning and a definite ending. A project is over when the product, service, or result is created, the scope is fulfilled, and the customer has accepted the end result. Or, in not-so-pleasant times, it's over when it becomes evident that the project won't be able to create the desired product, service, or result for whatever reason (skills, cost, schedule, or the business case is no longer supported).

Projects can be launched, managed, and executed by an organization, by a collection of organizations, or even by a single person. A project to update your company's computer software, for example, could be launched and managed through the IT department.

Or this project could be initiated by the sales department, managed by a project manager in the IT department, and led to completion by a group of people from a vendor, the IT department, and the sales department on the project team. There are so many different combinations of people, organizations, contractors, and vendors that can contribute to a project—and that contributes both to the challenges and opportunities of project management.

Projects Are Temporary

Some project managers get hung up on the idea of a project being temporary. After all, some projects can last for years or decades—but they don't last forever. Projects are *temporary* in that they have a definite ending somewhere in the future. Projects—at least, most projects—create something that will last for some time, usually longer than the project team or longer than the time it took to complete the project itself. Consider a project to build a house, create a park, or develop a software application—these deliverables will be utilized for some time. In other words, the project ends, but the benefits and deliverables of the project continue.

Notice that I said that project deliverables usually last longer than the project itself. For some special projects, this isn't true—such as for a project to host a trade show, an event, or a fantastic party. Once the event is over, the project is also over.

"Temporary" can also refer to the market window status. Remember the Internet dot-com boom? It was definitely temporary. I'm sure in your business you can identify examples of market windows that were temporary. Project teams are also examples of temporary structures: the team comes together, does the work of the project, and then, once the project is over, so is the project team.

Defining a Project's Uniqueness

Each project should be unique and separate from the rest of your organization's operations. Consider the creation of a new car. The designing, drafting, modeling, and creative process of creating a new car could be a project. The manufacturing of the automobile, however, typically isn't a project—that's operations. Here are a few unique things that a project can create:

- Products such as software
- Products that are components for other projects, such as the blueprints for a new warehouse
- A new service that will be integrated into your organization's functions, such as a help desk or an Internet application
- A result: feasibility study, research and development outcomes, or trend analysis

Progressively Elaborating a Project

Progressive elaboration is a process that all projects move through. The project manager and the project team start very broadly—typically with a project's concepts—and then refine the concepts with details, studies, and discussion until a project *scope statement* is formed. The scope statement may pass through additional steps to continue to refine the project's objectives.

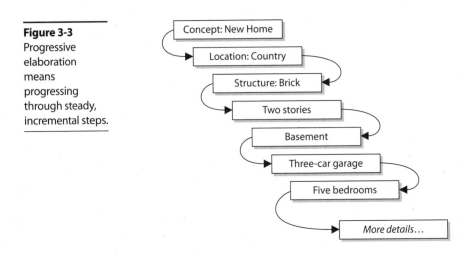

Figure 3-3
Progressive elaboration means progressing through steady, incremental steps.

Did you ever read any of Arthur Conan Doyle's stories featuring the detective Sherlock Holmes? Holmes would create a very broad theory of the mystery's solution and then, through a scientific approach and deductive reasoning, narrow his theory more and more until he finally solved the case. He started very broad and then narrowed his hypothesis. This is one example of progressive elaboration (although Doyle never called it that). Basically, progressive elaboration means that you start with a very broad concept, and then, through steady progressions, you gather more detail to clarify the concept your project centers on. Figure 3-3 shows a simple example of progressive elaboration with a project to create a new home.

In the Real World
It is important to let your project stakeholders know that projects are generally iterative and subject to progressive elaboration, to counter the expectation that you can plan everything at the beginning of a project.

Why Do Projects?
Projects are typically endeavors that aren't part of an organization's normal operations. Basically, projects are chunks of work that need to be completed, but the work doesn't necessarily fit into any predefined function of an organization, such as accounting or sales.

Projects can also be managed by external organizations that complete projects for other organizations. Consider an IT consulting company that swoops into company after company to install and configure new networks, servers, or computer software. Or consider an architectural firm that designs buildings for other companies. Or think of practically any service-based business, and you'll find a performing organization that completes projects for other entities.

Organizations that treat practically every undertaking as a project are likely participating in *management by projects*. This means they operate by relying heavily on project management principles to complete their work. This isn't unusual in consulting agencies, construction firms, or IT shops—they exist through management by projects.

Projects are most likely undertaken for any of the following reasons:

- **Opportunity**   The market demand may call for a project to create a new product, service, or solution.

- **Organizational needs**   I bet you can identify some needs within your organization that would make dandy projects, such as upgrading computers or training staff. Usually, organizational needs focus on reducing costs or increasing revenue, and sometimes both (bonus!).

- **Customers**   Your customers have things that they want you to create for them. Sometimes these requests develop into projects. Stakeholders can request the project be initiated to achieve a goal.

- **Technology**   Technology seems to change and advance daily, and this often spurs new projects to keep up with or ahead of competitors. Know any IT gurus out there managing technical projects?

- **Legal requirements**   Laws and regulations can give rise to new projects. Publicly traded companies have been required to secure their IT data in compliance with the Sarbanes-Oxley Act. Healthcare organizations must adhere to HIPAA (Health Insurance Portability and Accountability Act of 1996) requirements. And U.S. companies have been working with Occupational Safety and Health Administration (OSHA) requirements for years and years. Initial conformance to these requirements often creates new projects.

Projects create value for organizations. The following are examples of ways projects create value:

- **Improved efficiency**   Projects can create value by streamlining processes and reducing waste, leading to increased efficiency and productivity.

- **Enhanced customer experience**   Projects aimed at improving customer satisfaction and experience can create value by increasing customer loyalty and attracting new business.

- **Increased revenue**   Projects that result in new products, services, or markets can create value by driving increased revenue and growth.

- **Competitive advantage**   Projects that result in unique capabilities or processes can create value by providing a competitive advantage and differentiating the organization from its competitors.

- **Improved employee satisfaction**   Projects that improve the work environment, processes, or training can create value by increasing employee satisfaction and retention.

- **Better quality**   Projects aimed at improving product or service quality can create value by reducing defects, increasing customer satisfaction, and reducing warranty costs.

- **Better decision-making**   Projects that improve data collection, analysis, and reporting can create value by providing more accurate and timely information for decision-making.

What Is a Subproject?

A *subproject* is a smaller project that's been lopped off from a larger project. For example, a project to build a new house may create a subproject for all of the home automation, home theater, and home network installation. The subproject is managed as its own project but has constraints and requirements within the confines of the larger project to create the new home. Here are some other examples of subprojects:

- **A single phase within a project life cycle**   Consider, for example, the phases of construction on a new home: permits, excavation, foundation, framing, and so on. Each phase could be a subproject.

- **Human resource skill sets**   Consider all of the work that plumbers, electricians, carpenters, and other skilled workers can do. The related work of each professional could form a subproject.

- **Specialized technology, materials, or activities**   The installation of a new type of siding for a home construction project could be considered a subproject, in which a team of specialists would manage and complete the subproject.

Distinguish Between a Project and Operations

Task 1, Enabler 2

Projects are temporary endeavors; operations are ongoing. Projects can be initiated to upgrade equipment and processes within operations, for example. Operations describe the ongoing overall activities of the business, such as manufacturing, constructing, consulting, and other application areas. Project resources, such as team members on the project, often have responsibilities in operations as well—the team members may have day-to-day work for operations in addition to assignments for the project.

Although projects and operations are distinct, they usually interact in most organizations. As a project manager, one of the most common times you'll work directly with operations is at the end of a project, when you transfer the deliverables from the project ownership into operations. This is called *operational transfer* and usually is done as part of the project closure. Depending on what the project has created, resources from the project team may be required to support the solution, train the staff on the deliverables, or just be available as part of a service-level agreement (SLA) with the recipients of the deliverable your project has created.

NOTE There are only two types of work in the world, according to the *PMBOK Guide*. All work is either operational work or project work. If it is operational work, then it is repetitive and ongoing. If it is project work, then it has a defined start, middle, and end and delivers a product, service, or result.

In the Real World

You may find a degree of overlap between project work and operational work. There are certainly some projects that bear a striking resemblance to each other and perhaps could be construed as ongoing work. It is the unique aspect of each—and that it is done slightly differently, in a different location, to produce a slightly different product, service, or result—that makes it a project.

Distinguish Between Predictive and Adaptive Approaches

Task 1, Enabler 3

A development approach is the means used to create and evolve the product, service, or result during the project life cycle. The project life cycle provides a framework and also describes the generally sequential activities undertaken in any project, beginning with the process of starting or initiating the project, organizing and preparing to do the work of the project, then carrying out the defined project work, and finally recognizing the closeout of a project.

A *predictive* approach, more commonly called a plan-driven or traditional approach, "predicts" the work that will happen in each phase of the project. Through a series of waterfalls, where the outputs of one phase enable the next phase to begin, the project moves through a defined approach in each phase. Each phase in this approach usually requires different resources and skills, so the project team may be large, but the team members may not necessarily all work on the project together other than on scope definition activities. Changes to the scope are more tightly controlled in this plan-driven approach than in other project management approaches.

An *adaptive* approach is used when there is a great deal of uncertainty and a recognition that very little planning work can be done up front. An adaptive approach is useful when requirements are subject to a high level of uncertainty and volatility and are likely to change throughout the project. For example, an adaptive approach typically is used in highly complex information technology projects.

An *iterative* approach starts with a vision of the project scope, but the schedule and cost estimates are still pretty rough. The project work is divided into chunks of time, called *iterations*, that allow the project team to tackle the top requirements first and also apply lessons learned to future iterations of project work. Iteration cycles have predefined types of work to create the project requirements, such as features defined, designed, developed, and tested. You might know iterations as timeboxed periods or sprints.

An *incremental* approach is similar to an iterative development approach, but the difference is that the project deliverables are created in increments. A few more features are added incrementally until the project is completed. An incremental approach is almost like an assembly line process: the features are added in predefined increments from the start until the final finished product.

 EXAM TIP Many of the adaptive approaches, such as Scrum and XP, don't include the specific role of project manager. For your exam, however, remember that the project management principles still apply. You'll need to recognize the characteristics of the adaptive approach and how you'll get things done as a project manager in that life cycle.

A *hybrid development* approach is a combination of predictive and adaptive development approaches. Depending on the organization and the discipline, the components of the project that are established will follow a predictive approach, while the project components that are not fully defined may follow the adaptive approach.

 EXAM TIP You will be tested on the idea of hybrid development approaches on your CAPM exam. Pay close attention to the idea of helping the team and stakeholder transition between the predictive and adaptive project management approaches. Communication, planning, and engaging the stakeholders will be key activities to manage the transition between the approaches.

Here's a very basic way of identifying these different life cycles. A predictive approach predicts as much as possible and then uses baselines to minimize changes later in the project. An iterative approach repeats the same steps for each iteration, building the outcome in "chunks" or portions of the deliverable (which may be for different "chunks" of the project requirements, or improvements of previous work when more information is available.) An incremental approach builds the project deliverable in increments—successively, adding functionality until the deliverable contains the necessary and sufficient capability to be considered complete. An adaptive approach uses iterative and incremental approaches. A hybrid approach is a combination of predictive and adaptive approaches.

Distinguish Between Issues, Risks, Assumptions, and Constraints

Task 1, Enabler 4

Issues, risks, assumptions, and constraints are all factors that can impact the success of a project. However, they are different concepts and must be addressed separately in the planning and execution of a project.

Identifying Issues

Issues are unexpected events that you must document and manage to prevent them from causing risks, causing other problems within the project, and keeping the project team from reaching the project objectives. Issues are events that have happened, that reoccur, or that are going to happen and will likely disrupt the project.

Creating a Project Issue Log   When an issue occurs, the project manager documents the issue in the issue log, assigns an issue owner, and starts tracking the issue through its resolution. Each issue identified in the issue log includes the following information:

- Date identified
- Person identifying the issue
- Details about the issue
- Summary of the issue
- Prioritization
- Issue owner
- Target resolution date
- Current status
- Final outcome

Common issues include the following:

- Differences of opinion
- Situations to be investigated
- Unanticipated responsibilities that need to be assigned to someone on the project team

Managing Project Risks

A *risk* is an uncertain event or condition that could have a positive or negative impact on the project. Risks that have a negative impact are also known as *threats*. That's correct—it's possible for a risk to have a positive impact. Risks that have a positive impact are also known as *opportunities*. Technically, risk isn't a bad thing. It's the impact of a realized risk that can be painful, be costly, or delay the project work. Most project managers look at risk the same way they'd look at leftover shrimp cocktail. Yuck. Some risks, though, are good for the project, and the project manager wants to accept them; other risks aren't so welcome.

Let's look at this from another point of view. Imagine a golfer teeing up. The fairway doglegs to the right, around a water hazard that sits in the direct path of the green. The golfer can either avoid the water and take more strokes to get to the green or try to shoot over the water and get to the green in fewer strokes. Driving up the fairway is the safer play, but cutting directly over the water will likely improve the golfer's score. The risk with the water hazard is that if the ball falls short of the green and ends up in the water, the golfer is assessed a penalty stroke.

Risk, as in the golfing scenario, must be in proportion to the reward the risk-taker can realize as a result of taking the chance. The willingness to accept the risk is called the *utility function*. Some call the utility function your *risk tolerance*—the amount of risk you'll take on in relation to the impact the risk event may bring. Your risk appetite is how much risk you'll accept in relation to the reward the risk may bring. An experienced golfer may have a high-risk appetite and so be willing to accept the water hazard. A golf hack like me would likely have a low risk tolerance and drive up the fairway away from the water. Someone with a high tolerance for risk is called a *risk-seeker*, while someone with a low tolerance for risk is called *risk-averse*.

Risk works this way in project management, too. With some projects, you and your organization are willing to accept risks to realize rewards such as cost savings, time savings, or on-the-job training opportunities. On other projects—typically, those projects with high-impact and high-profile characteristics—you're not so willing to accept the risks.

Risks that exist within your project are individual risk events that can affect, for better or worse, the project objectives. The overall project risk, however, is the cloud of risk surrounding even doing the project. The overall project risk describes the risk of project success or failure, the risk of not meeting the project objectives, and the risk of other factors that expose the organization to positive or negative outcomes. Risks can exist in the organization, in a program, in a portfolio, and in a project. Integrated risk management is an organizational approach to managing the overall risk distribution and risk exposure through all of the organization's activities.

Let me be very clear: The risks you can readily identify are the *known risks*. The risks that are more ambiguous, such as weather events or vendor delays, are called *known unknowns*. You can anticipate and plan for the known unknowns, but the planning is about the probability of the event and the impact the risk might have on the project objectives. Project risk describes the likelihood of the overall project being successful for the organization. Individual project risks are the risks within the project. When a risk event actually happens, it can shift from being just a risk to being an issue in the project.

The project manager will need several project documents to identify project risks: assumption log, cost estimates, duration estimates, issue log, lessons learned register, resource requirements, requirements documentation, and the stakeholder register. Examine all of these documents for risk events, ambiguity, risk sensitivity, and insight to positive or negative risks for the project objectives.

One of the first steps the risk identification participants can take is to review the project documentation, including the project plan, scope, and other project files. Constraints and assumptions should be reviewed, considered, and analyzed for risks. This structured review takes a broad look at the project plan, the scope, and the activities defined within the project.

Examining the Assumptions

An *assumption* is something that you believe to be true but that hasn't been proven to be true. Assumptions can include expected performance of a vendor, reliability of equipment, access to resources, the weather, and more. In projects, there are often some things that you have to assume to be true just to function; for example, you assume that the people on the project team are going to be involved in the project for the duration of the project.

Or some project managers may assume just the opposite—that some of the people on the project team will leave the project or organization before the project is done.

All projects have assumptions. *Assumption analysis* is the process of examining the assumptions to see what risks may stem from false assumptions. Examining assumptions is about gauging the validity of the assumptions. For example, consider a project to install a new piece of software on every computer within an organization. The project team has made the assumption that all of the computers within the organization meet the minimum requirements for installing the software. If this assumption is wrong, cost increases and schedule delays will occur.

Examining the assumptions also requires a review of assumptions across the whole project for consistency. For example, consider a project with an assumption that a senior employee will be needed throughout the entire project work; the cost estimate, however, has been billed at the rate of a junior employee.

Creating the Assumption Log   Whatever assumptions you have about the project—especially at the initiation stage of the project—you document in the assumption log. Assumptions can also be examined a bit later for risk, but as the project gets started, you'll just jot down the assumptions in the assumption log and keep moving forward. You can't worry about everything, but chances are some assumptions will hold true and some will not.

Constraints

Constraints are factors that limit the options of the project manager and the project team and can quickly endanger a project's success. Common constraints—such as schedule, budget, requirements, resources, or risks—can dramatically impact the results, like customer satisfaction. It is management's responsibility to know all of the possible constraints, their influences on one another, and set the priority of each constraint within a project. It is the project manager's and project team's responsibility to analyze the impacts that any changes will have according to the project constraints.

Communication constraints can be anything that limits the project management team's options when it comes to communication. Communication constraints, such as geographical locales, incompatible communications software, and even limited communications technology, can affect the project team. Communication constraints can also include technology, regulations, political and cultural differences, policies, and other enterprise environmental factors.

While predictive projects use the Triple Constraints of Project Management, agile projects use an inverted triangle to represent the constraints, as in Figure 3-4. Rather than viewing scope as fixed at the start, Agile sets time (iterations) and cost (team members) as fixed; scope is then adjusted to focus on the highest priorities. Agile is built with the expectation that scope will evolve over time. The goal is to deliver the client's most important requirements within the budgeted cost and time.

As the team creates the prioritized items in the product backlog, the time and costs are eaten up—until all of the time and costs are gone, and then the project is done. Unlike predictive projects, agile projects don't usually have milestones, as the milestones would likely change anyway. In agile projects, the focus shifts. Agile projects have roadmaps that attempt to lay out release points like milestones.

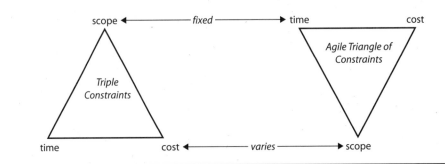

Figure 3-4 Agile uses an inverted triangle to represent the flexible and fixed constraints.

Balancing Constraints

One of the tasks of project management is the balancing of competing constraints on a project. Traditional projects are often defined as successful if the project's objectives are achieved by the due date and completed within budget...on target, on schedule, on budget. Apart from scope, schedule, and cost, the additional constraints of quality, resources, and risk limit the process of properly accomplishing the project's goals. If any one of these constraints changes, it will likely place additional pressure on one or more of the other constraints. For example, if you have to deliver a project in a shorter time period, you may need additional budget to complete the work, and your known risks may increase while quality decreases.

NOTE   You should know that one important aspect of project management is about recognizing and navigating your way through competing constraints on a project. This is evident in planning a project and also when considering a request for a change to a project, where a request for more time may impact schedule, risk, or quality.

Review/Critique Project Scope

Task 1, Enabler 5

Suppose you're the project manager of a large, complex project. You've worked with the project team and the key stakeholders to define the project scope, and the project is moving along. Everyone agrees that the project must be completed within one year, the budget is tight, and there's little room for error. One of your project team members, Antonio, has taken it upon himself to incorporate "extras" into the project deliverable to make it snappier, better, and easier for the product customer to use. Though his project additions are clever, they aren't in the project scope.

Antonio argues that his creative additions don't cost the project anything extra and the customer will love what he's come up with. The trouble for you, the customer, and Antonio, however, is that the time he's spent changing the scope should have been spent doing the things that are in the scope. In addition, the extras weren't managed and reviewed as change requests, so they will likely be a surprise to the project customer— not to mention the added risks, potential for defect, and the contempt shown for an established change control system.

Managing the project scope is the project manager's job; it ensures that all the required work—and only the required work—is done to complete the project successfully. Project scope management doesn't permit Antonio's, or anyone else's, additions without proper change management. Scope management involves agreeing on what's in the scope and then defending that agreement.

Antonio's additions are what is called *scope creep*: the project team is doing what should never have entered the scope in the first place—and that means wasted time and dollars. That's one sure way for a project to be late and over budget.

In managing scope, there is a difference between managing a project with a predictive, plan-based approach versus managing a project with an adaptive approach. A *predictive, plan-based approach*, as in the preceding example, predicts what the project will create and how the project will create it. An *adaptive approach*, like you'll find in an iterative or incremental environment, expects change to happen in the project. The scope in an adaptive approach is defined and decomposed into the product backlog. With each iteration, the project team will collect requirements, define scope, and create the work breakdown structure (WBS) for that iteration of the project. Basically, you'll take the product backlog, prioritize the items, and then choose what items can feasibly be accomplished in the next iteration of the project.

Some of the items from the product backlog are requirements, also called *user stories*. User stories are quick descriptions of the requirement from the user's perspective. Each user story receives *story points* from the project team. Story points represent how much effort is required to create the user story, and there are only so many points available for each iteration, called *sprints* in a true agile project. The number of available story points is determined by the project team and will vary by project. Some requirements for adaptive projects can be so big that they can't fit into one iteration—these are called *epics*. Epics describe really big requirements that are broken down into user stories and can span multiple iterations of the project.

Adaptive life cycles keep the project sponsor and customer representative engaged and involved throughout the project. One role, the product owner, works closely with the project team and the project manager to help prioritize the product backlog and answer questions for the project team. The Validate Scope and Control Scope processes happen with each iteration of the project; the project team creates the items from the product backlog, and they'll review the results with the project manager and the product owner at the end of each iteration.

Team members can't just add changes to the project because they seem like good ideas. Both predictive, plan-based and adaptive approaches allow, or at least entertain, changes to the project scope. Proposed changes might be great, but it's not the team member's role in the project to make that determination. Any team member or stakeholder must get their changes documented and reviewed to be included in the project scope.

Examining the Requirements Traceability Matrix

The requirements traceability matrix (RTM) is an essential tool for controlling project scope as it helps to ensure that all project requirements are addressed and fulfilled throughout the project life cycle. It provides a clear and organized way to track the relationship between project requirements and their corresponding deliverables, tasks, or test cases. Because requirements can comprise a long, long list, it's better to record them in a table called a *requirements traceability matrix*. This table documents and numbers each requirement and its status in the project and shows how each requirement is linked to a specific deliverable that the project will create or has created. You'll also, usually, provide a little narrative about the requirement in the matrix as a point of reference, current status of the requirement, owner, and status date. For more detail, you'll reference the actual requirements documentation. The traceability matrix helps the project manager and the project customer see the product of the project and compare it against the requirements to confirm that all of the requirements have been met and are in existence in the final deliverable for the customer.

Tracing requirements in project scope control provides several benefits, including:

- **Improved project planning**   By tracing requirements, project managers can ensure that all necessary tasks are identified and incorporated into the project plan.
- **Enhanced communication**   Tracing requirements helps stakeholders understand the project's goals and objectives, which leads to better communication and collaboration.
- **Better risk management**   By tracing requirements, project managers can identify potential risks early on and put mitigation strategies in place.
- **Increased project visibility**   Tracing requirements provides project managers with better visibility into the project's progress, making it easier to identify any issues or discrepancies.
- **Improved quality assurance**   Tracing requirements helps to ensure that all project deliverables meet the specified requirements, leading to improved quality assurance.
- **Better stakeholder engagement**   Tracing requirements helps stakeholders stay informed and engaged, which can lead to higher levels of satisfaction and stakeholder buy-in.

Apply the Project Management Code of Ethics to Scenarios

Task 1, Enabler 6

Several years ago, the CAPM exam included distinct questions about ethics and professional situations. However, questions regarding these topics now are incorporated into the main body of questions and may lie hidden within a question that appears to be about estimating, or risk, or quality, or customer relations, or any other topic. Thus, it is very important that you read each question carefully to determine if it is presenting you with a scenario that requires you to specify how you would act ethically and professionally.

Chapter 7 focuses on the topic of ethics and professional conduct and how a professional project manager is expected to act in many different situations. As explained in Chapter 7, both mandatory and aspirational standards are captured in the PMI Code of Ethics and Professional Conduct. The Code of Ethics and Professional Conduct, and the behavior of professional project management practitioners, reflects the values of responsibility, respect, fairness, and honesty.

A breach of this code can result in an ethics complaint to the Project Management Institute, which has the ability to consider the complaint and take action against anyone found to have breached the code.

In the Real World

I have always found that the Code of Ethics and Professional Conduct serves as a very valuable reference to guide my own decisions and behaviors in real-world situations where perhaps I might be tempted to act differently. It has also served as a guide to the behaviors I expect of other professional project managers. Keep in mind that sometimes the right course of action isn't the easiest course of action. When considering what is best to do in an ethical situation, one approach is to look at what the impact of a bad decision will have on your professional and personal reputation and credibility. Always select an answer that will enhance your credibility and reputation.

As mentioned, the four key foundational values for any project manager are responsibility, respect, fairness, and honesty. Though these may all seem to be fairly straightforward concepts that you think you both understand and apply consistently, you may not fully understand the implications and expected behaviors. Individually they describe specific behaviors, and collectively they present a unified code by which any professional project manager can guide and assess their own actions and the actions of others. Therefore, it is worth taking the time to download the PMI Code of Ethics (https://www.pmi.org/codeofethics#) and study it carefully to investigate each value and review the specific actions and behaviors that each demands of a professional project manager.

EXAM TIP   Take time when reading each exam question to determine if it is presenting you with a technical situation or an ethical situation. If it is an ethical situation, then answer according to the PMI Code of Ethics and Professional Conduct.

Explain How a Project Can Be a Vehicle for Change

Task 1, Enabler 7

Change means uncertainty; uncertainty breeds opportunity. All projects introduce some form of change within your organization, and that change invariably alters the way people work. Change on projects is inevitable! We all understand that Agile "embraces change." "Controlled" change is always allowed in predictive, plan-based and hybrid projects.

Project leaders must prepare to tailor project change management by development approach. They should define, articulate, and support a change control process, even when using an agile development approach. Project change management is a skill that sets leaders apart from the average project manager. Anticipating change, developing a change strategy, and supporting the change process during the project can help deliver project success.

Projects are really about changing the organization by achieving a measurable outcome. From a business perspective, projects are initiated to move the organization from its current state to the desired future state. Think of a project to create new software; the current state is missing the benefits the app will bring, and the future state has the app in production and it benefits the organization. Projects drive change by undertaking the work to achieve the specific goals of the project. If you achieve the goals of the project, specifically the scope of the project, then the goal becomes a reality for the organization and the business will achieve the desired future state.

A project can be a vehicle for change by providing a structured approach to addressing a problem or addressing a need. Through the defined goals, tasks, resources, and timelines of a project, individuals and organizations can work together to create solutions that have a lasting impact. The process of working on a project can also build skills, foster relationships, and increase awareness of the issue being addressed, all of which can contribute to larger-scale changes beyond the scope of the project itself. By successfully implementing and completing a project, it can demonstrate the feasibility and benefits of a new idea or approach, serving as a model for future change efforts.

Projects are important vehicles for change because they provide a structured and organized approach to achieving specific goals and objectives. They allow for the systematic planning, implementation, and monitoring of change initiatives, which helps to ensure that change is implemented efficiently, effectively, and with minimal disruption. Projects also provide a platform for collaboration and teamwork, enabling stakeholders to work together to achieve common goals. Additionally, projects help to establish clear accountability and responsibility, allowing individuals and organizations to track progress and measure success. By providing a framework for change, projects help to create a more stable and predictable environment, which is essential for making lasting change.

Project management can be used to drive organizational change by defining and executing projects that align with the desired change objectives. It provides a structured approach to planning, executing, and closing projects while considering constraints such as resources, schedule, budget, and scope. Effective project management helps organizations achieve their goals by aligning the efforts of stakeholders, ensuring clear communication and collaboration, and minimizing risk. By using project management methodologies, organizations can achieve lasting change by breaking down complex transformations into manageable tasks and tracking progress toward achieving their desired outcome.

You can tailor the change management approach and governance within the project. Project change management, like all processes, is not universal and can always be tailored to fit your organization, rather than changing your organization to fit a project management approach.

Agile project life cycles rely on the team members, including the project manager, to define how plans and components will integrate. In agile, product planning and delivery are completed by the project team, while the project manager oversees the project and promotes collaboration for decisions and change management. Agile environments welcome change, with some rules, and change can happen throughout the project.

NOTE For a deeper dive into this topic, see "How to change the world with project management" by Jack Duggal (go to https://www.pmi.org and enter the title in the search box).

Demonstrate an Understanding of Project Management Planning

Task 2

Project management planning involves defining the goals, tasks, resources, and timeline of a project. It involves identifying what needs to be done, who will do it, how it will be done, and when it will be completed. This stage is critical in ensuring that the project is delivered on schedule and within budget and meets quality standards. It involves developing a detailed project plan that outlines the steps needed to achieve the project goals and establishes the timeline for completion. The project plan should also include risk management, quality management, and communication plans. Effective project management planning helps in ensuring project success by reducing uncertainty, improving accountability, and establishing a clear path for project execution.

The project management planning processes are iterative, as you know, and will happen over and over throughout the project. You and the project team—and even some key stakeholders—will work together to define the project's schedule management plan. This will happen early in the project's planning processes, but you'll probably need to return to schedule management planning to adjust, replan, or focus on the schedule you've created for the project.

Schedule management planning is not the creation of the actual project schedule. That'd be too easy. Instead, the schedule management plan defines how the project's policies and procedures for managing the project schedule will take place. You'll define the procedures for completing schedule management.

Of course, agile projects don't include the overhead of detailed project schedule planning. You'll instead work with a fixed schedule and then complete as many requirements as time allows and that the development team can deliver during a single sprint. With a fixed schedule, or deadline, you'll start with the most important requirements first so there's less risk of running out of time and not creating value—something we always fear in predictive environments.

NOTE Sprint planning in Scrum is about creating a basic schedule to build the user stories. The schedule can change in each sprint. It is lighter and does not require as much detail as the predictive schedule. In Scrum, once agreed, the duration of the sprint is fixed.

To do this planning, you'll gather your project team, key stakeholders, and subject matter experts (SMEs) such as people from management and consultants to help you plan what it is you're about to schedule. You'll need the project management plan, the project charter, enterprise environmental factors, and organizational process assets.

 EXAM TIP For your exam, you'll need to know both the predictive and agile approaches to project scheduling management, even if you don't use both approaches on your projects. Just remember that agile projects have a fixed schedule, while predictive projects predict duration.

Developing the Project Management Plan

You wouldn't go about building a house, creating a new piece of software, or launching any project without a project plan, right? The project management plan, however, is more than how the *work* will be done; it's how the *project* will be done. That's right, the project management plan defines how the project is executed, monitored and controlled, and then closed. It's a multifaceted plan on how to manage, coordinate, and integrate all the different knowledge areas and processes within a project. Figure 3-5 shows the process necessary before the project management plan can be developed. Think of all the things a project manager and the project team will decide within the project plan that need to be documented:

- Which project management processes and their level of implementation are appropriate for the project?
- What tools and techniques will be used with which processes?
- How will the selected processes be used to manage the project, including how the processes will interact as the project moves through its phases?
- How will the project work be completed?

Figure 3-5
It's a logical approach to get to the project management planning phase.

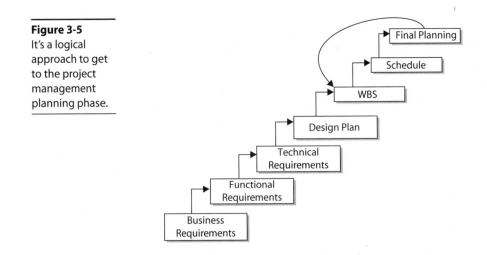

- How will change control happen?
- How will configuration management be performed?
- Who will maintain the integrity of the project's baselines and how will the measurements be used to manage the project better?
- What are the communication demands and techniques from the project stakeholders?
- How will the project phases commence and proceed?
- How much stakeholder inclusion and management will occur?
- When and how will management review the project performance?

Creating the Project Management Plan

The team creating the project management plan has many things to consider when it comes to staffing the project and utilizing physical resources for the project.

Creating the project plan can involve multiple tools and techniques. Brainstorming, focus groups, expert judgment, and interviews are tools that also can be used with project planning. Another tool, checklists, is ideal to use when an organization is doing several of the same types of projects. The checklist can guide the project manager and project team to ensure that all of the required project management plan components have been addressed and included in the plan.

As the project team completes project planning activities, the outputs will be assimilated into a collection of subsidiary project plans. The collection of these subsidiary project plans will address all of the previous points and help the project manager and the project team know where the project is going and how they will get there.

Let's take a moment and look at each of the minimum project management subsidiary plans the project management plan will include:

- **Scope management plan** This plan defines how the project scope will be planned, managed, and controlled. This plan is included because the project team will be doing the work to create the things the scope promises, and physical resources are likely needed to satisfy the scope.

- **Requirements management plan** This plan defines how the project requirements will be defined, gathered, documented, and managed.

- **Schedule management plan** This plan defines how the project schedule will be created and managed. The availability of, and the demand for, the project team and physical resources are influenced by the schedule management plan, and vice versa.

- **Cost management plan** This plan details how the project costs will be planned for, estimated, budgeted, and then monitored and controlled. In most projects, the project manager will need to account for the cost of the project team and their contributions to the project work. The cost management plan will also address the cost of the physical resources.

- **Quality management plan**   Quality is expected on every project. This plan defines what quality means for the project, how the project will achieve quality, and how the project will map to organizational procedures pertaining to quality. The project team members will need to adhere to quality expectations, which may include training, team development, peer reviews, and inspections.

- **Resource management plan**   This plan defines how project team members will be brought onto the project team, managed, and released from the project team. It also defines team training, safety issues, roles and responsibilities, and how the project's reward and recognition system will operate. Because resources aren't just people, this plan will also address physical resources, such as equipment, tools, and facilities.

- **Communications management plan**   This plan defines who will get what information, how they will receive it, and in what modality the communications will take place. The project team will need to communicate with the project manager, the sponsor, stakeholders, vendors, and one another.

- **Risk management plan (RMP)**   The RMP identifies, assesses, and addresses potential risks that could impact the project's objectives, timeline, budget, or quality. Project team members will need to know what risks are within the project, which risk owners are identified, and how risk responses will be planned and communicated.

- **Procurement management plan**   This plan outlines the processes, procedures, and guidelines for acquiring goods, services, or resources from external suppliers or vendors that are necessary for the successful completion of a project. The project team may need to interact with vendors, consultants, and even internal stakeholders, such as a procurement office or purchasing department.

- **Stakeholder engagement plan**   The stakeholder engagement plan defines how stakeholders will be included, managed, and prioritized for the project.

Each plan can be adapted from previous projects or templates within the company that the performing organization has created as part of its organizational process assets. While the project management is, for the most part, a compilation of project plans, additional plans and documents are included that you should know for your CAPM certification:

- **Scope baseline**   This is a combination of three project documents: the project scope statement, the work breakdown structure, and the WBS dictionary. The creation of the project's deliverable will be measured against the scope baseline to show any variances from what was expected and what the project team has created.

- **Schedule baseline**   This is the planned start and finish of the project. The comparison of what was planned and what was experienced is the schedule variance.

- **Cost baseline**   This is the aggregated costs of all the work packages within the WBS—excluding management reserves.

- **Performance measurement baseline**   This is the baseline that combines scope, schedule, and cost to compare what's planned and what's being experienced in the project.

- **Quality baseline** This documents the quality objectives for the project, including the metrics for stakeholder acceptance of the project deliverable.

- **Change management plan** Changes are likely to happen on the project, so you'll need to communicate the change management process to the project team. The change management plan explains how all changes will be captured, analyzed, and then, if approved, implemented into the project. Changes can affect what the project will create and how it is created, and you don't want this to be a surprise to the project team.

- **Compliance plan** This document outlines the actions, processes, and procedures that a project team must follow in order to meet regulatory requirements, ethical standards, and organizational policies. The plan serves as a roadmap for ensuring that the project complies with all relevant laws, regulations, and guidelines, and helps the team to minimize risk and avoid costly fines and penalties.

- **Configuration management plan** Documentation, control, and confirmation of the features and functions of the project's product are needed. Tied to scope management, the configuration management plan communicates how changes to the product may be permitted.

- **Risk response plan** This plan defines the risk responses that are to be used in the project for both positive and negative risks.

- **Milestone list** This list details the schedule milestones and their attributes. It is used for several areas of project planning but also helps determine how quickly the project may be achieving its objectives. The milestone list is in the WBS dictionary.

- **Resource calendar** Resources are people and things, such as equipment, rooms, and other facilities. This calendar defines when the resources are available to contribute to the project.

- **Stakeholder register** This document identifies all the project stakeholders, their interests in the project, and their roles. The stakeholder register can help identify who has control over physical and human resources in the project.

- **Risk register** The risk register is a centralized database consisting of the outcome of all the other risk management processes. It considers the outcome of risk identification, qualitative analysis, and quantitative analysis.

Another common tool and technique for creating project management processes is expert judgment. Expert judgment comes from SMEs, consultants, project team members, or other groups or individuals who can help you, the project manager, make the best decisions in the project. When it comes to creating the project management plan, expert judgment can help the project manager formulate the project plan by offering advice and insight on the following:

- Tailoring the project management processes
- Developing portions of the project management plan

- Determining which processes and associated tools and techniques are needed for the project
- Identifying resources and skill sets needed to complete the project work
- Defining how project documents may be changed
- Prioritizing project work

Describe the Purpose and Importance of Cost, Quality, Risk, Schedule, etc.

Task 2, Enabler 1

Cost, quality, risk, schedule, and other factors are all important considerations in the planning and execution of a project. Effective management of these factors is critical to ensuring that the project is completed on schedule, within budget, and to the desired quality and delivers value to the organization.

Cost

It's often the project manager's job to estimate, control, and account for the finances a project demands, from start to completion. Projects consume the project budget during execution, when all those project management plans we've discussed are put into action, and the project budget is monitored and controlled during, well, the monitoring and controlling processes. Project cost management is all about how much the resources—physical resources and human resources—will cost to complete the project.

What's that you say? You don't have any control over the monies your project requires? Management gives you a predetermined budget, and it's up to you to make it all work out? Yikes! Financing is always one of the scariest things I hear about. Or is it? If management's decision is based on previous projects, business analysts' research, or should-cost estimates from experts, then financing is not so scary. I'll give you this much, however: a predetermined project budget is always a constraint, and it's rarely fun for the project manager.

And what about those projects that don't have any monies assigned to the project work? You know, the projects for which the project scope is completed just by the project team's work, and there really aren't any materials or items to purchase. That's okay—there are still costs associated with the project, because someone, somewhere, is paying for the project team's time. Salaries can also be considered a project cost. After all, time is money.

Finally—and here's the big whammy—it doesn't really matter where your project monies come from, whether you actually control them, and what processes your organization uses to spend them. Your CAPM exam requires that you understand the appropriate processes in *Process Groups: A Practice Guide* of how projects are estimated, budgeted, and then financially controlled.

Your cost management plan defines and outlines your organization's and project's procedures for cost management and control.

Quality

What good does it do if a project launches and the project execution consumes the monies and time, but the project deliverable is of unacceptable quality? Imagine a project to build a new house, and at the project completion, the house is tilting to one side, the windows all have cracks and holes in them, and the roof has obvious gaps through which rain and birds can enter. This is not what the homeowners had in mind.

Fortunately, project management—that is, *good* project management—has mechanisms in place to plan and implement quality throughout the project, and quality is not just an afterthought. Project quality management is all about the project manager, the project team, and the performing organization working together to ensure that the project performs as the project plan calls for, so that the project deliverable aligns with the project scope statement. Quality in a project is really all about getting the project done and creating a deliverable that satisfies the project requirements and that can actually be used by the project customer.

According to the American Society for Quality (ASQ), quality can have two meanings: "1) the characteristics of a product or service that bear on its ability to satisfy stated or implied needs; 2) a product or service free of deficiencies." Well, isn't that interesting? Let's go back in time. A project is launched, and a project charter is issued to the project manager. Then the project manager and the project team create the *project scope statement*, which defines all the requirements for the project, including what's in scope and what's out of scope. Quality means, therefore, satisfying everything that the project scope statement requires.

In the project scope statement, we define what the project will create, its requirements for acceptance, and the metrics to measure project success. In project quality management, we plan quality into the project, inspect the project and deliverables for the existence of quality, and then move toward the scope validation process, which confirms that we've created what our customer expected. Quality is about delivering on promises.

No discussion on quality is complete without a nod to W. Edwards Deming. You likely won't need to know much about Deming for the exam, other than his famed plan-do-check-act (PDCA) cycle (refer back to Figure 3-1). For your CAPM exam, know that Deming's philosophy on quality management considers of paramount importance customer satisfaction, prevention over inspection, a call for management responsibility, and a desire to do the work correctly the first time.

Quality, even in agile and adaptive projects, is about meeting the project requirements. Of course, the project requirements are defined in the iteration planning sessions and directly before the project team takes on the work for the current iteration. As the product owner and the development team review the number of user stories that can be completed within the current iteration, the team, product owner, and project manager seek clarification on what exactly is required to deliver on the selected user stories.

In agile and adaptive environments, quality reviews are conducted throughout the project rather than occurring only at the end of the project or iteration. At the end of each iteration, a special meeting, called a *retrospective*, looks back on what worked (or didn't work) in the last iteration. This enables the project manager and team to make changes to processes and adjustments to improve upon the project processes and the execution of the work to create the user stories.

Quality is directly affected by all of the areas of project management, and all of the areas of project management are affected if quality is missing. It's a busy, two-way street.

Risk

The purpose of addressing risk in a project is to proactively identify, assess, and manage potential threats and opportunities that could impact the project's objectives, timeline, budget, or quality. Risk management helps to minimize the adverse effects of negative events while maximizing the likelihood of project success.

The importance of risk in a project can be summarized in the following points:

- **Improved decision-making**   By identifying and assessing risks, project managers and stakeholders can make more informed decisions regarding project scope, schedule, budget, and resources. This helps to ensure that the project remains on track and is better prepared for potential challenges.

- **Proactive risk mitigation**   Addressing risks proactively allows the project team to develop and implement risk mitigation and response strategies, reducing the likelihood and impact of negative events. This helps to prevent issues from escalating and causing significant disruptions to the project.

- **Enhanced communication and collaboration**   Effective risk management fosters open communication and collaboration among the project team and stakeholders. This ensures that everyone is aware of potential risks and their corresponding mitigation strategies, leading to a more unified and prepared team.

- **Increased project success**   By proactively managing risks, the likelihood of achieving project objectives on time and within budget while maintaining quality standards is increased. This contributes to the overall success and positive outcomes of a project.

- **Continuous improvement**   Addressing risk in a project enables the project team to learn from past experiences, identify trends, and implement improvements in their risk management processes. This helps to enhance the overall project management practices and the organization's capability to manage future projects effectively.

- **Stakeholder confidence**   Effective risk management demonstrates to stakeholders that the project team is well-prepared and capable of handling potential challenges. This can build stakeholder confidence in the project's ability to achieve its objectives, leading to increased support and engagement.

Schedule

 CAUTION   Dates on the calendar are closer than they appear!

Time has a funny way of sneaking up on you—and then easing on by. As a project manager, you have stakeholders, project team members, and management all worried about your project deliverables, how the project is moving forward, and when, oh when, the project will be done. You also have to deal with vacations, sick days, demands from other project managers, delays from vendors, and so on.

Management frets over how much a project will cost. Project customers fret over the deliverables the project will create. Everyone, as it turns out, frets over how long the project will take. Of course, I'm talking about the Triple Constraints of Project Management: scope, schedule, and cost. If any one of these constraints is out of balance with the other two, the project is unlikely to succeed. The schedule, as it happens, is often the toughest of the three constraints to manage, because interruptions come from all sides of the project.

The processes within project schedule management, like much of project management, are interdependent on one another and on other processes in the project management life cycle. In a predictive, plan-based project, you'll likely be using the critical path approach to project schedule management. In an agile project, you'll use timeboxed iterations or sprints to manage the project schedule and the project execution.

Adaptive environments use a product backlog, unlike a predictive environment. Recall that the product backlog is a list of prioritized requirements called user stories. The project team assigns story points to the user stories as a way to estimate the amount of effort required to create the user stories, and there are only so many story points available per timeboxed iteration. In other words, the team defines how much they can feasibly get down in an iteration based on the complexity and size of the user stories. This agile approach helps ensure realistic expectations of what can be completed in an iteration and assures the product owner that the most important requirements are built first.

Project management aims to accomplish the project objectives. Projects that are not well planned or that do not operate within a defined framework will suffer from missed due dates, cost overruns, poor quality in the project and the project deliverables, rework, frustration among the project team and stakeholders, and a host of other problems. It's the complete management of the project that's needed to ensure project success. Complete chaos isn't typical in most projects, but most projects experience success in some areas and failure in others.

Distinguish Between the Different Deliverables of a Project Management Plan Versus Product Management Plan

Task 2, Enabler 2

Project management and product management are two distinct fields within the larger field of project management. While they share some common goals and objectives, there are also key differences between project management and product management, including the deliverables they produce.

Scope and deliverables are closely related, as they both define key aspects of a project and product. The relationship between project scope and deliverables is that the project scope defines the overall work to be done, and the deliverables are the specific outputs or results that the project team must produce to fulfill the project scope. In other words, deliverables are a subset of the project scope. The relationship between product scope and deliverables is that the product scope defines the desired features, functions, and characteristics of the end product, while the deliverables are the specific outputs or results that the project team must produce to achieve the product scope. In other words, deliverables are the means through which the product scope is realized.

Defining Project and Product Scopes

Building a skyscraper has to be one of the largest projects a project manager could manage. Think of all the different facets of the project: the art and design of the building, the structural requirements, the government building regulations, and the concern and interest of all the stakeholders within the project. The skyscraper would require months, if not years, of serious planning, tight change control, and incredible organization to complete. The scope of the skyscraper would be massive, and any change within the scope could have ramifications further down the blueprinted line.

Now imagine a project to build a barn. It would still require considerable planning, and the stakeholders of the barn might be concerned with its planning and construction, but probably not to the same depth as with the skyscraper project. The priority and impact of each project are important to the key stakeholders of each, but no doubt the skyscraper has a much broader impact than a barn. My point? Larger projects require more detail when it comes to scope creation and planning. Lots more.

Let's define scope—er, scopes—before moving forward. Project scope and product scope are different entities.

Project scope deals with the required work to create the project deliverables. For instance, our projects to create a new barn and the new skyscraper would focus only on the work required to complete the projects, with the specific attributes, features, and characteristics called for by the project plan. The scope of the project is specific to the work required to complete the project objectives. The project scope focuses on what must be done to create the deliverable.

Product scope, on the other hand, refers to the attributes and characteristics of the deliverables the project is creating. In the preceding barn or skyscraper project, the product scope would define the features and attributes of the barn or skyscraper. In this instance, the project scope to create a barn would not include creating a flower garden, a wading pool, and the installation of a fence, and the skyscraper project scope would not include a neighboring park. There would be specific requirements regarding the features and characteristics of each project: the materials to be used, the dimensions of the space, the function of each building, and all the related details that make a skyscraper a skyscraper and a barn a barn. The product scope is what the customer of the project envisions.

The project scope and the product scope are bound to each other. The product scope constitutes the characteristics and features of the product that the project creates. The end result of the project is measured against the requirements for that product. The project scope is the work required to deliver the product. Throughout the project execution, the work is measured against the project management plan to validate that the project is on track to fulfill the product scope. The product scope is measured against requirements in the product management plan, while the project scope is measured against the project management plan.

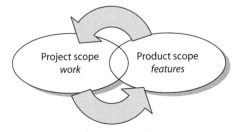

Project scope
work

Product scope
features

EXAM TIP When it comes to *project* scope management, focus on the work required to complete the project according to the project plan. The *product* scope, meanwhile, is specific to the deliverable of the project. Just remember, the CAPM exam will focus on both the product management plan and the project management plan.

Controlling the Project and Product Scopes

Scope control is about protecting the project scope and the product scope from change and, when changes do happen, managing those changes. Ideally, all requested changes follow the scope change control system, which means that change requests must be documented. Those changes that sneak into the project scope are lumped into that project poison category of *scope creep*—undocumented, unapproved changes to the project scope. Scope creep is bad, bad news. Of course, if you're working in an adaptive environment, there is still change control to the product scope and project scope, but change is managed through refinements of the product backlog. Change in a predictive environment is anticipated, but change follows the integrated change control process.

Corrective actions—steps taken to move the project back into alignment with the project scope—do require formal change requests, because the project manager isn't changing the scope, but rather the work that's outside of the project scope. Corrective actions are a part of scope control because you're nudging, and sometimes shoving, work back into alignment with the project scope. The trouble with scope creep and corrective actions is that the project team is doing or fixing work that should never have entered the scope in the first place—and that means wasted time and dollars. That's one sure way for a project to be late and over budget.

Distinguish Differences Between a Milestone and a Task Duration

Task 2, Enabler 3

A milestone and a task duration are two different concepts. Milestones are used to track progress and measure performance, while task durations are used to estimate the time required to complete individual tasks and to develop the project schedule.

Milestone

Milestones are significant points or events in the project's progress. If you're building a house, you could say the first milestone will be the finalization of the design of the house. The next milestone will be securing the permits from your city government. The next will be completion of building the foundation. And you'll continue to identify the milestones that represent the big successes within the project. Milestones are often, but not always, created at the end of a phase in the project life cycle.

A milestone list and milestone chart are tools used to visualize and track significant events or achievements within a project. These tools help project managers and stakeholders monitor progress, ensure timely completion of critical tasks, and maintain focus on important project goals.

The milestone list identifies all the milestones you've designated in the project and when you're expected to reach each milestone. As things progress, the milestone list also can show any variances between the planned date of the milestone and the actual realization of the milestone. The milestone list can help you identify and estimate activity durations for activities needed to reach the project milestones.

The milestone chart depicts the promised milestone completion and the actual milestone completion dates. A milestone chart is sometimes called a milestone schedule. A summary milestone schedule is a schedule of when the project management team can expect the milestones within the project to be reached. The summary milestone schedule is part of the project charter.

The milestone chart plots the high-level deliverables and external interfaces, such as a customer walkthrough, against a calendar. Milestone charts are similar to Gantt charts, but with less detail regarding individual activities. The following is an example of a milestone chart:

Milestone	July	Aug	Sep	Oct	Nov	Dec
Customer sign-off	△▼					
Architect signature		△	▼			
Foundation			△			
Framing					△▼	
Roofing						△

Legend
△ Planned
▼ Actual

Task Duration

How many times have you heard management ask, "How long will all of this take?" Countless times, right? Let's talk about the schedule.

The answer to the question "How long will it take?" depends on the accuracy of the estimates, the consistency of the work, and other variables within the project. The best a project manager can do is to create honest estimates based on the information provided. Until the schedule is finalized, no one will know the duration of the project.

Activity duration estimates, like the activity list, describe the activities on the schedule, with details on dates, resources, costs and dependencies, and the WBS, don't come from the project manager—they come from the people completing the work. The estimates may also undergo progressive elaboration. In this section, we'll examine the approach to completing activity duration estimates and the basis of these estimates.

> **NOTE** To be clear, milestones are just markers—no duration is assigned to the milestone; duration is assigned to activities, not milestones.

Considering the Activity Duration Estimate Inputs   The importance of accurate estimates is paramount. The activity duration estimates will be used to create the project schedule and to predict when the project should end. Inaccurate estimates could cost the performing organization thousands of dollars in fines, missed opportunities, lost customers, or worse. To create accurate estimates, the project manager and the project team will rely on several inputs:

- **Project team assignments**   The project team members who have been assigned to the project team make up the roles to complete the project work.

- **Resource breakdown structure**   This diagram shows a hierarchy of the resources, both physical resources and human resources, that are utilized on the project.

- **Resource requirements**   Activity resource requirements define the resources (human or physical) needed to complete a particular activity. For example, a project to build a home will require lots of different resources: plumbers, electricians, architects, framers, and landscapers. The project manager would not, however, assign all the different resources to every task, but only to the tasks that the resource was qualified to complete. Remember that resources also include equipment and materials, so those are identified as part of the resource requirements as well.

- **Resource calendars**   The project manager will need to know when resources are, or are not, available for utilization on the project.

- **Risk register**   The risk register can help the project manager and the project team identify key activities and their associated risks. This information may influence the constraints and task relationships in the project. Should risks come true, there may also be consideration of the timing of risk responses.

- **Organizational process assets (OPAs)**   Recall from Chapter 2 that OPAs include organizational processes, policies, procedures, and items from a corporate knowledge base. In the context of estimating activity duration, the most important OPA is historical information. Historical information is always an excellent source of data on activity duration estimates. It can come from several sources, such as the following:

    - Historical information can come from project files on other projects within the organization.

    - Commercial duration-estimating databases can offer information on how long industry-specific activities should take. These databases should take into consideration the materials and the experience of the resources and define the assumptions the predicted work duration is based upon.

    - Project team members may recollect information regarding the expected duration of activities. Though these inputs are valuable, they are generally less valuable than documented sources, such as other project files or the commercial databases.

- **Enterprise environmental factors**   Your organization may require the project manager to use duration-estimating databases, productivity metrics based on your industry, or other commercially available information.

You'll need to consider the resource capabilities of your project team. Consider a task in an architectural firm. Reason says that a senior architect assigned to the task will complete it faster than a junior architect will. Material resources can also influence activity time. Consider predrilled cabinets versus cabinets that require the carpenter to drill into each cabinet as it's installed. The predrilled cabinets enable the job to be completed faster.

Using Analogous Estimating   *Analogous estimating* relies on historical information to predict current activity durations. Analogous estimating is also known as *top-down estimating* and is a form of expert judgment. To use analogous estimating, activities from the historical project that are similar in nature are used to predict similar activities in the current project.

A project manager must consider whether the work has been done before and, if so, what help the historical information provides. The project manager must consider the resources, project team members, and equipment that completed the activities in the previous project compared with the resources available for the current project. Ideally, the activities should be more than similar; they should be identical. And the resources that completed the work in the past should be the same resources used in completing the current work. When the only source of activity duration estimates is the project team members, instead of expert judgment and historical information, your estimates will be uncertain and inherently risky.

NOTE   Analogous estimating uses historical information to predict what activity durations should be and is more reliable than team member recollections.

Workers	Units per Hour	Duration for 100,000 Units	Effort
Press operators (two)	5000	20 hours	40 hours
Bindery experts (two)	4000	25 hours	50 hours
Totals		45 hours	90 hours

Table 3-1 Decomposed Work with Quantitative Factors

Applying Parametric Estimating Parametric estimating is an estimating technique that uses a statistical relationship between historical data and other variables to calculate *an estimate for activity parameters*. Quantitatively based durations use mathematical formulas to predict how long an activity will take based on the "quantities" of work to be completed. For example, a commercial printer needs to print 100,000 brochures. The workers include two press operators and two bindery experts to fold and package the brochures. The duration is how long the activity will take to complete, while the effort is the total number of hours (labor) invested because of the resources involved. The decomposed work, with quantitative factors, is shown in Table 3-1.

NOTE *Duration* is how long an activity takes, while *effort* is the billable time for the labor to complete the activity. Consider an activity that is scheduled to last 40 hours. The project manager must consider the cost of the time of the person assigned to complete the project work. For example, a senior engineer may be able to complete the activity in 40 consecutive work hours, but the cost of this employee's time may be more than the value of the activity. A part-time employee may be able to complete the task in two segments of 20 hours, at a substantially lower rate.

Estimating from the Bottom Up If you were to start at a zero duration for your project and then begin adding up the duration of each of the work packages, you'd be creating a bottom-up estimate. A bottom-up estimate is the most reliable type of duration estimate because you are aggregating the predicted duration of each work package in the WBS. The challenge with a bottom-up estimate, however, is that you first need to create a WBS and the activity list to produce the estimate. That's right—before you can create a bottom-up estimate, you must first have the WBS.

This creates challenges for project managers and stakeholders alike. The stakeholders, such as management, want you to tell them how long the project will take to complete—and they want that prediction right now. Project managers want to provide an accurate estimate, but to do so, they must first create the project scope statement, decompose that into the WBS, then break down the work packages into the activity list, and then begin adding up the duration—that's no easy task.

The challenge is that giving an accurate duration estimate when there isn't much information, such as early in the planning stage, is nearly impossible. Later in the planning stage, however, when the WBS is created, the project manager can provide a much more detailed duration estimate because there's more information available. In addition to this, you truly don't know how long (or really how much) a project will take until you've completed the project work—there's uncertainty in the endeavor. But, as you know, no stakeholder is going to take as an answer "I'll tell you how long the project takes to complete when I'm done."

Activities are typically completed on schedule or later, but rarely early. Workers who have bloated the activity duration estimates may finish their task ahead of when they promised, but they tend to hold onto those results until the activity's due date. This is because workers aren't usually rewarded for completing work early. In addition, workers don't want to reveal the inaccuracies in their time estimates. Workers may believe future estimates may be based on actual work durations rather than estimates, so they'll "sand-bag" the results to protect themselves—and finish "on schedule."

So, what's a project manager to do? First off, the project manager should strive to incorporate historical information and expert judgment on which to predicate accurate estimates. Second, the project manager should stress a genuine need for accurate duration estimates. Finally, the project manager can incorporate a reserve time.

A *reserve time* is a percentage of the project duration or a preset number of work periods, and it is usually added to the end of the project schedule or just in front of reaching project milestones. Reserve time may also be added to individual activity durations based on risk or uncertainty in the activity duration. When activities are completed late, the additional time for the activity is subtracted from the reserve time. As the project moves forward, the reserve time can be reduced or eliminated as the project manager sees fit. Reserve time decisions should be documented.

Evaluating the Estimates   Estimating activities provides three outputs:

- **Activity duration estimates**   Activity duration estimates reflect how long each activity will take to complete. Duration estimates should include an acknowledgment of the range of variance. For example, an activity whose duration is expected to be one week may have a range of variance of one week plus or minus three days. This means that the work can take up to eight days or as few as two days, assuming a five-day workweek.

- **Basis of estimates**   Any supporting detail and approach you utilized during the creation of the duration estimates should be documented. This includes not just the basis of your estimates but any constraints or assumptions you used, the range of possible variations attached to your estimates, and your confidence level for the final duration estimate.

- **Project documents updates**   Activity attributes are updated with the duration estimates. The assumption log is updated to reflect any assumptions about the activities that may have been used to predict durations, such as resource availability. You might also need to update the lessons learned register with any effective methods you and your team have developed to improve duration predictions.

Determine the Number and Type of Resources in a Project

Task 2, Enabler 4

Your project relies on people doing the work, but these people also need the correct tools, equipment, software, materials, and other necessary resources to complete the project work. For example, you cannot install meters and meters of electrical wiring without the correct people, tools, and equipment.

First, people—specifically those on your project team—look to you, the project manager, to provide leadership, direction, and motivation. Your job is to help them know what their project assignments are, get their work done, and resolve issues and dilemmas within the project. In reality, and on your CAPM exam, the people involved with the project know what is expected of them by the project manager, management, and the stakeholders, and then they complete those expectations. And if they don't complete them? Then it's up to the project manager, the functional managers, and even the other project team members to enforce the project's ground rules so that all team members work toward the requirements in the project scope statement.

Second, physical resources are needed for the project team to do their work. It's frustrating for everyone involved when the project team is ready to do the work but doesn't have the equipment, tools, or materials available to do the work. It means wasted time and money for the project—and it's not helping the project be successful. The project manager must ascertain what physical resources are needed and then deliver those resources to ensure that the project moves forward as expected. In addition, it's critical to get the correct physical resources. This means that each resource is the one that's actually needed, it meets the quality expected, and it's available on time. Availability, with regard to materials, can often mean inventory: too much inventory and your funds are tied up in resources; too little inventory and you're waiting for resources to be replenished. Having the right resources available, at the right time, is often harder than it might seem.

The type of organizational structure, from functional to project-oriented, will influence how the project manager may discipline, motivate, and manage the project team. In a functional environment, the project manager won't have much autonomy to discipline or offer rewards beyond what management has deemed appropriate. In a project-oriented structure, for example, the project manager has much more autonomy both to discipline and to reward.

Your project team may be assigned to you, or you may have to build the team one person at a time. Chances are that you'll have a core project team at the beginning of the project and then more and more team members will join as the project scope is defined and the activities are identified. Adding people to the project team can influence how you do the work and introduce new risks and opportunities—based on their interest in the project, experience levels, and, frankly, their competency regarding the project work. An analysis of the project team can help you plan your team development approach.

 EXAM TIP   For your CAPM examination, you'll need to know some details about managing the project team and controlling the project resources.

Planning for Resource Management

Planning for project resources is vital to a successful project. After all, you've got to plan how the project work will be completed and which resources will complete that work.

When it comes to planning resources, the project manager is aiming to plan for several facets of the project. Specifically, this planning process answers the following questions:

- What project roles and physical resources are needed on the project?
- What is the responsibility of each role on the project?
- To whom does each role report?
- Will resources on the project come from inside or outside of the organization?
- How will project team members and physical resources be acquired?
- How will project team members and physical resources be released from the project?
- What training does the project team need to complete?
- What rewards and recognition systems may the project utilize?
- What compliance and safety issues must be addressed?
- How will the use of the resources affect the operations of the organization?

Phew! That's a bunch of questions the project management team must answer during this portion of planning. The good news is that you can answer some of these questions when you're doing other project management planning exercises, such as time and cost estimating. All of the answers to these questions are documented in the resource management plan. The resource management plan is the primary output of the Plan Resource Management process.

Identifying an Organizational Approach for Managing Resources

Project management is becoming more and more about empowering the project team members to make decisions rather than the project manager making all the project decisions. This collaborative approach fosters trust, shared ownership, and a reliance on experts on the project team. You'll need to know which approach your organization prefers, and for your CAPM exam, you should be familiar with these trends in managing resources:

- **Just-in-time (JIT) manufacturing**   Resources are in place only as they are needed. This approach reduces waste, keeps inventory at a minimum, and helps the project manager forecast resource utilization more accurately.
- **Kaizen**   Small changes to the organization and project team over time result in large changes overall. Kaizen posits that small changes in processes are easier to accept and incorporate than large, sweeping changes for the organization or project.
- **Total productive maintenance**   Continuous maintenance on equipment and quality systems keeps equipment working well and efficiently. This approach aims to reduce downtime by avoiding equipment failure.

- **Emotional intelligence**   A person is aware of their inbound and outbound emotions; by becoming emotionally competent, the person can better control their emotions and understand the emotions of others.

- **Self-organizing teams**   In agile environments, the project manager may be called a scrum master or servant leader. The project team takes charge of deciding who'll do what tasks to accomplish the project objectives.

- **Virtual teams/distributed teams**   These teams are not colocated, can be dispersed around the globe, and rely on technology to interact, communicate, and contribute to the project. Communication becomes a central focal point in virtual teams.

Resource management is a process that can be tailored to fit your project and organization. The project manager will consider the diversity of the project team and the strengths, weaknesses, opportunities, and threats (SWOT) that the diverse group may bring to the project. When work is completed by virtual teams, the physical location of each team member is also evaluated for how best to manage the resources.

Your industry may have special resource considerations, such as unions or inspectors. All project managers, regardless of the industry, will also have to follow the organization's policies for acquiring and managing the project team. Finally, the project life cycle can affect how you manage project team members. Specifically, you'll consider the peaks and valleys of team utilization depending on the type of work that's taking place in the project at any given time.

Use a Risk Register in a Given Situation

Task 2, Enabler 5

The only output of the Identify Risks process is the project's risk register. The risk register is a component of the project management plan that contains all of the information related to the risk management activities. It's updated as risk management activities are conducted to reflect the status, progress, and nature of the project risks. The risk register includes the following:

- **Risks**   Of course, the most obvious output of risk identification is the risk that has been successfully identified. Recall that a risk is an uncertain event or condition that could potentially have a positive or negative effect on project success.

- **Risk owners**   Risk owners, or potential risk owners, are identified in the risk register. The risk owner is the person who will be accountable for the risk and for tracking the risk, and who typically has authority to respond to the risk event should the risk be moving from uncertainty to certainty within the project.

- **Potential responses**   The initial risk identification process may yield solutions and responses to identified risks. This is fine, as long as the responses are documented in the risk register. Along with the risk responses, the identification of risk triggers may also occur. *Triggers* are warning signs or symptoms that a risk has occurred or is about to occur. For example, should a vendor fail to complete their portion of the project as scheduled, the project completion may be delayed.

- **Root causes of risk**   Risk identification can identify why risk conditions exist. Project managers can also use *if-then* statements based on the *cause* of the risk event to predict the *effect* of the risk event.

- **Risk categories**   Within the risk register, categories of risks should be created. The idea is that not only will related risks be lumped together but some trend identification and root cause analysis of identified risks may be possible as well. Having risks categorized should also make it easier to create risk responses.

- **Updated risk categories**   Risk identification may prompt the project team to identify new categories of risks. These new categories should be documented in the risk register, and if a risk breakdown structure is used, it will need to be updated as well.

Updating the Risk Register

Every time new information about the project's risks is learned, the risk register has to be updated. Updates to the risk register with regard to risk responses include the following:

- Identified risks and how each one can threaten the project
- Risk owners and their responsibilities for the risk events
- Risk response strategies and the responses to risk events
- Symptoms and warning signs of risk
- Budget and schedule impacts of the risk response activities
- Contingency reserves for time and costs
- Contingency plans and triggers to implement the plan
- Fallback plans
- Residual risks (risks that are expected to remain after a risk response)
- Secondary risks (new risks created as a result of a risk response)

A failure to update the project plan and the risk register may cause risk reactions to be missed—and skew performance measurements.

 NOTE   You'll always update the risk register when any new information about a risk is discovered.

Use a Stakeholder Register in a Given Situation

Task 2, Enabler 6

A stakeholder register is an important tool for project managers that helps to keep track of all the individuals and groups who have an interest in the project and its outcomes.

The stakeholder register documents each stakeholder's contact information, position, concerns, interests, and attitude toward the project. The project manager updates the register as new stakeholders are identified and when stakeholders leave the project.

Creating the Stakeholder Register

Stakeholder identification is only as good as the documentation that comes out of the process. The stakeholder register is the only output of stakeholder identification. It's a log of all the stakeholder information you've gathered in the project. It will help you communicate with project stakeholders; help ensure that you understand the stakeholders' needs, wants, and expectations; and help you classify stakeholder objectives and priorities.

The stakeholder register is a document that includes at least three types of information about your project stakeholders:

- **Identification**   You'll need to capture the stakeholder names, project role, company position, contact information, and where they're located should you need to meet with them face to face.

- **Assessment information**   Stakeholders' expectations are documented in the stakeholder register. You'll capture the stakeholders' primary expectations, their expected contributions to the project, their influence, and the periods during the project when you anticipate the stakeholder to be most involved and interested.

- **Stakeholder classification**   A primary activity of stakeholder identification is to classify each stakeholder by their role, position, attitude toward the project, and other factors.

The creation of the stakeholder register isn't a one-time event. You'll refer to the stakeholder register throughout the project and update it as new information becomes available. For example, stakeholders may leave the project, new stakeholders could be identified in the project, and stakeholder attitudes and influences can evolve as the project is in motion. Change requests might be generated as a result of stakeholder identification, though not in the initial round of identification. As you identify more and more stakeholders and they learn about the project, they may want additions or modifications to the project requirements.

Communications Planning

The stakeholder register defines whom you'll communicate with as a project manager. Based on the stakeholder register and the stakeholder analysis you've completed, you'll know which stakeholders are most interested in your project and how much influence they have over your project. For each stakeholder, you should record the following information in the stakeholder register:

- Their interest in the project
- Their influence over the project
- Strategies for gaining their support

Strategies for overcoming obstacles, blockers, and impediments that hinder the progress of a project or prevent the project team from achieving their goals. Some common obstacles, blockers, and impediments include poor communication, insufficient resources, competing priorities, skill gaps, and insufficient training.

This information can be sensitive, so it's important for the project manager to guard this information and share it only with the people who need to know this information. In other words, you don't want to document how difficult it is to work with the IT director and then post it on your blog. Though it's important that you create a definitive strategy for managing stakeholders' fears, threats, concerns, and objections, it's just as important that you guard the strategy from reaching the wrong people in your organization.

Knowledge Management

The stakeholder register will help you understand what knowledge stakeholders bring to the project. Stakeholders have insight into the project scope and requirements, and they can contribute to the project planning.

Procurement Process

The project manager and team will need the contact information for the stakeholders interested in the procurement decisions. Some decisions in procurement may affect the interests of stakeholders—consider costs, materials, schedules, and contractual obligations.

Quality Planning

You'll need to know which stakeholders have a specific interest in the quality objectives of the project and how to contact them. Some stakeholders may have concerns about specific deliverables, so you'll want to communicate with those folks when quality issues arise.

Requirements Elicitation

You'll have to work with the project stakeholders to identify the requirements your project needs. This is where the stakeholder register comes in very handy, because you'll need to contact the stakeholders to schedule times to elicit their project requirements. One favorable approach is to categorize the types of users and stakeholders to streamline your requirements collection process. By grouping similar stakeholders together, you can save time and effort and keep the project moving along.

Resource Planning

The stakeholder register identifies all the project stakeholders, their interests in the project, and their roles. The stakeholder register can help identify who has control over physical and human resources in the project.

Risk Management

The stakeholder register is referenced for stakeholder concerns, threats, perceived threats, contact information, and roles involved in the project.

Organizational Process Assets

Remember to look at past projects to identify current stakeholders. If you've done similar work in the past, your current project will probably include some of the same or similar stakeholders. Your organizational process assets can also include stakeholder identification approaches, a stakeholder register template, and lessons learned. Use what already exists so you can work smarter and not harder.

Explain Project Closure and Transitions

Task 2, Enabler 7

Project closure and transitions refers to the process of bringing a project to an orderly end, documenting its results, and ensuring a smooth transition to operations or to a follow-on project. The purposes of project closure are to formally close the project, to ensure that the project's objectives have been met, and to archive project documentation for future reference.

The transition phase of the project is important because it ensures a smooth handover of the project's deliverables to the stakeholders, including customers, clients, or operations. This phase involves making sure that the project's deliverables are accepted and integrated into the stakeholders' systems and processes and that the project team is disbanded.

Project closure and transition activities include the following, among others:

- Conducting a final review of the project to identify lessons learned
- Archiving project documents and records
- Obtaining formal acceptance of the project deliverables from stakeholders
- Transferring ownership of project deliverables to stakeholders
- Disbanding the project team and releasing team members to other projects

Closing the Project or Phase

Every project manager that I know loves to close a project. Completing a project and then transferring the deliverable to the customer or project user is a rewarding experience. I've also learned from participant feedback in my CAPM seminars that closing the project is the category in which they missed the most questions on their way to their CAPM certification. I believe it's because folks have a tendency to study in the order of the process groups: Initiation, Planning, Executing, Monitoring and Controlling, and then (finally) Closing. I imagine they're winded by the time their studying efforts get to Closing. With that in mind, give yourself a stretch, have another sip of coffee, and really home in on this discussion of closing a project or phase. I want you to pass your exam!

The Closing process group may be applied to the end of a project or to the end of the project phase in a multiphased project. Closing the project or phase means that the project manager confirms that all of the needed activities within the other process groups have been completed and that the project deliverables have been handed over to the customer. If a project is terminated for any reason, the project manager should still close the project to account for the work that has been performed on the project and to learn why the project may have failed.

 NOTE Projects can be moving along swimmingly and still get terminated. Consider an organization's cash flow or the project's priority, or perhaps the project deliverable may not be needed any longer. Just because a project was canceled doesn't always mean the project was a failure.

Documenting the Closing

You can close the entire project or, in larger projects, you can close just a phase of the project. The process of closing the project or phase is about finalizing everything in the project and ensuring that there are no loose ends, that everyone has the information they need, and that the project is officially done. The project manager documents everyone who is involved in the project closure: team members, vendors, management, the sponsor, and often the project customer. Part of this documentation defines each person's role and related responsibility to close out the project. Consider a large construction project. Lots of people are involved in the formal closing proceedings, so documentation explaining who'll be needed, what they'll be doing, and when they'll be doing it makes great sense for the project manager.

When the project manager prepares to close the project or phase, they'll need to gather eight specific items as process inputs:

- **Project charter**   The project charter defines what the project will accomplish, what constitutes project success, and who will sign off on the project completion.

- **Project management plan**   The project management plan includes the project scope, the project requirements, and expectations for the project objectives. When a project is being completed for another organization, the contract serves as a guide for how the project may be closed. The project plan may also reference the enterprise environmental factors to consider as part of project closing.

- **Project documents**   You may rely on some (or all) of the project documents to close the project. This can include the assumption log, basis of estimates, change log, issue log, lessons learned register, milestone list, communications, quality control measurement, quality reports, requirements documentation, risk register, and any risk reports.

- **Deliverables**   The project has to create something, so it's no surprise that the deliverables serve as input to the project closing processes.

- **Business documents**   The business case that justified the need for the project and the benefits management plan are referenced in closing.

- **Agreements**   Any contracts or similar documents that need to be closed are included as part of the closing project phase or project process. The terms of contract closure should be part of any contract.

- **Procurement documentation**   All procurement documentation is gathered and filed. This includes all vendor performance information, contract change information, payments, and inspection results. Your project may also have "as-built" or "as-developed" plans, drawings, and documentation that need to be archived.

- **Organizational process assets**   An organization may have procedures and processes that every project manager must follow to close a phase or project. These can include financial, reporting, and human resource obligations.

Project closure includes analyzing the success of the project through data analysis. One of the most common approaches is *regression analysis*, which is a mathematical model to examine the relationship among project variables, such as cost, schedule, labor, and other project metrics. For regression analysis, you can use a scatter diagram to help visualize the correlation between the dependent variables, such as the project's budget, against the independent variables, such as errors in the project, changes to the project, and any delays stakeholders may have caused to the project. This helps to identify trends, especially in phases, and helps you prepare for future projects and other phases yet to begin within the project.

The goal of project closure is to obtain acceptance of the deliverables: The project manager must obtain formal acceptance of the project deliverables from the stakeholders and the customer, ensuring that they meet the required standards and specifications. *Formal acceptance* means that the project customer or sponsor agrees that the deliverable provided is in alignment with the project scope and that it is acceptable. A formal documentation of project acceptance, such as a project certificate of closure or a project closure sign-off, is needed to confirm that the project deliverable has been transferred from the project manager to the recipient of the project.

Creating the Final Project Report

When you've confirmed that the project deliverables have been transferred to the customer or organizational party, ensured that the project resources have been released from the project, and obtained project sign-off from the key stakeholders such as the project sponsor, you'll create the final project report. This final report is a summation of the entire project and the experience of the project manager and the project team. The final report is all about determining how well the project performed and how efficiently the project was managed to reach its objectives.

The final project report typically includes the following:

- Summation of the project

- Scope objectives and evidence of when the scope objectives were met or missed

- Quality performance of the project and its deliverables

- Schedule performance, milestone delivery dates, and overall schedule management

- Cost performance, actual costs, cost variances, and earned value management performance

- Final product, service, or result performance and ability to meet the scope objectives and business objectives of the organization

- Summation of project risk management and how risks were managed within the project
- Success or failure status of the project and reasons

Should the project be cancelled during its execution, the project manager should still follow the Close Project or Phase process and create the final project report. After creating the project report, the project manager will submit it to the project sponsor and any other key stakeholders who require the document. Typically, not all stakeholders receive the final project report—only the key stakeholders who are privy to the information, such as the project sponsor, receive it. Finally, all of the project documentation, support materials, and lessons learned information are entered into organizational process assets to help future projects.

More on Project Closure and Transitions

Project closure and transitions are the final stages of the project management life cycle. They involve formally completing the project, reviewing its performance, documenting lessons learned, and transitioning the project deliverables to the intended recipients or operational teams. These steps are crucial to ensuring that the project's goals have been met and that the organization can benefit from the knowledge gained during the project.

Project Closure

Project closure involves formally completing the project, reviewing its performance, documenting lessons learned, and transitioning the project deliverables to the intended recipients or operational teams. These steps are crucial to ensuring that the project's goals have been met and that the organization can benefit from the knowledge gained during the project.

Key activities of project closure include:

- **Confirm completion of project deliverables** The project manager and team review and confirm that all project deliverables have been completed according to the project scope and quality requirements.

- **Obtain final acceptance** The project manager works with the project sponsor and key stakeholders to obtain their formal acceptance of the project deliverables, signifying that they meet the desired outcomes and objectives.

- **Conduct a project review** The project team conducts a thorough review of the project's performance, comparing planned vs. actual results in terms of scope, schedule, budget, and quality. This helps identify any variances, success factors, and areas for improvement.

- **Document lessons learned** The project team gathers and documents lessons learned throughout the project, focusing on what worked well, what didn't, and what can be improved for future projects. This information is typically stored in a lessons learned repository to help the organization improve its project management practices.

- **Release resources**   The project manager releases project resources, such as team members, equipment, and facilities, back to their respective departments or makes them available for new projects.

- **Celebrate success and recognize team members**   The project manager acknowledges the team's efforts and accomplishments, often through a project celebration.

Transition Plan

A transition plan is a document that outlines the steps, processes, and activities required to transfer the project deliverables from the project team to the intended recipients, such as operational teams or end users. The purpose of a transition plan is to ensure a smooth handover, minimize disruption, and facilitate the successful integration of the project deliverables into the organization's ongoing operations. A transition plan ensures the stakeholders in the receiving organization who will facilitate the ongoing realization of benefits are prepared to receive the benefits of the project. This plan is addressed in both *The Standard for Program Management* and *Business Analysis for Practitioners: A Practice Guide*. The transition plan identifies how, when, and to whom the results and benefits are to be delivered. It may also include identification of training, documentation, conversions, or other activities that should be conducted before the benefits are provided to the receiving organization.

Two more plans are essential components for ensuring the long-term success and value of a project: a sustainment plan and a benefits management plan. These plans focus on maintaining the project deliverables and maximizing the benefits derived from the project, respectively.

Sustainment Plan

In addition to the transition plan, a sustainment plan should be developed to identify and implement tracking methods to ensure continued realization of the benefits delivered. A sustainment plan outlines the strategies, processes, and resources required to maintain and support the project deliverables after the project has been completed and handed over to the operational teams or end users. This plan includes risks, processes, measures, metrics, and tools to ensure the realization of the expected benefits. The sustainment plan ensures that the deliverables continue to function effectively, providing value to the organization.

Benefits Management Plan

A benefits management plan focuses on identifying, tracking, and maximizing the benefits derived from a project. This plan defines what benefits the project will create, when the benefits will be realized, and how the benefits will be measured. I'll share more details about the benefits management plan later in this chapter.

Final Product, Service, or Result Transition

The final product, service, or result is the whole point of the project, the reason it was initiated in the first place. This is the deliverable the entire project was planned to provide the customer with. In the case of phase closure, it is the milestone that is expected before approval is given to proceed to the next phase. The final product, service, or result is handed over to the customer as the final part of contractual closure.

Demonstrate an Understanding of Project Roles and Responsibilities

Task 3

An understanding of project roles and responsibilities is essential for the successful completion of a project. Different team members have distinct roles and responsibilities, which, when fulfilled effectively, contribute to the project's overall success. There are several key roles and responsibilities that need to be defined and fulfilled to ensure a successful outcome. Some of the most common roles include the following:

- **Project manager** The project manager is responsible for leading the project team, defining the project scope, developing the project plan, and ensuring that the project is completed on schedule, within budget, and to the required quality standards.

- **Project team** The project team is responsible for executing the project plan and delivering the project's deliverables. The size and composition of the project team will vary depending on the size and complexity of the project.

- **Sponsors/stakeholders** Sponsors are the individuals or organizations that provide funding and support for the project, while stakeholders are individuals or organizations that have an interest in the project's outcome. Both sponsors and stakeholders play an important role in ensuring that the project meets their needs and expectations.

- **Customer/client** The customer or client is the individual or organization that will benefit from the project's deliverables. They are responsible for defining their requirements and working closely with the project team to ensure that the project meets their needs.

- **Subject matter experts (SMEs)** SMEs are individuals who have specialized knowledge or expertise in specific areas related to the project. They play an important role in providing technical guidance and support to the project team.

By understanding the roles and responsibilities of each of these key players, project managers can ensure that everyone is working together effectively and that the project is moving in the right direction. They can also identify any areas where additional support or resources may be needed and take action to address these issues before they become problems.

Compare and Contrast the Roles and Responsibilities of Project Managers and Project Sponsors

Task 3, Enabler 1

Project managers and project sponsors play different but complementary roles in the success of a project.

Project managers are responsible for the day-to-day management of a project, including planning, execution, monitoring, and controlling the project. They ensure the project stays on track, on budget, and within scope, and are accountable for delivering the project outcomes. Key responsibilities of project managers include

- Defining project scope, goals, and deliverables
- Developing project plans and schedules
- Managing project budgets and resources
- Overseeing project execution and ensuring project tasks are completed on schedule and within budget
- Communicating project progress and status to stakeholders

Project sponsors, on the other hand, are responsible for providing the resources and support necessary for a project to succeed. They play a strategic role in the project and provide the vision, leadership, and decision-making necessary to keep the project on track. Key responsibilities of project sponsors include

- Providing strategic direction and support for the project
- Approving project budgets and resources
- Providing project funding
- Ensuring the project aligns with the organization's goals and objectives
- Acting as a champion for the project and promoting it to key stakeholders

In many organizations, the project manager is the person who writes the project charter, and that's fine—really!—but the charter cannot be signed by the project manager. Though the project may be backed by the project customer, the project champion, or the organization's project management office, the charter is officially backed the project sponsor. In other words, the project manager can't sign the charter because they are not "powerful" enough within the organization to assign resources and funds to their own project.

NOTE "ponor$" is a cute way to remember that project sponsors control the money.

A popular way of displaying the separate responsibilities of not only the project manager and project sponsor roles but also the other project roles is a matrix-based chart called a *RACI chart*. A RACI chart is a type of *responsibility assignment matrix (RAM)*. A RACI chart describes (as the acronym indicates) who is *responsible*, who is *accountable*, who will be *consulted*, and who will be *informed* on different activities. The difference between the "responsible" and "accountable" designations is that being responsible for an activity means producing or actually completing the work, whereas being accountable for an activity means having to answer for the work being done or not being done on time. A single person can be both responsible and accountable for an activity, and if your project is large enough to have many team members, you can split the responsibility and accountability as a means of ensuring better management of activities. However, only one person can be designated as accountable for an activity in a RACI chart.

NOTE Here is an easy way to remember RACI. Responsible: does the work; Accountable: approves the completed work; Consulted: gives expert judgment; Informed: kept in the loop.

A RACI chart is depicted in Figure 3-6. You may need to update the roles and responsibility charts, such as your RACI chart, to reflect the changes within the project and/or project team.

In the Real World
I have used several forms of the RACI chart on different projects. Some smaller projects simply have an RA chart. I also did some work for a large company that had their own variant, an RASCI chart, with the "S" standing for "Support," to indicate which team members were providing technical support.

	Project Team Member				
Activity	Dylan	Alexa	Chase	Naeem	Faisal
Foundation	A	R	C	I	C
Framing	R	A	C	I	C
Wiring	A	C	C	R	C
Testing	R	I	A	C	C

Figure 3-6 RACI charts show the relationships among activities and project team members.

Compare and Contrast the Roles and Responsibilities of the Project Team and the Project Sponsor

Task 3, Enabler 2

The project team and project sponsor both play important roles in the successful completion of a project, but they have different responsibilities and focus areas. The project manager has roles and responsibilities, but so do people on the project team. Roles are assigned to determine who does what on the project: developer, app tester, plumber, or technical writer, for example. In many projects, project team members, like the project manager, play multiple roles on a project. While the project manager is responsible for leading and managing the project team, the project team is responsible for completing their work assignments.

During planning, which is an *iterative* activity, the project manager and the project team will plan the work; next, they'll execute the project work. As the project manager leads and manages the project team, they will rely on the project team's expertise, experience, skills, and technical abilities to complete assignments. It's unrealistic for the project manager to have the skills and depth of knowledge of each project team member. The project manager should rely on the expertise of the project team when it comes to planning, and then the project team members must complete their assignments as promised.

The project sponsor is a high-ranking individual within the organization, often an executive or senior manager, who serves as the project's champion and primary decision-maker. They are responsible for ensuring the project aligns with the organization's strategic objectives, providing support and resources, and overseeing project success.

Project Team

The project team consists of individuals with diverse skill sets and expertise, who are responsible for executing the project. It may include project managers, team leads, technical experts, business analysts, and others.

The project team's primary role is to execute the project according to the project plan, meeting the defined objectives, scope, timeline, and quality standards. And the project team's responsibilities include the following:

- Developing the project plan, including scope, schedule, resources, and budget
- Collaborating with stakeholders to gather requirements and expectations
- Identifying and managing risks and issues
- Monitoring and controlling project progress, ensuring the project remains on track
- Regularly reporting project status to the project sponsor and other stakeholders
- Ensuring deliverables meet quality standards and stakeholder expectations
- Implementing changes as required, while managing scope and schedule
- Closing the project upon completion and conducting a post-project review

Project Sponsor

The project sponsor is typically a senior executive or key stakeholder who champions the project within an organization. They provide strategic guidance, support, and resources to ensure the project's success.

The project sponsor's responsibilities include

- **Project advocacy**   The project sponsor serves as the primary advocate for the project, promoting its importance and benefits to the organization's leadership and stakeholders. They help secure buy-in and support from various parties.

- **Strategic alignment**   The project sponsor ensures that the project aligns with the organization's strategic goals and objectives. They work with the project manager to clarify the project's purpose, scope, and desired outcomes.

- **Resource provision**   The project sponsor helps secure necessary resources, such as funding, personnel, and equipment, to support the project's completion. They may also help remove organizational barriers that could impede the project's progress.

- **Decision making**   The project sponsor is responsible for making high-level decisions that impact the project's direction and outcomes. They may need to resolve conflicts, approve changes to the project scope, and make critical decisions that cannot be made by the project manager or team.

- **Risk management**   The project sponsor plays a role in identifying and addressing potential risks that could jeopardize the project's success. They help the project manager and team develop strategies to mitigate or avoid these risks.

- **Governance and accountability**   The project sponsor is accountable for the project's success and ensures that it adheres to organizational policies and procedures. They provide oversight and guidance to the project manager and team to ensure that the project stays on track and delivers the expected outcomes.

The project team is responsible for executing the project plan, while the project sponsor provides the necessary resources and support to ensure the project's success.

Explain the Importance of the Role the Project Manager Plays

Task 3, Enabler 3

The project manager plays a crucial role in ensuring the success of a project by performing several important functions. These functions include the following:

- **Initiator**   The project manager is responsible for defining the project scope, identifying project objectives, and establishing a project plan.

- **Negotiator**   The project manager must negotiate with stakeholders, including team members, customers, and suppliers, to resolve conflicts and ensure that everyone is working toward a common goal.

- **Listener**   The project manager must be a good listener, able to understand the needs and concerns of all stakeholders and respond to their questions and issues in a timely manner.

- **Coach**   The project manager must motivate and coach team members, helping them to develop their skills and achieve their full potential.

- **Working member**   The project manager must be an active member of the project team, participating in project activities and working alongside other team members to ensure project success.

- **Facilitator**   The project manager must facilitate communication and collaboration among team members, ensuring that everyone is informed and engaged throughout the project.

- **Model**   The project manager uses their own behavior to shape others' performance.

- **Steward**   A steward is a person who takes responsibility for ensuring the efficient and responsible use of resources, safeguarding the interests of the project stakeholders, and promoting the project's long-term sustainability and success. The steward role is often implicitly embedded in the project manager's responsibilities, but it can also be a separate role or shared among team members.

Initiator

Rather than tell people what to do, an initiator draws attention to actions that must be taken for team goals to be met. The role of the project manager as an initiator is crucial in the initiation phase of a project. The initiation phase is the first stage in the project life cycle, where the project manager is responsible for defining the project scope, identifying stakeholders, and establishing the project objectives and goals.

The importance of the project manager's role as an initiator is highlighted by the following:

- **Project definition**   The project manager is responsible for defining the project scope, objectives, and goals. This sets the foundation for the rest of the project and helps to ensure that everyone is aligned and working toward the same end goal.

- **Stakeholder identification**   The project manager is responsible for identifying all of the stakeholders involved in the project, including internal and external stakeholders, and establishing their level of involvement in the project.

- **Project charter**   The project manager is responsible for creating the project charter, which is a document that formally recognizes the existence of the project and provides a high-level overview of the project scope, objectives, and goals.

- **Project team formation**   The project manager is responsible for selecting and forming the project team, including selecting the project sponsor, stakeholders, and project team members.

- **Budget and schedule development**   The project manager is responsible for developing the project budget and schedule, including identifying the resources required to complete the project and estimating the project duration.

PART II

Negotiator

A negotiator gets what they need from resource providers by framing the project as mutually beneficial.

The project manager plays a critical role as a negotiator. Negotiations are a common occurrence in projects, and the project manager is often the primary negotiator for the project team. The importance of the project manager's role as a negotiator is highlighted by the following:

- **Resource allocation**   The project manager often negotiates with stakeholders, suppliers, and team members to allocate resources such as budget, personnel, and equipment to ensure the project is completed on schedule and within budget.

- **Conflict resolution**   Projects often involve conflicting goals and interests among stakeholders and team members. The project manager is responsible for mediating and resolving these conflicts through negotiations to ensure that the project remains on track.

- **Scope management**   The project manager is responsible for negotiating the project scope with the customer or client to ensure that all requirements are captured and that the project remains within the defined constraints.

- **Risk management**   The project manager is responsible for negotiating risk mitigation strategies with stakeholders and team members to ensure that the project remains on track and that potential risks are managed effectively.

- **Stakeholder management**   The project manager is responsible for negotiating with stakeholders to align their interests with the project goals and objectives and to ensure that the project remains aligned with their expectations.

 NOTE   The purpose of negotiations is to reach a fair agreement among all parties. Be respectful of all involved; you may have to work with them throughout the project and beyond.

Negotiation, communication, and political savvy are key to getting the desired resources on the project.

Listener

A listener gathers from the environment signals of impending trouble, employee discontent, and opportunities for gain. As a listener, the project manager can foster collaboration, build trust, and ensure that everyone's input is valued and considered during the decision-making process. Here are three key aspects of the project manager's role as a listener:

Active Listening   With this technique, the listener takes active steps to ensure that the message was understood correctly. The result is that the listener is more engaged and there is a much better transfer of information between sender and receiver.

When communicating, the project manager needs to be an active listener; this means the project manager is engaged and involved in the conversation. In some instances, the project manager must be aware of cultural and personal differences that can affect the message meaning and understanding between the parties in the conversation. Active listening also helps the PM persuade and motivate when fulfilling the negotiator and coach functions

In the Real World

Throughout my career as a project manager, the ability to listen and understand what it is that people are actually communicating has played an important role in the success of projects I have managed. I remember when I was younger and perhaps a little more headstrong, and I would simply take shortcuts when receiving information from people, assuming I understood what they were trying to communicate. This, of course, led to many misunderstandings and many inefficiencies and mistakes that affected the chances of project success. I have since learned that being an active listener is more important than being an active talker.

Effective Listening   Similar to active listening, this technique also involves the listener or receiver monitoring nonverbal and physical communication. Effective listening is the ability to watch the speaker's body language, interpret paralinguistic clues (pitch, tone, inflections), and decipher facial expressions. Following the message, effective listening has the listener asking questions to achieve clarity and offering feedback.

Empathic Listening   Empathic listening is a communication technique where the listener actively tries to understand the speaker's feelings, thoughts, and experiences by putting themselves in the speaker's shoes. It involves paying close attention to what the speaker is saying, both verbally and nonverbally, and trying to understand their perspective.

Empathic listening can help in communications in several ways:

- **Building trust**   When people feel heard and understood, they are more likely to trust and feel valued by the listener. This can improve relationships and create a more positive atmosphere.

- **Resolving conflicts**   Empathic listening can help to resolve conflicts by allowing both parties to express their perspectives and feelings, helping them to find common ground.

- **Improving understanding**   By actively trying to understand the speaker's perspective, the listener can gain a deeper understanding of the issue being discussed, which can lead to better decision-making and problem-solving.

- **Enhancing relationships**   Empathic listening can help to build stronger relationships by demonstrating respect and caring for others and by creating an environment where everyone feels valued and heard.

Coach

A coach finds ways to help team members maximize their potential and achieve agreed-upon goals. Coaching opportunities are abundant within teams because the skills that members eventually need are often ones they don't already have.

The role of a project manager as a coach is crucial to the success of a project. A coach is someone who provides guidance, support, and encouragement to help individuals or teams achieve their goals. In the context of project management, the project manager acts as a coach in several ways:

- **Team development** The project manager is responsible for coaching and developing the project team to ensure that they have the skills and knowledge necessary to perform their roles and responsibilities effectively.

- **Performance improvement** The project manager is responsible for coaching team members on their performance and providing feedback and guidance to help them improve. This can help to increase individual and team productivity and drive project success.

- **Career development** The project manager can act as a mentor and coach for team members, helping them to develop their careers and prepare for future opportunities.

- **Motivation** The project manager is responsible for coaching and motivating the project team to ensure that they are committed and engaged in the project. This can lead to higher levels of employee satisfaction and reduced turnover.

- **Problem-solving** As a coach and mentor for team members, the project manager can help them to identify and solve problems and to develop new skills and knowledge.

The OSCAR Model The OSCAR model is a coaching tool used to help project managers improve their coaching skills and support their team members in achieving their goals. The acronym OSCAR stands for

- **Outcome** The desired result or goal that the team member wants to achieve
- **Situation** The current situation or problem that the team member is facing
- **Causes** The underlying causes of the situation or problem
- **Actions** The specific actions that the team member needs to take to achieve their outcome
- **Review** The process of reviewing the outcome and situation after the actions have been taken to determine what worked well and what can be improved

The OSCAR model provides a structured approach to coaching that can help project managers to provide more effective support to their team members. By using the OSCAR model, project managers can help their team members to

- Define their goals and desired outcomes
- Identify the underlying causes of their situation or problem
- Develop a plan of action to achieve their goals

- Monitor their progress and make adjustments as needed
- Reflect on their performance and identify areas for improvement

Working Member

In addition to providing direction, a working member must do a share of the work, particularly in areas where they have special competence. Ideally, they should also take on one or two of the unpleasant or unexciting jobs that no one else wants to do.

The role of the project manager as a working member of the team is critical in ensuring the success of the project. The project manager is responsible for leading and managing the project, but they must also be an active and engaged participant in the day-to-day activities of the project team. The importance of the project manager's role as a working member of the team is highlighted by the following:

- **Understanding the work**   The project manager must have a deep understanding of the work being performed by the project team, including the tasks, processes, and challenges faced by team members. This knowledge helps the project manager to make informed decisions and provide effective leadership and support.

- **Building relationships**   The project manager must build strong relationships with the project team and stakeholders, including regular communication and collaboration. This helps to create a positive and productive work environment, which can lead to higher levels of employee satisfaction and engagement.

- **Providing support**   The project manager must provide support to the project team, including assisting with the resolution of issues and challenges, providing resources and tools, and facilitating communication and collaboration.

- **Demonstrating flexibility**   The project manager must demonstrate flexibility and adaptability, including being willing to roll up their sleeves and help with the work when necessary. This helps to create a sense of shared responsibility and reinforces the idea that everyone is working toward the same goal.

- **Building collaboration**   The project manager must facilitate collaboration and teamwork, including encouraging communication and collaboration between team members and fostering a culture of collaboration and cooperation.

Facilitator

Through meetings and messages, a facilitator builds consensus on project goals.

The role of the project manager as a facilitator is critical in ensuring the successful execution of the project. The project manager is responsible for facilitating communication, collaboration, and decision-making between the project team, stakeholders, and other key groups involved in the project. The importance of the project manager's role as a facilitator is highlighted by the following:

- **Improving communication**   The project manager must facilitate communication and ensure that all parties are kept informed about the project status, risks, and issues. This helps to reduce misunderstandings and promotes a culture of transparency and accountability.

- **Facilitating decision-making**   The project manager must facilitate decision-making and help to resolve disputes or conflicts that may arise during the project. This helps to ensure that the project is completed on schedule, within budget, and to the required quality standards.

- **Encouraging collaboration**   The project manager must encourage collaboration and teamwork, including facilitating communication and collaboration between team members and stakeholders. This helps to create a positive and productive work environment, which can lead to higher levels of employee satisfaction and engagement.

- **Streamlining processes**   The project manager must streamline processes and ensure that the project is executed in an efficient and effective manner. This includes facilitating the identification of bottlenecks and roadblocks and working with the project team to develop solutions to overcome these challenges.

- **Supporting change**   The project manager must support change and help to manage the transition from the current state to the desired future state. This includes facilitating the identification of change requirements, managing the change process, and communicating changes to all relevant parties.

Model

Aside from the previously described roles listed in Enabler 3, there are two other roles for you to consider—model and steward (described in the next section).

A model, in the context of leadership or management, is an individual who influences others through their actions and behavior. They set a positive example by embodying the values, principles, and practices that they wish to see in their team members or colleagues. By modeling desired behaviors, they shape the performance of others and create an environment that fosters growth, collaboration, and success.

Leaders often rely heavily on this tactic, since they typically cannot use promotions, compensation, or threats of dismissal to influence team members.

The role of the project manager as a model is critical in leading and inspiring the project team to achieve success. The project manager serves as a role model for the project team by demonstrating the values, behaviors, and attitudes that are essential for success. The importance of the project manager's role as a model is highlighted by the following:

- **Setting the tone**   The project manager sets the tone for the project and establishes the culture and expectations for the project team. This helps to create a positive and productive work environment, which can lead to higher levels of employee satisfaction and engagement.

- **Demonstrating best practices**   The project manager is responsible for demonstrating best practices and processes, such as project management methodologies, risk management, and change management, to the project team. This helps to ensure that the project is managed effectively and efficiently.

- **Leading by example**   The project manager leads by example and demonstrates the behaviors and attitudes that they expect from the project team. This can help to inspire and motivate the project team to perform at their best.

- **Building trust**   The project manager is responsible for building trust and credibility with the project team and stakeholders. By serving as a role model and demonstrating integrity, the project manager can help to build a culture of trust, which can lead to higher levels of employee engagement and satisfaction.

- **Supporting professional development**   Supporting professional development is a modeling behavior because it demonstrates a commitment to continuous learning, improvement, and growth, which are essential traits for successful project management. By actively encouraging and fostering professional development within the project team, the project manager sets an example for others to follow and helps create a positive, growth-oriented culture within the organization.

Steward

One of the 12 project management principles in the *PMBOK Guide* is "Be a diligent, respectful, and caring steward."

The steward role involves safeguarding the interests of the project stakeholders, managing resources responsibly, and promoting the project's long-term sustainability and success. A steward promotes the sharing and application of knowledge within the project team and the broader organization. They facilitate the documentation and dissemination of lessons learned, best practices, and innovative solutions to support organizational learning and continuous improvement. A steward is responsible for fostering positive relationships with the project's stakeholders, including clients, team members, suppliers, and regulatory authorities. They ensure that stakeholders are informed, engaged, and their concerns and expectations are addressed throughout the project life cycle. A steward acts as a role model for ethical behavior, demonstrating integrity, fairness, and respect in all their actions and decisions. They create a culture of accountability and trust within the project team, encouraging all team members to adhere to the highest standards of professional conduct. Additionally, stewards can serve as mentors and guides, sharing their experiences and wisdom with others to help them achieve their own goals.

Explain the Differences Between Leadership and Management

Task 3, Enabler 4

Project leadership and project management are two distinct, but related, aspects of successfully delivering a project. While both are important for the success of a project, they focus on different aspects of project delivery.

Project management is focused on the day-to-day planning, execution, and control of the project. It involves developing and following a project plan, tracking progress, and making adjustments as necessary to ensure that the project stays on track and meets its objectives. Project management tasks include

- Developing the project plan
- Tracking progress and performance
- Managing risks and issues

- Allocating resources and managing budgets
- Monitoring and controlling quality

Project leadership, on the other hand, focuses on the strategic direction and vision of the project. Project leaders set the tone and provide guidance and direction to the project team, and are responsible for ensuring that the project aligns with the organization's goals and objectives. Project leadership tasks include

- Setting the project vision and goals
- Inspiring and motivating the project team
- Building and maintaining stakeholder relationships
- Providing strategic guidance and decision-making
- Fostering a culture of teamwork and collaboration

Leadership requires the following qualities in a project manager:

- Respect for others
- Integrity and cultural sensitivity
- Problem-solving abilities
- Ability to give others credit
- Desire to learn and improve

Explain Emotional Intelligence and Its Impact on Project Management

Task 3, Enabler 5

As a project manager, you need interpersonal skills to lead the project team. You might know these as *soft skills, emotional intelligence,* or *emotional quotient (EQ)*—they're about understanding what motivates people, how you can lead people, and how to listen to people on your project team. Emotional intelligence helps you identify who you are and how you can better interact with others. Though project management is about getting things done, you're dealing with people who have issues, concerns, stresses, anxieties, and lives beyond your project. You need to listen to the project team, empathize with them as needed, and help them manage their project work and assignments. An experienced project manager can shift from the project manager role and see the project from the perspectives of the team members.

There are four quadrants that define emotional intelligence, as shown in Figure 3-7. The four quadrants of emotional intelligence are as follows:

- **Self-awareness**   Individuals have an understanding of how their behavior affects others. Self-awareness requires an honest assessment of one's emotions and an understanding of how emotions affect others. This is an inward-facing component of emotional intelligence.

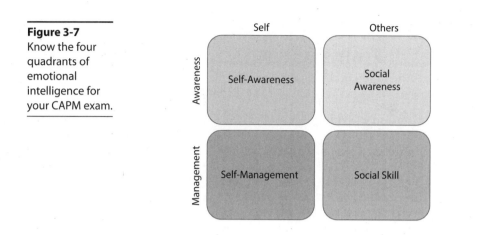

Figure 3-7
Know the four quadrants of emotional intelligence for your CAPM exam.

- **Self-management**   Individuals have self-control, are conscientious of others, can adapt their behavior to the situation, and have some level of drive, ambition, and motivation to accomplish tasks. This is an inward-facing component of emotional intelligence.

- **Social awareness**   Social awareness is the empathy one feels toward other people. Understanding the organizational context, the situation, and the protocol to behave in a working environment is social awareness. This is an outward-facing component of emotional intelligence.

- **Social skill**   Another outward-facing component, social skill is the culmination of the other dimensions of emotional intelligence. It is concerned with managing groups of people, such as project teams, building social networks, finding common ground with various stakeholders, and building rapport.

 EXAM TIP   You'll likely encounter at least a few questions about emotional intelligence, so it's good to have a high-level understanding. Be sure to also have a look at page 6 of the memory card included with this book.

Another chunk of project management relies on interpersonal skills. Specifically, the project manager relies on the following:

- **Conflict management**   Project managers cannot allow conflicts to hinder progress. Sure, some conflicts are serious, but the goal of management is to get things done. The project manager isn't a counselor, however, so you'll need to balance the emotional intelligence of leadership with the desire to get things done.

- **Influencing**   Project managers use their influence to get things done.

- **Motivation**   Good project managers master the art of establishing direction, aligning people, and motivating the project team to complete the project work.

- **Negotiating**   Project managers will likely negotiate for scope, cost, terms, assignment, and resources.

Determine How to Follow and Execute Planned Strategies or Frameworks

Task 4

By following the steps described next, project managers can ensure that they are effectively following and executing planned strategies or frameworks and that they are able to deliver a successful project outcome.

To follow and execute planned strategies as a project manager, you can take several steps:

- **Clearly define the strategy**   Before starting to execute a strategy, it's important to understand what it is, what it aims to achieve, and how it should be implemented. You can do this by reviewing the strategy document, engaging in discussions with key stakeholders, and asking questions to clarify any uncertainties.

- **Assign roles and responsibilities**   Assign roles and responsibilities to team members to ensure that everyone knows what is expected of them and how they contribute to the success of the strategy.

- **Develop an action plan**   Develop a detailed action plan that outlines the steps needed to implement the strategy. The plan should include a timeline, a list of tasks, and the resources required.

- **Implement the strategy**   Start executing the strategy by carrying out the tasks outlined in the action plan. Regularly check progress against the plan and make adjustments as needed.

- **Monitor and evaluate progress**   Monitor the implementation of the strategy and evaluate progress regularly to ensure that the strategy is on track and achieving the desired outcomes.

- **Communicate progress and results**   Regularly communicate progress and results to key stakeholders to keep them informed and engaged. Share both positive and negative results, and discuss any challenges or opportunities for improvement.

- **Continuously refine and adjust**   As the strategy is being implemented, be prepared to continuously refine and adjust it based on feedback, changes in circumstances, or new insights.

To follow and execute planned frameworks as a project manager, take these steps:

- **Choose the right framework**   Choose the project management framework that best aligns with the project goals, constraints, and organizational culture.

- **Understand the framework**   Study the framework in detail to understand its processes, procedures, and tools. This will help you to implement the framework correctly and achieve the desired outcomes.

- **Develop a project plan**   Develop a detailed project plan that incorporates the processes and procedures of the project management framework. The plan should include a timeline, a list of tasks, and the resources required.

- **Assign roles and responsibilities**   Assign roles and responsibilities to team members to ensure that everyone knows what is expected of them and how they contribute to the success of the project.

- **Implement the framework**   Start executing the framework by carrying out the tasks outlined in the project plan. Regularly check progress against the plan and make adjustments as needed.

- **Monitor and evaluate progress**   Monitor the implementation of the project management framework and evaluate progress regularly to ensure that the project is on track and meeting its goals.

- **Communicate progress and results**   Regularly communicate progress and results to key stakeholders to keep them informed and engaged. Share both positive and negative results, and discuss any challenges or opportunities for improvement.

- **Continuously refine and adjust**   As the project management framework is being implemented, be prepared to continuously refine and adjust it based on feedback, changes in circumstances, or new insights.

Give Examples of How It Is Appropriate to Respond to a Planned Strategy or Framework

Task 4, Enabler 1

The key to responding to a planned strategy or framework is to have a clear plan in place and to regularly review and update it as necessary to ensure that the project remains on track and achieves its objectives.

   Here are some examples of appropriate responses to a planned strategy or framework:

- **Active participation**   Engage in active participation by taking on tasks, providing input, and contributing to the overall success of the strategy or framework.

- **Constructive feedback**   Provide constructive feedback that helps to refine the strategy or framework and improve its effectiveness. This can include giving suggestions for improvement, pointing out potential challenges, and sharing best practices.

- **Supportive attitude**   Adopt a supportive attitude and work with other stakeholders to implement the strategy or framework successfully. This includes helping to overcome obstacles, providing resources, and collaborating to achieve the desired outcomes.

- **Flexibility**   Be flexible and open-minded about changes to the strategy or framework. Be prepared to adapt to new circumstances and adjust the plan as needed to achieve the desired outcomes.

- **Communication** Communicate effectively with stakeholders to ensure that everyone is on the same page and has a clear understanding of the strategy or framework.

- **Compliance** Comply with the processes and procedures outlined in the strategy or framework to ensure that the implementation is consistent and effective.

- **Continuous improvement** Continuously seek ways to improve the strategy or framework and make it more effective over time. This can include making adjustments based on feedback, changes in circumstances, or new insights.

The following are examples of communication when responding to a planned strategy or framework:

- **Stakeholder communication** Communicate the planned strategy or framework to key stakeholders, including customers, employees, partners, and investors, to build support and buy-in.

- **Project update communication** Regularly communicate progress updates and changes to the planned strategy or framework to keep everyone informed and on the same page.

- **Feedback communication** Encourage and solicit feedback from stakeholders to identify areas for improvement and make necessary adjustments to the plan.

- **Risk communication** Communicate identified risks and mitigation plans to stakeholders to proactively manage potential roadblocks and challenges.

- **Change management communication** Communicate the changes associated with the planned strategy or framework, including the impact on employees and processes, to help manage resistance to change.

- **Celebration communication** Communicate and celebrate successes and milestones achieved through the implementation of the planned strategy or framework to keep morale high and motivate the team.

- **Crisis communication** Have a plan in place for communicating in the event of a crisis, such as a significant setback or unexpected challenge, to minimize damage and maintain trust.

EXAM TIP Most project managers are good communicators to begin with. You're probably going to do fine on this exam topic if you do fine in your role as project manager, but don't let your guard down. Pay attention to the terms and communications management plan. These may be things you don't use in your day-to-day role as a project manager, but you'll find them on your exam. Use positive self-talk. You can pass this exam!

The following are examples of risk when responding to a planned strategy or framework:

- **Implementation risk** The risk of not being able to successfully execute the planned strategy or framework due to unforeseen technical or operational challenges

- **Resistance-to-change risk**   The risk of stakeholders or employees resisting the change associated with the new strategy or framework, leading to decreased engagement and potential failure

- **Budgetary risk**   The risk of not having sufficient budget or resources to fully implement the planned strategy or framework, leading to incomplete or inadequate execution

- **Market risk**   The risk that external market conditions or competitive actions may negatively impact the planned strategy or framework, making it less effective or even irrelevant

- **Political risk**   The risk of changes in government regulations, policies, or political climate affecting the viability or success of the planned strategy or framework

- **Reputation risk**   The risk of the organization's reputation being negatively impacted by the implementation of the planned strategy or framework

- **Technical risk**   The risk of new technology not performing as expected or not being compatible with existing systems, leading to disruptions in operations

Explain Project Initiation and Benefit Planning

Task 4, Enabler 2

Project initiation and benefit planning are essential early stages in the project management process, as they lay the foundation for the project and set the direction for its successful execution. They provide a clear direction, establish a solid foundation, and ensure that the project delivers the intended value to the organization.

Project Initiation

Project initiation, called "Starting the Project" in *Process Groups: A Practice Guide*, is the first stage of the project management life cycle and involves defining the purpose, scope, and objectives of the project. It's the process of defining and setting up a new project and getting it off the ground.

The main activities involved in project initiation include the following:

1. *Define the problem or opportunity.* Identify the problem or opportunity that the project is meant to address. This will help to define the purpose and objectives of the project.

2. *Perform a project assessment.* Assess the project based on the available information, the lessons learned from previous projects, and the meetings held with relevant stakeholders.

3. *Conduct a feasibility study.* Evaluate the feasibility of the project, including technical feasibility, economic feasibility, and operational feasibility. This will help to determine whether the project is viable and worth pursuing.

4. *Identify stakeholders.* Identify the key stakeholders who will be impacted by the project and determine their needs, expectations, and level of involvement.

5. *Identify high-level risks, assumptions, and constraints.* Use the current environment, organizational factors, historical data, and expert judgment to propose an implementation strategy. Critical to this activity is that the team selects the appropriate strategy to deliver the expected business value. The team must understand the potential bumps their project might encounter and select an appropriate strategy.

6. *Define the high-level project scope.* Identify the key deliverables based on the business requirements to manage customer expectations and direct the achievement of project goals. Define the boundaries of the project and determine what is included and excluded from the project.

7. *Develop a project charter.* Develop a project charter that defines the purpose, objectives, stakeholders, and scope of the project. The charter should also outline the roles and responsibilities of key stakeholders and the authority of the project manager. Most project managers find that the charter is rarely completed before they are assigned to it. More often than not, they are required to work with the sponsor and other stakeholders to create a charter.

8. *Obtain approval.* Obtain project charter approval from the sponsor to formalize the authority assigned to the project manager and gain commitment and acceptance for the project. This may involve getting sign-off from a sponsor, steering committee, or other key decision-makers. This step is important because it informs the team about the sponsor's expectations and the limits of their authority. The level of authority given to the project manager and team often provides critical information to everyone else about how important the project truly is to the sponsor and organization.

Benefit Planning

Benefit planning is a key aspect of project management that involves defining and documenting the benefits that will be realized from a project. The goal of benefit planning is to ensure that the project delivers the intended outcomes and provides value to the stakeholders. It focuses attention on the need to align the project with the organizational strategy. That's right! Project managers are supposed to be part of the strategic leadership team, and every project is supposed to be aligned with the organization's strategy.

Benefit planning involves several key activities:

- **Defining the benefits** Define the benefits that the project is expected to deliver. This may include tangible benefits such as cost savings, increased revenue, or improved efficiency, as well as intangible benefits such as improved customer satisfaction or increased employee engagement.

- **Assigning responsibility** Assign responsibility for delivering each benefit to a specific person or team. This helps to ensure accountability for delivering the benefits and helps to ensure that everyone is working towards the same goals.

- **Tracking and monitoring**   Develop a system for tracking and monitoring the benefits to ensure that they are delivered as expected. This may involve setting up KPIs (key performance indicators), conducting regular status updates, and conducting regular reviews to assess the benefits delivered.

- **Evaluating the benefits**   Regularly evaluate the benefits to ensure that they are delivering the expected outcomes. This may involve conducting a formal benefits review at the end of the project or on a regular basis to assess the impact of the project.

- **Realizing the benefits**   Ensure that the benefits are realized and embedded into the organization's operations and processes. This may involve making changes to processes, systems, or organizational structures to ensure that the benefits are sustained over time.

Project Benefits Management Plan   The project benefits management plan is created and maintained by the project sponsor and the project manager. The project sponsor is generally accountable for the development and maintenance of the project business case document. The project manager is responsible for providing recommendations and oversight to keep the project business case, project management plan, project charter, and project benefits management plan success measures in alignment with one another and with the goals and objectives of the organization. This plan defines what benefits the project will create, when the benefits will be realized, and how the benefits will be measured. The plan typically includes these elements:

- **Processes**   How to create, maximize, and sustain project benefits
- **Target benefits**   The benefits the project aims to achieve
- **Strategic alignment**   How the benefits the project creates support the business strategies
- **Time frame**   When the short- and long-term benefits will be available; some projects may have intermittent benefits as opposed to all benefits being realized only at the conclusion of the project
- **Benefits owner**   An accountable person who will monitor, track, and measure the benefits of the project
- **Metrics**   How the benefits will be measured
- **Assumptions**   Things believed about the project and benefits that can affect the benefits realization if the assumptions prove otherwise than what is believed
- **Risks**   Uncertain conditions that can affect the realization of the benefits

The benefits management plan is a business document, not part of the project management plan. The maintenance of the benefits management plan is an ongoing activity throughout the project's life cycle.

Demonstrate an Understanding of Common Problem-Solving Tools and Techniques

Task 5

Various tools and techniques can be employed to identify, analyze, and address problems that may arise during the project life cycle. These problem-solving tools and techniques can be adapted to suit the specific needs of a project and can be used in combination to address complex problems effectively. Effective problem-solving requires clear communication, collaboration, and critical thinking among project team members.

Active Problem-Solving

Projects can be cumbersome and tedious, can have competing objectives, and can have constraints that seem to box in the project manager. Project management demands *active problem-solving*, which is the ability to understand the problem, identify a viable solution, and then implement a solution. Though you want to be accurate in your decision, you don't want to take too long to act. This is why many project managers will say it's better to fail early and fail often—try your best option, and if it doesn't work, adapt. In any project, countless problems require viable solutions. And like any good puzzle, the solution to one portion of the problem may create more problems elsewhere.

Active problem-solving requires a clear understanding of what the problem is—this means first defining the problem. A viable solution focuses on more than just the problem. In defining the problem, you must discern between its causes and effects. This requires root cause analysis to identify the effects, which include the problem plus all the possible causes and combinations of causes. If a project manager treats only the symptoms of a problem rather than the cause of the problem, the symptoms will perpetuate and continue throughout the project's life. Root cause analysis looks beyond the immediate symptoms to the cause of the symptoms—which then affords opportunities for solutions.

Root cause analysis doesn't solve the problem, however; you'll still need to implement your solution. Solutions can be presented from vendors, the project team, the project manager, or various stakeholders, which the *PMBOK Guide* refers to as "expert judgment."

Project management often involves solving problems and making decisions, and there are a number of common tools and techniques that can be used to support effective problem-solving and decision-making. The following are some of the most commonly used problem-solving tools and techniques:

- **Root cause analysis**   This involves identifying the underlying cause of a problem, rather than just treating its symptoms. Root cause analysis can be done using tools such as the Ishikawa diagram (also known as a fishbone diagram) or the 5 Whys technique.

- **SWOT analysis**   SWOT stands for strengths, weaknesses, opportunities, and threats. This tool is used to assess a project's internal and external environment and identify potential challenges and opportunities.

- **Mind mapping** This involves creating a visual representation of ideas and information related to a problem. Mind maps can be used to organize thoughts, identify relationships between different ideas, and support decision-making.

- **Decision tree** A decision tree is a graphical representation of the options available for solving a problem and the expected outcomes of each option. This tool can be used to assess the risks and benefits of different solutions and support informed decision-making.

- **Force-field analysis** This tool is used to identify the factors that are driving and resisting a change and to assess the potential impact of a change. Force-field analysis can be used to support decision-making and problem-solving in projects.

In addition, a timely decision is needed, or the window of opportunity may pass and then a new decision will be needed to address the problem. As in most cases, the worst thing you can do is nothing.

Evaluate the Effectiveness of a Meeting

Task 5, Enabler 1

Ever attend a WOT meeting? That's a "waste of time" meeting. Meetings should have an agenda and order, and someone needs to keep the meeting minutes for the project. Meetings are forms of communication. How the meeting is led, managed, and controlled all influence the message being delivered. Agendas, minutes, time boundaries, and order are mandatory for effectively communicating project information.

Evaluating the effectiveness of a project meeting is important to continuously improve the meeting process and make sure that it is contributing to the success of the project. Here are some key factors and questions to consider when evaluating the effectiveness of a project meeting:

- **Objectives** Did the meeting achieve its stated objectives? Were all the necessary discussions and decisions made?

- **Attendance** Was the right mix of people in attendance? Did the right people attend the meeting, and were they involved in the discussions and decisions that were made?

- **Preparation** Were the participants prepared for the meeting? Were the necessary materials and information available for the discussions and decisions that needed to be made?

- **Time management** Was the meeting run efficiently? Was enough time allocated for each agenda item, and did the meeting stay on schedule?

- **Communication** Was the communication during the meeting clear, concise, and effective?

- **Participation** Did everyone have an opportunity to express their opinions and ideas, and were they listened to and considered?

- **Action items**   Were action items clearly identified during the meeting and assigned to the appropriate people? Were the action items followed up on in a timely manner?

- **Feedback**   Did the participants provide feedback on the meeting and suggest ways to improve it in the future?

Hosting the Project Kickoff Meeting

The project kickoff meeting is usually held when the project is ready to begin executing. The kickoff meeting is all about communicating the project's intent, to explain the roles and responsibilities and the expectations for the project stakeholders, and to define how the project will be executed, monitored, and controlled. Some organizations may have a kickoff meeting right after project initiation, but usually it's a bit deeper into the project when the project manager and team have created a clear vision of where the project is going and who'll do what on the project.

On larger projects, there may be two different project teams: one that undertakes the planning processes and another that executes the plan. Construction is a great example of this approach: architects, structural engineers, and draftsmen do the planning, and then the professional builders create the structure based on the plan. In these types of environments, the kickoff is associated with the executing processes as the project execution is launching. Finally, if a project has multiple phases in its life cycle, there can be a kickoff meeting for each phase of the project.

When a project is initiated, the focus is on what the project will deliver: the product scope. It's all dreamy and blue sky. After the project has moved into planning, things are tightened through the project scope statement. The project scope statement is built on the foundations defined in the project's initiation: major deliverables, constraints, and assumptions. The scope statement is also built on the output of the collect requirements process. In planning, more information about the exactness of the project deliverables comes to light through planning, research, stakeholder analysis, and product analysis. The wants and needs of the stakeholders are considered, and eventually they evolve into the project requirements.

Risk Planning Meetings

Planning for risk happens in—surprise, surprise!—planning meetings, where the project team develops the risk management plan and analyzes the inputs previously mentioned to make the best decisions for the current project. It's possible that the risk management plan was already developed, or at least started to be developed, in the project's kickoff meeting. More likely, you'll host risk planning meetings to dig into the risk management. Though the project team comprises the primary participants at the risk management planning meeting, attendees may include the project manager, stakeholders, and other subject matter experts within an organization who influence the risk management processes.

The point of the risk management planning meetings is to plan an approach for how risks will be managed in the project. This is not the same as risk identification; in risk management planning, the focus is on how to manage, monitor, and track risks.

You'll also likely do some stakeholder analysis to get a sense of the stakeholder concerns, threats, and perceived threats for the project objectives. You'll want to define the stakeholder appetite for risk and how that'll affect the depth of risk management.

The purpose of these risk management planning meetings is to create the risk management plan and to define the cost and schedule for risk management activities. Let's face facts: It'll take time and monies for most projects to identify, test, and challenge the risks that may exist within the project. The decisions made in these initial meetings enable monies and time to be incorporated within the project. Risk responsibilities are also assigned in these meetings, as are the risk terminologies the project will use. Risk management planning also defines and tailors the following for the project:

- Risk templates the project should use
- Definitions and terms for risk levels
- Probability according to risk type
- Impact of the risks
- Guidelines for the probability and impact matrix to be used during risk analysis

---

In the Real World

I have often found that meetings are a great way to not only solicit technical input from people with relevant experience but also to generate buy-in and commitment. This is especially important in the area of risk management, because giving team members and relevant stakeholders the opportunity to contribute to the management of project risk helps keep them involved and also allows them to understand the importance of being proactive rather than reactive when managing risk.

Stakeholder Identification Meetings

One of the tools and techniques for stakeholder identification is meetings. Stakeholder identification meetings, sometimes called profile analysis meetings, help the project manager and the management team realize the expectations and interests of the key project stakeholders. These meetings are useful to identify and document the different roles in the project, the types of stakeholders you'll work with, and all the differing objectives, interests, and inputs for the project.

The Stakeholder Engagement Plan Meeting

After you've gathered the necessary inputs to planning stakeholder engagement, you'll need to gather the correct experts to help. Stakeholder engagement planning isn't a solo activity—you'll need experts from within your organization and possibly outside consultants to help with the planning. Subject matter experts for creating the stakeholder engagement plan include senior management, consultants, the project team, leaders within the organization, other project managers with similar project experience, and other needed and identified experts within your organization. The goal is to include as many readily available experts to help you accurately plan an approach to engage your stakeholders.

After you have decided which experts to include, you'll gather these experts together, either one-on-one or through a group format, by hosting meetings. Meetings are one of the tools and techniques for creating the stakeholder engagement plan. Stakeholder meetings can be traditional conference room events, focus groups, or even panels. The goal isn't to get fancy, but to define the needed engagement level for the stakeholders. Engagement levels define the amount of interest each stakeholder has in the project, but also the stakeholder's level of engagement for the project. There are five engagement levels:

- **Unaware**   The stakeholder doesn't know about the project and the effect the project may have on them.

- **Resistant**   The stakeholder knows about the project and doesn't want the change the project may bring.

- **Neutral**   The stakeholder knows about the project but neither supports nor resists the project.

- **Supportive**   The stakeholder knows about the project and is supportive of the change the project will bring about.

- **Leading**   The stakeholder knows about the project, is supportive of the change the project may bring about, and is working to make the project successful.

In larger projects with lots of different stakeholders, you may find it beneficial to create a stakeholder engagement assessment matrix. This is a table that defines all of the stakeholders and their engagement levels in the project. This can help you identify stakeholder trends, commonalities, and group stakeholders by their levels of support for the project. Stakeholders are tagged in the matrix, with C for current engagement level and D for their desired engagement level. Not all stakeholders need to be in the leading category, but your strategy may work to get most stakeholders to at least the supportive level for the project.

Communications Meetings

Stakeholders expect you to keep them abreast of the project's performance, issues, conditions, changes, risk, and other concerns about the project. Meetings enable the project manager, project team, stakeholders, and experts to have conversations about the project. Meetings can help you and the stakeholders determine whether the current communications approach is working or whether refinements regarding how you and the stakeholders communicate are necessary.

Cost Management Plan Meetings

The actual creation of the cost management plan relies heavily on information you gather at meetings. Nothing like some meetings about the project budget, right? You'll need meetings specifically with your key stakeholders and subject matter experts. These people can help guide and direct you about the organization's environment, tell you about similar projects they've worked on or sponsored, and help with the enterprise environmental factors and organizational processes you'll have to adhere to in cost management.

These meetings will likely include the use of some analytical techniques to analyze the anticipated cost of the project, the return on investment, and how the project should be funded. The following are some funding options:

- *Self-funding* means the organization pays for the project expenses from their cash flow.

- *Funding with equity* means the organization balances the project expenses with equity they have in their assets.

- *Funding with debt* means the company pays for the project through a line of credit or bank loan.

There are pros and cons to each approach, and an analysis of the true cost of the project, the cost of the funding, and the risk associated with the project are examined as part of the decision.

Face-to-Face Meetings

Face-to-face meetings are gatherings where team members, stakeholders, or project participants come together in person to discuss project-related issues, share updates, make decisions, and collaborate on various aspects of the project. These meetings hold significant value in the project management process for several reasons:

- **Enhanced communication**   Face-to-face meetings allow for better communication as they facilitate verbal and nonverbal cues, such as tone, body language, and facial expressions, which can help in conveying and understanding messages more effectively.

- **Relationship building**   Meeting in person helps to build trust, rapport, and camaraderie among team members, which is essential for the success of the project. Face-to-face interactions foster a sense of team spirit, belonging, and shared ownership of the project.

- **Immediate feedback and clarification**   In-person meetings enable real-time feedback and the opportunity to address any questions, concerns, or misunderstandings promptly. This ensures that all participants are on the same page and can move forward with a clear understanding of the project's objectives and tasks.

- **Improved problem-solving and decision-making**   Face-to-face meetings facilitate brainstorming, open discussions, and collaborative problem-solving. Participants can present their ideas, debate different approaches, and make decisions more effectively when they are in the same physical space.

- **Increased accountability**   When team members meet in person, they are more likely to feel responsible for their commitments and actions, as they can see the impact of their work on their colleagues and the project as a whole.

- **Reduced miscommunication** Face-to-face meetings help minimize miscommunication that can occur through written or virtual communication channels. In-person discussions allow for immediate clarification, reducing the risk of misunderstandings and errors.

- **Enhanced creativity and innovation** In-person meetings can promote a more open and creative environment for ideation and innovation, as team members can bounce ideas off one another, share insights, and explore new concepts together.

While face-to-face meetings offer many benefits, they may not always be feasible due to geographical constraints, budget limitations, or other factors. In such cases, virtual meetings, video conferences, and other remote collaboration tools can be employed to bridge the gap and maintain effective communication within the project team. However, it is essential to recognize the value of face-to-face meetings and, whenever possible, integrate them into your project management process to maximize their benefits.

 EXAM TIP If an exam question asks which type of communication is best for project communications, face-to-face meetings is correct.

Knowledge Management Meetings

Knowledge management is also dependent on the size of the project and the number of stakeholders involved. Projects with a large number of stakeholders will likely need a more formal strategy for knowledge management than is required for smaller projects. Though expert judgment is an accessible tool for knowledge management, there are many other tools and techniques to consider, especially in a larger project:

- **Networking (live and web-based)** Informal conversations and open-based questions can provide knowledge.

- **Communities of practice** Sometimes called special interest groups, these can be live or web-based.

- **Meetings** Both live and web-based meetings can help inform and educate.

Project Charter Meetings

Project charter meetings are essential during the initial stages of a project to bring together stakeholders, project sponsors, and the project team to discuss, develop, and approve the project charter. In project charter meetings, stakeholders discuss the project objectives, the requirements, success criteria, assumptions, constraints, and all aspects of the project.

Performance Review Meetings

The project manager will host performance review meetings to ascertain the progress and level of success the project team is having with the project work. Performance review meetings focus on the work that has been completed and how the work results are living up to the time and cost estimates. In addition, the project manager and the project team will evaluate the project scope to protect it from change and creep. The project manager and the project team will also examine quality and its effect on the project as a whole.

Lessons Learned Meetings

Lessons learned meetings, also known as post-project reviews or project retrospectives, are an essential part of project management. These meetings take place after the completion of a project or at the end of project phases to evaluate the project's performance, identify successes and challenges, and gather insights that can be applied to future projects. Lessons learned meetings aim to foster a culture of continuous improvement and learning within an organization.

Explain the Purpose of Focus Groups, Standup Meetings, Brainstorming, etc.

Task 5, Enabler 2

Focus Groups

Focus groups are a common tool used to gather information and insights from a specific group of stakeholders. A focus group is a collection of stakeholders that interacts with a trained moderator. The moderator leads the group through a conversation, engages all of the participants, and remains neutral about the topic at hand. Focus groups can build trust, create new relationships, and help the group of stakeholders reach consensus on the project requirements. A scribe or recorder documents the conversation for analysis after the focus group is concluded.

The purpose of focus groups is to achieve the following:

- **Gather feedback**   Focus groups provide an opportunity to gather feedback from stakeholders on a particular aspect of the project, such as the project scope, schedule, budget, or risks. This feedback can help project managers to make informed decisions and improve the project.

- **Understand perspectives**   Focus groups allow project managers to understand the perspectives of different stakeholders on a project. This can be particularly useful when trying to resolve conflicts or address concerns that stakeholders may have.

- **Validate assumptions**   Focus groups can be used to validate assumptions that project managers may have about a project. For example, a focus group may be used to confirm that a proposed solution will meet the needs of stakeholders.

- **Generate ideas**   Focus groups can be used to generate ideas and suggestions for improving a project. This can help project managers to identify new opportunities and innovative solutions that may not have been considered previously.

- **Build relationships**   Focus groups can help project managers to build relationships with stakeholders. By involving stakeholders in discussions and decision-making, project managers can show that their opinions and perspectives are valued and that their contributions are important to the success of the project.

NOTE You might know a focus group through a facilitated workshop called the Joint Application Design (JAD) session. These software development workshops enable the designers and the users to interact and discuss the software requirements.

Standup Meetings

Standup meetings are short, daily meetings held to provide an update on the progress of a project. The purpose of standup meetings is to achieve the following:

- **Provide a daily update** Standup meetings allow project team members to quickly and efficiently provide a daily update on the status of their tasks and any progress they have made. This helps to keep everyone on the same page and ensure that any obstacles or issues are identified and addressed in a timely manner.

- **Facilitate communication** Standup meetings promote communication between team members and help to build a culture of collaboration. By providing regular updates and opportunities for discussion, standup meetings can help to identify and resolve any issues or problems that may arise during the course of a project.

- **Improve accountability** Standup meetings help to improve accountability among team members by requiring them to provide a daily update on their progress. This can help to keep team members focused and motivated and ensure that the project stays on track.

- **Highlight dependencies** Standup meetings provide an opportunity to highlight any dependencies between tasks or team members. This helps to identify any potential roadblocks or delays and ensures that everyone is aware of their role in the project.

- **Identify risks** Standup meetings allow project team members to identify any risks or obstacles that may arise during the course of a project. This helps to ensure that these risks are addressed and mitigated in a timely manner.

The Agile Daily Standup Meeting Every day during the sprint is the *daily scrum*, a 15-minute meeting in which each team member describes what they have accomplished since yesterday, what they are working on today, who they may need to see, and whether they've encountered any impediments. The team usually stands up during the meeting, so sometimes it's called the daily standup. Stakeholders are regularly invited, but they don't speak in the meeting.

When colocation isn't feasible, virtual teams are the norm. The team can leverage technology using web collaboration software, webcams, and apps to work together. Virtual teams can do their daily standup meetings online, but attendees will need to consider time zones and possibly language differences. It's always a good idea to get all the team members together for face-to-face, in-person meetings throughout the project, if that's possible.

Brainstorming

Brainstorming is a creative problem-solving technique used to generate a large number of ideas in a short period of time. Led by a facilitator, the group creates as many ideas as possible and then the ideas are analyzed.

Here are the ground rules:

- Negative responses or criticisms are not allowed.
- Participants are safe to present their own creative ideas even though some ideas may be unrealistic/absurd.
- All generated ideas/requirements are recorded without any assessments.

The uses of brainstorming are

- **Problem-solving**   Brainstorming is often used to generate ideas and solutions to specific problems or challenges that may arise during the course of a project. This can help project managers to identify innovative and effective solutions that may not have been considered previously.
- **Decision-making**   Brainstorming can be used to gather input and insights from team members on important decisions related to the project. This can help project managers to make informed decisions that are supported by the team.
- **Risk management**   Brainstorming can be used to identify potential risks and develop strategies to mitigate these risks. By generating a large number of ideas and solutions, brainstorming can help project managers to identify the most effective strategies for managing risks.
- **Requirements gathering**   Brainstorming can be used to gather input and insights from stakeholders on project requirements. This can help project managers to ensure that the project meets the needs of stakeholders and is aligned with their expectations.
- **Team building**   Brainstorming can be used to build teamwork and improve collaboration among project team members. By involving team members in the brainstorming process, project managers can show that their opinions and perspectives are valued and help to build a positive team dynamic.

Nominal Group Technique   This approach builds on brainstorming by adding a vote to each idea to rank the ideas for acceptance, for more brainstorming, or just to prioritize the identified requirements. Here's how it works:

1. The participants silently write down their ideas.
2. The participants share their ideas with the group, and the moderator writes down the ideas on a whiteboard until all of the ideas have been captured.
3. Each idea is discussed for clarity.

4. Individuals vote privately on the ideas, with 1 being the lowest score and 5 being the highest score.

5. Voting and conversation can take place over many rounds to gain consensus on each item's score and prioritization.

Delphi Technique

The Delphi technique is a problem-solving method that addresses the issue of people being less forthcoming and truthful when their superiors or rivals are present. Anonymity is the crucial aspect of this approach; the identities of the participants remain confidential, eliminating any concerns about facing criticism or retribution for their ideas. The implementation can be as straightforward as requesting individuals to e-mail their ideas, which can then be compiled into a list with the names removed, or it can be more intricate.

Chapter Summary

In this chapter, we talked about what a project is—and is not. You now know that a project is a temporary endeavor to create a unique product or service. Projects are created for any number of reasons, from responding to marketplace demand, to solving a problem within an organization, to following laws and regulations.

Three pre-work activities are important steps in ensuring the success of a project: the business case justifies the project to stakeholders, the feasibility study evaluates the viability of the project, and the SOW defines the scope and objectives of the project.

Projects, regardless of why they were created, move through a progressive elaboration to provide accurate and complete descriptions of their goals and objectives. Recall that progressive elaboration typically starts with a broad synopsis of a project's goals, and through rounds of discussion, analysis, and brainstorming, the characteristics of a project become more detailed until, finally, the scope statement is formed.

The project life cycle is made up of the phases of the project. Each phase describes the work that will happen within that phase of the project. At the end of a project phase, known as a stage gate or go/no-go point, a decision is made at the phase-end review to determine whether the project is ready to move forward in the project life cycle, rework needs to be done in the phase, or the project should be terminated.

A predictive, plan-based approach predicts what the project will create and how the project will create it. An *adaptive approach*, like you'll find in an iterative or incremental environment, expects change to happen in the project.

Portfolio management ensures that all projects selected to be completed by the organization align with the organizational strategy. Portfolio management has an organizational scope that reflects the organizational strategy. Often projects or programs are grouped together into a single portfolio that reflects a specific strategy.

 EXAM TIP The *PMBOK Guide* places a great deal of emphasis on the alignment of organizational strategy and the profession of project management as a strategic enabler for delivering the strategy. Always assume that the default position in a question is that an organization has a strategy and is using project management to achieve that strategy.

Program management focuses on managing interdependencies within projects with a common goal or capability. Program managers are skilled at forecasting, anticipating, and dealing with real or perceived conflict between projects in the same program. All programs have projects, but not all projects are part of programs.

The purpose of a project life cycle is to provide a structured and standardized approach to managing projects, ensuring that they are delivered on schedule, within budget, and to the required quality standards. The project life cycle focuses on managing the project from start to finish, while the product life cycle focuses on managing the product from development to retirement.

As the project manager, you'll need to manage and lead the project—yes, there is a difference between management and leadership. Management is about getting things done. Leadership is about aligning, motivating, and directing people. People tend to work harder, smarter, and better for someone they want to work for than for someone they are required to work for. As part of your leadership and management, you want to maintain a professional and ethical behavior. Avoid playing favorites, balance the tasks among the project team, and get involved in the work when the team needs your help.

Project management is focused on the tactical implementation of a project, while project leadership focuses on the strategic direction and leadership of a project. Both are important for the success of a project and work together to ensure that the project is completed on schedule, within budget, and to the satisfaction of all stakeholders.

The roles and responsibilities of each person involved in the project can vary depending on the size and complexity of the project, as well as the organization's policies and procedures. Nevertheless, it's crucial for project managers to clearly define and communicate the roles and responsibilities of each person involved in the project to ensure that the project is completed successfully.

Project managers are responsible for the day-to-day execution of a project, while project sponsors provide the overall vision, support, and resources necessary for the project to succeed.

The project team focuses on the tactical implementation of the project, while the project sponsor focuses on the strategic direction and leadership of the project. Both work together to ensure the successful completion of the project.

The project manager plays a key role in defining the project scope, resolving conflicts, motivating team members, and facilitating communication and collaboration. These functions are critical to the success of a project and help ensure that the project is completed on schedule, within budget, and to the satisfaction of all stakeholders.

Empathic listening is an important communication skill that can improve relationships, resolve conflicts, and enhance understanding. It requires active engagement and a willingness to understand others, which can lead to more positive and productive communication.

Emotional intelligence is the ability to recognize and manage your emotions, other people's emotions, and the emotions of groups involved in the project. Emotional intelligence recognizes that emotions are real, can affect the project success, and can affect relationships with the project team, stakeholders, and the project manager.

Through effective negotiations, the project manager is able to ensure that the project remains on track, that stakeholders are engaged and aligned with the project goals, and that potential risks are managed effectively.

Through effective initiation, the project manager is able to define the project scope, identify stakeholders, and establish the project objectives and goals, which sets the foundation for the rest of the project.

Through effective coaching, the project manager can help to develop and improve the skills and performance of the project team and increase employee satisfaction and motivation.

The OSCAR model is a useful tool for project managers to use in coaching their team members and supporting them in achieving their goals. The model provides a structured approach to coaching that can help to improve the performance and productivity of the project team.

The role of the project manager as a model is critical in leading and inspiring the project team to achieve success. By serving as a role model, the project manager is able to set the tone for the project, demonstrate best practices, lead by example, build trust, and support professional development.

By actively participating in the day-to-day activities of the project team, the project manager is able to build relationships, provide support, demonstrate flexibility, and build collaboration.

By facilitating communication, decision-making, and collaboration; streamlining processes; and supporting change, the project manager is able to drive project success and deliver the desired outcomes for the project stakeholders.

To successfully follow and execute planned strategies, it's important to have a clear understanding of the strategy, assign roles and responsibilities, develop an action plan, monitor and evaluate progress, communicate regularly, and be prepared to continuously refine and adjust the strategy as needed.

To successfully follow and execute project management frameworks, it's important to choose the right framework, understand the framework, develop a project plan, assign roles and responsibilities, implement the framework, monitor and evaluate progress, communicate regularly, and be prepared to continuously refine and adjust the framework as needed.

Appropriate responses to a planned strategy or framework include active participation, constructive feedback, supportive attitude, flexibility, effective communication, compliance, and continuous improvement.

Project initiation is the process of defining the purpose, scope, and objectives of a new project and getting it off the ground. It involves defining the problem or opportunity, conducting a feasibility study, identifying stakeholders, defining the project scope, developing a project charter, and obtaining approval to proceed.

Benefit planning is the process of defining and documenting the benefits that will be realized from a project. It involves defining the benefits, assigning responsibility, tracking and monitoring the benefits, evaluating the benefits, and realizing the benefits. The goal of benefit planning is to ensure that the project delivers the intended outcomes and provides value to the stakeholders.

There are a number of common problem-solving tools and techniques that project managers can use, including root cause analysis, SWOT analysis, mind mapping, decision trees, and force-field analysis. These tools and techniques can help project managers to identify and solve problems, make informed decisions, and support the successful delivery of projects.

Evaluating the effectiveness of a project meeting is important to continuously improve the meeting process and make sure that it is contributing to the success of the project. The key factors to consider when evaluating the effectiveness of a project meeting include objectives, attendance, preparation, time management, communication, action items, and feedback.

Focus groups are a useful tool for gathering feedback, understanding perspectives, validating assumptions, generating ideas, and building relationships with stakeholders.

Standup meetings are a valuable tool for providing a daily update, facilitating communication, improving accountability, highlighting dependencies, and identifying risks.

Brainstorming is a valuable tool for problem-solving, decision-making, risk management, requirements gathering, and team building.

The Delphi Technique uses rounds of anonymous surveys to gain consensus.

Questions

1. The collection of generally sequential and sometimes overlapping project phases differentiated by a distinct work focus is known as what?

   A. Project management information system

   B. Project management methodology

   C. Project management office

   D. Project life cycle

2. All of the following are basic characteristics of the project life cycle except?

   A. Closing the project

   B. Checking the project work

   C. Starting the project

   D. Carrying out the project work

3. Sayed is looking at his project budget and notices that the cost and staffing levels are high. At which point in the project would this generally be?

   A. Starting the project

   B. Organizing and preparing

   C. Carrying out the work

   D. Closing the project

4. What is the name of the document that lists any problems that stakeholders may have and records what is being done about them?

   A. Change log

   B. Issue log

   C. Stakeholder register

   D. Stakeholder management plan

5. Sumith and his project team are currently breaking down all the project deliverables into the smallest useful units so that they can then estimate costs for each of these units and then aggregate these estimates into a total project cost estimate. What is the name of the technique that Sumith and his team are using to estimate costs?

A. Parametric estimating

B. Bottom-up estimating

C. Low-level estimating

D. Project management software

6. While developing individual cost estimates for work packages on his project, Varun uses a technique that requires him to use a statistical relationship between historical data and other variables to calculate a cost estimate for a schedule activity resource. What is this estimating technique more commonly referred to as?

A. Statistical estimating

B. Bottom-up estimating

C. Parametric estimating

D. Top-down estimating

7. Marissa's project sponsor has asked her to provide a cost estimate quickly to give the project steering group an idea of what the costs for a particular work package will be. Which of the following estimating techniques would Marissa choose to use?

A. Analogous estimating

B. Parametric estimating

C. Resource rate estimating

D. Bottom-up estimating

8. Daryl has completed his activity list and is explaining to his team members what it contains. Which of the following is not contained in the activity list?

A. Milestone list

B. Scope of work description

C. All schedule activities required on the project

D. Activity identifier

9. Assad's project has been underway for nine months when a major problem occurs that is not included in the risk register. What is his *best* course of action?

A. Conduct perform qualitative risk analysis and then perform quantitative risk analysis.

B. Conduct perform quantitative risk analysis and then perform qualitative risk analysis.

C. Create a workaround.

D. Contact his project sponsor.

10. Lenell is the project manager for the GBK Project. This project affects a line of business, and the customer is anxious about the success of the project. Which of the following is likely not a top concern for the customer?

    A. Project priorities

    B. Schedule

    C. Cost

    D. Personality conflicts

11. Brenda is the project manager of the PLN Project. She is using a RACI chart to organize roles and responsibilities for project assignments. In a RACI chart, what is the maximum number of people that can be accountable for an assignment?

    A. One

    B. Two

    C. Two, if one of the two people is also responsible

    D. As many people that are on the project team

12. Aileen knows she can present project information in many different ways. Which one of the following is not a method Aileen can use to present project performance?

    A. Histograms

    B. S-curves

    C. Bar charts

    D. RACI charts

13. The project team is experiencing some trouble with a new material that the project will use. The project manager, Ali, gathers the team to lead an active problem-solving session. Which one of the following is the best definition of active problem-solving?

    A. Define the problem and the desired solution.

    B. Discern the cause and the effect of the problem.

    C. Document the problem and its characteristics to see the whole effect.

    D. Test the materials to identify the solution.

14. Amer is the project manager of the BHY Project. His project customer has demanded that the project be completed by December 1. December 1 is an example of which one of the following?

    A. A constraint

    B. An assumption

    C. A project boundary

    D. Product acceptance criteria

15. Alicia is the project manager on a project to develop a new piece of customer management software for an external client. Through the approved change control process, Alicia is considering a request to alter the scope of the project. While considering the impact of the request upon the project scope, she must also consider the impact upon other areas of the project such as quality, schedule, budget and risk. These other areas that Alicia is considering represent what to the project?

A. Opportunities

B. Constraints

C. Constrictions

D. Risks

16. Although people may say they can identify, assess, and manage their personal feelings, many teams experience tension and uncooperative behaviors among teammates. Nicole has recognized this on projects where she has been a team member, especially virtual teams. Now that she is a project manager, Nicole wants to establish an environment in which teammates can reduce tension and increase cooperation. Which of the following is a best practice to promote such an environment?

A. Use emotional intelligence to control the sentiments of team members.

B. Focus on goals to be served and ask that emotions be left outside the project.

C. Emphasize areas of agreement rather than areas of difference.

D. Maintain a good relationship with the project sponsor.

17. Project sponsors have the most influence on the scope, quality, schedule, and cost of the project during which phase?

A. Initiation

B. Planning

C. Execution

D. Closure

18. While working as a project manager for a secret government agency, Doc discovers that a previous project that was very successful had a stakeholder, Winston, who was unhappy with the benefits received. Winston can have a significant impact on Doc's current project. What should Doc do next?

A. Review the stakeholder register to determine exactly how much impact Winston has.

B. Communicate and work with Winston to meet his needs and expectations.

C. Ensure that the communications management plan addresses Winston's information needs.

D. Review the stakeholder management plan to determine Winston's engagement level.

19. Teresa and her project team have produced a requirements traceability matrix that links requirements to their origin and traces them throughout the project life cycle. Which statement describes the purpose of the requirements traceability matrix?

   A. It describes in detail the project's deliverables and the work required to create those deliverables and includes product and project scope description.

   B. It ensures that requirements approved in the requirements documentation are delivered at the end of the project and helps manage changes to the product scope.

   C. It is a narrative description of products or services to be delivered by the project and is received from the customer for external projects.

   D. It provides the necessary information from a business standpoint to determine whether the project is worth the required investment.

20. Kevin has just joined your project and asks what is involved in this project. You refer him to the project scope statement, which contains all the following except:

   A. Deferred change requests

   B. Product scope description

   C. Project assumptions

   D. Product acceptance criteria

Answers

   1. D. Knowing the project life cycle and how projects and project management fit gives you context and provides a basic framework for managing a project, regardless of the specific work involved. Do not confuse this with the *product* life cycle. A is incorrect because the project management information system is an example of an organizational process asset and does not refer to a collection of overlapping phases. B is incorrect because project management methodology is a prescribed and standardized approach to project management and does not describe overlapping project phases. C is incorrect because a project management office (PMO) is the center of excellence for project management within an organization and does not refer to a collection of overlapping phases.

   2. B. The generic level of the project life cycle features four key characteristics: starting the project, organizing and preparing, carrying out the project work, and closing the project. Checking the project work is part of Deming's plan-do-check-act (PDCA) cycle, which elaborates on the basic characteristics of a project life cycle. A is incorrect because closing the project is the final step in the project life cycle. C is incorrect because starting the project is the first step in the project life cycle. D is incorrect because carrying out the project work is a characteristic of the project life cycle.

3. C. Generally speaking, cost and staffing levels are highest during the phase in the project life cycle where work is being carried out. A, B, and D are incorrect because the costs associated with each of these phases of the project life cycle are not as high as the costs of carrying out the project work, which has the greatest assignment of resources and activities.

4. B. The issue log records any issues that stakeholders may have and what is being done about them. A is incorrect because the change log records information about change requests and their status. C is incorrect because the stakeholder register records specific information about each stakeholder but does not list any problems or issues they may have. D is incorrect because the stakeholder management plan sets out how stakeholders' expectations and engagement will be proactively influenced and managed.

5. B. Bottom-up estimating is a technique for estimating the cost of individual work packages with the lowest level of detail. A is incorrect because parametric estimating is an estimating technique that uses a statistical relationship between historical data and other variables to calculate an estimate for activity parameters. C is incorrect because low-level estimating is not a term referenced in the *PMBOK Guide*. D is incorrect because project management software may be useful for developing cost estimates, but it is a tool, not a technique.

6. C. Parametric estimating is a technique that uses a statistical relationship between historical data and other variables to calculate *an estimate for activity parameters*. A is incorrect because statistical estimating is not a term referenced in the *PMBOK Guide*. B is incorrect because bottom-up estimating is a technique for estimating the cost of individual work packages with the lowest level of detail. D is incorrect because top-down estimating (aka analogous estimating) is a macro estimating technique that assigns costs to particular deliverables and work packages.

7. A. Analogous estimating can be done faster than the other techniques and is generally less costly than other estimating techniques, but it is also generally less accurate. B is incorrect because parametric estimating requires access to estimating databases and as such generally takes longer than analogous estimating. C is incorrect because resource rate estimating is a made-up term. D is incorrect because the time and cost involved in decomposing the WBS in bottom-up estimating mean that it takes longer than analogous estimating.

8. A. The milestone list would be found in your WBS dictionary. B is incorrect because the scope of work description is contained in the activity list. C is incorrect because all schedule activities required on the project are contained in the activity list. D is incorrect because activity identifiers are contained in the activity list.

9. C. In this case the risk has occurred and created an impact on the project, so there is no need to begin formal evaluation processes. Assad's risk response plan would identify that a workaround is the best option for unanticipated risks. A is incorrect because, given that the question outlines that this is a major problem, Assad will not have time to evaluate the risk in any manner. B is incorrect because, given that the question outlines that this is a major problem, Assad will not have time to evaluate the risk in any manner (and if he were to do so, he would perform qualitative analysis first). D is incorrect because, given that this has been identified as a major problem, Assad's best course of action in this instance is to create a workaround first and then contact his project sponsor.

10. **D.** Personality conflicts may be a concern for the customer, but they are not as important or as likely to be of concern as project priorities, schedule, and cost. The customer hired Lenell's company to solve the technical issues. A, B, and C are all incorrect. These are most likely the top issues for a customer in a project of this magnitude.

11. **A.** In a RACI chart, which stands for responsible, accountable, consulted, and informed, only one person can be designated as accountable for an assignment. B, C, and D are incorrect because these choices enable more than one person to be accountable for an assignment.

12. **D.** RACI charts do not show project performance, but instead show accountability of the resources involved in the project. A, B, and C are incorrect because these choices do present project performance.

13. **A.** Active problem-solving begins by defining the problem, which requires discerning between the cause of the problem and the effect of the problem, accomplished through root cause analysis. B, C, and D are incorrect because these approaches don't first define the effect and the causes, which is crucial to active problem-solving.

14. **A.** A definitive project deadline is an example of a project constraint. B is incorrect because this deadline is a requirement, not an assumption. C is incorrect because project boundaries define things that are within and outside of the project scope. D is incorrect because product acceptance criteria are functions and features the product must have to be acceptable to the customer.

15. **B.** Constraints is correct because central to any successful project management is an awareness that a project manager must balance competing constraints on the project. A change in one area can and usually does also mean a potential change in another area. A is incorrect because opportunities are the opposite of constraints. C is incorrect because the correct terminology is constraints, not constrictions. D is incorrect because risks refer to any areas of positive or negative uncertainty on the project.

16. **A.** Emotional intelligence (the ability to manage your emotions and others' emotions) leads directly to reducing conflict and making positive decisions. B is incorrect because focusing only on the goals is too "task" oriented and not enough "relationship" oriented. C is incorrect because this is the definition of the smoothing technique used in conflict resolution. D is incorrect because it is one of the factors that influence conflict resolution methods.

17. **A.** The project sponsor is the key stakeholder in the initiation phase. The project charter is agreed to by the project sponsor and represents what they want out of the project; it also drives the direction of the project. B is incorrect because the project manager, not the sponsor, has the greatest influence during the planning phase. C is incorrect because the execution phase is carrying out what has been agreed on in the project charter during initiation and in the project plan during planning. D is incorrect because in the closure phase the project deliverables have been created and scope, quality, schedule, and cost are now actuals that can no longer be influenced.

18. **A.** The stakeholder register contains the stakeholder classification, which includes the stakeholder engagement assessment matrix. B is incorrect because meeting with Winston will enable you to identify the appropriate focus for his engagement, not his impact on the project. C is incorrect because the communications plan describes how project communications will be planned, structured, implemented, and monitored for effectiveness; it will be used later. D is incorrect because reviewing the stakeholder management plan comes after you classify stakeholders in the stakeholder register.

19. **B.** The requirements traceability matrix ensures that requirements approved in the requirements documentation are delivered at the end of the project. The requirements traceability matrix also provides a structure for managing changes to product scope. A is incorrect because it describes the project scope statement. C is incorrect because this is the project statement of work used in developing the project charter. D is incorrect because it describes the project business case. Identifying all stakeholders is the only way to uncover all project requirements.

20. **A.** Deferred change requests could be approved at some time in the future, but have not yet been approved and do not authorize the work that implies a change in scope. B, C, and D are incorrect because the detailed project scope statement does include the product scope description, project assumptions (as well as deliverables, exclusions, and constraints), and product acceptance criteria.

References

- *Agile Practice Guide* (2017)
- *Business Analysis for Practitioners: A Practice Guide* (2015)
- *CAPM Certified Associate in Project Management Practice Exams* (2019), Haner and McCoy
- *Effective Project Management, Eighth Edition* (2019), Wysocki
- *PMBOK Guide* (2021)
- *Process Groups: A Practice Guide* (2022)
- *PMIstandards+*
- *The PMI Guide to Business Analysis* (2017)
- *The Project Management Answer Book* (2015), Furman
- *The Standard for Program Management – Fourth Edition* (2017)

4

Predictive, Plan-Based Methodologies

This chapter covers the tasks in Domain 2:
- Explain when it is appropriate to use a predictive, plan-based approach
- Demonstrate an understanding of a project management plan schedule
- Determine how to document project controls of predictive, plan-based projects

This domain represents approximately 17 percent of the CAPM examination.

Explain When It Is Appropriate to Use a Predictive, Plan-Based Approach

Task 1

A predictive, plan-based approach is appropriate when the project's objectives and scope are well-defined and the project team has experience in executing similar projects. In this approach, the project's objectives, scope, and deliverables are defined at the beginning of the project, and the project team follows a detailed plan to achieve them.

> **In the Real World**
>
> It is very rare that you will ever begin a project with a complete and detailed description of the scope. Often this will only occur as a result of lengthy contractual negotiations. In almost every other situation you will begin a project with enough of the scope defined to allow you to begin, and then you will undertake successive iterations of definition and documentation as you go. You may also decide to commit time and energy to defining the scope for the immediate time frame, and leave definition of the remainder of the scope until you get closer to the time of delivery.

This approach is appropriate when the project has a low degree of uncertainty and the project team can accurately predict the project's outcomes, costs, and timeline. A predictive approach is commonly used in industries such as construction, manufacturing, and software development, where projects are repetitive and the processes and procedures are well-established.

A predictive, plan-based approach requires a detailed project plan that outlines the project's scope, schedule, budget, quality standards, and risks. The plan serves as a roadmap for the project team to execute the project efficiently and effectively. The project plan is usually developed at the beginning of the project and is updated throughout the project's life cycle.

This approach is useful when the project has a fixed budget and timeline and there is little room for change. A predictive, plan-based approach provides stakeholders with a clear understanding of the project's progress and enables them to make informed decisions about the project's direction.

Identify the Suitability of a Predictive, Plan-Based Approach for the Organizational Structure

Task 1, Enabler 1

The suitability of a predictive, plan-based approach for an organizational structure depends on the organization's culture, industry, and project characteristics. The organizational structure, including virtual, colocation, matrix structure, and hierarchical, can also influence the suitability of a predictive, plan-based approach.

In general, organizations with a hierarchical and traditional structure are more suited to a predictive, plan-based approach. In this structure, decision-making is centralized and there is a clear chain of command. This allows for a top-down approach to project management, where project managers have a clear understanding of the project's objectives, scope, and deliverables. In this case, a predictive, plan-based approach may be suitable regardless of whether the organization is virtual or colocated.

Organizations with a matrix structure may also be suited to a predictive, plan-based approach. A matrix structure combines functional departments and project teams to optimize resources and expertise. In this structure, project managers have some degree of authority over resources, allowing for more control and predictability. However, the complexity of the matrix structure may make it difficult to implement a predictive approach effectively.

Virtual organizations, where teams are geographically dispersed, may be more suited to an adaptive approach. In this structure, decision-making is distributed and teams have more autonomy in managing projects. A predictive, plan-based approach may not work well in these environments because it does not allow for flexibility or adaptation to changing circumstances.

In a colocated organization, a predictive, plan-based approach may be suitable if the project's objectives, scope, and deliverables are well-defined and the project team has experience in executing similar projects. However, a colocated organization with a flat or collaborative structure may not be suited to a predictive approach.

Other factors to consider when determining the suitability of using a predictive, plan-based approach are

- **The nature of the projects**   If the projects are well defined and have a clear set of requirements and objectives, a predictive, plan-based approach may be more suitable.

- **The organizational culture**   If the organization values structure, predictability, and control, a plan-based approach may align well with the organization's culture.

- **The level of change and uncertainty**   If the projects are subject to significant change and uncertainty, a plan-based approach may not be suitable, as it assumes a certain level of stability in the requirements and goals.

- **The level of control**   If the organization wants to maintain a high level of control over the project, a plan-based approach may be more suitable.

- **The level of collaboration and flexibility**   If the organization values collaboration and flexibility, a plan-based approach may not be the best fit, as it tends to be more structured and rigid.

- **The level of risk**   If the projects involve a high level of risk, a plan-based approach may be more suitable, as it provides a clear framework for managing and mitigating risks.

- **The size and complexity of the projects**   If the projects are large and complex, a plan-based approach may be more suitable, as it provides a clear framework for managing the various activities and dependencies.

Determine the Activities Within Each Process

Task 1, Enabler 2
Determining the activities within each process in the *Process Groups: A Practice Guide* is essential for effective project planning and execution. Each process in the *Process Groups: A Practice Guide* consists of a set of activities that must be completed to achieve the project's objectives. This typically involves breaking down each process into smaller, more manageable activities or work packages, which can then be assigned to team members or scheduled on a timeline.

The following are some reasons why it is important to determine the activities within each process:

- **Planning**   Helps in developing an accurate project management plan. A project management plan outlines the project's scope, schedule, budget, quality standards, and risks. The activities within each process are the building blocks of the project plan, and they help in estimating the project's duration, resources, and costs.

- **Resource allocation**   Resources such as time, personnel, equipment, and materials are required to complete each activity. By determining the activities within each process, you can allocate resources efficiently and avoid overburdening resources.

- **Tracking progress** You can monitor the completion of each activity to ensure that the project is on track. Tracking progress also helps in identifying delays, deviations from the project management plan, and potential risks.

- **Quality control** Each activity has specific quality standards that must be met to ensure that the project's objectives are achieved.

- **Communication** You can communicate the project's progress, status, and risks to the team and stakeholders.

As introduced in Chapter 3, *Process Groups: A Practice Guide* is a PMI publication that provides an overview of the five process groups, which are used to organize and manage the various processes involved in a project. The guide uses a popular Process Groups model Processes are grouped into one of three categories. Those that are performed

- **Only once or at predefined points** Example processes are Develop Project Charter, Develop Project Management Plan, and Close Project or Phase.

- **Multiple times as needed** Example processes include Conduct Procurements, Acquire Resources, and Monitor and Control Project Work.

- **Continuously** Example processes include Identify Risks, Define Activities, and Perform Integrated Change Control.

Determining activities within the processes of a plan-based approach involves several steps:

1. *Identify the project scope.* The first step in determining activities is to define the scope of the project. This includes defining the objectives, deliverables, and timeline for the project.

2. *Break down the project into smaller parts.* Next, decompose your primary deliverables into smaller, more manageable parts. If you are using phases in your project life cycle, this will help you to better understand the activities that need to be completed in each phase.

3. *Create a work breakdown structure.* A work breakdown structure (WBS) is a hierarchical decomposition of the project into smaller, more manageable parts. This structure should be used to identify all the activities that need to be completed in each phase.

In the Real World

I always use my project team members who are responsible for completing the work to help complete the WBS. Not only does this give me the right technical input from the people responsible for completing the work, but it also creates commitment to the process of completing the work, because people feel they have made a significant and personal contribution.

4. *Identify dependencies.* Identify the dependencies between activities. This will help you to better understand the sequence in which activities need to be completed.

5. *Develop a project schedule.* Use the WBS and the dependencies between activities to develop a project schedule. This schedule should include the start and end dates for each activity, the duration of each activity, and the sequence in which activities need to be completed. (If you are using Microsoft Project, an activity is a "task.") The Develop Schedule process is the final stage in the Planning process group for schedule management. It takes all the previous information from the previous planning processes and makes the project schedule. This process will be quite iterative because at the start of the project the information you have available is less accurate.

6. *Assign resources.* Assign resources to each activity, including staff, equipment, and materials. This will help you to determine the cost of each activity and the overall cost of the project.

7. *Monitor and control the project.* Regularly monitor (measure) and control (correct) the project to ensure that it stays on track. This includes monitoring the progress of each activity, controlling the budget, and adjusting the project management plan as needed.

By following these steps, you can ensure that your project stays on track and achieves its objectives.

Give Examples of Typical Activities Within Each Process

Task 1, Enabler 3

Activities in a plan-based approach are performed in a sequential and structured manner, with a focus on predictability and control. This approach is often used in projects with well-defined requirements and constraints and where a high degree of control is necessary to ensure the success of the project.

- Each process group in project management consists of a set of processes that must be completed to achieve the project's objectives. Determining the activities within each process is essential for effective project planning, execution, and control. You must identify and manage the activities within each process to ensure that the project's objectives are achieved within the defined scope, budget, and timeline.

- The following are examples of typical activities within each process of a process group:

  - **Initiating**   Authorizing the project or a project phase to begin.
    - Developing the project charter
    - Identifying stakeholders and their needs
    - Defining the project's objectives and scope
    - Assessing the project's feasibility and risks
    - Developing the preliminary budget and schedule

- **Planning**   Defining and refining the project goals and objectives. Once the project objectives have been defined, you and the key stakeholders will plan how to reach those objectives.
  - Developing the project management plan
  - Defining the project's detailed scope, objectives, and deliverables
  - Developing the work breakdown structure
  - Identifying and sequencing project activities
  - Estimating the duration and resources required for each activity
  - Developing the project budget and schedule
  - Identifying and analyzing project risks
  - Developing the quality management plan
  - Developing the human resource management plan
  - Developing the communication management plan
  - Developing the procurement management plan
- **Executing**   Now that you have a project plan, it's time to put the plan into action. You've heard the saying, "Plan your work and now work your plan?" This is the "working your plan" part.
  - Assigning tasks and responsibilities to project team members
  - Acquiring and managing project resources
  - Developing and managing project deliverables
  - Performing quality assurance activities
  - Implementing the project's change management processes
  - Conducting stakeholder meetings and communication activities
  - Performing project status reporting
- **Monitoring and Controlling**   Your project team is doing the work, but it's up to you to measure and monitor things to ensure that the project team is doing the work as it was planned. The results of your measurements—primarily in cost, time, scope, and quality—will show discrepancies between what was planned and what was experienced. These discrepancies are your project variances.
  - Measuring project performance against the project management plan
  - Monitoring and controlling project scope, schedule, budget, and quality
  - Managing project risks
  - Managing changes to the project management plan
  - Managing project issues and defects
  - Performing project status reporting

- Analyzing project performance data
- Performing trend analysis to identify potential issues
- **Closing**   Focuses on formal acceptance of the project's final deliverable. Note that technically the approval of the deliverable is the result of the Validate Scope process, a process in the Monitoring and Controlling process group. The Close Project or Phase process makes that acceptance formal with a project sign-off. The Closing process group also focuses on bringing the project or project phase to a tidy ending by finalizing all project activities and wrapping up the project, including archiving project documents and conducting a post-project review.

  - Conducting final project activities
  - Completing project deliverables
  - Conducting project performance reviews
  - Documenting project lessons learned
  - Archiving project information
  - Closing out project contracts and agreements
  - Obtaining customer acceptance of project deliverables
  - Closing out project accounts and financial records

NOTE   The generally accepted flow of the process groups can also apply to more than just projects. A project manager can use the processes within these groups for each phase of a project.

Distinguish the Differences Between Various Project Components

Task 1, Enabler 4

In a predictive, plan-based approach, the differences between various project components are well defined and managed to ensure that the project stays on track and achieves its objectives. The project scope, schedule, budget, risks, resources, and quality are all closely monitored and controlled to ensure that the project stays on track and achieves its goals.

In a predictive, plan-based approach, the differences between various project components are as follows:

- **Scope**   The project scope is well defined and clearly outlines the objectives, deliverables, and timeline for the project.
- **Schedule**   The project schedule is a detailed and accurate timeline for the project that includes start and end dates for each activity, the duration of each activity, and the sequence in which activities need to be completed.

- **Budget** The project budget is a detailed estimate of the costs associated with the project and is based on a thorough analysis of the project requirements and resources. The budget is closely monitored and controlled to ensure that the project stays within its budget.

- **Risks** Project risks are identified, assessed, and managed through the development of contingency plans. This helps to minimize the impact of potential problems on the project.

- **Resources** Project resources are clearly defined and allocated in accordance with the project schedule. This includes the allocation of staff, equipment, and materials to each activity.

- **Quality** Project quality is a key consideration throughout the project, and quality assurance processes are established and followed to ensure that the project meets its objectives and delivers the desired results. Quality is the degree to which a set of inherent characteristics fulfills requirements—remember this definition for the exam.

Demonstrate an Understanding of a Project Management Plan Schedule

Task 2

The project schedule is one of the major elements in the project, along with scope and cost. Project managers need to understand how to manage and control the project schedule. The project schedule includes *all* the activities—and *only* the activities—to be completed to meet the project objectives. Developing the project schedule starts with understanding the project scope, requirements, and objectives. This information is decomposed into work packages through a WBS (introduced in the Task 1, Enabler 2 section). The project manager then meets with the project team to identify for each work package the specific activities required to complete the deliverable. Once the activities have been identified, the project manager and the team will work on sequencing and establishing resource/duration estimates.

These are the basic steps to creating a project schedule. Throughout this chapter, we will do a deeper dive into working with the project schedule and gain a better understanding about schedule components and how the schedule integrates with other aspects of the project.

Apply Critical Path Methods

Task 2, Enabler 1

If you've ever worked as a project manager of any sort, you've most likely had some executive ask you if an activity was "on the critical path." What the executive was asking was whether the activity was "critical" to the project success. PMI has a very specific definition of a *critical path activity*: "the longest (time) sequence of activities in a project plan, which must be completed on time, for the project to be completed by the due date." Remember, *all activities* must be completed on the schedule to meet the project objectives. So, what is the big deal about these activities on the critical path? Read on to learn more.

The critical path method is used to help the project manager "manage" the schedule. This method identifies activities that *must* be done on the date in the schedule and the others that can be adjusted without impacting the project end date. The activities on the critical path have zero "float" (or slack). This means that any delay of these critical path activities has a corresponding delay to the project end date. It is a mathematical certainty! The critical path is the path with the longest duration. In addition, the activities on the critical path change during project execution. So, the project manager needs to continuously leverage the critical path method to understand these zero-float activities.

> **NOTE**   The *PMBOK Guide* rarely uses two terms to mean the same thing. The case of slack and float is one of those rare exceptions. Here are two types of slack or float. *Free slack* (or *free float*) indicates the amount of time an activity can be delayed before that affects the next activity on the path. *Total slack* (or *total float*) indicates the amount of time an activity can be delayed before it affects the total project duration. If an activity has zero total float, it means that if it is delayed, it will automatically increase the duration of the project. The critical path or paths through a project are those upon which there is no slack or float.

In Microsoft Project, the critical path method analyzes the tasks on the schedule using forward pass and backward pass calculations.

Forward pass and backward pass are two techniques used in project management to determine the project's critical path and calculate the earliest and latest start and finish times of activities.

The forward pass is a technique used to calculate the earliest start and finish times for each activity in the project network diagram. This technique starts at the project's beginning and moves forward through the network diagram, calculating the earliest start and finish times for each activity based on the previous activities' completion time. The earliest start time of an activity is the earliest possible time that the activity can start, given its predecessor activities' completion times. The earliest finish time is the earliest possible time that an activity can be completed, given its earliest start time and duration.

The backward pass is a technique used to calculate the latest start and finish times for each activity in the project network diagram. This technique starts at the project's end and moves backward through the network diagram, calculating the latest start and finish times for each activity based on the successor activities' latest start and finish times. The latest finish time of an activity is the latest possible time that the activity can be completed without delaying the project's completion date. The latest start time is the latest possible time that the activity can start without delaying its successor activities' start time.

The critical path is the sequence of activities that have zero slack time, which means that any delay in the critical path activities will cause a delay in the project's completion date. The critical path can be identified by comparing the earliest and latest start and finish times of each activity. If an activity has a difference between its earliest and latest start and finish times, it means that it has slack time and it is not critical to the project's completion date.

Any scheduling software (e.g., Microsoft Project) will produce a network diagram that shows every task on the schedule and the relationships (i.e., dependencies) of each task. The software will then do a forward pass and a backward pass and calculate the float of every task. This is how it determines the critical path. Of course, on the CAPM exam, you will not have to do this manually, but you at least need to understand how it is done.

NOTE   When we are talking about scheduling software, "activities" are called "tasks."

Knowing this information, the project manager can now monitor those critical path tasks and make certain they are completed as per the project schedule.

EXAM TIP   For the CAPM exam, remember that the critical path is used to determine which activities have no float. You can also use the critical path to determine the earliest date for when the project may be completed. There can be more than one critical path in a project, as two paths can have the same duration, and it's possible for the critical path to change.

Calculate Schedule Variance

Task 2, Enabler 2

Projects all have a starting point, called a *baseline*, that measures progress … or delays. The three major baselines are scope, schedule, and cost. This is where the concept of the performance measurement baseline comes into play. The performance measurement baseline (PMB) is the analysis of schedule, cost, and scope, which are three defined factors in a predictive, plan-based project.

The schedule baseline is the planned start and finish of the project. The comparison of what was planned and what was experienced in the schedule is called the schedule variance. The schedule baseline is created in the scheduling software and is determined at various points throughout the project. When the project manager and project team determine the schedule is ready to be executed, they establish a baseline. Then as activities are executed, they compare the actual results against the baseline to determine the *schedule variance*. The scheduling software computes the schedule variance when the actual activity completion date and effort are entered. Often, through approved changes, a new schedule baseline is set.

Control Schedule is a process that involves monitoring the status of project activities to update project progress and manage changes to the project schedule. This process is performed throughout the project life cycle and focuses on ensuring that the project remains on schedule and any schedule deviations are identified and addressed promptly.

NOTE You never *change* a baseline, but you set new ones. This is important for the retrospective at the end of the project to see how well the schedule was estimated and how many times a new baseline was set.

Explain Work Breakdown Structures

Task 2, Enabler 3

The work breakdown structure (WBS) is exactly what its name suggests. You take the project work (scope) and break it down into smaller components (*work packages*) using a specific structure. This process is known as *decomposition*. This structure could be based on tasks (task-oriented), components (physical or functional), time-phased, organization types, geographical types, cost breakdown types, or profit-center types. A task-oriented WBS defines the project work in terms of the actions that must be done to produce the deliverable. The first word in a task-oriented WBS element usually is a verb, such as design, develop, optimize, transfer, test, etc. The component-oriented WBS defines project work in terms of physical or functional components that make up the deliverable. The first word in a given WBS element is a noun, such as Element X or Subunit 1.

In any case, the goal of a WBS is to identify all of the work packages needed to achieve the project objectives. These work packages are then used to determine the specific activities required to achieve the work packages, and those activities are incorporated into the project schedule when it is created.

You probably have done *decomposition* if you ever did an outline for a term paper. The subject of the term paper was the scope, and the outline elements created the work packages. Then you wrote the words that described the outline work packages. It is the same concept. Remember, the WBS includes *all* the work to be done to achieve the project objectives, and nothing should be done that is not included in the WBS.

Figure 4-1 shows an example of a simple WBS. In the figure, the house project has five major categories of components: project management, paperwork, construction, interior design, and landscaping. Each of these first-tier deliverables can be broken down into smaller components. The construction deliverable has been broken down into several smaller components: the basement, first floor, and second floor. Each of these components could be broken down further to another level, and so on. As previously mentioned, the smallest item in the WBS is called a *work package*, which can be used effectively to estimate cost and time and can be monitored and controlled within the project.

The predictive, plan-based approach takes the WBS work package (noun/deliverable) and moves it to the schedule to identify the "activities" (verb-noun) needed to complete the work package. The *work* in the WBS refers to the deliverables the project will create, not the effort your project team will have to put forth to create the deliverables.

EXAM TIP The work package is just a label for the smallest component within the WBS that creates a deliverable. For your CAPM exam, know that the smallest component in the WBS is a work package and that it can be scheduled, estimated for costs, and then monitored and controlled.

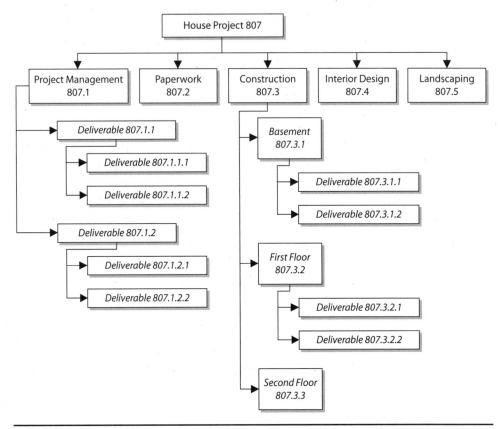

Figure 4-1   WBS construction example

Explain Work Packages

Task 2, Enabler 4

As just described, the work package is the smallest component in the WBS and can be used effectively to estimate cost and time and can be monitored and controlled within the project. So, how far must the project scope be broken down? There's no right answer that fits every project: each project scope should be broken down to the level of detail that's appropriate for the project priority, scope, and objectives.

A guideline for WBS breakdown is the *8/80 rule*, which states that the labor to create a work package should equate to no more than 80 hours and no fewer than 8 hours of labor for the associated activities. Of course, this is just a guideline, not a regulation. Some projects may call for work packages that take far less time than 8 hours.

Work packages are often related to control accounts that are used to aggregate costs of the activities completed for a specific deliverable.

Apply a Quality Management Plan

Task 2, Enabler 5

Quality management is about applying the appropriate level of quality to meet the customer's needs. Too much quality is a waste of resources, and not enough quality can lead to rework and scrap.

One of the major outputs of quality planning is the quality management plan. This document describes how the project manager and the project team will fulfill the quality policy. In an ISO 9000 environment, the quality management plan is referred to as the "project quality system."

The quality management plan addresses the following things about the project and the project work:

- Quality standards the project will utilize
- Quality objectives the project must achieve
- Quality roles and responsibilities among the project team and key stakeholders
- Deliverables and processes that will be reviewed for quality
- How quality process activities will be controlled
- Quality tools the project will utilize
- How the project will address nonconformance to quality issues, corrective activities, and continuous process improvement

Quality management includes the Manage Quality and Control Quality processes. The Manage Quality process includes the planned activities to meet the customer quality needs. The Control Quality process involves monitoring and recording the results of quality management activities to ensure deliverables are complete and meet customer requirements.

A major tenet of quality is that preventing a mistake is cheaper than correcting a mistake. Therefore, quality management focuses on prevention over inspection. The project manager will always try to implement strategies to prevent errors, rather than finding errors through inspection techniques like testing. The latter is always more disruptive and expensive.

Quality management is not something that happens only once; it is ongoing throughout the life of the project, and it is iterative. Not only is quality management highly iterative, like other project management processes, one of its central elements is the concept of continuous improvement. *Continuous improvement* is an iterative process of always seeking to improve your approach to, and results obtained from, quality management processes, and has the goal of improving the quality of the project processes as well as the project deliverables.

EXAM TIP For your CAPM exam, *quality* means delivering the project at the exact level of the design specifications and the project scope—no more, no less.

Quality is not free. There is a cost to implement, monitor, and control quality. This is called the *cost of quality (COQ)*. The COQ considers how much must be spent to achieve the expected level of quality within the project. There are two types of costs directly tied to quality:

- **Cost of conformance to quality** This cost is associated with the monies spent to attain the expected level of quality, such as the cost of training, complying with safety issues, and purchasing the appropriate equipment and materials, which all contribute to the expected levels of quality. The cost of conformance includes prevention costs for training, documenting processes, procuring the appropriate equipment, and having the time to do the work correctly. The cost of conformance is also where you'll determine appraisal costs to test the product, complete destructive testing loss, and perform inspections. These all require that money be spent to avoid failures.

- **Cost of nonconformance to quality** This cost is associated with not satisfying the quality expectations. The cost of nonconformance is evident when the project must spend money because of failures within the project. Internal failure costs are in the form of rework and scrap. External failure costs happen when the customer finds the defects, which can mean your organization will incur liabilities, warranty claims, and even lost business. The cost of nonconformance to quality is also known as the *cost of poor quality* or the *cost of failure*.

 EXAM TIP Technically, when it comes to the cost of quality, you need to be familiar with three specific terms for the exam. *Prevention costs* are monies spent to prevent poor quality. *Appraisal costs* are monies spent to test, evaluate, measure, and audit the product, deliverables, or services of the project. *Failure costs* are related to nonconformance to quality.

You should be familiar with basic quality tools for your CAPM exam. These methods will help you visualize data and information. You can use these tools in quality planning, managing quality, and most likely with controlling quality:

- **Cause-and-effect diagrams** Also known as fishbone, Ishikawa, or why-why diagrams, these help you determine causal factors for a problem you'd like to solve. These diagrams show the relationship between the variables within a process and how those relationships may contribute to inadequate quality. They can help organize both the process and team opinions, as well as generate discussion on finding a solution to ensure quality. Figure 4-2 shows an example of a cause-and-effect diagram.

Figure 4-2
A cause-and effect diagram shows the relationship of process variables to a problem.

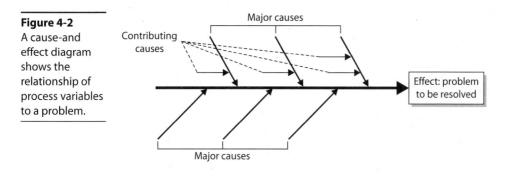

- **System or process flowcharts** A flowchart shows the sequence of events with possible branching and loopbacks to reach an end result of a process or a series of processes. These flowcharts illustrate the flow of a process through a system, such as a project change request through the change control system or work authorization through the Control Quality process. A process flowchart does not have to be limited to the project management activities; it could instead demonstrate how a manufacturer creates, packages, and ships the product to the customer (as shown in Figure 4-3).

- **Check sheets** These are used to tally up problems, effects, conditions, or other aspects about a project's product during inspection. The results of check sheets help project managers quickly ascertain problems within the project.

- **Pareto diagrams** A Pareto diagram is somewhat related to Pareto's Law: 80 percent of the problems come from 20 percent of the issues. This is also known as the 80/20 rule. A Pareto diagram illustrates the problems by assigned cause, from largest to smallest, as Figure 4-4 shows. The project team should first work on the larger problems and then move on to the smaller problems.

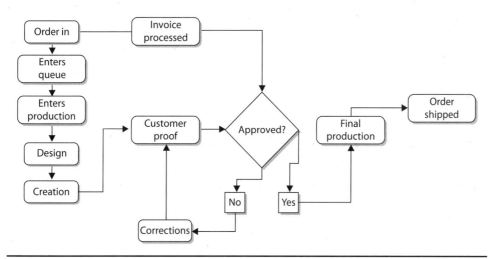

Figure 4-3 A flowchart demonstrates how processes within a system are related.

Figure 4-4
A Pareto diagram is a histogram that ranks the issues from largest to smallest.

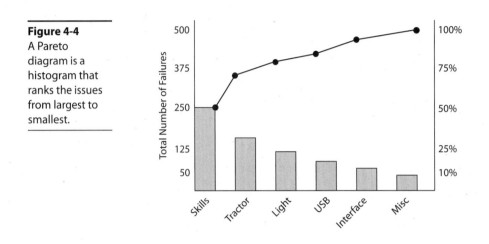

- **Histograms** A histogram is a bar chart that can be used to show frequency of problems, ranking of services, or any other distribution of data. Consider this an unordered Pareto diagram.

- **Control charts** Ever feel like your project is out of control? A control chart can prove it. Control charts illustrate the performance of a project over time. They map the results of inspections against a chart, as shown in Figure 4-5. Control charts are typically used in projects or operations that include repetitive activities—such as product manufacturing, a series of tests, or help desk issues. The outer limits of a control chart are set by the customer requirements. Within the customer requirements are the upper control limits (UCLs) and the lower control limits (LCLs). The UCL is typically set at +3 or +6 sigma, while the LCL is set at −3 or −6 sigma. Sigma results show the degree of correctness. Table 4-1 outlines the four sigma values representing normal distribution.

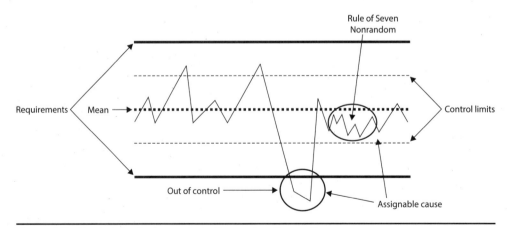

Figure 4-5   Control charts demonstrate the results of inspections.

Table 4-1	Value	Percent Correct
The Four Sigma Values Representing Normal Distribution	+/– 1 sigma	68.26 percent
	+/– 2 sigma	95.46 percent
	+/– 3 sigma	99.73 percent
	+/– 6 sigma	99.99 percent

Control charts show trends over time and help a project manager determine the stability of a process, an improvement, or other analysis of the project work. These are ideal for repeatable processes, such as in manufacturing.

- **Scatter diagrams** These charts measure the relationship between a dependent project variable and an independent project variable. The closer the variables trend, the more likely there is a connection.

Apply an Integration Management Plan

Task 2, Enabler 6

Project integration management refers to the project manager's responsibility to make the best decisions for work, resources, project issues, and all the logistics of the project so that it is completed as planned. Project integration management is undertaken specifically by the project manager.

Project integration management works across all the other process areas. By analogy, project integration management is the forest, whereas the other process areas are the trees. Project integration management recognizes that the processes are all interdependent and rely on each other to a greater or lesser extent. They are also able to affect each other, which a project manager must recognize when defining, planning, executing, and controlling the project and thus take an integrated point of view.

Additionally, project integration management reinforces the fact that there are many successful ways to manage a project. Projects vary considerably in terms of depth, complexity, size, industry, and deliverables. As such, the level of interaction between selected processes will also be different. This process is called *tailoring* and involves selecting those processes that are appropriate to a project and ensuring throughout the life of the project that constant checking is done to ensure the selected processes and their application are still appropriate. Having a broad oversight of the project via project integration management helps in selecting the right processes and applying them appropriately.

In the Real World

I am a big advocate of tailoring the tools, techniques, and processes to appropriately fit your organization and your project. There are all sorts of potential problems that arise from simply applying too many, or too few, project management practices to a project.

(continued)

> Take the time at the beginning of the project to choose those processes, tools, and techniques that will actually add value to your project and throughout the life of the project. Be prepared to reexamine your decisions to ensure that they are still correct. For example, on one small IT project I worked on, our project management methodology was tailored to be flexible and very simple because the project was simple and over a short time frame. A larger IT project I worked on had a very rigid methodology with many processes, reflecting the complexity of the project.

Project integration management includes seven processes:

1. **Developing the project charter** The project charter authorizes the project. It names the project manager and enables the project to commence. Projects are chartered for varying reasons: to satisfy market demand, to respond to customer requests, to solve a problem, or to address a social need. While the charter authorizes the project, it also defines the requirements for stakeholder satisfaction, the project purpose, and the project assumptions and constraints.

NOTE Remember that the project charter authorizes the project, names the project manager, and defines the project manager's level of authority. Project charters are not contracts, because no payments are exchanged or detailed in the charter.

2. **Developing the project management plan** Project management plan development is an iterative process that requires input from the project manager, the project team, the project customers, and other key stakeholders. It details how the project work will accomplish the project goals. The project management plan comprises subsidiary plans and several other documents.

NOTE Agile projects often don't have a project management plan because change is welcome and expected.

3. **Directing and managing the project work** Once the project management plan has been created, the project manager and the project team can implement the plan. Directing and managing the project work creates the project deliverables for the project or phase. Corrective actions, preventive actions, and defect repair all happen through directing and managing the project work.

NOTE Agile project teams are self-organizing, and the team will decide in each iteration who'll do what work.

4. **Managing project knowledge**   The project manager and the project team members come into the project with knowledge about the work, but that knowledge isn't always easily shared with one another. Explicit knowledge—knowledge that can be quickly and easily expressed through conversations, documentation, figures, or numbers—is easily communicated. However, tacit knowledge is more difficult to express because it's about personal beliefs, values, knowledge gained from experience, and "know-how" when doing an activity.

5. **Monitoring and controlling the project work**   This process starts with the project's conception and finishes with the project completion. Its goal is to make certain that the project stays on track and finishes according to the project plan. Measurements for project performance, schedule, cost, and quality are implemented. If there are variances, responses to these will happen through preventive, corrective, or defect repair actions.

6. **Performing integrated change control**   Changes can kill a project. Change requests must be documented and sent through a formal change control system to determine their worthiness for implementation. Integrated change control manages changes across the entire project. Change requests are evaluated and considered for impacts on risk, costs, schedule, and scope. Not all change requests are approved—but all change requests must be documented and reviewed.

NOTE   To help you remember the concept of integrated change control, think of the domino effect. Any proposed changes to the project can have serious impacts on other areas of the project. Because of this, all the project areas must be evaluated with each project change.

7. **Closing the project or phase**   Projects and phases are closed. Administrative closure confirms that all the needed processes for each process group have been completed. Administrative closure also gathers all project records for archival purposes, including documentation of the project's success or failure. Contract closure involves contracts and agreements, when used, which must also be closed after inspection of the contract deliverables. Contracts are always closed according to the agreed-upon terms.

In the Real World

Project closure is one of those processes that we know we should do, but usually by the time we move into the part of the project where the bulk of our effort is on project closure, we are being called away to start a new project. I have learned that there are tangible benefits in staying focused on project closure in the face of these calls to join new projects. It is important to make sure you get formal signoff that the project is complete, collect and store lessons learned, and, if possible, hold a post-implementation review sometime later to determine if the deliverable is actually doing what it was supposed to do.

Project integration management is an ongoing process completed by the project manager to ensure that the project moves from initiation to closure. It is the gears, guts, and grind of project management—the day-in, day-out business of completing the project work. Project integration management coordinates the activities, project resources, constraints, and assumptions of the project plans and massages them into a working model. Once the model exists, it's up to the project manager and project team to monitor and control the project from initiation to closure.

Determine How to Document Project Controls of Predictive, Plan-Based Projects

Task 3
Predictive, plan-based projects were the standard type of projects in the early days of project management. The predictive, plan-based approach remains the most common type of project development approach. Projects with clear scope and execution according to a defined set of specifications are prime for the predictive, plan-based approach. Construction projects are a good example of projects that work well with a predictive, plan-based approach.

Identify Artifacts That Are Used in Predictive, Plan-Based Projects

Task 3, Enabler 1
An *artifact* is a template, document, output, or project deliverable. Artifacts are considered part of the organizational process assets and can be reused and tailored on future projects. Many organizations have databases to store and retrieve these artifacts for reuse. These actions would be part of the configuration management plan, which is part of the project management plan.

Artifacts are common across multiple project development approaches. The following sections describe common artifacts in predictive, plan-based projects.

Strategic Artifacts
Strategic artifacts involve documentation that relates to a project's initiation. Creating these artifacts is usually the first step of a project, as they help guide a team's work moving forward. Prior to a formal project charter, these documents describe the business purpose, proposed value, and link to strategic objectives. The information in these documents during this time frame is at a high level, as there may be considerable uncertainty. These artifacts are made prior to the start of a project and remain fairly static but are often referenced throughout the project to ensure things are going as planned.

Three critical strategic artifacts of project management that play an essential role in ensuring project success are the needs assessment, business case, and benefits management plan. Here's a brief overview of each:

- **Needs assessment**   Before initiating a project, it's important to conduct a needs assessment to determine the project's objectives and scope. A needs assessment involves identifying the gap between the current state and the desired state and determining the resources needed to achieve the desired state. The needs assessment helps to ensure that the project aligns with the organization's strategic goals and that it meets the stakeholders' needs.

- **Business case**   A business case is a document that justifies the project's investment and outlines the expected benefits, costs, and risks associated with the project. It helps stakeholders understand the rationale behind the project and provides a basis for decision-making. The business case should include a cost-benefit analysis, a feasibility study, and an evaluation of the project's impact on the organization.

- **Benefits management plan**   A benefits management plan outlines the process for identifying, tracking, and measuring the project's benefits. It defines the benefits to be realized, who is responsible for realizing them, and how they will be measured. The benefits management plan ensures that the project's benefits are aligned with the organization's strategic goals and that they are realized in a timely and effective manner.

Logs and Registers

Logs and registers are part of your daily management process. They are artifacts used to record the events, points of contention, and experiences on the project and are updated constantly throughout the project. These documents aren't set in place and are continuously updated throughout the project. The terms *log* and *register* are often used interchangeably; for instance, the risk register and the risk log are the same artifact.

Several project management logs and registers are listed next:

- **Assumption log**   Records all assumptions and constraints throughout the project. Assumptions are things related to the project that are considered true but are not directly supported by fact or proof. Constraints are factors that limit the project options.

- **Change log**   Documents all requested, approved, and rejected project changes and their status.

- **Issue log**   Documents and tracks events that have a negative impact on the project and require a workaround.

- **Lessons learned register**   Records experiences and conclusions gathered throughout the project to aid in improving future project executions.

- **Risk register**   Documents and tracks all risks and responses throughout the project. Includes risk ID, risk description, prioritization, root causes of risk, probability, ownership, potential response, possible impact, and updated risk categories.

- **Stakeholder register**   Documents information about all project stakeholders, along with their influence and interest in the project.

Plans

Plans are written documents that describe the rules around how various aspects of the project will be accomplished. Plans are often updated throughout the project to reflect approved changes. The project management plan may include subsidiary management plans and other planning documents.

Let's take a moment and look at each of the minimum project management subsidiary plans the project management plan can include for a predictive, plan-based project:

- **Change control plan**   Describes how changes will be documented, reviewed, and implemented

- **Communications management plan**   Includes what is communicated, to whom, when, and why.

- **Configuration management plan**   Describes how the project will track and control changes to important project documents and products. Coordinates with the change management plan.

- **Cost management plan**   Describes how costs are collected, reviewed, monitored, and reported.

- **Procurement management plan**   Describes how resources are acquired and the various contractual approaches used in the organization.

- **Project management plan**   Integrated document for all other management plans that describe the complete rules on how the project will be conducted.

- **Quality management plan**   Describes a project's quality policies, procedures, criteria for and areas of application, and roles, responsibilities, and authorities.

- **Requirements management plan**   Describes how requirements will be identified, managed, and tracked from initiation to closure of the project.

- **Resource management plan**   Describes how to identify, organize, schedule, and manage a project's resources—people, tools, equipment, tech, and facilities.

- **Risk management plan**   Describes how to identify, evaluate, and plan for potential risk events.

- **Scope management plan**   Describes how the scope will be defined, developed, monitored, controlled, and validated.

- **Schedule management plan**   Describes how the schedule will be defined, developed, monitored, controlled, and modified.
- **Stakeholder engagement plan**   Describes the various stakeholders and how they are identified, categorized, assessed, and controlled.

Hierarchy Charts

These documents break down higher-level information into more detail to allow for identification of specific project activity. Hierarchy charts include all project objectives and serve as a check and balance for the project manager to ensure the project is conforming to the project goals.

- **Organizational breakdown structure**   Describes the structure of the project organization and where authority resides.
- **Product breakdown structure**   Describes the various requirements of the product solution.
- **Resource breakdown structure**   Describes resources by category and type.
- **Risk breakdown structure**   Describes the various areas of potential risk.
- **Work breakdown structure**   Decomposes the project scope into actionable work packages that provide the specific project activities.

Baselines

Baselines are approved snapshots of plans or work products used to compare against actual performance to identify variances. Baselines are used to monitor progress after project execution has begun. The completion of the work is measured and then compared against the cost, schedule, and scope baselines as documented in the project plan. Should there be—gasp! —discrepancies between the project work and the baselines, prompt and accurate reactions are needed to adjust the slipping components of the project.

The project baseline concept includes five different types of baselines:

- **Cost (budget) baseline**   Combined costs of all activities and milestones that the project must fulfill.
- **Scope baseline**   Includes approved scope statement, WBS, and associated WBS dictionary. Modified through integrated change control.
- **Schedule baseline**   The final approved version of the project schedule used to track actual progress against planned progress.
- **Performance measurement baseline**   Combination of cost, scope, and schedule baselines used to monitor overall project performance.
- **Quality baseline**   Documents the quality objectives for the project, including the metrics for stakeholder acceptance of the project deliverable.

NOTE All project baselines form part of the overall project management plan, because they provide information about what is intended.

In the Real World
The most often used form of schedule baseline is the Gantt chart. However, be aware that the Gantt chart is also an exceptional communications tool. On many projects I have worked on, I have used the Gantt chart for both reasons with great success. The Gantt chart presents different levels of information graphically, which means it is easily understood by both technically minded and nontechnically minded stakeholders.

Visual Data and Information
Visual data and information, such as charts, graphs, matrices, and diagrams, play a crucial role in project management. They help you communicate complex information effectively and efficiently to stakeholders, team members, and clients. Visually presenting information provides alternatives for communicating and understanding information, which can aid in decision-making and prioritization.

The following are some examples of visual data and information used in project management:

- **Cause-and-effect diagram** Breaks down the causes of the problem statement identified into discrete branches, helping to identify the main or root cause of the problem. Refer back to Figure 4-2.
- **Dashboard** Displays project progress or performance.
- **Flowchart** Visualizes a sequence of steps to be followed to complete a goal.
- **Gantt chart** Illustrates work completed over a period in relation to the time planned for the work.
- **Histogram** Displays the frequency distribution of a variable's data points.
- **Project schedule network diagram** Represents the logical relationships among project activities; produced using scheduling software.
- **Requirements traceability matrix** Describes the two-way link between requirements and deliverables.
- **Responsibility assignment matrix (RAM)** Documents stakeholders and clarifies responsibilities among cross-functional teams and their involvement level in a project. Also known as a RACI chart, which is an acronym for responsible, accountable, consulted, or informed.
- **Stakeholder engagement assessment matrix** Documents and manages stakeholder interest and influence over time.

Reports

Schedules and reports are critical elements of project management. They help you to plan, execute, monitor, and control projects effectively. Various types of schedules and reports can be used, including project schedule, resource schedule, budget schedule, risk management report, progress report, and status report. The use of these schedules and reports can help ensure that the project is completed within the allocated budget, timeline, and scope.

The following are some examples of schedules and reports used in project management:

- **Milestone schedule**   A milestone schedule is a type of project schedule that identifies specific significant events or achievements in a project. These events are significant to the project and usually represent critical decision points, deadlines, or the completion of a significant deliverable. Milestone schedules are often included in the project management plan and used to track project progress, communicate progress to stakeholders, and help ensure that the project stays on track.

- **Project schedule**   A project schedule is a plan that outlines the project's activities, duration, and sequence. It includes start and finish dates for each activity, dependencies, and milestones. The project schedule helps you to estimate resources, manage risk, and track progress.

- **Resource schedule**   A resource schedule is a plan that outlines the availability and allocation of resources for the project. It includes the types and number of resources required, their availability, and their assignment to specific activities. The resource schedule helps you to manage resources efficiently and avoid overburdening them.

- **Budget schedule**   A budget schedule is a plan that outlines the project's financial resources and expenses. It includes the project's total budget, funding sources, and expenses. The budget schedule helps you to manage costs and ensure that the project is completed within the allocated budget.

- **Quality report**   A quality report is a document that provides an overview of the quality of a project's deliverables, processes, and outcomes. It is used to communicate the project's quality status to stakeholders, including project sponsors, customers, and project team members. The quality report is an important component of the project management plan and should be updated regularly throughout the project life cycle.

- **Risk management report**   A risk management report is a document that outlines the project's risks, their likelihood, and potential impact. It includes the risk mitigation strategies and contingency plans. The risk management report helps project managers to manage risks proactively and avoid potential issues.

- **Progress report**   A progress report is a document that outlines the project's progress against the project plan. It includes a summary of completed activities, milestones achieved, and any issues or delays encountered. The progress report helps project managers to track progress and identify any deviations from the project plan.

- **Status report:** A status report is a document that outlines the project's status, including progress, budget, and risks. It provides an overview of the project's health and helps you to communicate effectively with stakeholders and team members. A status report describes how the project is meeting its scope, schedule, and cost targets with comparison to historical data and future forecasting.

Agreements and Contracts

A *contract* is a formal agreement between a buyer and a seller. It obliges the seller to perform certain services requested by the buyer to achieve an objective. An *agreement* is any document or communication that defines the intentions of the parties. There are various types of contracts:

- **Fixed-price contract** Provides a price that is not subject to any adjustment based on the seller's cost experience in carrying out the contract.

- **Cost-reimbursable contract** Provides payment for allowable costs incurred by the other party. These contracts are often used when the project scope is not well defined or is subject to frequent change.

- **T&M, time and materials** Provides a fixed hourly rate for the time the seller spends fulfilling the contract; it does not include a strict scope definition. Often used for staff augmentation, subject matter expertise, or other outside support.

- **IDIQ, indefinite delivery/indefinite quantity** A type of contract used in government procurement that allows for an indefinite quantity of goods or services to be provided during a specified period of time.

- **MOU, memorandum of understanding** A nonbinding agreement between two or more parties that outlines the terms and details of a cooperative relationship or project.

- **MOA, memorandum of agreement** A document that outlines the terms and conditions of a formal agreement between two or more parties.

- **SLA, service level agreement** A contract between a service provider and a client that specifies the level of service that will be provided, as well as the remedies or penalties that will be imposed if the service level is not met.

- **BOA, blanket order agreement** A type of purchasing agreement between a buyer and a supplier that establishes terms and conditions for the purchase of goods or services over a specified period of time.

Other Artifacts

The documents in this category are used for a variety of purposes.

- **Activity list** Describes the activities on the schedule, with details on dates, resources, costs, and dependencies.

- **Bid documents**   Procurement-related documents used to acquire goods or services:
  - Request for information (RFI)
  - Request for quotation (RFQ)
  - Request for proposal (RFP)
- **Metrics**   Describes an attribute and how to measure it.
- **Project/resource calendar**   Documents available workdays and hours for the overall project and for specific resources.
- **Requirements documentation**   Describes project requirements used to confirm product completeness and track impacts to changing requirements.
- **Project team charter**   Describes how the team will work together with operating guidelines and clear expectations regarding acceptable behavior.

Calculate Cost and Schedule Variances

Task 3, Enabler 2

Reporting on project progress is one of the major activities performed by the project manager. The reporting includes how much work has been completed and how much it has cost to complete. Further, management wants to know how much work is left to do and how much it will cost to complete. This reporting is not straightforward. For example, if you have expended 50 percent of the project budget, is the project 50 percent done? Or if you have used 50 percent of the estimated project time, is the project 50 percent complete? It might be, or it might not. Using earned value analysis provides more accurate progress reporting.

Earned value analysis (EVA) is a tool that measures how much work has been completed, how much it cost to complete, and whether that cost was the same as what was budgeted. It also helps estimate how much work still needs to be completed and estimates the cost to complete.

 NOTE   Adaptive projects don't typically use EVA because it's tough to say where a project should be at a certain point in time and what the work should be worth, and the estimate at completion is already determined as the project budget. A hybrid project, however, could use EVA because it will have a blend of adaptive and predictive approaches.

All this analysis is done through the project scheduling software ... assuming you have developed a complete project schedule.

There are basically four elements to EVA:

- **Planned value (PV)**   The work scheduled and the budget authorized to accomplish that work. For example, if a project has a budget of $500,000 and month six represents 50 percent of the project work, the PV for that month is $250,000.

- **Earned value (EV)**   The physical work completed to date and the authorized budget for that work. For example, if your project has a budget of $500,000 and the work completed to date represents 45 percent of the entire project work, its earned value is $225,000. You can find EV by multiplying the percent complete times the project budget at completion (BAC).

- **Actual cost (AC)**   The actual amount of monies the project has required to date. In your project, your BAC, for example, is $500,000 and your earned value is $225,000. As it turns out, your project team had some waste, and you spent $232,000 in actual monies to reach the 45-percent-complete milestone. Your actual cost is $232,000.

- **Budget at completion (BAC)**   The total budget or cost allocated to complete a project or project phase. It is a critical metric used to measure the overall financial performance of the project and to track the project's progress against the budget. The BAC is set during the project planning phase and can be compared to the actual cost incurred during the project to determine the project's financial performance. From the actual cost description earlier, in this case, the BAC is $500,000.

With these four elements, you can compute variance at completion (VAC), estimate to complete (ETC), estimate at completion (EAC), performance indexes (CPI and SPI), and estimate cost and schedule for project completion. Table 4-2 shows all the earned value elements, their definitions, and the information they provide. You can also find this information in the memory card included with this book.

Name	Formula	Sample Mnemonic Device
Planned value	PV = percent complete of where the project should be	Please
Earned value	EV = percent complete × budget at completion	Eat
Cost variance	CV = EV – AC	Carl's
Schedule variance	SV = EV – PV	Sugar
Cost performance index	CPI = EV / AC	Candy
Schedule performance index	SPI = EV / PV	S (this and the following two spell "SEE")
Estimate at completion	EAC = BAC / CPI	E
Estimate to complete	ETC = EAC – AC	E
To-complete performance index (BAC)	(BAC – EV) / (BAC – AC)	The
To-complete performance index (EAC)	(BAC – EV) / (EAC – AC)	Taffy
Variance at completion	VAC = BAC – EAC	Violin

Table 4-2   A Summary of the Most Common EVA Formulas

PART II

EXAM TIP There won't be as many questions on these EVA formulas as you might think, but knowing these formulas can help you nail down the few questions you'll likely have.

EVA is a "point in time" analysis, meaning you, as the project manager, perform the EVA at various dates within the project life cycle. At each date, you determine the progress of work completed and cost expended and predict the project completion cost and time. This provides you with knowledge to manipulate the project schedule factors to improve the project outcome.

Two analysis outcomes are variances and performance indexes. Variances are calculated by subtracting AC or PV from EV. Performance indexes divide EV by AC or PV and can be used to estimate project completion time and cost.

Finding the Project Variances

Out in the real world, I'm sure your projects are never late and never over budget (ha ha—pretty funny, right?). For your CAPM exam, you may need to find the cost and schedule variances for your project. Finding the variances helps the project manager and management determine a project's health, set goals for project improvement, and benchmark projects against each other based on the identified variances. Negative numbers are bad, positive numbers are good.

Finding the Cost Variance Let's say your project has a BAC of $500,000 and is 40 percent complete. However, you have already spent $234,000 in real monies (actual cost). To find the cost variance (EV – AC), you need to calculate the earned value, which is 40 percent of the $500,000 budget. As Figure 4-6 shows, EV is $200,000. In this instance, the cost variance is –$34,000.

Finding the Schedule Variance

The schedule variance is basically the same as the cost variance, only this time, we're concerned with planned value instead of actual costs. Let's say your project with the $500,000 budget is supposed to be 45 percent complete by today, but it's only 40 percent complete. We've already computed the earned value as $200,000.

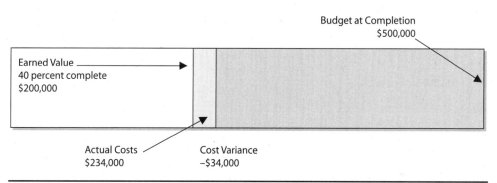

Budget at Completion
$500,000

Earned Value
40 percent complete
$200,000

Actual Costs
$234,000

Cost Variance
–$34,000

Figure 4-6 Cost variance is the difference between earned value and actual costs.

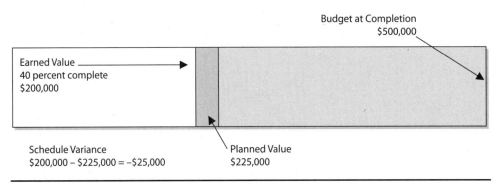

Figure 4-7 Schedule variance is the difference between earned value and planned value.

Recall that planned value, where you're supposed to be and what you're supposed to be worth, is percent complete of where the project should be. In this example, it's 45 percent of the $500,000 BAC, which is $225,000. Uh-oh! You're behind schedule. The schedule variance formula, as Figure 4-7 demonstrates, is earned value minus the planned value. So, in this example, the schedule variance is –$25,000.

Finding the Schedule Performance Index and Cost Performance Index

Along with computing the cost and schedule variances, as just described, EVA also computes two performance indexes: schedule performance index (SPI) and cost performance index:

- **Schedule performance index (SPI)** A measure of how close the project is to performing work as it was scheduled. If you are ahead of schedule, EV will be greater than PV, and therefore the SPI will be greater than 1. Obviously, this is desirable. Conversely, an SPI below 1 indicates that the amount of work performed was less than the work scheduled—not a good thing. SPI is computed as follows:

  $$SPI = EV / PV$$

- **Cost performance index (CPI)** A measure of how close current project spending is to planned project spending at this point. If you are spending less on the work performed than was budgeted, the CPI will be greater than 1. If not, and you are spending more than was budgeted for the work performed, then the CPI will be less than 1. CPI is computed as follows:

  $$CPI = EV / AC$$

 EXAM TIP Here are a few EVA tips for the exam. For variances (subtraction), EV is always on the left. Negative is bad and positive is good. For indexes (division), EV is always on the top. Over 1 is good, under 1 is bad.

These indexes can be used to calculate estimate at completion (EAC), which computes the estimated final cost of the project at any point in time. The formula is EAC = BAC / CPI.

EXAM TIP   There are several ways to compute EAC. As of this writing, you only need to know one!

Chapter Summary

In this chapter, we focused on predictive, plan-based approaches. Projects that follow a predictive, plan-based approach have well-defined project goals and outcomes. The project requirements are clear, as well as the project goal. There is a clear sequence of steps or stages, and they flow from one to another. The project team has well-defined roles and responsibilities and clear lines of communication and reporting. In general, a predictive, plan-based approach is best suited for projects that are structured, predictable, and controllable, with limited scope for change and ambiguity.

Predictive, plan-based projects have processes that may be performed only once or at predefined points, such as Develop Project Management Plan or Develop Project Charter. Other processes may be performed multiple times as needed, such as Conduct Procurements or Acquire Resources. And some processes may be performed continuously throughout the project, such as Identify Risks or Perform Integrated Change Control.

Determining the activities within each process is essential for effective project planning, resource allocation, progress tracking, quality control, and communication. Project managers must identify the activities within each process to ensure that the project's objectives are achieved within the defined scope, budget, and timeline.

All projects are concerned with scope (what to do), cost (how much), and schedule (when). The project schedule drives the *when* and includes the *what* through all of the specific activities. The *how much* is determined by executing each of the activities and accumulating the related costs of human and physical resources. Project managers create a schedule management plan to develop, manage, and control the schedule.

Project schedule development starts with the project scope statement. The scope is then decomposed into work packages that are organized into a work breakdown structure (WBS). The project team then takes each WBS work package and identifies the specific activities needed to complete the work package. These activities are sequenced along with estimates of time (duration/work effort) and resources (human/physical). Once the schedule is developed, the project manager uses analysis tools, such as the critical path method and earned value analysis, to control the schedule to ensure the project is delivered on schedule and within the project budget. Many other factors can consume a project's schedule: change request reviews, corrective and preventive actions, defect repair, defect repair review, and scope verification.

Project integration management is about bringing all the schedule, cost, resource, quality, and other elements together. Integration recognizes, and is focused on, the realization that project work is not completed in discrete chunks and that activities in one area may influence activities in another area, thus requiring a high-level view across all project activities.

Project integration begins with the project charter, which is the foundational document for the project, and all projects must have a project charter. The project charter is a formal document that authorizes the project to go forward and gives the project manager authority over the project resources.

Project integration management requires the project manager to make the best decisions for work, resources, project issues, and all the logistics of the project so that it is completed as planned. Project integration management is the project manager's responsibility.

One output of project integration is the project management plan. This document contains all the elements of integrated project planning and all the other outputs from the other planning processes. It describes *how* the project will be done. It includes rules for executing each of the other aspects of the project (scope, cost, time, quality, etc.). The project management plan is a team document and is often referred to and updated throughout the project.

The suitability of a predictive, plan-based approach for an organizational structure depends on various factors, including the organization's culture, industry, project characteristics, and organizational structure. A hierarchical and traditional structure may be more suited to a predictive approach, while a virtual or colocated organization may be more suited to an adaptive approach. A matrix structure may be suitable for a predictive approach, but its complexity may make it challenging to implement.

Schedules and reports are critical elements of project management. They help project managers to plan, execute, monitor, and control projects effectively. Various types of schedules and reports can be used, including project schedule, resource schedule, budget schedule, risk management report, progress report, and status report. The use of these schedules and reports can help ensure that the project is completed within the allocated budget, timeline, and scope.

Projects develop and update many documents or artifacts that serve to provide the project manager with tools to control and manage the overall project. Project artifacts can be of a strategic nature that match project objectives with corporate goals, such as the needs assessment, business case, or benefits management plan. Many artifacts support the day-to-day operation of the project and document project actions, such as issues, risks, changes, and so forth. These artifacts are called logs or registers. Much of the project manager's job is communication and reporting. Several artifacts provide the tools to report project progress and activities through narrative and visual means, such as dashboards and Gantt charts. Artifacts also include tools to control the major project elements, scope, schedule, cost, and quality.

Visual data and information are essential in project management. They help you communicate complex information effectively, identify issues, and ensure that the project stays on track. Various tools and techniques can be used to create visual data and information, including Gantt charts, network diagrams, status reports, risk matrices, swimlane diagrams, and process flowcharts.

Earned value analysis is one tool that project managers rely on to understand and control the value or work completed through execution of the schedule activities. Through computed variances from cost and schedule baselines and predictive analysis of project completion using computed performance indexes, the project manager can manipulate and control the schedule to drive the project toward completion on schedule and within budget.

Questions

1. Bill's current project was originally estimated to cost $1.5 million, with a completion target of six months. Bill is three months into the project and has performed an earned value analysis with the following results: EV = $650,000, PV = $750,000, and AC = $800,000. What are the schedule and cost variances?

    A. SV = $100,000 / CV = $150,000

    B. SV = $150,000 / CV = –$100,000

    C. SV = –$50,000 / CV = $150,000

    D. SV = –$100,000 / CV = –$150,000

2. Which value for CV indicates that the project is over budget?

    A. CV = 0

    B. CV > 0

    C. CV < 0

    D. CV = 1

3. Which of the following is an example of a strategic project artifact?

    A. Business case

    B. Stakeholder register

    C. Project management plan

    D. Organizational breakdown structure

4. The project management plan provides a baseline for several things. Which one of the following does the project management plan not provide a baseline for?

    A. Scope

    B. Cost

    C. Schedule

    D. Control

5. Sally is the project manager for her organization. A change has recently been approved by her organization's change control board. What document will Sally update first?

    A. The cost baseline

    B. The quality baseline

    C. The risk management plan

    D. The change log

6. Tamika is the project manager of a new project to develop a new software product. Management has not required a formal project management plan in the past, but they'd like Tamika to develop a project management plan to serve as a model or template for all other projects in the organization. What is the primary purpose of Tamika's project management plan?

   A. To define the work to be completed to reach the project end date

   B. To define the work needed in each phase of the project life cycle

   C. To prevent any changes to the scope

   D. To provide accurate communication for the project team, project sponsor, and stakeholders regarding how the project will be executed, controlled, and closed

7. What is the best definition of quality?

   A. Quality is whatever the customer says is right.

   B. Quality is the degree to which a product can be used for its intended purpose.

   C. Quality is the degree to which a set of inherent characteristics fulfills requirements.

   D. Quality is the number of features that the product has.

8. Which of the following answers best describes a key benefit of the Develop Project Charter process as described in the *Process Groups: A Practice Guide*?

   A. Assesses and manages all change requests.

   B. Defines the project start and creates a formal record of the project.

   C. Iteratively prepares plans for execution throughout a project.

   D. Ensures all projects are closed.

9. Which project integration process deals with making decisions on change requests?

   A. Monitor and Control Project Work

   B. Develop Project Charter

   C. Direct and Manage Project Work

   D. Perform Integrated Change Control

10. José is explaining to his project team that all changes to the project must be documented and assessed in relation to any extra costs incurred. This is particularly important at what point in a project's timeline?

    A. At the beginning of the project

    B. Toward the end of the project

    C. During the project execution

    D. It is equal throughout a project

11. Which of the following artifacts is not a valid project log or register?

    A. Assumption log

    B. Lessons learned register

    C. Cost register

    D. Risk register

12. Sean is newly appointed to a project and is reading the project charter to gain an understanding of what is known about the project at this point. The project charter should contain enough information to do all but which one of the following?

    A. Complete the WBS.

    B. Initiate the project.

    C. Describe the high-level project scope.

    D. Appoint the project manager.

13. Carlo has completed a business case for his proposed project and is presenting it to senior management for consideration and approval. Which of the following should Carlo include in this document?

    A. The project management plan

    B. A copy of the stakeholder register

    C. Any blank project templates his organization says he must use in completing the project charter

    D. A description of the expected market demand for the product of the project

14. Arial has just taken over a project that has been underway for ten months. The previous project manager left the project for health reasons. The project is performing well, but Arial would like to become familiar with the way in which this project is being executed, monitored and controlled, and closed. What document will help Arial in this instance?

    A. Quality management plan

    B. Project statement of work

    C. Project charter

    D. Project management plan

15. Franklin and his team are considering making an early change to a part of the project management plan, when one of Franklin's team members says that it is too early to be considering any changes. At what point in the project would Franklin perform integrated change control?

    A. During project execution

    B. From project start to completion

    C. During project monitoring and control

    D. From project execution through to project closure

16. Roberta is using the work packages from her WBS to assist with creating her project schedule. Roberta begins breaking down the work packages into the actual work necessary to complete the work package. What is Roberta in the process of defining?

   A. WBS dictionary items

   B. Project work

   C. Activities

   D. Work package assignments

17. What is the *Process Groups: A Practice Guide* process of analyzing activity sequences, durations, resource requirements, and scheduled constraints to create the project schedule?

   A. Project Schedule Development

   B. Create Project Schedule

   C. Develop Schedule

   D. Schedule Management

18. What is the name of the process in the *Process Groups: A Practice Guide* that monitors the status of the project to update project progress and manage changes to the schedule baseline?

   A. Develop Schedule

   B. Monitoring and Controlling

   C. Verify Schedule

   D. Control Schedule

19. Management has asked that Veronica create the schedule management plan to identify the different processes and procedures her project will require. During the creation of the plan, Veronica needs to identify schedule change control and its components. Schedule change control is part of which process in *Process Groups: A Practice Guide*?

   A. Change control

   B. Cost control

   C. WBS refinements

   D. Integrated change control

20. Rachel is a project manager for a construction project. The project will be using new material that the project team has never worked with before. Rachel allotted $10,000 to train the project team on working with the new material so that the project will operate smoothly. The $10,000 for training is known as what?

   A. Cost of quality

   B. Cost of poor quality

   C. Sunk costs

   D. Contingency allowance

Answers

1. **D.** Using the values provided and the respective formulas for schedule variance and cost variance of $SV = EV - PV$ and $CV = EV - AC$, $SV = -\$100,000$ and $CV = -\$150,000$. A, B, and C are incorrect because these answers do not result from using the numbers provided in the correct formulas.

2. **C.** For cost variance analysis ($CV = EV - AC$), negative values are bad and positive values are good. When $CV < 0$, the project is over budget. A is incorrect because a project is on budget when $CV = 0$. B is incorrect because a project is under budget when $CV > 0$. D is incorrect because when the $CV = 1$, which is greater than zero, the project is under budget.

3. **A.** The business case is a strategic artifact that outlines the proposed value of the project solution and describes the business need or gap that will be filled. B, C, and D are incorrect because they are not strategic project artifacts; they are other types of artifacts.

4. **D.** The project management plan provides baselines for the schedule, cost, and scope. Control is a project activity and part of the Monitoring and Controlling process group. A, B, and C are incorrect because scope, cost, and schedule do have associated baselines. Recall that a baseline is what's predicted, and the actuals are the experiences of the project. The difference between the baseline and what happened reveals the variances of the project.

5. **D.** When a change enters the project, the change log must be updated to reflect the change. A change log is a record of all changes made to a project, system, or process over time. It provides a chronological history of the changes, including details such as the date of the change, who made the change, the reason for the change, and any other relevant information. The change log is always updated first, after which the cost baseline, quality baseline, or risk management plan might need to be updated depending on the type of change the board approved, but that isn't specified in the question. A and C are incorrect because the question did not indicate that new costs or risks will be entering the project. B, the quality baseline, is not a valid answer because quality reflects the completion of the project scope.

6. **D.** The primary purpose of the project management plan is to define how the project will be managed and to communicate that information to project stakeholders. A and B are incorrect because they address only the project work. C is incorrect because this answer addresses the project's change control system.

7. **C.** Quality is the degree to which a set of inherent characteristics fulfills requirements—remember this definition for the exam. A is incorrect because quality doesn't necessarily relate to what the customer says is right, unless what the customer says is right is captured in the requirements. B is incorrect because quality is more than the degree to which a product can be used for its intended purpose. D is incorrect because the amount of features a product has, or does not have, refers to grade, not quality.

8. **B.** The Develop Project Charter process results in outputs that define the start of the project and create a formal record of the project with the project charter. A is incorrect because the Perform Integrated Change Control process assesses and manages change requests. C is incorrect because the Develop Project Management Plan process iteratively prepares the different plans to guide project execution. D is incorrect because the Close Project or Phase process ensures all projects are formally closed.

9. **D.** The Perform Integrated Change Control process uses change requests as an input and, with the appropriate tools and techniques, makes decisions on whether to accept or reject the change requests. A is incorrect because the Monitor and Control Project Work process focuses on monitoring the actual work being done against the planned work. Change requests are an output from this process. B is incorrect because the Develop Project Charter process is focused on project selection methods and the development of the project charter. C is incorrect because the Direct and Manage Project Work process is focused on executing the work contained in the project management plan.

10. **B.** As you near the end of the project, both the cost and impact of any requested changes increase. A is incorrect because the cost of changes is lowest at the beginning of the project, as very little commitment has been made at this point to resources and executing the work. C is incorrect because there will be significant cost of changes during project execution, but they won't be as much as toward the end of the project. D is incorrect because the cost of changes increases as greater commitment is made to the deliverable and the resources to produce the deliverable.

11. **C.** A cost register is not a valid project artifact. A, B, and D are valid project logs or registers.

12. **A.** The project charter is like the birth certificate for a project. You need it to prove the project exists and to provide basic but extremely important information about the project. The information it contains is generally quite high level; it is the first document developed in an iterative process, so it won't contain enough information to complete a WBS. B is incorrect because the project charter should always contain information about the project initiation. C is incorrect because the project charter should contain a high-level description of the work to be done on the project. D is incorrect because the project charter should be the document that appoints the project manager.

13. **D.** The business case contains information to enable the project sponsor to authorize the project from a business perspective and therefore must contain information about expected market demand for the product. A is incorrect because the project management plan is done after the development of the business case and therefore would not be included in the business case. B is incorrect because there is no need for the business case to have a copy of the stakeholder register. C is incorrect because blank templates will not necessarily be part of the business case.

14. **D.** The project management plan is a product of all the different management plans and contains the information required to execute, monitor and control, and close the project. A is incorrect because the quality management plan relates to project quality and will not be detailed enough to give Arial all the information she requires. B is incorrect because the project statement of work will not be detailed enough to give Arial all the information she requires. C is incorrect because the project charter will not be detailed enough to give Arial all the information she requires.

15. **B.** Changes can affect a project at any point in the life cycle, and therefore Franklin must be ready to proactively influence, monitor, and control change requests. A is incorrect because integrated change control is performed from project inception to completion and not just during project execution, so this is not the best possible answer of the choices given. C is incorrect because Franklin would perform integrated change control during the monitoring and controlling phase as well as performing it from inception to completion, so this is not the best of the possible answers. D is incorrect because it does not acknowledge that integrated change control is also performed during project initiation and project planning phases.

16. **C.** The next step in the decomposition process is to break down the work package into activities that represent the actual work needed to complete the work package. This is essential to achieve a robust project schedule. A is incorrect because WBS dictionary items provide more detailed information about each node of the WBS. They do not refer to any work below the level of the work package. B is incorrect because project work is a scheduling term. For the exam, the correct term to use is activities. D is incorrect because work package assignments refer to the resources allocated to complete the work packages.

17. **C.** The Develop Schedule process is the final stage in the Planning process group for schedule management. It takes all the information from the previous planning processes and makes the project schedule. This process will be quite iterative because the information you have available at the start of the project is less accurate. A is incorrect because Project Schedule Development is not the name of a *Process Groups: A Practice Guide* process. B is incorrect because Create Project Schedule is not the name of a *Process Groups: A Practice Guide* process. D is incorrect because Schedule Management is not the name of a *Process Groups: A Practice Guide* process.

18. **D.** Control Schedule is the only schedule management process that appears in the Monitoring and Controlling process group. A is incorrect because the Develop Schedule process produces the project schedule and schedule baseline. B is incorrect because Monitoring and Controlling is a process group, not an individual process. C is incorrect because it is a made-up process name.

19. **D.** Schedule change control is part of the integrated change control process. A, B, and C are incorrect because they are not part of the integrated change control process.

20. A. Training for the project team is known as the cost of quality. B is incorrect because this would be the costs the project would incur if it did not attain the expected level of quality. C is incorrect because sunk costs describes the monies that have been spent on a project already. D is incorrect because contingency allowance is an amount of funds allotted to cover cost overruns in a project.

References

- *CAPM Certified Associate in Project Management Practice Exams* (2019), Haner and McCoy
- *Effective Project Management, Eighth Edition* (2019), Wysocki
- *PMBOK Guide* (2021)
- *PMIstandards+*
- *Process Groups: A Practice Guide* (2022)
- *The Project Management Answer Book* (2015), Furman

Agile Frameworks/ Methodologies

This chapter covers the tasks in Domain 3:
- Explain when it is appropriate to use an adaptive approach
- Determine how to plan project iterations
- Determine how to document project controls for an adaptive project
- Explain the components of an adaptive plan
- Determine how to prepare and execute task management steps

This domain represents approximately 20 percent of the CAPM examination.

Agile project management is a broad topic—and it's evolving daily in the project management space. It's difficult to describe a definitive approach to agile project management because there are many different approaches to agile project management. Approaches splinter into new approaches all the time. Unlike traditional project management, where it's easy to see the project from initiating to closing, some agile projects flow through repetitive cycles, called *iterations*, and other approaches, while following repetitions of work, create increments of deliverables.

Agile project management is all about value realization and welcoming change and is not as document heavy as predictive, plan-based project management. As a project manager for a predictive project, such as building a new house, you' plan everything up front, in detail, down to the cabinets in the kitchen. Once you have a solid set of plans, stakeholder approval, a budget, and a schedule, you become averse to change. Agile projects, which typically have been in the software development arena, don't do as much up-front planning as predictive projects. Certainly, there's a sense of where the project is going, but agile projects begin by prioritizing stakeholder requirements from most important to least important, build out the deliverables based on priorities, and welcome change throughout the project. Obviously, there are some project types for which agile is inappropriate.

You're familiar with my classic example of building a house. Building something physical is easy to assess; you can drive by the job site, take a quick peek on the construction project, and determine whether the crew has made progress. These physical projects describe industrial work. Industrial work is typically centered on physical labor, and it's easy to see results and predict time and cost, and everyone has a good sense of where the project is going.

With other projects, such as software development, creative work, and writing, it isn't always easy to see progress. You can see someone staring off into space in front of their computer, and you really don't know if they are working out a solution or daydreaming about sugary beaches in Florida. This type of work is knowledge work and is sometimes called *invisible work*. With knowledge work, you cannot always see what people are about to create. Therefore, knowledge work expects changes, has agility to move directions quickly, and is easier to adapt, change, and do rework than changing the floorplan for a new home construction project.

An industrial project, such as building a house or a skyscraper, is very visible. It is stable. It has structure. There are definite yes and no answers, and there are industry standards with codes for compliance that you must follow. It is task-driven because you install the foundation and build the framework. You have one person in charge, command, and control. Performance is easy to measure because you can look at the project and see how far along you are. For a task, such as installing light fixtures, you can say how much it will cost because you have an hourly rate for your workers.

Knowledge work is much less visible. When a programmer is coding an app and making lots of changes, the user can't see those changes until the app is functional. Agile expects change, which includes the environment. There is less structure. There are lots of questions in knowledge work. Agile encourages empirical processes, which are decisions and action based on observation and experience. Agile project management drives team autonomy, meaning the team is self-led and self-organizing, rather than led by a command-and-control approach. Agile leaders want the team to experiment and to use innovation. The agile team is seen as an asset, not a cost.

Hybrid projects are a combination of predictive, plan-based, and agile—where you might do a bit more planning up front than a typical agile project, but you'll shift into agile principles thereafter. Or you might start with agile prioritization of requirements and then plan and become averse to change. Hybrid approaches are custom approaches to specific projects—and there are no steadfast rules in hybrid, other than the focus is on delivering value to stakeholders. This chapter will help you create a strong foundation of agile frameworks/methodologies for the CAPM exam.

EXAM TIP   This brief overview of agile project management probably all sounds tricky—and it can be—but you'll be happy to know that the CAPM exam will be much more direct and question you only about the mainstream concepts of agile project management.

Explain When It Is Appropriate to Use an Adaptive Approach

Task 1

An adaptive approach to project management is most appropriate when the project requires flexibility, responsiveness, and an ability to adapt to changing circumstances. An adaptive approach requires both high coordination with the business unit and executive buy-in to the methodology and framework. Here are some scenarios in which an adaptive approach may be more suitable:

- **Complex and uncertain projects**   Projects with a lot of complexity or uncertainty are often better suited to an adaptive approach. In these situations, it is difficult to predict everything up front, so an adaptive approach allows for ongoing refinement and adjustment as the project progresses.

- **Fast-paced environments**   In industries where new technologies, market trends, or customer needs are rapidly changing, an adaptive approach can help teams stay ahead of the curve. By delivering value quickly and responding to feedback, teams can adapt to changing circumstances more easily.

- **Projects with changing requirements**   If the requirements for the project are likely to change over time, an adaptive approach can help the team respond to those changes more effectively. By focusing on delivering value in small increments and prioritizing the most important features first, the team can ensure that they are meeting stakeholder needs as they evolve.

- **Creative or experimental projects**   Projects that involve creative work or experimentation may benefit from an adaptive approach that allows for more freedom and exploration. By encouraging collaboration, feedback, and iteration, the team can find new and innovative solutions to complex problems.

- **Projects with high uncertainty**   Projects with a high degree of uncertainty or risk may be better managed with an adaptive approach. By breaking down the project into smaller, more manageable pieces, the team can learn more quickly and adjust the approach as they go.

Compare the Pros and Cons of Adaptive and Predictive, Plan-Based Projects

Task 1, Enabler 1

The suitability of adaptive and predictive, plan-based approaches for a project depends on the specific needs of the project and its stakeholders. For complex and evolving projects, an adaptive approach may be more suitable, while projects with well-defined requirements and a fixed timeline may be better suited for a predictive, plan-based approach. It is crucial to carefully assess the project's needs and the stakeholders' requirements to determine the most appropriate approach.

There are multiple ways to approach a project, often depending on the level of knowledge required for the work and the understanding of the outcome.

Adaptive Approach: Pros

An adaptive approach is a flexible and responsive way of handling situations, problems, or tasks. It allows for adjustments to be made in real time based on changing circumstances, which can be beneficial in many different contexts.

Here are some potential pros of an adaptive approach:

- Adaptive projects can respond to change and new information as the project progresses. The adaptive approach prioritizes decision-making regarding change, which can result in faster decision-making. When the project work is not understood, is complex, can change, and/or contains risks, a more flexible approach is advantageous.

- Adaptive projects encourage a culture of continuous improvement through reflection and adaptation. These types of projects require more "agility" and therefore often utilize agile approaches to address the work in smaller "chunks," enabling the project team to quickly respond to feedback and incorporate changes.

- An adaptive approach is very similar to an exploratory approach where results are presented, reviewed, and adapted based on the feedback received. The frequent feedback and checkpoints allow the team to detect issues early and address them before they become bigger problems.

- With the adaptive approach, results can be delivered to the customer in smaller, more frequent increments. It is up to the business to determine how the increment is presented, as it may not always be an actual deliverable, but rather a potentially deliverable item. This supports the ability to adapt to changes and deliver value earlier and more frequently, often resulting in increased customer satisfaction. Adaptive projects promote collaboration between team members and stakeholders, which can lead to more effective solutions.

Adaptive Approach: Cons

While an adaptive approach can offer many benefits, it is not without its potential drawbacks. Here are some cons of an adaptive approach:

- An adaptive approach can be more difficult to plan for and may require more ongoing monitoring and adjustment. For projects that are unable to be planned up front, additional change, complexity, and risks often are encountered during the project delivery. By not having more detailed understanding of the purpose and activities to be delivered, there may be changes and rework needed to meet the final expectation. This may also require modifications to existing organizational artifacts and activities.

- The flexibility and responsiveness to changes afforded by an adaptive approach also can cause uneasiness among team members. Some individuals feel uncomfortable without having a clear idea of the purpose and activities prior to starting work. An adaptive approach also often requires additional subject matter experts (SMEs) to collaborate and explore multiple options needed to meet the needs of the customer.

- The ability to adjust the project can make it difficult to predict the timeline or cost of the project. And frequent engagement with stakeholders may be time-consuming and require more coordination.

By understanding the pros and cons of an adaptive approach, individuals and organizations can make informed decisions about when and how to use it.

Predictive, Plan-Based Approach: Pros

A predictive, plan-based approach can be a valuable tool in many different contexts because it allows individuals or organizations to plan, clearly define requirements, and provide a project roadmap.

- Predictive, plan-based projects are more predictable in terms of timeline, cost, and deliverables. When the work has been done previously and procedures and activities are available, the project work can be planned, reducing uncertainty and risk. This is often based on clear procedures from similar past projects that have been successful. This allows work to utilize a plan to manage the work throughout the life cycle of the project.

- Predictive, plan-based projects often have more clearly defined requirements, which can make planning and execution more straightforward.

- And predictive, plan-based projects require detailed planning at the beginning, which can provide a roadmap for the project.

Predictive, Plan-Based Approach: Cons

While a predictive, plan-based approach can offer many benefits, it is important to be aware of its potential drawbacks.

Here are some cons of a predictive, plan-based approach:

- Predictive, plan-based projects may be less able to adapt to change, which can make it difficult to respond to new information or requirements. When changes to preplanned activities are discovered, there is often an impact to the schedule and/or the budget (which is identified and controlled by a change control process). Issues may be detected later in predictive, plan-based projects, which can make them more difficult and costly to address.

- Predictive, plan-based projects may prioritize following the plan over delivering value to stakeholders. The product, service, or result of the predictive approach is delivered to the customer at the end of the project.

- And the structured nature of predictive, plan-based projects may limit collaboration between team members and stakeholders.

You can make informed decisions about when and how to use a predictive, plan-based approach by being aware of its advantages and disadvantages.

Identify the Suitability of Adaptive Approaches for the Organizational Structure

Task 1, Enabler 2

The suitability of adaptive approaches to project management in different organizational structures depends on the specific needs and characteristics of the project and the organization. It's important to consider the communication channels, decision-making processes, and stakeholder engagement practices within the organization to determine the most appropriate approach.

Virtual Structure

In a virtual structure, team members may be geographically dispersed and work remotely. An adaptive approach can be suitable for virtual teams because it allows for more frequent check-ins and communication, which can help to build trust and maintain momentum. However, it's important to ensure that communication channels are in place to facilitate collaboration and feedback. If team members come from different geographic locations, there may be language barriers, cultural and time zone differences, or collaboration challenges. These challenges can be reduced when the team can be either colocated in a single area or near each other.

Colocation Structure

In a colocation structure, team members work in the same physical location. An adaptive approach can be suitable for a colocated team because it promotes collaboration, communication, and transparency that increase the team's effectiveness. However, it's important to ensure that team members are empowered to make decisions and that feedback loops are in place to allow for continuous improvement. When this colocation is not possible, the use of "tooling" and communication platforms can help provide a way for team members to virtually communicate and collaborate.

Matrix Structure

In a matrix structure, team members may report to multiple managers or departments. An adaptive approach can be suitable for matrix teams because it allows for more flexibility in responding to the needs of different stakeholders. However, it's important to ensure that roles and responsibilities are clearly defined and that communication channels are established to avoid confusion or conflict. The collaboration and transparency inherent in agile approaches is often more difficult to accomplish across department boundaries.

Hierarchical Structure

In a hierarchical structure, there is a clear chain of command and decision-making authority is concentrated at the top. This structure is often subject to the formal policies and procedures for the organization. These "ways of working" are well established and often provide a challenge to changes in the ways projects are performed. An adaptive approach can be challenging in a hierarchical structure because it requires more collaboration and decision-making at all levels of the organization. However, it may be possible to implement an adaptive approach in certain departments or teams within the organization.

Project-Oriented

An adaptive approach is particularly beneficial in project-oriented structures, where teams may be working on complex, time-sensitive projects that require a high degree of collaboration and coordination. Teams that have been established and utilize a project-oriented structure can determine the best approach to use to deliver the project, based on the context, change, complexity, urgency, and risk. Adaptive approaches can be a good fit for project-oriented organizational structures, as they promote flexibility, collaboration, and continuous improvement.

Identify Organizational Process Assets and Environmental Factors that Facilitate the Use of Adaptive Approaches

Task 1, Enabler 3
In Agile methodology, adaptive approaches are used to continuously improve and adjust the project processes and deliverables based on feedback and changing requirements. However, the success of these adaptive approaches depends on the presence of supportive enterprise environmental factors and access to appropriate organizational process assets.

Enterprise Environmental Factors
Enterprise environmental factors refer to areas that cannot be controlled by the project team, but rather influence or constrain the way the project is performed. Here are some factors that can facilitate the use of adaptive approaches:

- **Stakeholder engagement**   Active engagement with stakeholders throughout the project life cycle can facilitate the use of adaptive approaches by providing regular feedback and guidance.

- **Dynamic and changing project requirements**   Projects with requirements that are subject to change, either due to technological advancements or evolving business needs, are well-suited to an adaptive approach.

- **Small-to-medium sized projects**   Smaller projects with a limited scope and fewer stakeholders are often more suitable for adaptive approaches, as they may have less complexity and can be more easily adjusted.

- **Highly skilled and empowered teams**   Teams with high levels of skill and expertise, as well as a strong sense of empowerment and ownership over the project, are well-suited to adaptive approaches.

- **Marketplace conditions**   Marketplace conditions can facilitate the use of adaptive approaches by creating a need for businesses to respond quickly to changing demands, innovate to stay ahead of the competition, focus on customer needs, and take advantage of new technologies. As the various marketplace conditions change, the organization in general, and the project specifically, may need to make continued adjustments. These may be the work that a competitor is producing as well as the changing needs of stakeholders which need to be supported in shorter time frames through smaller delivery increments. This often includes a trade-off between costs of delay from planning to the risk of potential quality issues requiring rework.

- **Risk appetite**   Risk appetite can facilitate the use of adaptive approaches in Agile methodology by promoting experimentation, quick decision-making, embracing change, and learning from failure. When an organization has a high risk appetite, it is more willing to take the necessary risks to achieve its goals and adapt to changing circumstances. Risk appetite can vary based on a range of factors, such as the industry, organizational culture, and individual stakeholder preferences. Those stakeholders who appreciate the importance of continuous improvement often will be willing to absorb a few additional risks to achieve the value desired. By taking the time to understand stakeholder preferences and concerns, project managers can develop more effective risk management plans and risk response strategies.

Organizational Process Assets

As described in Chapter 2, organizational process assets are grouped into two categories: processes, policies, procedures, and items from a corporate knowledge base.

Organizational process assets can play a significant role in facilitating the use of adaptive approaches in project management. Here are some assets that can be particularly helpful:

- **Culture of collaboration and continuous improvement**   An organizational culture that values collaboration and embraces change is well-suited to an adaptive approach. This can be reflected in processes such as regular team retrospectives, open communication channels, and cross-functional teams. Governance processes that allow for flexibility and adaptation, such as lightweight reporting and feedback loops, can support the use of adaptive approaches.

- **Agile methodology frameworks**   Frameworks such as Scrum, Kanban, and Lean are designed to support adaptive project management and provide guidance on best practices and processes. Best practices can include plans, templates, artifacts, policies, and procedures established to support project efforts. They also include information available from previous projects through historical information, often referred to as *knowledge repositories*.

- **Agile coaching and training**   Providing coaching and training on agile methodologies and adaptive project management can help teams to build skills and knowledge, as well as promote a culture of continuous learning and improvement. This culture may include additional experimentation and prototyping to capture feedback on a more frequent basis—enabling small changes to be easily incorporated into the result.

Even in adaptive methods, an organization may still require some documentation and adherence to policies and activities—but they should be more focused on the purpose and value of those organizational requirements than on just developing artifacts to meet previous deliverables.

Determine How to Plan Project Iterations

Task 2

Project iterations involve breaking down the project work into smaller, manageable units to deliver value to the customer in shorter intervals. Here are the steps to plan project iterations:

1. *Define the project scope.* Define the project's boundaries, objectives, goals, deliverables, and stakeholders' expectations. This will provide clarity on what needs to be delivered within each iteration.

2. *Create a prioritized product backlog.* Create a list of all the features and requirements that need to be implemented. Prioritize them based on the value they provide to the customer and their dependencies. This will serve as the basis for planning the iterations.

3. *Define the iteration length.* Define the length of the iteration, which can range from a few days to several weeks, depending on the project's complexity.

4. *Select the work for the iteration.* Based on the prioritized product backlog, select the work that can be completed within the iteration. This should include a mix of features, bugs, technical debt, and other work items.

5. *Break down the work into smaller units.* Break down the selected work items into smaller units, such as user stories or tasks. This will make it easier to estimate and track progress.

6. *Estimate the effort required.* Estimate the effort required to complete each work item using techniques such as planning poker, T-shirt sizing, or story points.

7. *Plan the iteration.* Plan the iteration by assigning work items to team members, setting realistic goals, and defining the acceptance criteria for each work item.

8. *Execute the iteration.* Work on the assigned items during the iteration, collaborate with the team, and ensure that the acceptance criteria are met.

9. *Review and retrospect the iteration.* At the end of the iteration, review the work done, evaluate the results, and retrospect on what worked well and what needs to be improved.

By following these steps, teams can plan project iterations effectively, deliver value to the customer incrementally, and continuously improve their processes.

Distinguish the Logical Units of Iterations

Task 2, Enabler 1

When planning project iterations, it is essential to define the logical units of iteration to ensure that the work is organized, structured, and delivered efficiently. The following are the logical units of iteration:

- **Epics**   Epics are the highest-level of logical units and are often used to describe large and complex features that require significant development effort. Epics are typically broken down into smaller units, such as user stories, to facilitate iterative development.

- **User stories**   User stories are a common method for breaking down epics into smaller, more manageable units. User stories define requirements from the end-user perspective. They represent a specific feature or functionality that needs to be delivered, and they should be small enough to be completed within an iteration. User stories typically include acceptance criteria, which define when a story is considered complete.

- **Tasks**   Tasks are the smallest unit of work in an iteration. They represent individual activities that need to be completed to deliver a user story. Tasks should be estimated in hours, and they are typically assigned to a specific team member.

When planning project iterations, epics are broken down into user stories, which are further broken down into tasks. The goal is to have a set of well-defined user stories that can be completed within a single iteration. This allows for better visibility into the progress of the project and provides an opportunity to adjust the plan if necessary.

Epics represent the highest level of iteration, followed by user stories, and tasks as the smallest logical unit of iteration. Breaking down development work into logical units allows for greater agility and flexibility in responding to changing requirements and helps teams to deliver software more quickly and efficiently.

Interpret the Pros and Cons of the Iteration

Task 2, Enabler 2
In Agile frameworks and methodologies, project iterations are a core component of the development process. Here are the pros and cons of using iterations in Agile project planning:

Pros:

- **Early and continuous delivery of value**   Iterations in Agile allow for the early and continuous delivery of value to the customer. By delivering working software incrementally, the customer can provide feedback, and the team can make adjustments to meet customer needs.

- **Adaptability and flexibility**   Agile iterations allow for flexibility and adaptability to changing requirements. The team can adjust the project plan based on customer feedback and emerging requirements.

- **Improved visibility and predictability**   Agile iterations provide better visibility and predictability into the project's progress. By measuring progress at the end of each iteration, the team can identify potential issues early and take corrective action.

- **Continuous improvement**   Agile iterations allow for continuous improvement of the development process. The team can reflect on the previous iteration's results and adjust the process to improve performance.

- **Increased collaboration**   Agile iterations encourage collaboration and communication among team members and stakeholders, leading to better teamwork and a more cohesive team.

Cons:

- **Increased planning overhead** Agile iterations require more planning and coordination than traditional project management. This can increase the overhead and administrative burden of the project.

- **Risk of scope creep** Agile iterations can increase the risk of scope creep, where additional requirements are added to the project scope, leading to delays and increased costs.

- **Dependency management** Agile iterations require effective management of dependencies between work items, which can be challenging and time-consuming.

- **Inflexibility** Agile iterations can be inflexible if the work items are not well-defined or estimated. This can lead to delays and missed deadlines.

Translate This WBS to an Adaptive Iteration

Task 2, Enabler 3

In agile frameworks, the work breakdown structure (WBS) is typically replaced with a product backlog, which is a prioritized list of features or user stories that describe the functionality that the product should have.

To translate a WBS to an adaptive iteration, we would first need to break down the WBS tasks into smaller, more manageable pieces of work that can be completed in a single iteration. This breakdown would involve identifying the specific features or user stories that would be required to complete each task.

Once you have identified the features or user stories, the development team prioritizes them based on their value to the customer and their level of effort. This prioritization would be used to create an initial product backlog for the iteration.

During the adaptive iteration, the team would work on completing the highest-priority features or user stories from the product backlog. As they work, they would regularly review their progress and adjust the backlog as determined by the business, adding or removing items based on changing priorities, or new information.

At the end of the iteration, the team would deliver a potentially shippable working product that includes all the completed features or user stories. They would then conduct a retrospective to reflect on what worked well and what could be improved for the next iteration. This process would continue until the product is complete or the team decides to stop development.

Determine Inputs for Scope

Task 2, Enabler 4

In an adaptive project, *scope* refers to the boundaries of the project and what is and is not included in the project. The scope is developed and refined throughout the project based on the project's objectives, goals, and requirements.

PART II

Here are some inputs for defining and refining the scope in an adaptive project:

- **Stakeholder requirements**   Stakeholder requirements are a critical input for defining the scope of the project. These requirements come from the individuals or groups who have a stake in the project, which can include customers, end users, sponsors, and other stakeholders. The project team must understand these requirements and ensure that the project scope addresses them.

- **Project objectives**   The project objectives provide a high-level view of what the project is intended to achieve. These objectives are typically defined at the beginning of the project and can guide the project scope. The scope should align with the project objectives and contribute to their achievement. Even though most adaptive projects don't refer to inputs for scope specifically, there is still some need to understand why the project is being done, the vision of the result, and what objectives are to be met.

- **Business case**   The business case is a document that outlines the justification for the project. It includes the expected benefits, costs, and risks associated with the project. The business case can help to clarify the scope by identifying what is and is not included in the project. As just mentioned, understanding why the project is being done, the vision of the result, and what objectives are to be met is usually part of the business case. In addition, at a very high level, what is to be "in scope" and what is considered "out of scope" is included in these initial documents.

- **Constraints**   Constraints are factors that limit the project team's ability to complete the project. They can include things like time, budget, resources, or technical limitations. The project scope must consider these constraints to ensure that the project is feasible and achievable.

- **Lessons learned**   Lessons learned from previous projects or iterations can be used to refine the scope for the current project. By identifying what worked well and what didn't work in previous projects, the team can adjust the scope to better meet the needs of the current project.

- **Change requests**   Adaptive projects may not have a clear definition of the result. Therefore, the various items that may be included in the scope are continually prioritized, developed, reviewed, and accepted. These items are often identified as epics, or large user stories, at the beginning of the project and then continually prioritized and decomposed into smaller user stories. The detail for each user story is not developed until the story is ready to be developed, allowing changes to be incorporated as more information becomes available. As the project progresses, stakeholders may identify new requirements or changes to existing requirements. These change requests should be evaluated to determine if they should be incorporated into the project scope.

- **Project team expertise**   The expertise and knowledge of the project team can also be an input for defining and refining the project scope. Input and additional information from SMEs or domain experts are needed to help provide the detailed understanding of the individual stories. This is part of the definition of ready, including any required sequence, information needed, and business rules to be applied. The team's experience with similar projects can help to identify potential challenges and opportunities and guide the project scope accordingly.

Explain the Importance of Adaptive Project Tracking Versus Predictive, Plan-Based Tracking

Task 2, Enabler 5

Adaptive project tracking and predictive, plan-based tracking are two different approaches to project management. Adaptive project tracking is associated with agile and iterative methodologies, while predictive, plan-based tracking is associated with more traditional project management.

Adaptive Project Tracking

Here are some reasons why adaptive project tracking is important:

- **Flexibility**   Allows for greater flexibility in managing the project. The team can adjust their approach and priorities based on changing requirements or priorities, which is especially important in fast-moving industries or projects with evolving needs.

- **Focus on value**   Focuses on delivering value to stakeholders as quickly as possible. This helps ensure that the project is meeting stakeholder needs and that the team is delivering the most valuable features first.

- **Continuous improvement**   Encourages continuous improvement through frequent retrospectives and a willingness to adjust the approach. This helps the team learn from their mistakes and find ways to work more efficiently and effectively.

- **Collaboration**   Promotes collaboration between team members and stakeholders. By working closely together and sharing information in a transparent way, the team can ensure that everyone is aligned and working toward the same goals.

- **Early detection of issues**   Includes frequent checkpoints and opportunities for feedback. This can help the team detect issues early on and address them before they become bigger problems.

Adaptive project tracking is usually performed at the iteration level, to determine whether the expected results are delivered and accepted. As the user stories from each iteration are approved, they are accumulated into the overall functionality that can be delivered as part of a release.

The measurements of these results may take on different forms, as explained in the following sections.

PART II

Story Points   In Agile project tracking, story points are used as a relative estimation tool rather than an absolute measurement of time or effort. This allows for greater flexibility and adaptability in the project management process. User story points are assigned to user stories in relation to the size of the user stories.. Story points are a subjective measure that considers the complexity, effort, and uncertainty of a task. Story points are a way to estimate the complexity and effort required for individual stories. These are then combined to determine the velocity, or number of story points, that can be delivered during an iteration, based on previous results.

During the sprint, the team tracks the progress of each user story or task by updating its status and the number of story points completed. This helps to identify any delays or bottlenecks in the sprint.

Velocity   *Velocity* is the rate at which a team completes tasks in an agile project. It is measured by the number of story points completed in a sprint or iteration. If the velocity, or number of story points delivered, does not match the expected number, then a review, usually done during a retrospective, is conducted to identify the cause. It may identify that the stories were not defined well enough or were more complicated than expected, and changes to the initial estimating may need to be made. The progress to completion of the story points within an iteration is usually shown on a velocity chart. Later in this chapter, we'll take a deeper dive into velocity.

Kanban Board   A Kanban board is a visual tool used to manage work and workflow in a project. It allows team members to see the status of tasks and identify any bottlenecks or issues. Its emphasis is on just-in-time delivery and limiting work in progress (WIP). The Kanban board data is used to adjust the workflow or team processes. For example, adaptive methods using a timeboxed approach estimate the number of story points for a release, even baselining those stories and points, but to be truly adaptive, the determination of what is done within each iteration is based on the continual refinement and prioritization of stories by the product owner as well as incorporation of feedback received during the demonstration.

Burnup/Burndown   Burnup and burndown charts are visual tools used to track project progress against a set of goals or targets, typically toward a release. A burnup chart shows the work completed over time, while a burndown chart shows the remaining work to be completed.

Figure 5-1 is a burnup chart. Like the burndown chart, this chart shows the accumulation of completed features, completed tasks, or work hours completed. It's ideal for any time you want to show the accumulation of something rather than the completion of an item. You can use a burnup chart for the sprint backlog, product backlog, or tracking the total accumulation of work hours or workdays in an iteration or project. In this burnup chart, the total number of user stories completed for the product backlog is shown on the y-axis, and each iteration is plotted across the x-axis. The solid line represents the number of user stories in the product backlog, and the dashed line represents the user stories completed in each iteration.

Figure 5-1
Burnup charts show the accumulation of items completed.

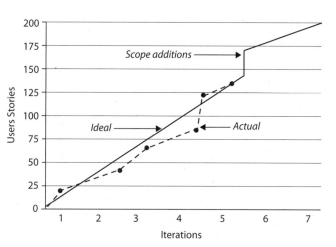

Notice how the solid line in Figure 5-1 moves upward from 130 to 170. This shows the addition of features needed during the project. Because agile expects and welcomes changes, the total number of user stories can increase, or decrease, during the project.

The burnup chart can track the total number of user stories in the product backlog, and when new stories, due to change requests, are added to the product backlog, the y-axis reflects this in the chart.

EXAM TIP A good exam question would be to define why the solid line changed during the project. And, of course, the answer is because there were additional features added to the product backlog.

A burndown chart is used when you have a long list of items, such as features in the product backlog, and by completing each item, the list is "burned down." As you complete more and more items in the list, the list sizzles down and down until you're done. In agile, a burndown chart can be used for the product backlog and the sprint backlog.

Figure 5-2 is a burndown chart for a sprint backlog. The y-axis represents the total number of tasks in the sprint backlog, and the x-axis represents the timeline for the sprint, 28 days in this scenario. The solid line in the chart is the ideal flow of work over the sprint—steady work each day to reach the iteration's end with all the tasks completed. The ideal line is just that: ideal. It is based on estimates and is not always accurate. The dashed line in the chart shows the actual work performed and correlates to the x-axis to show how much work is remaining and correlates to the y-axis to show how many days are left in the sprint to do the work. Every day in the sprint a point will be added to the actual line to show progress against the ideal line. If the dashed line, the actual work, is above the ideal line, then there is more work to do, and the team is running late on planned work for the sprint. If the dashed line is below the ideal line, then the team is

PART II

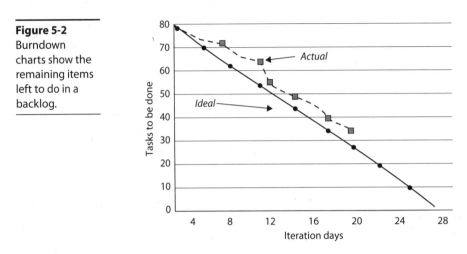

Figure 5-2
Burndown charts show the remaining items left to do in a backlog.

ahead of schedule on the project tasks. You don't want the actual work to be too far above or below the ideal line. A big fluctuation between the two can mean that the estimated work for the sprint wasn't accurate.

Cumulative Flow Diagram   You're most likely to use a cumulative flow diagram with tasks in a Kanban board. Recall that in Kanban, tasks are pulled from the queue into the WIP, moving from left to right through each phase of the project work. A cumulative flow diagram can seem overwhelming at first glance, but it's actually a simple stack diagram showing the number of tasks in each Kanban column. For example, a software development project can have a Kanban board with four columns: Backlog, Development, Testing, and Deployed. The chart will show how many items are in each column of the Kanban board.

In Figure 5-3, the cumulative flow diagram shows the total number of items on the y-axis and the total number of days on the x-axis. When you look at the cumulative flow diagram, each shaded shape in the chart is stacked according to the columns of Backlog, Development, Testing, and Deployed. The shaded areas within the chart show how many items are in each phase of the project work. For example, the product backlog has 200 items total, while there are a total of 85 items deployed from the project. The cumulative flow diagram can also show when there are significant changes to the product backlog. When the customer adds items to the project, this increases the number of user stories or features to be created. In a cumulative flow diagram, this displays as a stair step in the product backlog portion of the chart.

The WIP is represented by items in the chart that are between the product backlog and the deployment. At a glance, the number of items in the WIP should be uniform along the chart. Ideally, the shaded areas of the chart trend upward from left to right with the number of items deployed increasing, the number of items to do in the product backlog decreasing, and the phases representing the WIP staying uniform throughout the

Figure 5-3
Cumulative flow diagrams show the number of items in each phase of a project.

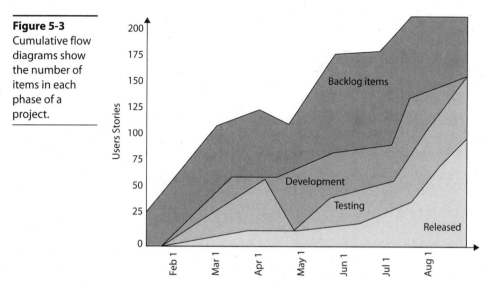

PART II

project. When there's a change between the items in WIP and deployment, there's likely a bottleneck or blocker in the project, and the issue should be addressed during your daily scrum meeting.

Earned Value Analysis   As covered in Chapter 4, earned value analysis (EVA) is a project management technique used to track the progress of a project and assess its performance in terms of schedule and cost. EVA provides insight into the efficiency and effectiveness of a project.

In adaptive project tracking, EVA can be used as a tool to monitor and control the progress of work within iterations or sprints.

To complete agile EVA, you'll need four things:

- **Actual cost of the release**   The costs are needed to calculate the suite of formulas. You'll need the anticipated cost per release, not just the cost for the entire project. You can predict this by the cost of each story point in an iteration and the velocity of the team.

- **Estimated product backlog**   The product backlog represents the remaining project scope.

- **Product release plan**   This is when the increments will be released and the expected number of iterations.

- **Assumed velocity**   This is the number of user story points the team can complete per iteration.

As presented in Chapter 2, the base formulas for agile EVA are like traditional earned value management:

- **Planned value (PV)** The value of the planned work to be completed in the iteration. For example, if the cost per user story point is $1,600 and there are 35 user story points, the planned value for iteration is $56,000.

- **Earned value (EV)** The value of the work actually completed in the iteration. If the team completes only 30 user story points, the earned value would be 30 times $1,600, for an earned value of $48,000.

- **Actual cost (AC)** The cost of the work actually completed in the iteration. This is the actual money spent in the project. If the team had to work overtime or hire a resource to help with the project and they spent $55,000, that would be the actual cost for the iteration.

- **Budget at completion (BAC)** The anticipated cost for the product release; there may be several iterations to get to a release. The product release plan will predict, though not always reliably, how many iterations will be needed. For example, if there are three iterations to get to the first release, you can predict the BAC for the release by taking the number of iterations times the velocity and then times the cost per user story point. Here's the formula:

  > Three iterations with a velocity of 35 equates to 105 story points ($3 \times 35 = 105$)
  > In this example, the cost for each story point is $1,600.
  > So, the BAC for the release is $168,000 ($105 \times \$1,600$).

With these metrics you can quickly perform EVA for the project. Table 5-1 shows a breakdown of earned value management for an agile project.

 EXAM TIP I'd expect a question or two on earned value analysis (CV, SV, CPI, and SPI) in agile or hybrid projects on your exam.

Predictive, Plan-Based Project Tracking

Predictive, plan-based project tracking is insufficient for adaptive projects because Agile is based on principles of adaptability, flexibility, and continuous improvement, which are not well-supported by a predictive, plan-based approach.

Predictive, plan-based tracking is useful in projects where the requirements are well-defined and stable and the project plan can be followed closely. This approach is particularly useful in projects with strict deadlines and budget constraints, where any deviation from the plan could have significant consequences.

In predictive, plan-based project tracking, the project plan is created at the beginning of the project and followed throughout the project, regardless of changes in requirements or feedback from stakeholders. This approach assumes that the requirements are

What is the expected velocity?	40
What is the cost per story point?	$1,000
How many iterations per release?	4
How complete is the project?	50%
How complete should the project be?	55%
How much has the project spent?	$83,000
Budget at completion (for the product release)	$160,000
Actual costs	$83,000
Earned value	$80,000
Planned value	$88,000
Cost variance	−$3,000
Schedule variance	−$8000
Cost performance index	0.96
Schedule performance index	0.91
Estimate at completion	$166,000
Estimate to complete	$83,000
To-complete performance index (BAC)	1.04
To-complete performance index (EAC)	0.96
Variance at completion	−$6,000

Table 5-1   Earned Value Analysis Applied to Agile

well-defined and stable and that the project can be completed according to a predefined plan and rolling wave planning.

However, in adaptive projects, the requirements are often not fully known or may change over time, and there is a need to be able to adapt to changing requirements and feedback from stakeholders. The adaptive approach is based on the idea of delivering value to the customer in small increments and continuously improving the product based on feedback and learning.

Adaptive project tracking is better suited for agile projects because it allows for flexibility and adaptability in response to changing requirements and feedback from stakeholders. This approach allows the team to make changes to the project plan as needed, without being tied to a predefined plan.

In addition, adaptive project tracking provides continuous feedback and improvement, which is a key principle of Agile. By adapting to changes in requirements and feedback, the team can continuously improve the product and ensure that it meets the needs of the customer.

Determine How to Document Project Controls for an Adaptive Project

Task 3

Project controls for an adaptive project are a set of tools and processes used to manage and monitor project progress in a flexible and responsive manner. Documenting project controls for an adaptive project is essential to ensure that the project stays on track and meets its goals.

Documenting project controls for an adaptive project typically includes but is not limited to:

- **Define project objectives and goals** Defining project objectives and goals in the project charter is critical to the success of the project. It provides a clear direction for the project team and helps to ensure that everyone is working toward the same outcomes. By following the SMART (specific, measurable, achievable, relevant, and time-bound) framework and obtaining stakeholder buy-in, project objectives and goals can be effectively defined and achieved.

- **Develop a project plan** The project plan is a dynamic document that outlines the approach, scope, timeline, budget, and resources needed to achieve the project objectives. It is flexible and responsive to changing requirements, allowing the project team to adapt to changing circumstances and emerging opportunities.

- **Define project roles and responsibilities** Clearly define the roles and responsibilities of the project team members, including the project manager, scrum master, product owner, and development team. This helps to ensure that everyone knows what they are responsible for and what is expected of them. The resource management plan is a formal document that outlines how resources will be managed and allocated within a project.

- **Document change control** In an adaptive project, changes are expected. However, it is important to have a change control process in place to ensure that changes are managed properly. The change control process should include a clear definition of how changes will be identified, evaluated, approved, and implemented. Use a change control plan to outline the process for managing changes within a project.

- **Establish communication protocols** Communication is crucial in an adaptive project. Establish clear communication protocols that define how information will be shared among the project team members, stakeholders, and other relevant parties. Communication protocols are typically documented in a formal communications plan.

- **Document project progress** Keep detailed records of project progress, including sprint backlog items completed, burndown charts, and retrospectives. This helps the project team to identify areas where they need to improve and to adjust their approach as necessary. Here are some places where project progress can be documented: project management software, shared documents, communication channels (such as e-mail, instant messaging, or video conferencing), project dashboard, and project meetings.

- **Conduct regular project reviews**   Regular project reviews are important to ensure that the project is on track and to identify areas for improvement. Conduct regular reviews with stakeholders and the project team to review progress and adjust the project plan, as necessary. Document project reviews in the lessons learned register.

Identify Artifacts that Are Used in Adaptive Projects

Task 3, Enabler 1

An artifact is a tangible or intangible item that is created, maintained, or used during an adaptive project. These artifacts help the team to manage work, track progress, and make adjustments based on changing requirements and feedback.

Here are some common artifacts that are used in adaptive projects:

- **Product backlog**   A product backlog is a prioritized list of features, requirements, and tasks that need to be completed to achieve the project objectives. It is used to manage and prioritize work and to ensure that the most valuable features are developed first.

- **Sprint backlog**   A sprint backlog is a list of tasks that are scheduled to be completed during a sprint. It is created at the beginning of each sprint and is based on the prioritized items in the product backlog.

- **User stories**   User stories are short, simple descriptions of a feature or requirement from the perspective of the end user. They are used to define the scope of work and provide a clear understanding of what needs to be delivered.

- **Burndown charts**   A burndown chart is a visual representation of the work remaining in a project. It tracks progress over time and helps the team to identify if they are on track to meet their objectives.

- **Definition of done (DoD)**   The definition of done is a shared understanding of what constitutes a completed task or feature. It ensures that everyone on the team understands what needs to be done to complete a task or feature.

- **Minimum viable product (MVP)**   A minimum viable product is the most basic version of a product that can be delivered to meet the needs of the end user. It is used to test the market, validate assumptions, and gather feedback to inform further development.

- **Minimum business increment (MBI)**   The smallest possible deliverable unit that provides some value to the customer and can be independently deployed, tested, and validated. MBIs are often used in agile methodologies to break down larger features or projects into smaller, manageable pieces that can be completed and delivered more efficiently.

- **Retrospective**   A retrospective is a meeting held at the end of a sprint or project phase to review what went well, what didn't go well, and what can be improved. It is used to identify areas for improvement and to make adjustments to the project plan as needed.

- **Continuous integration and continuous deployment (CI/CD) pipeline**
  A CI/CD pipeline is a series of automated processes used to build, test, and deploy software updates. It is used to ensure that changes are delivered quickly and consistently.

- **Agile release plan**   An agile release plan is a high-level plan that outlines the release schedule for the project. It provides a roadmap for the project team and stakeholders and ensures that everyone is aligned on the project objectives and timeline.

- **Velocity chart**   A velocity chart is a graphical representation used in agile project management to track the progress of a team's work. It shows the amount of work completed by the team over a specified period of time, typically in a sprint or iteration. The vertical axis of the chart represents the amount of work completed, often in story points or other units of work. The horizontal axis represents time, usually in days or weeks.

By using these artifacts, and others, teams can work more efficiently and effectively, while also ensuring that the project is aligned with stakeholder expectations.

Explain the Components of an Adaptive Plan

Task 4

An *adaptive plan* is a type of plan that can adjust to changing circumstances or new information. The components of an adaptive plan typically include the following:

- **Goals and objectives**   The goals and objectives of an adaptive plan provide a clear picture of what the plan is intended to achieve. These should be specific, measurable, achievable, relevant, and time-bound (SMART) and should be reviewed and updated as needed.

- **Key performance indicators (KPIs)**   KPIs are metrics that are used to measure progress toward the goals and objectives of the plan. KPIs help to track progress and identify areas where changes may need to be made.

- **Risk management**   An adaptive plan should include a risk management strategy that identifies potential risks and outlines actions to mitigate or respond to them. This helps to minimize the impact of unforeseen events and helps the plan to stay on track.

- **Resource allocation**   Resource allocation involves determining how resources, such as personnel, equipment, and finances, will be used to achieve the goals of the plan. An adaptive plan should be flexible enough to adjust resource allocation as needed to respond to changing circumstances.

- **Communication plan**   A communication plan outlines how information will be shared and disseminated among stakeholders, team members, and decision-makers. Effective communication is critical for ensuring that everyone is on the same page and that changes are implemented smoothly.

- **Evaluation and feedback mechanisms** An adaptive plan should include mechanisms for evaluating progress and gathering feedback from stakeholders. This allows for adjustments to be made based on real-time feedback and helps to ensure that the plan stays on track toward achieving its goals.

Distinguish Between the Components of Different Adaptive Methodologies

Task 4, Enabler 1

Agile project management is not just one approach to getting things done, but rather many different approaches and different philosophies to project completion.

All adaptive methodologies are largely based on the Agile Manifesto (https://agilemanifesto.org/), and they share three common actions:

- *Transparency* requires trust, agreement, and open communication throughout the project. One of the first examples of transparency begins with the project's definition of done (DoD), which defines how we know when the project is done.

- *Inspection* is the review of the artifacts, the progress, and the quality of the work. Consistent with maintaining transparency, you divulge discoveries, good or bad, to the rest of the project team. Inspection should not get in the way of the work, but inspection is most beneficial when you have skilled inspectors inspecting the work.

- *Adaptation* is needed when issues arise. In other words, if the solution is not going to be acceptable, fix the problem. Adjustments are made as soon as possible to minimize additional deviation. You fix the problem right now. Do not keep moving forward in the project with this problem because you will have more and more work based on the current faulty product. You don't want a future deliverable based on a past problem. Fix this problem as soon as possible to minimize additional deviations from what the customer expects.

 EXAM TIP All approaches to agile project management have these three principles—transparency, inspection, and adaptation (TIA). On your exam, when you're faced with a tough agile or hybrid question, think of TIA. You'll want to determine what the project manager can do to be transparent, what the team can do to inspect the work results and the approach, and what adaptations are needed to reach value within the project.

There are several different adaptive methodologies in Agile that are interpretations of how the Agile Manifesto and its companion 12 principles should be applied to actual project activities. These methodologies are based on the principles of Agile and are adapted to fit different types of projects and teams. Each methodology has its own approach and practices, but they all share a common focus on delivering value to the customer in a timely and cost-effective manner, while also adapting to changing requirements and feedback from stakeholders.

EXAM TIP Your CAPM exam will test you on the common principles of agile project management, and you may encounter a few specific questions from the different adaptive methodologies covered in this section.

Regardless of the methodology chosen, the goal is to deliver a continuous flow of value to customers on a timely basis, which in turn will result in better outcomes for the organization. They are based on values of Lean thinking.

The following are key aspects of Lean that are incorporated in the various agile frameworks:

- Delivering value
- Respect for people
- Minimizing waste
- Being transparent
- Adapting to change
- Continuously improving

Different adaptive methodologies, such as those specifically listed in Task 4—Scrum, Extreme Programming (XP), Scaled Agile Framework (SAFe), and Kanban—share some common components, but they also have unique features that distinguish them from one another. The following sections cover the unique features of many different adaptive methodologies that you should be familiar with for the CAPM exam. Note that these include methodologies that are not specifically listed in Task 4, which identifies Scrum, XP, SAFe, and Kanban as *examples*, not as an all-inclusive list. Scrum and XP are covered in the most depth because they have the most prominence both in the real world and on the exam.

 EXAM TIP Other than Scrum, XP is where you will probably have the next largest number of agile questions on your exam.

Scrum

Scrum is probably the framework most often associated with agile approaches, as it is one of the most well-known frameworks, both by project team members and management. Scrum defines project team roles, activities (referred to as ceremonies), and documents (referred to as artifacts) and provides an iterative approach for developing working results.

The scrum team includes the following members:

- **Product owner** Responsible for prioritizing the work to maximize the value of the result for the customer. The product owner owns the product backlog.

- **Development team members**   Cross-functional and self-organizing individuals who have the capability to deliver the results without requiring other resources outside the team

- **Scrum master**   Works with the team to remove any impediments while supporting and coaching on the understanding and adherence to the Scrum process

The scrum ceremonies are repeated for each timeboxed iteration and include

- **Sprint planning**   A meeting during which user stories for the upcoming sprint are discussed, sized, and committed to for the immediate sprint. This meeting is held with the product owner and development team members to help understand the detail behind the prioritized stories being presented for potential inclusion in the upcoming sprint. The team sizes the individual stories based on complexity and effort and often assigns story points to each story. The combination of the story points is then compared to the team "velocity" to help determine how much the team feels comfortable being able to complete. The agreed-upon stories are then placed on the sprint backlog.

- **Sprint**   The timebox during which the stories that have been selected during the sprint planning meeting, and now are identified on the iteration backlog, will be developed.

- **Daily scrum**   A daily collaboration meeting of the team members, facilitated by the scrum master, where team members individually identify what they worked on the previous day, what they are planning to work on today, and whether they are encountering any obstacles that the scrum master can help remove. They are often referred to as "stand-up" meetings, as they should be limited to 15 minutes with all team members standing and communicating with each other. These are *not* daily status meetings, but rather sharing of information among team members.

 NOTE   Some organizations are deprecating the term "stand-up meeting" to be inclusive of people who can't stand up.

- **Sprint review**   A meeting held at the end of each iteration during which the team demonstrates for stakeholders the work the team has done and, hopefully, receives the stakeholders' approval. Sprint reviews are attended by the team members, the product owner, and any other identified stakeholders. The sum of the story points for the stories that are completed becomes the velocity of that sprint.

- **Sprint retrospective**   A meeting held at the end of each sprint during which the team reflects on the work just completed, identifying things that went well and should be continued, as well as areas where improvements could be made. These reflections are often the result of analyzing why they were not able to finish a story or meet the expectations for the sprint. These short team meetings are usually facilitated by the scrum master and include the team members.

The scrum artifacts include the following:

- **Product backlog** Includes all the requests received for inclusion in the project. These items can vary in size and complexity, ranging from "epics" (vary large stories) to "user stories" that follow a format of "I (as a user) want to (requirement) so that (benefit)."

- **Sprint backlog** Includes the specific user stories that have been prioritized by the product owner, sized and analyzed by the team members, and committed to completion during an individual sprint.

- **Increments** Working software that is released to the customer at the end of an iteration or sprint. The software may not be complete, but it provides some value to the customer and can be used to gather feedback and make improvements.

 NOTE In agile project management, an iteration and a sprint are both timeboxed periods during which the team works on a specific set of tasks or objectives. However, there are some differences between the two.

An iteration is a fixed period of time, typically one to four weeks, during which the team works on a set of user stories or features. The goal of an iteration is to deliver working software that provides value to the customer. At the end of the iteration, the team reviews the work that was completed and determines what they can do better in the next iteration. Iterations are a key component of Agile and allow for continuous feedback and improvement.

A sprint is a specific type of iteration used in Scrum, which is a widely used agile methodology. A sprint is typically two to four weeks long and is focused on delivering a specific set of user stories or features. During a sprint, the team works to complete the work identified in the sprint backlog, which is a prioritized list of user stories or features. At the end of the sprint, the team holds a sprint review, where they demonstrate the working software that was completed during the sprint and gather feedback from stakeholders. The team also holds a sprint retrospective, where they review the process and identify areas for improvement.

 EXAM TIP Both iterations and sprints are timeboxed periods during which the team works on specific objectives. While iterations is a general term used in Agile, sprints are a specific type of iteration used in Scrum.

Diving into Scrum The Scrum framework is applied not only to project management but also to product management.. It is an agile approach that follows repeatable activities to move the project toward the definition of done. The project moves through iterations, called *sprints*, to work on the most important to least important requirements of the stakeholders.

While there are many different approaches to agile, all agile projects work in sprints, iterations, or increments. An *increment* is a chunk of usable product developed in each sprint. An increment is a potentially releasable part of the final product. Each increment is appended to the prior increments. Think of a freight train; each increment is just another boxcar in the train. In most incremental projects, several increments will create key, usable benefits that will then be released. The product owner will determine what qualifications must be in place before a release may occur. An increment is the sum of all the sprints that you have completed.

Iterations are also sprints, and they build on what's been completed in the past, but they refine and improve on the product. Imagine sketching out a painting and then refining the sketch, painting over the sketch, repainting the sketch, and so on, until the painting is perfected. That's the idea behind iterations—you iterate on what you've completed. Creating a website is a good example of an iterative project, as the team and product owner can quickly see a mockup and then a functional prototype, then the text is added, then more functionality is added, and so on. This is, unfortunately, where things get blurry in agile: iterations may, or may not, qualify for incremental releases to the customer. The product owner may determine some iterations create an increment and should be released. Other products may not be released until the entire product is created. Every project is different.

Before the team gets to the requirements in a sprint, the team needs a *vision statement*, which describes the goals and why the project exists. It's a simple document that keeps the purpose of the project and the value the project brings in the forefront. A vision statement is a short document that must have five elements to be considered good:

- Unambiguous definition of the project
- Clear and simple language
- Alignment with the organization's value
- Realistic expectations of the project
- Short and direct

Next, at the launch of the project's first sprint, there should be a product roadmap. The product owner is likely to work with the project manager, the scrum master, and the team to develop a product roadmap. This is one area where agile projects shine over predictive, plan-based projects. If you're building a house, there is no benefit to the homeowner until the house is completely done. The homeowner can't move into a portion of the house until the entire house is ready. In agile projects, the customer could begin using a portion of the software, such as version 1, while your team continues to build and create version 2. Each release of the software builds on what's already been created.

The product roadmap is a map of how the project should move from start to finish with intermittent deliverables to the stakeholders. It's an ideal document of how the team will get from the start to the end. It answers what conditions must be met to allow the product owner to do a release, what the components of a release are, and the result of the project.

Figure 5-4 is the big picture of Scrum, and it begins with the product backlog, which is all known requirements. The product backlog is owned and maintained by the product owner, a businessperson who knows what the business values and knows how a scrum project works. The product owner keeps the product backlog prioritized based on the business value and the expected monetary value of the item. When changes are requested,

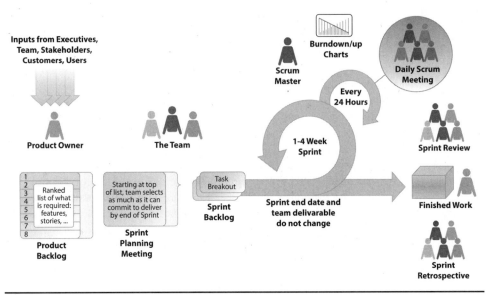

Figure 5-4 Scrum follows a logical and iterative approach throughout the project.

the product owner evaluates the change, puts it into the product backlog, and reprioritizes the list of requirements with the new addition. Adding a requirement does not mean it goes to the bottom of the product backlog; it could be an important change and be pushed to the top of the backlog, plopped in the middle, or appear somewhere near the bottom—it's all based on value.

NOTE User stories are predominantly prioritized based on the value to the customer, but some user stories carry significant risks and should be moved to earlier in the project. The product owner and team can calculate the expected monetary value of the risk for the user story as follows: probability × impact = expected monetary value.

As previously discussed, the actual work of creating how the deliverable is performed is called a *sprint*. In general, the most common sprint length in Agile is two weeks, but some teams prefer shorter sprints (e.g., one week) or longer sprints (e.g., four weeks). The key is to find a sprint length that works best for the team and the stakeholders while still allowing for effective collaboration and the delivery of high-quality work. At the start of each sprint, the product owner, the developers, and the scrum master all meet to plan out the work for the sprint. As mentioned earlier, this meeting, called *sprint planning*, focuses on the product backlog and how much work the developers believe they can accomplish. The team reviews the items in the prioritized sprint backlog, which are called *user stories*. The items are called user stories because they tell a little story about the user, how they'd use the action, and the value they'd receive from the action.

Creating the Sprint Backlog   The team, working with the product owner, will review the most valuable user stories from the product backlog and determine how many of the user stories they can complete during the sprint. This first meeting of each sprint is the sprint planning meeting. The team all agrees on the chunk of work that they feel they can accomplish during the next sprint. This chunk of selected user stories always starts with the most important items in the backlog first. Sometimes you'll see this concept referred to as "eating your dessert first," as the team first gets to the good stuff that creates the most value for the customers. The user stories that are selected for the sprint are now referred to as the *sprint backlog*. The sprint backlog does not change once it is created. The sprint backlog helps the team create a sprint goal: what the team will accomplish during the next sprint. Each sprint repeats this process of sprint planning, and this meeting typically lasts eight hours for a four-week sprint.

> **NOTE**   User stories should not be so big that they can't be completed during one sprint of the project. You do not want stories so big that they span several sprints. You want the story to be sized appropriately so that it can be done in one four-week iteration or however long the sprint is in your project.

Completing the Daily Work   Next, we get into our daily work. This is the heart of the project where the team is focused on getting the work done. In this part of the project, it's the team, not a project manager, that determines who'll do what in the project and what's important to get done next. This is why scrum teams are self-organizing and self-led. They don't look to a project manager to tell them what to do. However, early in a scrum project, the role of the scrum master, which is similar to a project manager, is to coach the team. The scrum master may help the team determine who'll do what task, coordinate events, and provide some control over the work. As the project moves along, the scrum master will control activities less, and the team will become more self-led.

Sometimes I am asked, "What if somebody wants to do a six- to eight-week sprint or even a ten-week sprint? What's the problem with that?" Longer sprints introduce risk, because it's a long time to work on a product without review and interaction from the customer. Longer sprints might also affect the ability to go to market because the team has a deliverable that could be a released increment at a two-to-four-week sprint, but the product owner must wait for the end of the ten-week sprint. Remember, the product owner and customer don't see or receive any value until the end of the sprint.

Another consideration for the sprint duration is that the team is likely going to change. Changing team members during a sprint is not recommended; people leaving or joining a team during the middle of a long sprint creates new risks and problems: learning curve, team formation phases, communication challenges, and work assignments. It's a mess—four-week sprints are ideal.

Hosting the Daily Scrum   Every 24 hours in a scrum project there is an event called the *daily scrum*. This is a meeting where the team can assess how they are doing for their sprint goal. The team can do some forecasting, discuss the likelihood of completing all items in the sprint, and discuss any roadblocks in the project. The daily scrum happens every day at the same time and same place throughout the sprint. In the daily scrum, the team answers four questions:

- What have you accomplished since we last met?
- What will you accomplish before our next daily scrum?
- Who do you need to see to make that happen?
- Are there impediments to your progress?

Extremely large projects, or even programs, could have multiple teams contributing to the customer's goal. In that case, you would have daily scrums happening in each project. To help coordinate all of the different projects, a representative from each project will also meet for a *scrum of scrums*. Each representative will discuss their project's accomplishments, next plans, and impediments, and they'll discuss if their project work could interfere with other project work. While it's unusual, a massive project could duplicate this effort and call for a scrum of scrum of scrums where multiple projects are grouped and have one representative to speak for all projects in their group to other representatives of grouped projects.

Leading the Sprint Review Meeting   At the end of the sprint is the *sprint review*, a four-hour meeting for a four-week sprint, where the developers review what's been completed in the sprint. Only completed items are demonstrated in the sprint review; if the item doesn't meet the definition of done, the item is returned to the product owner for prioritization in the product backlog. It's common for the project customers to request changes during the sprint review. The customer will see the demo, see what's possible, and have ideas for improvement to their value. This is fine because in agile we welcome and expect changes.

Performing the Sprint Retrospective   The final ceremony of the sprint is a three-hour meeting called the *sprint retrospective*. The sprint retrospective is a type of lessons learned meeting on what went well, or not so well, during the past sprint. The goal of the meeting is to look for opportunities to improve the product and the project. The product owner, the developers, and the scrum master attend this meeting to transparently inspect and review the communication, successes, and failures of the project. This is not an opportunity to place blame, but to honestly discuss the wins and losses of the sprint. The retrospective helps the team improve upon the project work for the next sprint. For purposes of your CAPM exam, retrospectives are required, but there are times when the product owner, the scrum master, and the development team agree that a retrospective isn't needed, so it can be skipped. Skipping a retrospective is a rare event.

NOTE   Only the product owner can cancel the sprint. This should not occur unless there is a drastic reason, such as the project goal has become obsolete. If the customer has changed their mind about the project, a technology has changed, or some other significant event has occurred, the product owner might choose to cancel the sprint. Anything that is done when the sprint is canceled should still go through the sprint review, and then the items that are not done should go back to the product backlog so that the product owner can reprioritize. It is unusual to cancel a sprint.

Working with User Stories   A user story, like its name implies, is a story of a role utilizing some functionality to get value from the functionality. User stories follow a formula of role, function, and value: "As a <role>, I want <function>, so I can realize <value.>" For example, "As a salesperson, I want to place orders via an app, so I can make more sales." User stories are the items in the product backlog, they are a small chunk of functionality, and they generally take up to 40 hours to create. User stories are written on sticky notes or index cards and are sometimes called *story cards*. You can even purchase preprinted sticky notes that guide you through the user story requirements.

Creating User Stories   User stories should be easy to understand by everyone on the team. Strictly speaking, user stories are created by the product owner, and they go into the product backlog. Realistically speaking, user stories are written by everyone on the team, though the product owner is responsible for the user stories and the prioritization of the user stories in the product backlog. Each user story should aim to create value. When a person proposes a user story and the value is being considered for project inclusion, it's called a *candidate story*—it is worth considering but hasn't yet been fully included in the project requirements.

In user story formats, you give the scenario of what the role is doing and the action that is happening, such as purchasing things from your website. And you provide the result, which is the realized value of the action. One of my favorite approaches to writing user stories is called the three Cs:

- **Card**   User story can fit on one card
- **Conversational**   Quick details that are easy to understand
- **Confirmation**   Customer confirms the user story has been completed

During the sprint review, the development team demonstrates the completed user story functionality. For example, say a company is selling car parts, and the user story reads: "As a customer, I want to search for a car part, so I can order it online." In the sprint review, the team could read the card and then show the action and the completed result. This is quick and easy to understand and simple to demonstrate as a user story that has met the definition of done. Of course, not all user stories are so simple, but the CAPM exam will test you on the concept.

Another common approach that you will see is to utilize the user story acronym of INVEST:

- **Independent**   This can be prioritized in any order in the product backlog.
- **Negotiable**   The team and product owner can make trade-offs for cost and function.
- **Value**   The value of the user story action is apparent.
- **Estimable**   The required effort to create the function can be estimated.
- **Small**   It should be able to be completed in one iteration.
- **Testable**   The results can be tested for completion and accuracy.

Estimating User Stories   The developers can do only so much work in a four-week time period, and we need a way to predict how much work the developers can take on. The developers need to look at the user stories in the prioritized product backlog and determine how big, or how small, the user stories are and assign points to stories based on the size of the user story. The bigger the story, the more story points it receives. A story point is just a way to size the stories we are about to take on, from large to small. This does not mean assigned story points reflect prioritization, but only reflects how big the user stories are. User story point sizing is all relative; for example, "This story point is really tricky, so we'll give it ten points, and this story point is tiny, so we'll give it two points."

Story point sizing helps the team predict how much work or, more precisely, how many story points they can complete in an iteration. When a scrum project launches, the team can look at a chunk of the project work in the prioritized backlog and determine if they can complete it over the next four weeks. Each user story in the chunk is sized based on effort, complexity, and duration to do the work, though it's not really a precise duration estimation, but a rough estimate of the amount of work the developers can realistically complete within the sprint.

It's tricky to do user story point sizing, so a good approach is to think in terms of T-shirts. "This story is a small; this story is an extra-large." User stories are relative to one another—the small story and the extra-large story can help you triangulate other stories for their size, also. You want to make certain that sizing is correct, but also uniform. This approach helps the team avoid incorrect sizing when they dread certain parts of the project: "I hate this activity, so this is a jumbo awning size" doesn't fit in proportion to the other user stories. T-shirt sizing for estimating is an example of *affinity estimating*, where all stories are estimated by the same types of rules.

In affinity estimating, the product owner, the development team, and the scrum master participate. The estimates are created from the top of the product backlog, and the process begins with some proven reference points, such as past projects or similar work, like analogous estimating. It is difficult to say this estimate is a definitive estimate. In the early sprints, it'll be tricky to predict how much work the developers can complete, but over time, this prediction will normalize. The number of story points a team completed in a sprint is called *velocity*. Velocity can be unpredictable to start, but over time, the velocity of the team will become stable.

Another approach to user story point sizing is the Fibonacci sequence. The Fibonacci sequence can be seen by examining the top of a seashell, the branching of a tree, and other places in nature. You take two consecutive numbers, starting with zero and one, and add them together to predict the next number in the sequence. For example, one and two is three. Then you add two and three for five. Then three and five for eight. This pattern forms a spiral, like the top shown in Figure 5-5. How this relates to affinity estimating is that each number in the pattern is relative to the other numbers—it's not random. When estimating user stories with the Fibonacci sequence, you'll generally use numbers 1, 2, 3, 5, 8, and 13, though some organizations take sizing out to 21 points. The bigger the user story, the bigger the number it receives in the sequence.

Figure 5-5
The Fibonacci
sequence creates
a spiraled pattern
as the numbers
grow in size.

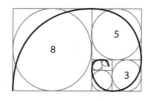

PART II

NOTE The number of user story points doesn't have to equal the expected velocity of the team. For example, if the team's velocity is 30, the selection of user stories should fit within the 30-story point velocity, not exactly 30, but approximately 30. That could be 28, could be 31, or might even be 33. It's approximate.

Extreme Programming

Extreme Programming (XP) is one of the oldest agile methodologies and is focused on software development with frequent delivery cycles, usually of one week in length. XP emphasizes continuous feedback, rapid iteration, and a high level of customer involvement.

XP focuses on the results of software projects and the continuous improvement of those results. The core values are communication, simplicity, feedback, courage, and respect. Key principles include humanity, economics, mutual benefit, self-similarity, improvement, diversity, reflection, flow, opportunity, redundancy, failure, quality, baby steps, and accepted responsibility.

The core value of XP is simplicity first. XP teams want to get rid of extra features, get rid of waste, keep things simple, and find the simplest thing that could possibly work to satisfy customer requirements. Like Scrum, XP expects changes to happen throughout the project, and the XP team welcomes change. A difference, however, is that XP acknowledges the risk that a deadline-driven project introduces. Projects that have deadlines are not realistic with the time it will take to create the deliverable, and there's added stress of the deadline for the project team.

EXAM TIP The deadline can also cause the XP team to feel overworked, under pressure, and afraid to innovate. Know that concept for your exam.

XP uses a weekly and quarterly cycle to describe its timeboxed approach. A weekly cycle, like a scrum sprint, is an iteration. On the first day of each week, the team meets to discuss what's been accomplished, choose the prioritized user stories to create during the week, and decide how the team will go about creating the selected user stories. This concept is similar to sprint planning, but it's shorter than a typical sprint. The quarterly cycle is a release, and it is planned and updated each week in the weekly cycle based on what the customer prioritization of requirements are. Basically, the accomplishments of each week help determine what will be released each quarter.

Figure 5-6
XP incorporates planning and feedback loops through its life cycle.

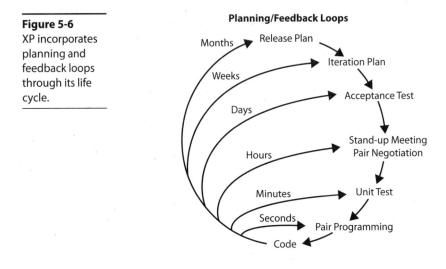

Planning/Feedback Loops

Months — Release Plan
Weeks — Iteration Plan
Days — Acceptance Test
Hours — Stand-up Meeting / Pair Negotiation
Minutes — Unit Test
Seconds — Pair Programming
Code

Slack in XP is created by adding in some low-level requirements that can be dropped from the weekly cycle if the schedule gets tight. If things are going smoothly, the low-level requirements can be added into the weekly cycle without creating a burden for the project team. In XP, another approach to manage time effectively is the "ten-minute build" concept. This involves designing the system to compile all code and run all tests within a ten-minute time frame.

A ten-minute build encourages the team to create an automated build approach, test frequently, and follow continuous integration. Continuous integration happens when the code is developed or changed, and then the code is tested immediately to find and fix integration errors.

The XP methodology adopts a "test-first" programming approach, which initially may seem counterintuitive. Under this policy, developers write the tests before writing the code, causing the tests to initially fail due to the absence of code to be tested. Subsequently, developers write the necessary code to pass the tests. By writing the test first, the paired programmers know what the code must be to pass the required test.

XP, as depicted in Figure 5-6, follows a logical approach to getting work done. There are loops built into the approach that make everything iterative as you move through the project.

 EXAM TIP The CAPM exam may lightly touch on the approach depicted in Figure 5-6, so you should be familiar with planning and feedback loops.

XP projects involve a number of activities, including planning, designing, coding, testing, and managing. Here's a brief overview of each activity:

Planning the XP Project

- User stories are written.
- A release schedule is created.

- Plans for frequent, small releases are developed.
- A project is segmented into iterations.
- Each iteration begins with an iteration planning session.

Designing

- Keep things simple.
- Create a system metaphor to quickly explain the project.
- Class, responsibilities, and collaboration (CRC) cards help design the system.
- Spike iterations are used to address risks.
- Don't add features and functions until they are requested.
- Refactor, which means cleaning up the code, happens throughout the project.

Coding

- A customer role should be available for input. Establish standards for all coding.
- Unit tests are written first.
- Programmers utilize paired programming.
- Code is frequently integrated, but by only one programming pair at a time.
- An integration server is required for the project.
- All code is collectively owned, and any programmer can review or edit code.

Testing

- Unit tests are required for all code.
- All code must pass the unit test before release.
- Bugs in the code require new tests to be created.
- Acceptance testing is required, and results are tracked and shared.

Managing the XP Project

- Colocated teams work in an open workspace.
- Establish a sustainable pace of work.
- Each day begins with a 15-minute meeting.
- Project velocity is frequently measured.
- Team members are trained in other roles.
- Retrospectives help fix problems in XP.

XP Core Values   As I mentioned at the beginning of this section, XP has five central values: communication, simplicity, feedback, courage, and respect.

- **Communication**   XP, like Scrum, relies heavily on face-to-face communication, even if it's over web conferencing software, like Zoom or Microsoft Teams. You know that when effective communication happens, you receive feedback. This is a core attribute of XP: get feedback early and often. This is part of XP's fail early, fail fast, fail often approach. When people fail fast, fail early, they get feedback as to what's working or isn't working so they can make adjustments and move forward in the project. XP also calls for a safe environment for people to experiment and to fail in. There's no negative feedback—if the experiment didn't work, the team knows what didn't work and they can move on without fear of retribution.

- **Keeping things simple**   Simple does not mean easy. Simple means not overengineering the solution, not creating complex code, and designing a solution that's direct and easy to implement. In XP, you'll ask for the simplest thing that will work to satisfy the customer requirements. A temptation I often see among developers is to assume requirements will be coming in the project, so they'll go ahead and address their assumptions. This is scope creep and is project poison. XP teams should only address requirements they know with certainty, not requirements they think may be coming later in the project.

- **Working with feedback**   Recall that in Scrum there is a sprint retrospective to give teams an opportunity to improve and work better in the next sprint. XP has a similar, though less formal, concept through immediate feedback. Feedback shouldn't be judgmental, but constructive, and it should guide the team to make better decisions. When giving feedback, team members should be respectful, honest, and focus on what's worked or didn't work—it's not all negative. This is not an opportunity to place blame, but an opportunity to move forward in the project.

- **Working with courage**   To fail early, fail fast, fail often, we need courage. When developers experiment, their work is visible to everyone on the team. That takes courage. The team openly shares code, collectively owns the code, and has the authority to correct each other's code. One approach in this concept is the previously mentioned *pair programming*. One programmer works as a developer, and a second programmer sits next to them and watches that person develop the code. Actually, it is more than just watching. The second programmer helps catch mistakes, offers improvements, and helps the programmer however it is needed. The person programming is called the *driver*, and the person helping is called the *navigator*. The driver and navigator switch roles every 1.5 to 3 hours.

- **Respecting the team**   To communicate effectively, work together through paired programming, and try new approaches, the team members must respect one another. XP embraces the concept that everyone is responsible, not any one individual, for the success or failure of the project. Everyone works differently, but the team must work together.

Reviewing the XP Roles and Responsibilities   There are eight roles in an XP project that you must know for the CAPM exam. You won't need to know these in depth, but you should be familiar with their responsibilities and be able to recognize what each role does in the project.

- **Customer or product owner**   This role, like the product owner in Scrum, represents the business values and is responsible for writing user stories, prioritizing the requirements, and helping programmers understand the value of user stories. While this role may not be the actual customer or businessperson, they serve as a representative for the business or customer, so they need good insight into what the customer values are and what's expected as an end result of the project.

- **Coach**   The XP coach coaches the team members on the XP approach, keeps things moving along, oversees the work of the project, and helps implement process improvements as a result of team feedback. The coach isn't the same as a project manager, but does help coordinate activities among the project and ensures everyone is following the rules and contributing.

- **Programmer**   The programmer programs the code to satisfy the requirements of the customer. Programmers also derive the tasks needed to complete user stories and work on unit testing in the project.

- **Tester**   The tester runs functional tests on the code the programmers have created. Functional tests are also called *integration tests* and are more robust than the unit tests the programmers do. The tester role also documents the test results.

- **Tracker**   This role has some project management duties as the person is responsible for tracking the work assignments to confirm things are "on track" in the project. If things aren't going as expected, the tracker works to ensure assignments are going to plan. The tracker also meets with programmers, the coach, and the customer to report on project progress.

- **Doomsayer**   The cheeriest role in XP projects, the doomsayer monitors risk, poor results, and issues with the project. The doomsayer communicates frequently about the conditions of events that could threaten the project's success. The role's objective is to be honest and transparent about the health of the project.

- **Manager**   The XP manager is responsible for delivering the project as promised. The manager is responsible for communicating status to the project customer, schedules meetings for release planning, and often serves as the doomsayer and tracker roles.

- **Gold owner**   The gold owner pays for the project and is often the project sponsor in an organization.

Traditionally, XP teams are colocated for face-to-face communication and osmotic communications. Osmotic communication is the useful sharing of information that flows between team members working near each other, as they can overhear each other's conversations. Of course, with more and more people working remotely, this is fading as an XP rule.

You'll also see that XP roles are sometimes called *generalizing specialists*, meaning a role can do more than one thing, rather than serving as a silo and doing only one thing.

 EXAM TIP One of the key things for your exam is the concept of a sustainable pace.

When the team examines the product backlog, they start with the items at the top, which are the most important, and determine how many story points they can complete in the iteration. When they go into that iteration, do not encourage the developers, "Well, how about you take on 30 or 35 story points?" Well, that is going to lead to overtime and long hours, and that is not sustainable. What we aim for is what will lead us to a sustainable velocity. Remember, velocity is how much a team can get done in an iteration, so we want something that is uniform and sustainable.

Kanban

Kanban originated in manufacturing and is used for knowledge work. This approach is less prescriptive and less disruptive than the predictive, plan-based approach since teams can apply the techniques to current ways of delivering project results. It is most applicable to those projects using a more continuous flow approach, rather than a timeboxed approach. Kanban instead "pulls" single items continuously from start to finish. This method stresses the importance of completing work and enables the team to work to together to get work to "done."

This method also uses the Kanban board to help visualize where a particular item is from when it is started until it has been successfully delivered. The effort required is divided into areas shown as columns on the chart, with a work-in-progress (WIP) limit to help optimize the flow of work. It utilizes a "pull" approach where individuals or groups within a "column" pull work from a queue when there is availability to work on a new item.

The Kanban method is best applied when a team requires the following:

- Flexibility to work on the highest-priority items in the backlog that often cannot be completed in a timebox period.

- Continuous delivery of prioritized items to completion, while not beginning new work until the completion of WIP.

- Increased productivity and quality through the limiting of WIP, allowing for adequate time to deliver quality results throughout the process.

- Increased efficiency by reviewing activities to ensure that non-value-added activities are removed, often utilizing value stream mapping techniques.

- Team members focus on current work through the limiting of WIP, rather than being concerned about what is coming from the previous activity having been completed.

- Variability to support work that arrives at different times, as well as with different priorities. This does prevent teams from making future commitments, since the amount and context of the work are unpredictable.

- Reduction of waste is visible so that it can be easily identified and removed as the work is performed.

The defining principles of Kanban include

- Start with the current state.
- Agree to incremental and often evolutionary change where needed for improvement and elimination of waste.
- Respect current processes, roles, responsibilities, and titles.
- Encourage leadership activities at all levels.

Core properties of Kanban, which are very similar to those of Lean, include

- Visualize the workflow through tracking of progress toward completion with transparency of bottlenecks, blockers, and current status of work.
- Establish limits for the work in progress.
- Manage the flow of work through the use of queues for finished work awaiting the next step.
- Make process policies explicit, including entry and exit to columns.
- Implement feedback loops to encourage and incorporate needed changes.
- Improve collaboratively (like the retrospective in Scrum, but done as needed rather than on a regular basis).

Utilizing a Kanban Approach   While not a robust approach like the other agile project management methodologies, Kanban is a framework for organizing work, being transparent, and showing the flow of the work. Kanban means signboard and is pronounced "con-bon." You can technically use Kanban in any agile and predictive, plan-based project management methodology, but it's most popular in XP. A Kanban board shows all stages of the work and where the work items are located in the workflow, as in the example in Figure 5-7.

Work begins on the left side of the Kanban board and flows from left to right. The goal is to limit the work in progress and allow anyone on the team who has the right skillset and capacity to take a card from the left and begin the workflow. When a person chooses a card and moves it into the workflow, this is known as the *commitment point*. Visual signals are the sticky notes that flow through the columns. Each column represents a phase of the project work, such as Backlog, In Progress, and Testing. The columns can be given any logical name that works for your project's workflow. Each card must flow through each column—no skipping over segments. When the card has passed through all of the columns and it is completed, it's known as the *delivery point*.

Figure 5-7
A Kanban board shows all the stages of the work.

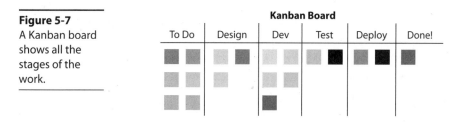

		Kanban Board			
To Do	Design	Dev	Test	Deploy	Done!

Scaled Agile Framework

Scaled Agile Framework (SAFe) is a set of practices for use at an enterprise level and often applied to agile projects across multiple levels of an organization. SAFe promotes alignment, collaboration, and delivery of results with a large number of individual agile teams.

As businesses grow in size, SAFe provides a structured approach for scaling agile, including Essential SAFe, Large Solution SAFe, Portfolio SAFe, and Full SAFe.

Principles of SAFe include

- Take an economic view to address the cost of delays.
- Apply systems thinking to the solution, the enterprise building the system, and the value streams, regardless of whether internal or external to the enterprise.
- Assume variability, preserving multiple requirements and design options until late in the process.
- Build incrementally with fast, integrated learning cycles incorporating the PDCA cycle for continuous quality improvement.
- Base milestones on an objective evaluation of working systems and stakeholder involvement in decisions.
- Visualize and limit WIP, reduce batch sizes, and manage queue lengths like Kanban practices.
- Apply cadence, and synchronize with cross-domain planning to enable activities to move like cogs in a wheel with learning applied to decisions and incremental planning.
- Unlock the intrinsic motivation of knowledge works by replacing a command-and-control approach to management with a coaching and servant leadership environment.
- Decentralize decision-making to allow teams the autonomy to get work done, with only strategic decisions being authorized by leadership.

Core SAFe values describing the leadership culture and behavior of individuals include

- Alignment with planning and cadences at all levels of an organization
- Built-in quality, with the definition of "done" for every task including flow architecture and design, code, system, and release quality
- Transparency with planning at smaller levels to expose problems and real-time visibility into progress for backlog items across all levels
- Program execution with regular delivery of quality, working software, and business value
- Leadership with a lean-agile behavior to create an environment that enables change to the system

Feature-Driven Development

Created specifically for software development projects, feature-driven development (FDD) is an agile approach that doesn't get much attention. While FDD does use short iterations and welcomes change, it can be a bit more rigid than Scrum or XP. FDD's rigidity is ideal for complex, long-term software development projects. FDD, unlike any other agile approach, skips meetings and utilizes documentation for communication.

While this can appear challenging for communication, it's actually ideal when the project team is large, there are multiple developers that aren't colocated, and you need a history of documented communication.

FDD has six roles you should recognize for the CAPM exam:

- **Project manager** Oversees the project as a typical project manager
- **Chief architect** Designs and models the system and leads planning with other developers
- **Development manager** Oversees the daily activity and coaches the development team
- **Chief programmer** Assists the chief architect and development manager and may lead smaller development teams within the project
- **Class owner** Works with the chief programmer and designs, codes, and tests the features of the system
- **Domain expert** Like the product owner role in Scrum, a businessperson who understands the customers' needs and what they value

FDD follows a strict, five-step approach to project management, unlike what you have seen in other agile approaches. FDD is ideal for large organizations engaging in projects that are extensive, may seem to be ongoing, and do not have developers colocated. The five steps of FDD are as follows:

1. *Develop the overall model.* Based on the customers' problem that the project should solve, the model is a big outline of what the solution should include. This is led by the chief architect.

2. *Build a features list.* Like the product backlog in Scrum, the features list is a prioritized list of project requirements that the client wants in the solution. Features in the list should take no longer than two weeks to create. If the feature is estimated to take longer than two weeks, the feature is too big and needs to be decomposed into smaller features.

3. *Plan by feature.* The team works with the domain expert to prioritize the features, but also with the chief architect to consider all the technical requirements needed to deliver the features. This step also considers the risks, technical dependencies, team bandwidth, and impediments that could threaten the feature's success.

4. *Design by feature.* This activity is led by the chief programmer, but the entire team is involved in the design review. The goal is to first determine which features the team can accomplish in a two-week iteration and then determine which developers will work together, or alone, to tackle the feature in the iteration.

5. *Build by feature.* The developers get to work creating the solution. A test for the feature is written, the code is written, and when the feature passes the test, the feature can be added to the build.

The core practices reflect software engineering best practices and include

- Domain object modeling
- Developing by feature
- Individual class ownership
- Feature teams
- Inspections
- Configuration management
- Regular integration and builds
- Visibility of progress and results

Dynamic Systems Development Method

Dynamic Systems Development Method (DSDM) is an agile project delivery framework that provides guidance on how to deliver projects in an agile way. DSDM is a great approach when working with vendors as part of your agile project. DSDM also offers a unique approach as it can be blended with Scrum. There are eight principles of DSDM that are similar to all agile project management approaches:

- Focus on the business need.
- Deliver the work on time.
- Collaborate.
- Do not compromise quality.
- Build incrementally.
- Develop iteratively.
- Communicate continuously, directly, and clearly.
- Demonstrate control.

This approach can be used for large, complex projects and smaller, quick projects. DSDM also leverages some of the tools and techniques of Scrum, XP, and hybrid project management such as timeboxing for iterations and the MoSCoW (Must, Should, Could, Won't) prioritization approach for requirements. DSDM has an overall goal of ensuring that every requirement and deliverable meet the organization's strategic goals. This helps prevent scope creep and ensures value for the customer. Finally, like other project management approaches, DSDM prioritizes requirements and delivers the most important features to the customer as soon as possible.

AgilePM

AgilePM and DSDM are closely related, as AgilePM is a project management framework based on DSDM.

AgilePM was developed as a subset of DSDM and is designed to provide a more focused approach to agile project management. AgilePM is based on the principles of DSDM, but it has been streamlined to provide a more accessible and practical approach to agile project management. AgilePM also provides more specific guidance on project management practices, such as risk management, planning, and governance.

Both AgilePM and DSDM are agile project delivery frameworks that provide guidance on how to deliver projects in an agile way. AgilePM is based on DSDM and provides a more focused approach to agile project management, while DSDM provides a more comprehensive approach to agile project delivery.

Determine How to Prepare and Execute Task Management Steps

Task 5

Preparing and executing task management steps in adaptive project management involve interpreting the success criteria of the tasks (enabler 1) and then prioritizing the tasks (enabler 2). The criteria for success can be established at multiple levels and with varying degrees of detail throughout a project. Prioritizing tasks is essential to ensure that the team is working on the most critical and valuable items in the first place.

Interpret Success Criteria of an Adaptive Project Management Task

Task 5, Enabler 1

Success criteria can be specified at many levels within a project as well as at various levels of detail. The measures described in the following sections can be used to interpret success criteria of an adaptive project management task.

Customer Satisfaction

In an adaptive project management approach, success is measured by the satisfaction of the customer. This means that the team should focus on delivering value to the customer through frequent and incremental releases, and the success of the project is determined by how satisfied the customer is with the final product. This could be measured through feedback from customers or stakeholders, surveys, or other forms of customer engagement.

The overall success criteria ensure alignment with the business goals and objectives of the project. At this level SMART objectives are developed and KPIs identified to further clarify the expected results. Roadmaps can also be used to show time frames when functionality is expected to be delivered. The actual value of work delivered may be perceived differently by different stakeholder groups.

It is critical that the team have a clear understanding of the requirements that support the user stories and acceptance criteria provided. This may include additional knowledge regarding any needed sequence, information, or business rules supporting the requirements. Clear understanding of those specifics is part of the definition of ready, prior to the team starting the work on an item.

Success at the iteration level is often equated to the quality of the delivered result. Some of the specific practices that can be used to verify the achievement of an expected result include

- **Continuous integration**   As individual portions of work are completed and initially tested by the developers, the result is combined with previous work to ensure that that entire work still performs as expected.

- **Testing at all levels**   Testing usually starts with the developer testing their own work, referred to as *unit testing*. Those individual portions are then combined with other individual results as part of *integration* or *system testing*. When the results are combined with previously accepted work, often through continuous integration, *regression testing* is performed. In addition, *interface testing* may be needed to ensure that inputs from other systems or areas, as well as outputs delivered as a result of the project, perform as expected. Based on the organizational methodology, additional testing must be done by a quality assurance function, in addition to actual *user acceptance testing (UAT)*. In agile UAT is done as part of the iteration review or demonstration.

- **Test-drive development (TDD)**   Tests are written prior to starting the development of the process. This can be done for non-software projects through the use of simulations to test design options.

- **Acceptance test–driven development (ATDD)**   This adaptation of TDD allows the team to create the test for the acceptance criteria and then develop just enough functionality to meet the criteria. For non-software projects, tests are developed to review chunks of work that have been completed.

- **Behavior-driven development (BDD)**   BDD and its associated testing include usage-based scenarios to help understand behavior and its implementation.

- **Spikes**   Spikes are short time frames used for additional learning of situations, especially risk and architectural areas. They can also be used to help understand sequence of usage of a product, estimation of effort, and definition of more detailed acceptance criteria factors.

- **Demonstration and review activity**   The demonstration and review activity allows the team to receive feedback on the work they have done. This feedback often is necessary more frequently than just at the end of the iteration, to ensure that they have understood the requirements and are working in the right direction. This enables frequent delivery of work that meets the stakeholder's expectations. These are measured not by what was predicted, but rather what is delivered. The smaller the chunk of work planned for an iteration, the better the chance of completing that satisfactorily.

Prioritize Tasks in Adaptive Project Management

Task 5, Enabler 2

Prioritizing tasks in adaptive project management is a crucial step to ensure that the team is working on the most important and valuable items first. Prioritizing tasks is important in adaptive project management for several reasons:

- **Focus on high-value work** Prioritizing tasks helps the team to focus on the work that provides the most value to the customer and the project. This ensures that the team is delivering work that aligns with the project's objectives and goals.

- **Efficient use of resources** Prioritizing tasks helps the team to allocate resources more effectively by focusing on the work that is most important and urgent. This ensures that the team is using their time and effort in the most efficient way possible.

- **Manage risk** Prioritizing tasks helps the team to identify and address potential risks early in the project. This allows the team to focus on the most critical tasks and reduce the risk of delays or failures that could impact the project's success.

- **Enable flexibility** Prioritizing tasks allows the team to be more flexible in their approach to the project. This enables the team to adapt to changing requirements and priorities as they emerge, without losing sight of the project's overall objectives.

Chapter Summary

Agile project management is about getting value to the customers as quickly as possible. Through increments, which are small releases, and iterations, which are repetitive cycles, agile teams create value for the customer. Most agile approaches follow an approach that's been dubbed as "eating your dessert first" (something I'm a fan of), which means you get the most desirable items to the customer as quickly as possible. Working from a big list of prioritized items, the team works from the top to the bottom of the list. If changes happen to the list, which is expected and is fine in Agile, the changes are prioritized in the list, and the team takes on the work in the next iteration.

We talked about the agile principles and the agile mindset you'll need to master for the CAPM exam. Agile projects are creative, knowledge-work projects that deal with invisible work and complex requirements to create value for the project customers. This complex work requires the use of trial and error, observation, and innovation through empirical processes (rather than through defined process like we see in industrial work).

Of course, your goal is to be agile, to embrace the agile mindset, and to create a safe environment for your team to create value for the project customer. You'll also work to educate others in your organization about Agile and why it's something the whole organization should embrace rather than just one individual or just one project team.

In this chapter you also explored how an adaptive approach to project management can be beneficial in a variety of situations where there is a need for flexibility, responsiveness, and an ability to adapt to changing circumstances. It is important to carefully consider the specific needs of the project and the stakeholders involved to determine whether an adaptive approach is the most appropriate.

PART II

The pros and cons of adaptive and predictive, plan-based projects depend on the specific needs of the project and the stakeholders involved. While an adaptive approach may be more suitable for complex and changing projects, a predictive, plan-based approach may be more appropriate for projects with well-defined requirements and a fixed timeline. It's important to carefully consider the needs of the project and the stakeholders to determine the most appropriate approach.

The suitability of adaptive approaches to project management in different organizational structures depends on the specific needs and characteristics of the project and the organization. It's important to consider the communication channels, decision-making processes, and stakeholder engagement practices within the organization to determine the most appropriate approach.

The use of adaptive approaches in project management can be facilitated by a combination of organizational process assets and environmental factors that support collaboration, flexibility, and ongoing improvement. By leveraging these assets and factors, organizations can build the necessary foundation to successfully execute adaptive projects.

The specific goals or outcomes that define an iteration will depend on the needs of the project and the specific methodology being used. Regardless of the specific goals or outcomes, the logical unit of an iteration is designed to be a self-contained, manageable chunk of work that can be planned, executed, and reviewed within a specific time frame. By breaking down larger projects into logical units of iterations, teams can more effectively manage the work and deliver value to stakeholders in a consistent and predictable way.

Epics represent the highest level of iteration, followed by user stories, and tasks as the smallest logical unit of iteration. Breaking down development work into logical units allows for greater agility and flexibility in responding to changing requirements and helps teams to deliver software more quickly and efficiently.

Project controls for an adaptive project are designed to enable flexibility, responsiveness, and collaboration. By using these tools and processes, teams can effectively manage and monitor project progress in a constantly evolving environment.

Planning project iterations involves breaking down a larger project into smaller, more manageable pieces, called iterations, and planning and executing them one at a time. By following the nine steps you can effectively plan project iterations and manage the project in a structured and organized way.

While iterations can be a powerful tool for agile teams, they require careful planning and management to be successful. By weighing the pros and cons of using iterations in agile frameworks/methodologies, teams can make informed decisions about whether to adopt this approach and how to optimize it for their specific needs.

Each iteration has a clear goal and set of deliverables that can be completed within the specified time frame. The team prioritizes the work based on the needs of the project and works to deliver value to stakeholders in a consistent and predictable way. By using adaptive iterations, the team can more effectively manage the work and respond to changing requirements or priorities.

By considering the inputs to scope, you and your team can develop and refine the project scope throughout the project in an adaptive way, ensuring that it aligns with the project's goals and objectives and addresses the needs of stakeholders.

The importance of adaptive project tracking versus predictive, plan-based tracking depends on the specific project and the needs of the stakeholders. However, in many cases, an adaptive approach can be more effective in managing complex projects and delivering value to stakeholders in a fast-moving environment.

Overall, prioritizing tasks is a key aspect of adaptive project management, as it enables the team to focus on the work that provides the most value to the customer and the project, while also ensuring efficient use of resources and effective risk management.

Next, you walked through the various agile project management approaches. This discussion included an in-depth look at adaptive approaches you'll likely see on the CAPM exam: Scrum, XP, Kanban, SAFe, FDD, DSDM, and AgilePM.

The success criteria of an adaptive project management task are typically focused on delivering value to the customer through frequent and incremental releases, ensuring the quality of deliverables, the team's ability to respond to change, timely delivery, and the satisfaction of the team.

Keep working toward your goal of earning the CAPM credential. You've already done more than many who say they want to earn the CAPM: you've read the first five chapters of this book that aims to get you there. Keep working smart, stay focused, and stay confident. You can do this!

Questions

1. Larad's team recently finished an agile project in which they created a grocery shopping application for the world's largest grocery store chain. A follow-up customer survey revealed that 76 percent of clients think the application has too many features and is too difficult to use. What shortcoming in the agile project likely led to these survey results?

   A. Larad did not effectively use scrum sprints.

   B. Larad failed to produce a minimum viable product (MVP) for his clients in sprints.

   C. Larad did not create an effective stakeholder engagement plan.

   D. The participating grocery stores did not make their requirements for the application clear.

2. Sally is a junior project manager and her organization wants to adopt more agile methodologies. However, before these methods can be implemented into any new project, what should Sally do first?

   A. Place current projects on hold and adjust them to the new agile changes.

   B. Assess organizational culture and readiness for the proposed agile shift in culture.

   C. Provide agile training for employees who are willing to participate in the first project team.

   D. Ask workers to vote on whether they want to participate in the new projects.

3. Mike, a new project manager, looks at the lessons learned for the two-year project and notices a high turnover rate for team members. He decides to switch from a predictive, plan-based development approach to adopt agile methodologies. What action should Mike take to shift to a hybrid approach?

   A. Evaluate the benefits of incorporating agile practices.

   B. Review a historically similar project to determine the current project's feasibility.

   C. Ensure the organization can continue funding the project.

   D. Downsize the number of team members to nine individuals, plus or minus two.

4. Petra, a project manager, is launching a project that will likely encounter technological changes, updates, and challenges during the next three years. Generally speaking, what mindset should Petra have in managing this project?

   A. An eye on the future because she knows change is coming.

   B. A fixed mindset because she can work only with the technology she has.

   C. An agile mindset because she should focus on the present with an eye to change.

   D. A traditional mindset because she should focus on one thing after another, in order. She should plan for the next three years.

5. The management team has tasked Matthew with conducting a pilot project using agile methods. Which of the following characteristics should Matthew *not* consider when selecting a pilot project?

   A. Three-to-six-month schedule

   B. Real business need

   C. High visibility

   D. A detailed project management plan

6. Lea is an agile project manager leading a team to develop a "silent" blender. The functional area demands extensive documentation before they will accept any changes. As an agile project manager, which action would *not* be an action Lea should take to create a shared understanding between the functional department and the agile team?

   A. Working with the functional department to review the required documentation

   B. Assisting with creating a shared understanding of how agile deliverables meet those requirements

   C. Evaluating the amount of documentation required, so teams are spending more time delivering a valuable product instead of producing exhaustive documentation

   D. Compromising with all parties so that everyone receives a feature they want

7. Leonardo recognizes that most of the members on his project team have little technical domain knowledge and are unfamiliar with how to employ agile methods effectively. What can Leonardo do to help adjust the team to agile methodologies?

   A. Let the team members figure everything out, as agile teams should be empowered and self-directing.

   B. Recommend terminating the project until the team members learn agile methodologies.

   C. Perform a retrospective to address the project team's deficiencies in agile methodologies.

   D. Assign and direct the team members until they gain the necessary skills to become self-directing.

8. The Preston Company is proficient in using a traditional project management approach and wants to incorporate scrum techniques in a new project. Kevin, a business analyst, is not familiar with scrum techniques. Which of the following actions should Kevin request to serve his role best?

   A. Request for the most proficient software development tester to approve or reject the minimum viable product (MVP) during each sprint review, as he is most familiar with the software.

   B. Request mentorship from an agile coach, as his role closely aligns with that of a product owner.

   C. Request to be assigned to another project, as he is only familiar with traditional project management.

   D. Request for one of the testers to take the role of the end user and prioritize the user stories in the product backlog.

9. Colleen is a project manager who also happens to be a scrum master for a small agile team. The team members want Colleen, as a project manager, to tell people what to do a little more. How should Colleen handle this dynamic?

   A. Assign roles and tasks.

   B. Work to remove impediments.

   C. Stop using scrum.

   D. Make a WBS.

10. Lindsay is looking to ensure that knowledge transfer is happening within her agile software project team. How can Lindsay encourage knowledge transfer engagingly?

    A. Ask each developer to write documentation on each process they complete.

    B. Encourage developers to pair together and program together.

    C. Make two developers on the team responsible for each process.

    D. Ensure that the functional manager knows how to complete each process.

11. In agile working environments, which of the following practices would be most effective for osmotic communication to work?

    A. Colocated teams

    B. Distributed teams

    C. Team members understanding each other's culture

    D. A team in the norming stage

12. Adam has joined an agile team. He approaches the agile coach to understand how stories and features are prioritized in the risk-adjusted backlog. Which one of the following would be the best answer?

    A. Risk impact or risk probability

    B. Expected monetary value or business value

    C. Cost-benefit ratio or customer value

    D. Risk mitigation impact or user impact

13. Near the completion of the first iteration, the agile project team must demonstrate the potentially shippable product increment to the project stakeholders. What scrum ceremony would be appropriate to conduct this demo?

    A. Sprint review

    B. Daily scrum

    C. Sprint retrospective

    D. Deliverables meeting

14. Marguerite is a new project manager. Her organization wants to adapt a Lean approach to the next project where the focus is on work stream improvement. Which of the following would not be considered an example of a form of waste?

    A. Code testing

    B. Task switching

    C. Code waiting for test results

    D. Assigning a developer to multiple projects at the same time

15. During the fifth sprint review meeting, one of the stakeholders is unsatisfied with the progress and advises the product owner that their most recent business requirement is missing from the product increment. What likely happened during the sprint planning meeting?

    A. The product backlog was not up-to-date.

    B. The sprint backlog was not prioritized.

    C. The stakeholder register was not up-to-date.

    D. The scrum master failed to identify priority.

16. Max is a developer on a software team. A person facilitates a daily 15-minute meeting, removes any blockers a teammate may have, and encourages the team to keep making progress. What kind of project methodology approach does Max's team have?

    A. Scrum

    B. Plan-driven

    C. Kanban

    D. Predictive, plan-based

17. Brittany meets with her team about once a week to review a board containing tickets that represent work items. After testing, the ticket is closed and goes into the Done column. What kind of project management approach does Brittany's project have?

    A. Scrum

    B. Kanban

    C. Hybrid

    D. Predictive, plan-based

18. Over lunch with your colleague, Bruce, the topic of iterative development arises. Bruce says that iterative development is better than incremental development when a usable delivery is needed early on for a project. Which of the following is true?

    A. Incremental development and iterative development mean the same thing and can be used interchangeably.

    B. Iterative development is planned in complete detail in the planning stage, while incremental development plans at a high level and develops the scope more and more over time.

    C. Incremental delivery yields a usable piece of the project in each iteration.

    D. Iterative delivery yields a usable piece of the project in each iteration.

19. Jane has joined an agile team as a replacement for a team member who has left the company. As an agile coach, what would you teach Jane to focus on as the highest priority?

    A. Create customer satisfaction by delivering valuable software early and often.

    B. Welcome change to requirements, even late in the development.

    C. Maximize the work done and complete as many requirements as is possible.

    D. Use iteration to plan the work effectively.

20. Mosiah has been assigned to lead a distributed agile team. Being an experienced agile project manager, Mosiah knows that agile project management approaches value face-to-face communication as the best way to convey information. However, it can be challenging for distributed teams since not all team members are in the same physical space. To help them communicate, the best option for Mosiah would be to do which of the following?

A. Ask the team to follow a common language for all project communications.

B. Inform the team members to share photos of themselves.

C. Set up a few initial face-to-face meetings for everyone to meet and get introduced.

D. Define common working hours so everyone on the team can better communicate.

Answers

1. B. In this scenario, Larad likely did not produce an MVP for his clients in regular sprints. As a result, he failed to capture the requirements of the most important stakeholder: the customer. A is incorrect because the sprints may or may not have been effective; the issue is in creating the product that is just enough for what the customer needs. C is incorrect because a comprehensive stakeholder engagement plan may have prevented the situation; it is more suited for more traditional project management than agile methods. D is incorrect because as the customer primarily measures value, they are ultimately the ones who decide how the application should be developed, not the grocery stores.

2. B. Sally should determine whether the organization is ready for the agile shift in culture. Choices A, C, and D are incorrect because they are viable solutions only after assessing the organizational culture. When an organization shifts to agile, there can be a disruption along with the learning curve agile approaches require.

3. A. Mike should review the benefits of incorporating agile practices. This action will ensure the requirements are defined and that the team can adjust to changing requirements through continuous feedback and delivery. B is incorrect because no two projects are exactly alike, and many external factors will need to be considered. C is incorrect because continuing to fund the project, although important, does not directly answer a hybrid approach. D is incorrect. It's true that the ideal team size for an agile project management team is between five and nine people, but simply reducing the team size won't address the root causes of the issues the project is facing.

4. C. Having an agile mindset means working on the most important items first and understanding and accepting that change is likely to happen in the project. B is incorrect because a fixed mindset is unlikely to help Petra in an agile or hybrid project. Not only are there known technological changes, but there are also known unknowns as well. D is incorrect because, although elements of the predictive, plan-based approach are likely to help Petra organize the project, it would be unwise to create fixed plans years ahead. Petra should not ignore the current technology that she has to work with and should focus on the immediate work through agile approaches. Petra should employ an agile mindset with an eye on current challenges and a willingness to adapt to the coming changes.

5. D. Matthew should not create a detailed project management plan, which is associated with a traditional methodology. A is incorrect because the project should be big enough to be deemed a real project but short enough to use the benefits quickly. B is incorrect because a pilot project should address a real business need that people know needs to addressed, one that is likely to be the focus of future projects. C is incorrect because the project should be one that people will see and notice, be easy to publicize its success, and have a good business spokesperson to spread the word.

6. D. The servant leader aims to make certain the team has what they need, but also keeps everyone focused on the primary goals of the project. Compromising usually involves parties agreeing to give up a feature they want, which results in a "lose-lose" situation. A, B, and C are incorrect because they are actions that Lea should take to create a shared understanding between a functional department and the agile team.

7. D. While assigning and directing team members may seem backward, Leonardo can more seamlessly transition from a traditional to an adaptive approach if he leads them at the start. When an organization or team first moves into agile, the servant leader should coach and direct the team initially. Over time and with experience the team will become more self-led and self-organizing. Choices A, C, and B are incorrect because they are forcing agile concepts onto the team instead of enabling the team members to adopt those methodologies themselves. The servant leader should neither threaten the team nor take a hands-off approach to the project.

8. B. For this scenario, Kevin should request and receive training and coaching from an agile coach, product owner, or scrum master. Kevin needs to learn how agile projects operate, and a coach can help him with the mechanics of agile and serving a product owner or working along with a product owner in the project. A is incorrect because testing the product is needed, but at the right level of testing. In addition, testing the product doesn't help Kevin navigate the Scrum approach in the scenario. C is incorrect because Kevin is needed on the current project and should work to learn and embrace agile in the organization. D is also incorrect because the tester has a different skillset than that of a product owner.

9. B. Having both of these roles can be problematic, especially if team members are not embracing agile. Colleen will likely need to remove the impediments by coaching the team on their responsibilities and tracking the velocity for the team members. The key is to find out what the team's obstacles are and work to remove them. In doing this, Colleen will be a helpful project manager and scrum master. A is incorrect because Scrum doesn't have roles and tasks like traditional project management. C is incorrect because, while Colleen could stop using Scrum, it's not a valid reaction to a few typical complaints. D is incorrect because a work breakdown structure (WBS) doesn't fit into the changing priorities and requirements of Scrum.

10. B. Of all the choices presented, pair programming ensures knowledge transfer between the two programmers. While none of the answers fully satisfies the question, this is the best of all choices presented. Remember, on your actual exam you will have to choose the best answer presented, not the best answer you have in your mind. Paired programming will ensure that multiple people understand and have experience completing the work. A is incorrect because comprehensive written documentation, although helpful to some extent, is not valued in agile practices. C is incorrect because having two people responsible for a process isn't a valid agile approach. D is incorrect because the functional manager does not need to know how to complete each process in the agile environment.

11. A. Osmotic communication is the useful sharing of information that flows between team members working near each other, as they can overhear each other's conversations. B is incorrect because distributed (or virtual) teams are not in the same physical environment and thus cannot experience osmotic communication. C is incorrect because understanding other team members' cultures, although valuable, does not ensure osmotic communication in a project. D is incorrect because even noncolocated teams move through the norming stage of team development.

12. B. Stories are prioritized in agile projects based on their expected monetary value and their business value. A is incorrect because it is not the best answer; it is partially correct, because the impact and probability do forecast the expected monetary value, but this is not done for all user stories. C and D are incorrect because the cost-benefit ratio, risk mitigation impact, and user impact are not valid assessments of value in the product backlog prioritization.

13. A. At the completion of each sprint, the developers demonstrate a potentially shippable product increment to the project stakeholders during a sprint review. During the review, the agile project team and stakeholders collaborate about what was done in the concluded iteration. Feedback from the product owner and customers is documented and prioritized into the product backlog after the sprint review. B is incorrect because the daily scrum meeting is a short (usually 15-minute) timeboxed event for the development team to inspect progress toward the iteration goal and plan work for the next 24 hours. C is incorrect because a sprint retrospective is an opportunity for the project team to inspect itself and create a plan for improvements to be enacted during the next iteration. D is incorrect because a "deliverables meeting" is not a valid agile project management meeting.

14. A. Out of all the listed options, testing the code would be the only necessary activity that would not be considered waste in Lean. B, C, and D are incorrect because task switching, waiting time, and having a developer move between projects are all considered examples of waste in Lean projects.

15. A. The development team sets sprint goals based on the product backlog, and it is up to the product owner to ensure it is prioritized. Given that the first four sprints were successful in delivering product increments, it is most likely that the product owner did not reprioritize the backlog with the stakeholders' changing requirements. B is incorrect because the sprint backlog is based on the selected user stories from the product backlog. C is incorrect because updating the stakeholder register would not affect the creation of the items in the product backlog. D is incorrect because the scrum master does not set priority in the product backlog; that's the responsibility of the product owner.

16. A. This is an example of a scrum project. In a scrum project, the team meets daily for a scrum meeting to discuss what work everyone is doing and to work through any blockers. There is a scrum master who is responsible for facilitating this meeting and motivating the team. B and D are incorrect because predictive, plan-based projects don't include short meetings such as this. C is also incorrect because in a Kanban-style stand-up daily meeting, the focus is on identifying issues and solving them, rather than discussing what everyone is working on.

17. B. This is a clear example of a Kanban project. The workflow presented describes a Kanban board in which work items are pulled into various statuses by the people doing the work. Choices A, C, and D are incorrect because none of these approaches uses a board with tickets as described in the scenario.

18. C. Incremental delivery yields a usable piece of the project in each iteration. A is incorrect because the terms incremental development and iterative development have similar but not identical definitions and cannot be used interchangeably. Iterative development means that the project is built in successive levels, but it is not always usable in the first few iterations. B is incorrect because neither iterative development nor incremental development involves detailed planning in the initial stages. Detailed planning is typical of traditional/predictive, plan-based development. D is incorrect because incremental delivery, not iterative delivery, yields a usable piece of the project in each iteration.

19. A. The foremost focus agile teams should have is delivering working software that brings value to the customer, resulting in high customer satisfaction. This is based on the first agile principle. B, C, and D are incorrect because, although they are valid and essential principles, they *do not* support this key-value delivery objective.

20. C. For distributed teams, setting up some initial face-to-face meetings for everyone on the team to meet is proven to be the best and most effective strategy to improve virtual and remote communication later in the project. It is easier for a team to connect and follow up with an e-mail or phone call once they have met face-to-face. A and D are incorrect because, although defining common working hours or language might be helpful, each can be viewed as rigid and disrespectful. B is incorrect because sending photos is unlikely to assist in this scenario and is certainly not the best option to follow.

PART II

References

- *Agile Practice Guide* (2017)
- *Business Analysis for Practitioners: A Practice Guide* (2015)
- *CAPM Certified Associate in Project Management Practice Exams* (2019), Haner and McCoy
- *Effective Project Management, Eighth Edition* (2019), Wysocki
- *PMBOK Guide* (2021)
- *Process Groups: A Practice Guide* (2022)
- *PMIstandards+*
- *The PMI Guide to Business Analysis* (2017)
- *The Project Management Answer Book* (2015), Furma

Business Analysis Frameworks

This chapter covers the tasks in Domain 4:
- Demonstrate an understanding of business analysis (BA) roles and responsibilities
- Determine how to conduct stakeholder communication
- Determine how to gather requirements
- Demonstrate an understanding of product roadmaps
- Determine how project methodologies influence business analysis processes
- Validate requirements through product delivery

This domain represents approximately 27 percent of the CAPM examination.

Business analysis is a distinct discipline. Its purpose is to identify which projects align with and deliver on the organization's strategic vision and business goals. It ensures the business need is properly identified, analyzed, and documented, and provides the effective design and development of the solution.

Business analysis comprises the tasks and techniques that stakeholders use to understand an organization's structure, policies, and operations. Business analysts work with stakeholders to use these tasks and techniques to suggest solutions that will allow the organization to achieve its goals.

 EXAM TIP   "BA" can stand for both "business analysis" (referring to the practice or discipline) and "business analyst" (referring to a role). The specific meaning can be determined based on the context in which it is used.

The PMI Guide to Business Analysis (PGBA) is a professional practice guide published by the PMI. The PGBA provides a framework for business analysts to follow when performing business analysis activities.

The PGBA covers the following topics:

- **Business analysis process**   Defines the business analysis process as a series of steps that business analysts follow to gather, analyze, and document business requirements.

- **Business analysis skills and knowledge**   Identifies the skills and knowledge that business analysts need to be successful.
- **Business analysis tools and techniques**   Describes the tools and techniques that business analysts can use to gather, analyze, and document business requirements.
- **Business analysis ethics and professionalism**   Provides guidance on ethical and professional behavior for business analysts.

Demonstrate an Understanding of Business Analysis Roles and Responsibilities

Task 1

Business analysis identifies business needs and determines solutions to business problems. The BA plays an essential role in this process, and responsibilities vary depending on the organization, project, and industry. The following are some of the primary responsibilities of the business analyst:

- **Requirements elicitation and analysis**   BAs work with stakeholders to identify business requirements and analyze them to determine the best solutions and ensure they align with business objectives.
- **Process improvement**   BAs continuously look for process improvement opportunities and recommend changes to streamline business processes and evaluate potential solutions and improvement opportunities to determine their feasibility, viability, and effectiveness.
- **Stakeholder management**   BAs must build and maintain strong relationships with stakeholders to ensure that their needs and requirements are met through facilitating communication, managing expectations, and negotiating requirements.
- **Change management**   BAs work closely with stakeholders to manage change and ensure that the solutions implemented are adopted successfully through training and support during the change transition.
- **Documentation**   BAs are responsible for documenting requirements, business processes, and other project-related information such as business requirement documents, process maps, and user stories.

It is important for the BA to understand the opportunity and the scope of that opportunity, as well as the benefits that would be associated with the realization of that opportunity. In this context, opportunity means business need/business problem. This allows the BA to embark on a focused piece of work. Figure 6-1 shows what is "in scope" for a BA.

The BA plays a crucial role in project management across all phases of the project life cycle, from development to implementation to maintenance or support. Here's how the BA role can be identified across each phase:

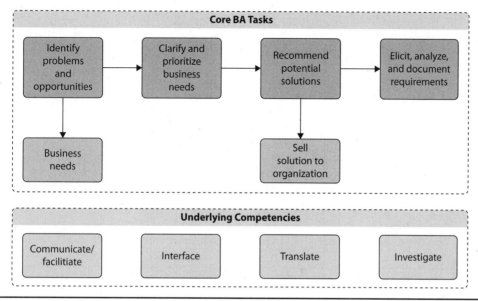

Figure 6-1 What a business analyst does (© 2023 C and P Dillon-Parkin. Used with permission.)

- **Development phase**   The BA role involves working closely with stakeholders to gather and document the project requirements. This includes defining the scope of the project, identifying the business needs and objectives, and translating them into detailed requirements that can be used by the development team. The BA also collaborates with the development team to ensure that the requirements are understood and that the solution is being developed in alignment with the business goals.

- **Implementation phase**   The BA role involves working closely with stakeholders and the development team to ensure that the solution is delivered according to the documented requirements. This includes verifying that the solution meets the business objectives, validating that the requirements are implemented correctly, and supporting the testing and deployment of the solution. The BA also collaborates with the project manager to ensure that the project is delivered on time, within budget, and to the required quality standards.

- **Maintenance or support phase**   The BA role involves working closely with stakeholders and the support team to ensure that the solution continues to meet the business needs and objectives. This includes analyzing and documenting change requests, validating that the changes meet the business requirements, and collaborating with the support team to ensure that the solution is functioning correctly. The BA also works with the operational manager to ensure that the solution is maintained and supported according to the service-level agreements.

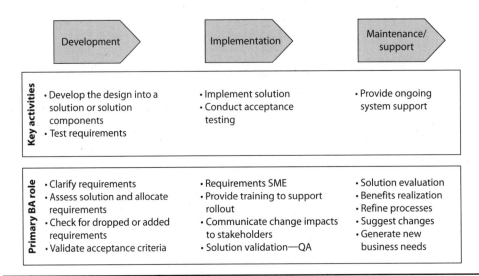

Figure 6-2 BA's role in project life cycle (© 2023 C and P Dillon-Parkin. Used with permission.)

EXAM TIP All change requests must go through a documented and agreed-upon change control process and be either approved, deferred, or declined.

Figure 6-2 identifies the BA role across the various phases of the project life cycle, including development, implementation, and maintenance or support.

Business analysts and project managers share some of the same skills. The common skills are communication, conflict resolution, facilitation, leadership, listening, time management, and problem-solving.

Figure 6-3 describes the business analysis process. Most BAs spend much of their time in the requirements engineering process. I will explain the items listed in the last column of the figure when we get to requirements management.

Business analyst activities and project manager activities have different focuses and responsibilities within a project. Table 6-1 contrasts these two roles and identifies some key differences between BA activities and PM activities.

People often confuse the BA and PM roles, and therefore the distinction calls for further explanation. Figure 6-4 further elaborates on Table 6-1 by showing the distinction between the roles of the BA and PM in the context of the preceding software product example. The "vs" indicates there is sometimes some confusion between the two roles.

EXAM TIP Business analysis precedes project management.

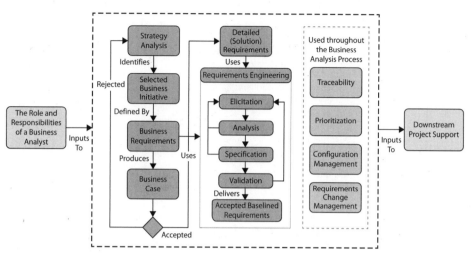

Figure 6-3   Business analysis process (© 2023 C and P Dillon-Parkin. Used with permission.)

	Business Analyst (BA)	Project Manager (PM)
Focus	On understanding the business needs and requirements of the project.	On planning, organizing, and managing the project to ensure it is completed on time, within budget, and to the required quality standards.
Requirements gathering	Heavily involved in requirements gathering and defining the scope of the project. BAs work closely with stakeholders to understand the business needs and translate them into detailed requirements for the project.	Involved in requirements gathering, but their focus is on ensuring that the requirements are clearly defined and achievable within the constraints of the project.
Documentation	Responsible for documenting requirements, functional specifications, and other project documentation to ensure that all stakeholders have a clear understanding of what is being delivered.	Involved in documentation, but their focus is on creating and maintaining project plans, schedules, and budgets.
Communication	Communicating requirements and project information to stakeholders, including developers and testers, to ensure that everyone is on the same page.	Communicating project progress, risks, and issues to stakeholders to ensure that the project stays on track.
Risk management	Identifying and mitigating risks related to the requirements and scope of the project.	Identifying and mitigating risks related to the overall project, including risks related to scope, schedule, budget, and quality.
Change management	Managing changes to requirements and scope throughout the project.	Managing changes to the project plan, schedule, and budget to ensure that changes are implemented in a controlled and effective manner.

Table 6-1   Key Differences Between BA Activities and PM Activities

Figure 6-4
The scope of business analysis work (© 2023 C and P Dillon-Parkin. Used with permission.)

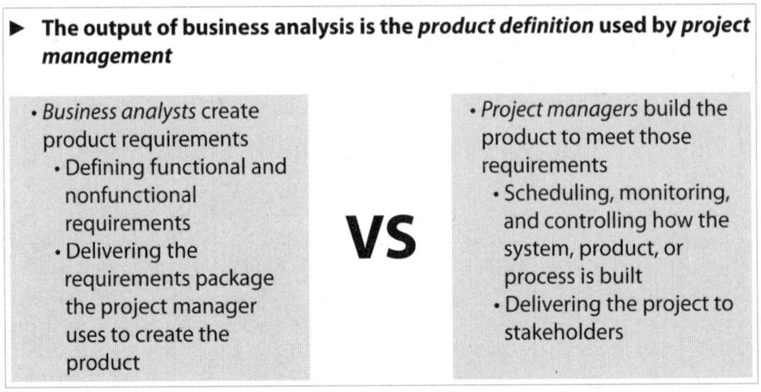

▶ **The output of business analysis is the *product definition* used by *project management***

- *Business analysts* create product requirements
  - Defining functional and nonfunctional requirements
  - Delivering the requirements package the project manager uses to create the product

VS

- *Project managers* build the product to meet those requirements
  - Scheduling, monitoring, and controlling how the system, product, or process is built
  - Delivering the project to stakeholders

Distinguish Between Stakeholder Roles

Task 1, Enabler 1

Stakeholder roles (e.g., process owner, process manager, product manager, product owner, etc.) vary depending on a project or business analysis effort, and it's important to understand the differences between these roles. Business analysts may work with any of the roles to implement a new product or process or change an existing one.

The role of the BA may not be well-defined in many organizations, especially if there are no collaboration points identified between other roles. Generally, a BA analyzes business needs and defines requirements for a project or product. In addition, they work with stakeholders to identify business problems and opportunities, develop solutions, and facilitate communication between different teams. Even though the work is similar among various roles, there is a perceived overlap, especially when defining approval levels for project work.

The *process owner* is often responsible for a specific process, including continual improvements and alignment to overall business objectives. In addition, they often set and monitor process performance targets.

The *process manager* reviews and reports on the end-to-end process activities and maintains the process map, a visual representation of a business process. They are responsible for ongoing process operations and optimization. Resources assigned to the process are managed and trained by the process manager. In smaller organizations, the same person may perform the role of the process owner and the process manager.

The *product manager* determines the overall direction and functionality delivered to the end user or customer through multiple releases. The product manager seeks a better understanding of the customer's needs and expectations. Those needs help identify the strategy of the product, including high-level functional requirements and management of product releases.

The *product owner* in projects using an adaptive approach plays a substantial role in determining and prioritizing the product backlog. The product owner, developers, testers, and BAs discuss user stories to maximize the value of the work delivered. The product owner is ultimately responsible for the product.

The *project manager* is responsible for ensuring that the project is completed on time, within budget, and to the satisfaction of the stakeholders. The project manager may work closely with the BA to

- Manage the requirements throughout the project life cycle.
- Confirm that any changes to the scope are properly evaluated and approved.
- Ensure that the communication plan is effective and that stakeholders are engaged throughout the project life cycle.
- Define acceptance criteria and ensure that the product meets the business requirements.

The *user* (end user or customer) is the person or group who will use the final product, service, or result of the project. Their primary focus is on the functionality, usability, and overall value of the product. Users are crucial in providing input on requirements, expectations, and priorities. It is essential to consider their preferences during the planning and executing phases.

As an example of how the various stakeholder roles work together, consider a company that wants to develop a new software product to improve the company's customer support process. The BA will collaborate with the process owner, process manager, product manager, product owner, and project manager to ensure the software product meets the needs of the business and its customers.

- **Process owner** The process owner is responsible for the overall performance and effectiveness of the customer support process. The BA will work with the process owner to understand the current state of the process, identify pain points, and gather requirements for the new software product. The BA will also keep the process owner informed about the progress and any changes in the project scope.

- **Process manager** The process manager oversees the day-to-day operations of the customer support process. The BA will work together with the process manager to gain a clear understanding of the specific challenges encountered by the support team. Additionally, the BA will gather input from the support team regarding potential enhancements or improvements. The BA might also work with the process manager to map the existing process, identify bottlenecks, and determine the most critical areas for improvement.

- **Product manager** The product manager is responsible for the overall strategy and vision of the software product. The BA will work closely with the product manager to ensure that the software product aligns with the company's business goals and customer needs. The BA and product manager will collaborate on defining the product roadmap, prioritizing features, and determining the minimum viable product (MVP) for initial release.

- **Product owner**   The product owner represents the customer, not the business unit or end user, and is responsible for defining and prioritizing the product backlog. The BA will collaborate with the product owner to translate the gathered requirements into user stories and acceptance criteria. The BA will also support the product owner in prioritizing the backlog based on business value, dependencies, and resource constraints.

- **Project manager**   The project manager is responsible for planning, executing, monitoring, controlling, and closing the project. They ensure that the project is completed within the defined scope, time, cost, and quality constraints. The BA will work with the project manager to help transition the work to operations once the project is complete and the product is launched.

- **User (end user or customer)**   The BA must consider their preferences and requirements during the planning and development processes. The BA will focus on the functionality, usability, and overall value of the product.

Throughout the project, the BA will continue to facilitate communication and collaboration between these stakeholders, ensuring that the software product meets the needs of the business and its customers.

Outline the Need for Roles and Responsibilities

Task 1, Enabler 2

This enabler poses the question "Why do you need to identify stakeholders in the first place?"

It is important to identify stakeholders because stakeholders are individuals or organizations who have a vested interest in the project and can be positively or negatively impacted by its outcome. Identifying stakeholders is a critical step in the project initiation phase, and it helps to ensure that the project is aligned with the needs and expectations of the stakeholders.

The project manager (PM) and business analyst (BA) play a critical role in identifying stakeholders. Identifying stakeholders early in the project helps to ensure that their needs and expectations are considered throughout the project life cycle.

The PM is responsible for identifying all stakeholders, both internal and external to the organization. This includes identifying people who will be directly affected by the project, as well as those who may experience an indirect impact.

The BA is responsible for gathering information about stakeholders, such as their needs, expectations, and influence on the project.

There are many key reasons for stakeholder identification. Here are some of the most important ones:

- **Ensuring project success**   Identifying stakeholders allows a better understanding of their needs and expectations, which in turn helps you to ensure that the project meets the requirements of all stakeholders. By aligning the project with the stakeholders' needs, you increase the chances of project success.

- **Managing expectations**   Identifying stakeholders helps manage their expectations by involving them in the project planning and decision-making process. By providing stakeholders with regular updates and involving them in the project, you reduce the risk of misunderstandings and increase their confidence in the project.

- **Managing risks**   Identifying stakeholders helps identify potential risks and issues that may impact the project. By involving stakeholders in the risk management process, you can proactively address these risks and reduce their impact on the project.

- **Building support**   Identifying stakeholders helps build support for the project. By involving stakeholders in the project, you increase their ownership and commitment to the project, which can lead to increased support and engagement throughout the project life cycle.

- **Enhancing communication**   Identifying stakeholders helps enhance communication by understanding their communication preferences and needs. By tailoring communication to the stakeholders' needs, you increase the effectiveness of the communication and reduce the risk of misunderstandings.

Stakeholders have specific needs, expectations, and concerns that must be acknowledged to ensure their support and buy-in for the project. Figure 6-5 depicts the overall stakeholder management process.

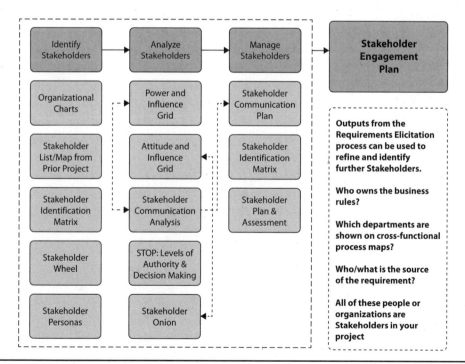

Figure 6-5   Stakeholder management process (© 2023 C and P Dillon-Parkin. Used with permission.)

Identifying stakeholders and defining their roles and responsibilities are critical aspects of project management to ensure everyone involved understands their specific roles, tasks, and deliverables. Roles and responsibilities ensure each stakeholder is accountable for their actions, tasks, and deliverables, which helps ensure tasks are completed on target, on schedule, and on budget. Figure 6-5 shows where identifying stakeholders fits in the stakeholder management process.

Here are some reasons why it is necessary to identify stakeholders and clarify their roles and responsibilities:

- **Align expectations and objectives**   Defining the roles and responsibilities of stakeholders helps ensure that their expectations, requirements, and objectives are aligned with the project's goals. This alignment is vital for delivering a successful project that meets stakeholder needs and expectations.

- **Effective communication**   Communication is improved between stakeholders and project teams by knowing who is responsible for what and ensuring that everyone is working toward the same goal. Knowing your stakeholders allows you to tailor your communication strategy to their specific needs and preferences, resulting in more effective and efficient information sharing.

- **Facilitate collaboration**   Defining roles and responsibilities fosters a collaborative environment by clarifying the tasks and functions each stakeholder is accountable for, which reduces confusion and promotes teamwork.

- **Resource allocation**   Resources are allocated more effectively, and the right people are assigned to the right tasks, which reduces the risk of delays or errors caused by inappropriate resource allocation.

- **Decision-making**   Having a clear understanding of stakeholder roles and responsibilities supports better decision-making by ensuring that the right people are involved in making decisions and providing input at the appropriate stages of the project.

- **Conflict resolution**   Identifying stakeholders and their interests can help to proactively address potential conflicts and manage them effectively if they arise.

- **Project buy-in and support**   Engaging with stakeholders early in the project to clarify their roles and responsibilities gets them involved early in the project life cycle and helps to ensure their full participation throughout the life cycle.

If you don't identify the stakeholders and the roles they represent, you'll likely miss or misunderstand requirements. If these requirements surface later in the project, they often require changes, which may negatively impact the project schedule and cost. Further, identification and analysis of stakeholders is an ongoing process jointly performed by both the business analyst and the project manager.

In addition to providing input regarding project needs and requirements, these stakeholders play an important part in providing feedback and approval of your work.

NOTE   To help you identify stakeholders, you may find it useful to ask known stakeholders who else should be involved in the project.

Differentiate Between Internal and External Roles

Task 1, Enabler 3

Business analysts work with organizations to analyze their processes, systems, and overall business environment to identify areas for improvement, develop solutions, and facilitate change. Business analysts can work in various capacities, including internal and external roles, depending on the organization's structure and the project's requirements.

Internal BAs are employees of the organization they work for. They are typically involved in all aspects of the business analysis process, from gathering requirements to developing solutions. Internal BAs have a deep understanding of the organization's culture, operations, and objectives, which allows them to provide more targeted recommendations and solutions.

External BAs are consultants who are hired by organizations to provide business analysis services. They typically have more specialized skills and experience than internal BAs, and they can provide an independent perspective on the business analysis process. External BAs have a broader perspective on industry trends, best practices, and market conditions, which allows them to provide more comprehensive recommendations and solutions.

The following explains the differentiation between internal and external roles for a business analyst.

Internal Business Analyst:

- **Employment**   An internal BA is typically a full-time employee of the organization for which they work. They may be part of a specific department or a centralized business analysis team.

- **In-depth knowledge**   Internal BAs have a deep understanding of the organization's culture, processes, systems, and stakeholders, enabling them to provide insights and recommendations tailored to the organization's needs.

- **Continuous improvement**   As a permanent member of the organization, an internal BA is often involved in ongoing process improvement initiatives, monitoring the impact of implemented solutions, and identifying new opportunities for enhancement.

- **Stakeholder relationships**   Internal BAs have established relationships with stakeholders within the organization, fostering trust and effective communication.

- **Long-term focus**   Internal BAs typically have a long-term perspective, working on projects and initiatives that support the organization's strategic goals and objectives.

External Business Analyst:

- **Employment**   An external BA is usually a consultant or contractor brought in for a specific project or a defined period. They may work for a consulting firm or operate as an independent contractor.

- **Broad industry knowledge**   External BAs bring a wealth of experience and expertise from working with various organizations and industries, enabling them to offer fresh perspectives and best practices.

- **Objective viewpoint**   As an outsider to the organization, external BAs can provide an unbiased perspective on the organization's challenges, opportunities, and potential solutions.

- **Project-based focus**   External BAs are typically engaged for specific projects or initiatives, with a focus on delivering tangible results and achieving project goals within the defined scope, timeline, and budget.

- **Knowledge transfer**   External BAs can share their expertise and introduce new methodologies, tools, and techniques to the organization, fostering continuous improvement and learning.

Determine How to Conduct Stakeholder Communication

Task 2

Effective stakeholder communication is a critical aspect of any project, and it helps to ensure that all stakeholders are informed, engaged, and aligned with the project goals and objectives. The following are steps to conduct effective stakeholder communication:

1. *Identify stakeholders.* Identify both internal and external stakeholders who are involved in or affected by the project. This includes project sponsors, project team members, employees, customers, suppliers, and regulatory bodies.

2. *Determine communication needs.* Understand what information stakeholders need, how often they need it, by which method they prefer to receive it (push, interactive, or pull), in what format they prefer to receive it, and where the information will be located.

3. *Develop a communication plan.* Develop a communication plan that outlines the communication purpose, audience, frequency, method, and format of communication.

4. *Use multiple communication channels.* Leverage a variety of stakeholder communication channels, such as e-mail, meetings, phone calls, newsletters, social media, and other online platforms, based on the stakeholders and the type of information being communicated.

5. *Be clear and concise.* Stakeholder communication should be clear, concise, relevant, accurate, and timely. Use simple language and avoid technical jargon or acronyms that stakeholders may not understand.

6. *Listen and respond.* Effective stakeholder communication is a two-way process. Understanding and responding timely to stakeholder feedback and concerns helps to build trust and credibility with stakeholders.

7. *Monitor and evaluate.* Monitor and evaluate the effectiveness of stakeholder communication by collecting stakeholder feedback and using this feedback to improve communication processes and ensure stakeholder needs are being met.

Recommend the Most Appropriate Communication Channel/Tool

Task 2, Enabler 1

Most business analysis work involves communication. Communication occurs at various times during the project, with various stakeholders and requires different methods of communication (e.g., reporting, presentation, etc.). Understanding the various communication channels available is an important first step. Communication channels have varying levels of information richness. Face-to-face and videoconferencing provide verbal and nonverbal communication, making them the most information rich. Written documents and spreadsheets have the lowest information richness, as they can be misunderstood or misinterpreted.

Knowing when to use verbal versus written communication is the next step. Verbal communication is generally faster and allows for immediate feedback and clarification, while written communication is generally more precise and creates a record of the conversation. Use verbal communication for conveying feelings and use written communication for conveying facts. Other considerations for choosing the communication channel should include the following:

- **Identify the audience** Consider who the communication is intended for. If the communication is for a large audience, a presentation or webinar may be appropriate. If the communication is for a small group or an individual, a phone call or one-on-one meeting may be more appropriate.

- **Consider the content** Determine the type of information that needs to be communicated. If the information is complex and detailed, a written report or memo may be more appropriate. If the information is visual, such as charts or diagrams, a presentation or infographic may be more effective.

- **Time constraints** Consider the time frame for the communication. If the communication needs to be delivered quickly, a phone call or e-mail may be more appropriate. If more time is available, a face-to-face meeting or presentation may be better.

- **Communication frequency** Determine how often the communication needs to be delivered. If the communication is a one-time event, a presentation or report may be appropriate. If the communication is ongoing, a combination of communication channels may be necessary, such as a regular e-mail newsletter or project status updates.

- **Communication culture** Consider the culture and preferences of the stakeholders. If the stakeholders prefer face-to-face communication, a meeting or presentation may be more appropriate. If they prefer digital communication, an e-mail or online platform may be more effective.

The most appropriate communication channel/tool is determined by who the various stakeholders are, their roles, and their interests. Choosing appropriate communication methods is important to ensure they meet their needs.

Organizational communication requirements and established capabilities may constrain methods of communication. These can include various communication technologies (including videoconferencing and remote collaboration tools) and security, information sharing, and record retention policies. Match the available methods to individual stakeholders' preferred methods of communication.

Demonstrate Why Communication Is Important for a Business Analyst Between Various Teams

Task 2, Enabler 2

The business analyst focuses on comprehending stakeholders and their connection to the "solution scope," which includes business objectives, features, and requirements necessary for delivering the solution.

A shared understanding of the project goals and objectives across teams is important from project initiation and should be continually reinforced throughout the project. This is because it helps to ensure that everyone is working toward the same thing and that there is no confusion or misunderstanding about what needs to be done. Often the project kick-off meeting is used to share this understanding, and it can be included in the project charter and product roadmap. This shared understanding across teams is important for the following reasons:

- **Understanding requirements** Working with different teams, including stakeholders, developers, testers, and project managers, requires the BA to understand each team's unique needs.

- **Collaborating with cross-functional teams** Working with cross-functional teams requires each team to understand their roles and responsibilities to work most effectively together.

- **Resolving issues** Many issues arise during a project, and the BA must communicate with various teams to come up with solutions.

- **Ensuring quality**   BAs must effectively communicate with developers, testers, and project managers to ensure that the level of product quality meets all requirements and specifications.

- **Managing expectations**   BAs must effectively communicate with stakeholders and project managers to ensure that everyone is on the same page about project goals, timelines, and budgets. As the project continues, there must be collaboration and open communication between all team members, with transparency regarding progress made and obstacles encountered.

As projects focus more on value delivery, BAs must clearly communicate work prioritization, including the prioritization and consensus for agreed-upon product requirements, features, and functions. BAs can show progress toward delivering those requirements established on visual artifacts, including task or Kanban boards, traceability matrices, burnup/burndown charts, or project network diagrams. Regardless of how information is displayed, BAs must update and show it openly and on time.

You should recommend that various teams be colocated to take advantage of osmotic communication. When teams (and possibly stakeholders) are colocated in their workspaces, communication ability increases through "osmosis." Osmotic communication is information that is heard in the common workplace—not eavesdropping, but just overhearing what others are saying. For example, Colleen tells James that she'll be out next week, and you overhear that message. Next week, Julie comes looking for Colleen and can't find her. You can help Julie because of osmotic communication—you heard that Colleen will be gone that week. It's like osmosis; you absorb the information because it's being communicated around you, not necessarily toward you.

Virtual conferencing technology can be a viable alternative to in-person meetings if it is used effectively. This technology may include fishbowl windows (a long-lived video conferencing link between the various locations in which the team is dispersed), virtual pairing (using virtual conferencing tools to share screens, including voice and video links), and videoconference meetings.

Peer reviews, frequent feedback among team members, and group decision-making techniques enable collaboration among multiple team members. In addition, BAs often identify usage and expectations in either the team charter for a predictive approach or the ground rules for an adaptive strategy.

Business analysts should encourage their teams to reflect on their work throughout the project. This reflection can help to identify successful practices that can be repeated in future work, as well as areas where improvements could be made. Additionally, the team should integrate key enhancements into the next work period and then review them to determine if they have been effective. By continuously trying out new changes and evaluating their effectiveness, the team can improve the process, the product, and their own effectiveness throughout the project.

Determine How to Gather Requirements

Task 3

Before the business analyst gathers, elicits, and engineers requirements, they can and should be classified according to both their level of detail and their source of discovery. Project requirements (see Figure 6-6) can be classified as follows.

Business Requirements   Business requirements outline the objectives, goals, and needs of a business and describe the business processes, workflows, and activities that are required to meet them. Business requirements are typically developed during the early stages of a project, and they form the foundation for the development of subsequent requirements. They may include elements such as:

- Business rules and constraints
- Performance metrics and key performance indicators (KPIs)
- Compliance requirements
- Stakeholder needs and expectations
- Budget and resource constraints

Stakeholder Requirements

Stakeholder requirements describe the needs and expectations of the stakeholders of a project or initiative. Stakeholders are individuals, groups, or organizations that have a vested interest in the project and can be impacted by its outcomes. Stakeholder requirements are typically gathered through stakeholder analysis and engagement activities.

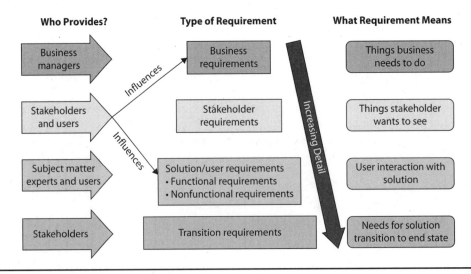

Figure 6-6   Requirement types

Solution/User Requirements

Solution/user requirements specify the characteristics, constraints, and other aspects of the solution that will address the needs or problems of the stakeholders. Solution/user requirements describe what needs to be done to solve a particular problem or meet a specific need (e.g., screen layouts and report formats). Solution/user requirements are typically developed after the problem or need has been identified and analyzed. Solution/user requirements help to ensure that the solution will meet the needs of the stakeholders and be feasible from a technical perspective. They provide the necessary guidance for the design, development, and testing of the solution.

Solution/user requirements decompose into functional and nonfunctional requirements.

Functional requirements describe what the system or product is expected to do or accomplish. They specify the features, functions, and capabilities that are required to meet the needs of the end users. Functional requirements are typically described in terms of inputs, processes, and outputs. Examples of functional requirements might include

- The ability to add items to a shopping cart
- The ability to search for products by name or category
- The ability to process payment transactions

Nonfunctional requirements describe how the system or product is expected to perform or operate. They are not related to the system's functions or features, but rather to the system's performance, usability, reliability, and other quality attributes. Examples of nonfunctional requirements might include

- Response time requirements
- Security requirements
- Usability requirements
- Reliability requirements

Nonfunctional requirements are often just as important as functional requirements because they help to ensure that the system or product operates as intended and meets the user's expectations. For example, a system may have all the necessary functional requirements, but if it's too slow or difficult to use, it may not be successful.

Transition Requirements   Transition requirements specify what should happen when transitioning from the current state to the desired future state. They outline the actions or changes you must make during the transition phase of a project or process.

For example, suppose your company moves from an old software system to a new one. In that case, a transition requirement might detail how you migrate data from the old system to the new system without information loss.

Transition requirements help to ensure that any transition is smooth and successful. They identify specific steps you should take during the transition and ensure all stakeholders know their roles and responsibilities.

Transition requirements also help to minimize the risks and disruptions that can occur during the transition phase. For example, identifying key actions you should take and ensuring you prepare all stakeholders for the transition reduce the likelihood of errors, delays, and misunderstandings.

Transition requirements help ensure our transition has successful outcomes.

Gathering the Project Requirements

It's great to have a project, but it's even greater to understand what the stakeholders want the project to create. The collect requirements process aims to identify and document what the stakeholders need from the project. The requirements you'll identify from the project sponsor, customer, and other stakeholders need to be quantifiable, measurable, and documented to confirm that the results of the project satisfy the needs of the stakeholder. You don't want requirements that use subjective terms to describe the project deliverables. What's "good" to you may not be "good" to someone else.

Requirements gathering is the process of collecting and documenting information from stakeholders about the desired functionality and features of a product or service. This process involves techniques such as interviews, surveys, and workshops. The goal of requirements gathering is to understand the needs of the stakeholders so that the product or service can be developed to meet those needs. The requirements gathered will be used to create a requirements specification, which is a document that describes the functionality and features of the product or service.

Requirements elicitation is the process of drawing out information from stakeholders about the product or service needs and desires. Elicitation is a more interactive process that involves active listening, asking questions, and clarifying requirements, so that the requirements gathering process can be more accurate and complete. It involves the business analyst leveraging their expertise to determine the most suitable approaches and techniques for gathering information from diverse sources. The primary goal is to establish a shared understanding through interactions between the business analyst and stakeholders.

Business Analysis for Practitioners: A Practice Guide includes the processes for identifying stakeholders, preparing for elicitation, and conducting elicitation to obtain information from sources. Figure 6-7 shows the three processes for requirements elicitation.

Further elaborating on effectively eliciting requirements, it involves the following steps:

1. **Determine the participants:**
   a. *Identify stakeholders.* Identify all stakeholders involved in the project, including users, customers, business owners, developers, and other key individuals who may have an interest in the project's success.

   b. *Categorize groups/classes.* Then categorize the identified stakeholders into groups or classes. By categorizing stakeholders, the BA can better understand their needs and interests.

   c. *Order elicitation activities.* Some information is necessary before other information can be understood. These dependencies can be documented in the elicitation plan to facilitate the organization of elicitation activities.

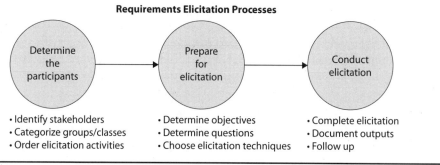

Requirements Elicitation Processes

- Identify stakeholders
- Categorize groups/classes
- Order elicitation activities

- Determine objectives
- Determine questions
- Choose elicitation techniques

- Complete elicitation
- Document outputs
- Follow up

Figure 6-7   Requirements elicitation processes

2. Prepare for elicitation:

a. *Determine objectives.* To ensure that elicitation activities are effective, it is important to set objectives for each session. The objective is the reason why the elicitation activity is being undertaken. Each session should provide some value and benefit to justify the time it takes to obtain the needed information.

b. *Determine questions.* When conducting elicitation activities, such as interviews, focus groups, or facilitated workshops, it is often helpful to prepare a list of questions in advance. This will help to ensure that the session objectives are achieved and that all relevant information is gathered. It is also important to be flexible and adaptable. The questions you ask may need to be adjusted based on the responses you receive. It is also important to be prepared to answer questions from the stakeholders.

c. *Choose elicitation techniques.* There are many different techniques that can be used for requirements elicitation. Some of the most common techniques include interviews, focus groups, brainstorming, observation, document analysis, prototyping, and requirements workshops. The best technique for requirements elicitation will vary depending on the specific situation. You should choose the technique that is most likely to gather the information you need from the stakeholders.

3. Conduct elicitation:

a. *Complete elicitation.* One guideline is to stop gathering information when the risk of problems emerging from the lack of complete information is acceptable. Another guideline is to stop gathering information when the analysis produces no further questions. This means that the business analyst has a good understanding of the stakeholders' needs and requirements and that there is no need to gather any more information.

 NOTE   In an adaptive project life cycle, the project team focuses on delivering working software increments to the customer as quickly as possible. This means that the team must be able to quickly gather requirements, design and build the working software increment, and test it to ensure that it meets the customer's needs.

b. *Document outputs.* It is important to document, whether formally or informally, the results of elicitation activities. The documentation can be as simple as a snapshot of a whiteboard or as formal as a requirements management tool. The primary goal of documentation is to capture the information gathered during elicitation so that it can be used to perform other business analysis tasks.

c. *Follow up.* Following up with all stakeholders involved in elicitation can help to ensure that elicitation activities are completed on time and to the best of your ability. It can also help to identify and resolve any problems that may arise.

EXAM TIP When taking the CAPM exam, you should assume that unless otherwise explicitly stated, you must go through a requirements eliciting procedure prior to completing the scope statement.

Match Tools to Scenarios

Task 3, Enabler 1

Requirements are gathered differently depending on the project approach used. The methods used are defined as part of the business analysis plan, including activities, time periods, and stakeholders' involvement. Even though the term "gather" is sometimes referred to this activity in project management, business analysis prefers to use the term "elicit" (or draw out), especially when the information is not readily available. These techniques are also referred to as *data gathering, data analysis,* and *data representation* in project management.

Use Cases (Predictive Approach)

When using a predictive approach, requirements can be gathered based on previous work that has been done on similar projects. This can be helpful in saving time and resources, as the business analyst can use the knowledge and experience gained from previous projects to inform the planning of the current project.

For example, if a company has previously developed a software application, the business analyst for a new software application project can use the requirements gathered from the previous project as a starting point for the current project.

Use cases describe the interactions between actors (users, systems, or external entities) and a system or application. They are often used to capture complex requirements and illustrate how a system will work from the user's perspective. Use cases are useful for scenarios where there are many stakeholders with different needs and perspectives and where the requirements are likely to remain stable over time. Figure 6-8 shows an example of a use case for an airline reservation system. The actors are the passenger and airline agent.

User Stories (Adaptive Approach)

Projects using an adaptive approach may utilize group sessions to develop requirements and document them as either epics or user stories. A *user story* is a brief, simple description of a feature or requirement that captures what the user wants to achieve. User stories are helpful for scenarios where the focus is on understanding the user's perspective and

Figure 6-8
Use case
example

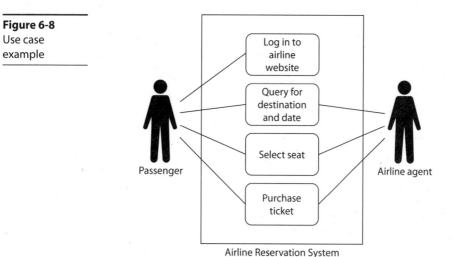

Airline Reservation System

needs and where the requirements are likely to change over time. These are often captured individually as needs are recognized by stakeholders and added to the product backlog. Figures 6-9, 6-10, and 6-11 show a user story example and criteria for creation.

User stories should be easy to understand by everyone on the team. Strictly speaking, user stories are created by the product owner, and they go into the product backlog.

Figure 6-9
User story
template card
(© 2023 C and
P Dillon-Parkin.
Used with
permission.)

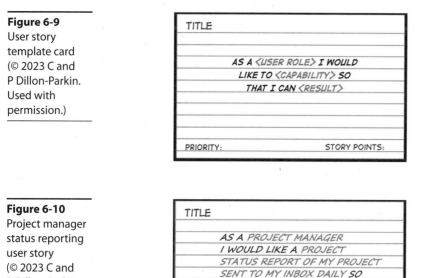

Figure 6-10
Project manager
status reporting
user story
(© 2023 C and
P Dillon-Parkin.
Used with
permission.)

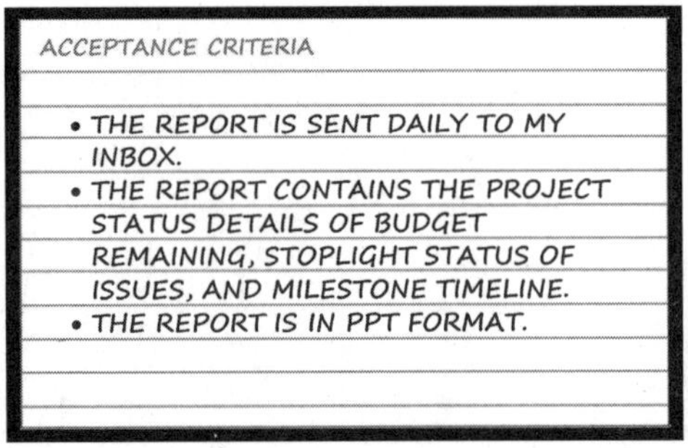

Figure 6-11
User story
acceptance
criteria (back of
card) (© 2023
C and P Dillon-
Parkin. Used with
permission.)

ACCEPTANCE CRITERIA

- THE REPORT IS SENT DAILY TO MY INBOX.
- THE REPORT CONTAINS THE PROJECT STATUS DETAILS OF BUDGET REMAINING, STOPLIGHT STATUS OF ISSUES, AND MILESTONE TIMELINE.
- THE REPORT IS IN PPT FORMAT.

Realistically speaking, user stories are written by everyone on the team, though it's the product owner who is responsible for the user stories and the prioritization of the user stories in the product backlog. Each user story should aim to create value. When a person proposes a user story and the value is being considered for project inclusion, it's called a *candidate story*—it is worth considering but hasn't yet been fully included in the project requirements.

In user story formats, you give the scenario of what the role is doing and the action that is happening, such as purchasing things from your website. And you provide the result, which is the realized value of the action. One of my favorite approaches to writing user stories is called the three Cs:

- **Card** The user story in its raw form fits on a single card.

- **Conversation** Eliciting further details about the card is necessary. The conversation promotes incremental and continuous collaboration among the team. This is needed to build a shared understanding around the problem and potential solution.

- **Confirmation** The customer confirms that the user story is complete and meets existing acceptance criteria. The user story captures the essential requirements and translates them into test criteria to ensure delivery of a successful user story.

During the sprint review, the development team demonstrates the completed user story functionality. For example, say a company is selling car parts, and the user story reads: "As a customer, I want to search for a car part, so I can order it online." In the sprint review, the team could read the card and then show the action and the completed result. This is quick and easy to understand and simple to demonstrate as a user story that has met the definition of done (DoD). For example, DoD refers to the agreement of the user acceptance being met—and decided jointly by the team and the stakeholder/PO. DoD is unique to each team, especially what the difference is between being completed rather than "done"—or maybe "done done." I finished writing my book (completed), I incorporate feedback (done; my interpretation), but my supervisor says it isn't "done" until it is published (my idea of "done done.")

 EXAM TIP Of course, not all user stories are so simple, but the CAPM exam will test you on the concept.

To organize these user stories, you can use a product roadmap to show sequentially when you plan to deliver themes or features/functions. The sections of the roadmap often represent dates of upcoming product releases.

You can use a story map to group user stories for an individual release. This technique sequences the key functionality you will deliver during the release. Then, you can group all appropriate user stories into a release backlog and prioritize them beneath the sequenced functionality. The release backlog and prioritization help to identify and prioritize user stories for individual iterations within a release.

The product owner prioritizes the release backlog, using the team members' estimates to determine the work they will commit to during an iteration. A BA can develop additional detail by working with the product owner through use cases, showing processes, information, and business rules required for the user story.

These stories become the iteration backlog and are tracked during the iteration to show progress. This can include task boards and burndown/burnup charts.

Identify the Requirements Gathering Approach for a Situation

Task 3, Enabler 2
The sequence and techniques used to gather requirements are basically the same regardless of whether an adaptive (time-bound), predictive, or hybrid approach is used. The difference is the amount of detail included. The adaptive continuous flow approach is based on prioritization of single requests, detail analysis, and tracking to completion and approval.

Table 6-2 shows a comparison of requirements gathering techniques. There are several tools that can be used regardless of the approach being employed, and they are described in the following sections.

Technique	Advantages	Disadvantages
Interview	Achieve a deeper level of engagement when talking to someone one on one.	It's more time-consuming than arranging one session with a group of people.
	It's easier to arrange a session with one person than to coordinate a group.	You miss out on people bouncing ideas off one another in a group session.
	Gain greater "buy in" from stakeholders. Helps them to feel like they are more valued and have greater ownership of the project. As a result, they could offer more support in the later stages of your project.	Interviewer's presence or characteristics may bias results.
		Requires trained interviewers.
		May only get a small sample because of time constraints.
		Being consistent across interviews is challenging.

Table 6-2 Comparison of Requirements Gathering Techniques

Technique	Advantages	Disadvantages
Observation	Get real-time specific insights from user behavior. Avoid the bias of people telling you want you want to hear, rather than what they need. Natural setting. Ability to choose interaction level of researcher.	Limited to a point in time. They require a large workforce. For example, if you are trying to observe a rare event, it may be necessary to have a large number of observers in order to increase the chances of seeing the event. Additionally, if you are trying to observe a large area, it may be necessary to have a large number of observers in order to cover the entire area. Recruiting participants and gaining approval to go ahead can be difficult. If researcher interacts with group, they may not be objective. Difficulty generalizing with large population. Requires skilled observer.
Prototyping	Get real-time, in-depth user feedback. It's the only way to really test how people use physical products. Works well in agile environments.	Only works for certain projects. It can be very expensive and time-consuming. Not always suited to waterfall-based project management.
Questionnaire/survey	It's quick and can be sent to a large database very quickly. Can tailor questions to different stakeholders to address different business objectives. Saves time from attending meetings and recording the information—the participants do it. Easy to use statistical analysis on results.	Designing and writing a good survey can be time-consuming. Participation can be limited. Return rate is low. It's one way: there's no opportunity to probe or clarify on the spot. Don't know if participants misinterpret questions.
Group-facilitated workshops	Able to bounce ideas off of multiple people. Can tap into diverse knowledge and experience. Can clarify response through probing.	Getting the best results requires an experienced facilitator. Without a facilitator, danger exists of quieter participants being drowned out by louder participants. Difficult to coordinate stakeholders' schedules. Difficulty with analyzing data.

Table 6-2   Comparison of Requirements Gathering Techniques (*continued*)

Interviews   Interviews can be formal or informal activities to help gather preliminary information, especially regarding the required vision, objectives, and critical functionality. They usually are done on an individual basis between the interviewer and interviewee. As a business analyst conducting an interview, structure and fully prepare the questions in advance or use unstructured questions employing a starting question that will allow appropriate follow-on questions.

Because of time and location constraints, conduct interviews synchronously or asynchronously. Synchronous interviews are performed live or in real time. They can be face-to-face or virtual. Asynchronous interviews involve preparing questions and distributing them to the interviewee, who in turn answers and returns the results to the interviewer.

Use interviews to gain further knowledge about a subject that can't be discussed appropriately in a group environment.

Observation   In observation, the observer views people in their work environment to understand actual activities and work within a context. The observer may observe workers by silently watching their steps or may ask clarifying questions as they observe. Workers may not express all of the information they know about a topic because they may not think all of the information is important. For example, a worker may not tell you about a problem they are having with a machine because they may think the problem is not important or that you will not be able to help them. Experienced workers often make decisions based on previous understanding—asking questions fleshes out areas they may not mention.

Observation often provides more insight into work that is difficult to explain, resulting in unbiased, objective, and factual information regarding current practices. In addition, observe workers by silently watching their steps or asking clarifying questions as they perform the process.

Passive observation means passively observing without interrupting the work with questions or requesting additional clarification. *Active observation* allows the observer to increase the information gathered through questioning. *Participatory observation* involves the observer participating in activities that are being observed, including getting answers to additional questions based on the work performed.

Simulation is a slightly different method of observation where the activities are simulated by a tool that performs the work, often in a training facility. Again, frequently ask follow-up questions of the worker for additional details.

NOTE   Sometimes, observing people changes how they perform.

Prototyping   Prototyping involves creating a preliminary version of a system or application to test the functionality and usability of the design. Prototyping is another method to gather feedback through review and experimentation of a working model before finalizing the product.

Prototyping can be *low-fidelity* and created with pen and paper, whiteboards, or a modeling tool to gather feedback with a visual representation of the product's functionality and look and feel. *High-fidelity* prototyping creates a final product over several iterations, allowing users to interact with the result to understand how it will work. These high-fidelity prototypes can be

- Throwaways that are disposed of after confirming the functionality
- Evolutionary with each session, including additional functionality

In agile projects, prototyping is often used to create a minimum viable product (MVP) or the initial release. Prototyping is helpful for scenarios where the requirements are complex and challenging to define and where stakeholders need to see a working system before providing feedback. Additional examples include storyboarding to show sequence or navigation through graphical representations.

Finally, wireframes are a low-fidelity method of prototyping that creates a skeleton of the product, e.g., static drawings of the user interface to help specify the sequence of steps, especially from one web page to another. Wireframing also serves as a simplified version of a portion of the product, depicting the look and feel of functionality and user experience.

Questionnaires and Surveys   Use a questionnaire or survey when gathering information from a large group of stakeholders, especially those from different geographical areas. This requires you to develop questions that can elicit useful information for analysis, often including closed-ended questions with little opportunity for clarification. Determining the makeup of the recipients is essential to elicit responses that reflect a cross-section sample. Since the return rate is often relatively low and may consist of very positive or very negative reactions, the results of a questionnaire or survey may be biased.

 EXAM TIP   Questionnaires and surveys are the quickest and most cost-effective way to collect data from a variety of people.

Group-Facilitated Workshops   A group-facilitated workshop is a meeting or event where a facilitator leads a group of people through a series of activities or exercises to achieve a specific goal. Use group-facilitated workshops to gather information from stakeholders, enabling the generation and capture of needs and requirements. A group-facilitated workshop can consist of a small group, preselected to represent diverse opinions, referred to as a *focus group*.

A group-facilitated workshop can also include a large cross-functional team that can use brainstorming, brainwriting, story mapping, and affinity diagrams to identify needs, risks, or potential solutions. Collaborative games, common in agile approaches, are often used to gather information from individual attendees. A facilitator runs these workshops and often includes subject matter experts (SMEs) to create a focus on the objectives of the workshop.

Explain a Requirements Traceability Matrix/Product Backlog

Task 3, Enabler 3

A requirements traceability matrix and a product backlog are two important tools used for managing requirements. A requirements traceability matrix and a product backlog can be used to improve the visibility, communication, efficiency, and risk reduction of a project.

Requirements Traceability Matrix

Requirements management is the process of gathering, documenting, and managing the requirements for a software system. It is a critical step in the software development process, as it ensures that the system meets the needs of the users. It also helps to identify and resolve any conflicts between requirements.

Requirements traceability is the ability to track the requirements throughout the software development process. This means that it is possible to see how each requirement was implemented and how it was tested. Traceability is important for ensuring that the system meets all the requirements and that it is free of defects.

I suggest two types of requirements traceability matrices to ensure your software development process is rigorous, your systems are reliable, and they meet the needs of your users: the bidirectional traceability matrix (BTM) and the requirements traceability matrix (RTM) for scope management.

The BTM is a tool that can be used to implement forward and backward traceability through the project life cycle. Forward and backward traceability are important for ensuring the quality of the software development process. They help to ensure that all the requirements are tested and that all the test cases are relevant to the requirements.

- **Traceable forward**   Each requirement should have a unique identifier that assists in identifying and maintaining change history and tracing the requirement through the system components.

- **Traceable backward**   Each requirement should be traced back to specific customer, user, or stakeholder input, such as a use case, a business rule, or some other origin.

Figure 6-12 is an example of a BTM showing forward and backward traceability. Tracing must be performed as requirements details are added at each level on the left side of the V. The higher-level requirements are decomposed and allocated to the more detailed requirements. The requirements must be traceable to the lower-level requirements and back to the higher level. This will ensure that the lower-level, detailed requirements do not introduce additional requirements not identified at the higher levels. The best traceability practice is to trace forward from detailed requirements to the design, development, integration, and testing of the deliverables. As components of the deliverables are developed and integrated into the final system solution, the deliverables must trace back to the requirements at the appropriate levels.

The RTM for scope management is a valuable tool for ensuring that the documented requirements are mapped directly back to business objectives. An RTM is a table that

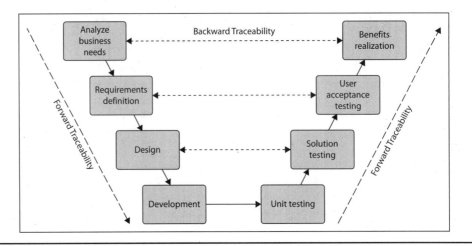

Figure 6-12 Forward and backward traceability

links the origins of individual product requirements to the expected deliverable that meets those requirements so that you can track requirements throughout the project life cycle. This is particularly important if you want to either change a requirement, assess the impact a requirement will have on deliverables, or check that a deliverable still meets the original requirement.

The RTM is a grid that is more often used in a project to capture and track requirements that have been approved as part of the project scope. The RTM links requirements to other artifacts, such as design documents, test cases, and business rules, to ensure that all requirements are covered and that changes to one requirement are reflected in all related artifacts. The formality and detail of the RTM will vary depending on the organizational methodology, the context of the project, and the needs of the project. Determination is also required as to when requirements are placed on the matrix. If a business analysis approach is being followed, the requirements are often approved and baselined by the stakeholders before being placed and traced on the RTM.

One of the key uses of the RTM is to support impact assessment of change requests through analysis of the relationships between requirements. For example, when a change request is received, you can review the requirements affected, and other associated requirements, to help provide additional insight into the overall impact of a change.

Adaptive projects use a simplified version of an RTM with task boards or Kanban boards, showing the requirements and where in the process toward completion they are at any point in time. These simplified versions may just identify columns including To Do, In Progress, and Done or they may show more detail representing the different groups working on portions of a request.

The determination of the attributes of an RTM for an individual project is conducted as part of the business analysis planning activities. Once identified, it is important that these attributes are tracked and that they do not overlap with information tracked and managed elsewhere. Once the attributes of the RTM have been identified, it is important

Trace ID	Requirement Source	Business Requirement (BR) ID	Stakeholder Requirement (SR) ID	UAT Case (TC) ID
T-1	Sponsor - DO	BR 1.0	SR 1.1	TC 1.1.1
T-2	Functional Mgr - MM	BR 1.0	SR 1.1	TC 1.1.2
T-3	Product Owner - CP	BR 1.0	SR 1.2	TC 1.2.1
T-4	CEO - DW	BR 1.0	SR 1.2	TC 1.2.2
T-5	US Congress	BR 2.0	SR 2.1	TC 2.1.1

Figure 6-13 Requirements traceability matrix (RTM) for scope management

to create a template for the RTM. The RTM should be updated as the project progresses. This will ensure that the information in the RTM is accurate and up to date.

Attributes most often include a unique identifier for the requirement, a short description, the creation date, last revision date, version number, and the current development stage (design, build, test, approval, or implementation). Additional attributes can include a WBS code of account or deliverable, status (active, approved, deferred, or cancelled), priority, owner, and source.

Since the RTM is often implemented via a spreadsheet, additional columns may allow mapping to other documents, including design documents, test cases, test results, approvals, and so forth. As individual requirements are broken into smaller components, the associations can be maintained in the RTM.

Requirements management tools or spreadsheets are commonly used by organizations to trace requirements. An example of a requirements traceability matrix for scope management with attributes is shown in Figure 6-13. This is one example and is only part of the complete requirements traceability practice for the project.

RTMs can be complex due to the large number and variety of traceable requirements, requirements levels, and elements. In certain cases, the RTM, stored in a spreadsheet, can become the primary requirements repository for some organizations.

Product Backlog

The product backlog is a key tool for managing the requirements of a project. It is a key part of agile development methodologies, such as Scrum. In Scrum, the product backlog is owned by the product owner, who handles gathering and prioritizing the requirements from the stakeholders to provide the greatest value to the organization or customer. As new items are added to the backlog, they are evaluated, and the backlog is continually sequenced based on business value. The development team then works from the product backlog to implement the features that are most important to the users.

The product owner is responsible for the product backlog, but they may not conduct all the activities in refining the backlog. In some organizations, the product owner may work with a team of stakeholders to evaluate new items and sequence the backlog. In other organizations, the product owner may delegate the refinement of stories to the development team.

PART II

A product backlog contains all the potential requirements or needs that have been identified by stakeholders. The potential requirements or needs can be merely functionality or features desired, or more detailed requirements in the form of an epic or a user story, with personas and benefits also identified. The product backlog is used to prioritize the work that needs to be done and to track the progress of the project. It is typically organized by priority and estimated effort.

The product backlog is a living document that is constantly being updated throughout the project as new requirements are identified and old requirements are changed or removed. Stories can be removed from the backlog and refined, often decomposing a story into smaller stories. It is an essential tool for communicating the project's goals to the team and to the stakeholders. And it ensures the product development process is aligned with the needs of the users and the business.

Here are some of the key benefits of using a product backlog:

- **Increased visibility** Provides increased visibility into the requirements and the project's progress. This helps to ensure that everyone is on the same page and that the project is on track.

- **Improved communication** Improves communication between the different stakeholders in the project. This helps to ensure that everyone's needs are met and that the project is successful.

- **Increased efficiency** Helps to increase the efficiency of the project by providing a way to track the requirements and the project's progress. This helps to identify and resolve any issues early in the process.

- **Reduced risk** Helps to reduce the risk of defects in the product by providing a way to track the requirements and the project's progress. This helps to identify and resolve any issues early in the process.

Here are some of the key elements of a product backlog:

- **Requirement** Requirements can be functional (what the product should do) or nonfunctional (how the product should do it).

- **Priority** Shows how important it is to the users. Requirements with a higher priority should be implemented before requirements with a lower priority.

- **Estimated effort** An estimate of how much time it will take to implement a requirement. This estimate can be used to prioritize the work that needs to be done and to track the progress of the project.

- **Status** Shows whether it is new, in progress, complete, or deferred. This information can be used to track the progress of the project and to identify any issues that need to be addressed.

Once the work has been agreed upon by the product owner and the delivery team, no changes are allowed. Work can be stopped on a story that has been determined to no longer be valuable, but few, if any, new items can be added to the work in progress during an iteration.

Demonstrate an Understanding of Product Roadmaps

Task 4

A *product roadmap* is a high-level strategic plan that outlines the vision, goals, and priorities for a product over a set period, typically 6 to12 months or longer. It is a living document that is constantly being updated as new features are added and old features are removed.

The product owner is likely to work with the BA, the scrum master, and the team to develop a product roadmap. Product roadmaps are used by product managers to communicate the product vision to stakeholders and to track the progress of the product development process. They are also used by development teams to prioritize work and to ensure that the product is developed in a way that meets the needs of the users and the business.

The product roadmap shows how the project should move from start to finish, with intermittent deliverables to the stakeholders. It's an ideal document of how the team will get from the start to the end. It answers what conditions must be met to allow the product owner to do a release, what the components of a release are, and the result of the project.

The product owner typically creates a product roadmap in collaboration with stakeholders. The product owner bases the roadmap on market research, customer feedback, and other relevant data sources. Finally, the product owner uses the roadmap to communicate the product vision and priorities to the development team, ensuring everyone is aligned and focused on delivering essential features.

This is one area where agile projects shine over predictive projects. If you're building a house, there is no benefit to the homeowner until the house is completely done. The homeowner can't move into a portion of the house until the entire house is ready. In agile projects, the customer could begin using a portion of the software, such as version 1, while your team continues to build and create version 2. Each release of the software builds on what's already been created.

Decomposition is the process of breaking down a complex problem or system into smaller, more manageable parts. In the context of product development, decomposition is used to break down a strategic roadmap into a tactical roadmap. In the example product roadmap shown in Figure 6-14, there are four epics targeted for delivery in release 1. Once the product roadmap is accepted, the product team will decompose those agreed-upon epics into stories required to deliver each epic. This populates the product backlog. The product owner then prioritizes those stories for the team to deliver.

The following are some key components of a product roadmap:

- **Product vision**   Brief description of the product's long-term goals.
- **Goals and objectives**   Clearly defines the goals and objectives of the product development, including sales targets, user engagement, or other metrics that are important to the success of the product.
- **Timeline**   Provides a timeline for the development of the product, including key milestones and deadlines when features will be released.

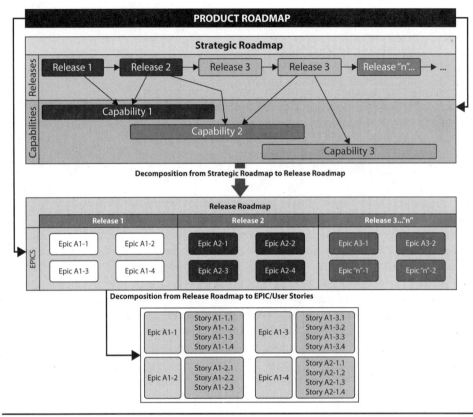

Figure 6-14 Product roadmap

- **Features** Identifies the key features that will be developed for the product, which may be grouped by release or by specific development phase.

- **Prioritization** Prioritizes the features that will be developed, based on their urgency and importance to the overall success of the product.

- **Risks and assumptions** Identifies any risks or assumptions that could impact the development of the product.

- **Feedback and iteration** Should be flexible and allow for feedback and iteration. This means that as the product is developed and tested, changes may be made to the roadmap to reflect new information or user feedback.

Here are some of the benefits of using a product roadmap:

- **Increased visibility** Provides increased visibility into the product development process. This helps to ensure that everyone is on the same page and that the product is on track.

- **Improved communication**   Improves communication between the different stakeholders in the product development process. This helps to ensure that everyone's needs are met and that the product is successful.

- **Increased efficiency**   Helps to increase the efficiency of the product development process by providing a way to track the progress of the product and to identify any issues early in the process.

- **Reduced risk**   Helps to reduce the risk of defects in the product by providing a way to track the progress of the product and to identify any issues early in the process.

Product roadmaps can be created using a variety of tools, including spreadsheets, project management software, and presentation software. The best tool for creating a product roadmap will depend on the specific needs of the team.

NOTE   A *product roadmap* is a high-level overview of the product's vision, strategy, and priorities. It is a visual representation of how the product will evolve over time. A *product backlog* is a list of all the features, bug fixes, and other work that needs to be done to complete a product. It is a living document that is continually updated as new requirements are identified and old requirements are changed or removed.

Explain the Application of a Product Roadmap

Task 4, Enabler 1

In adaptive projects you'll work with a product roadmap in lieu of a milestone list. A product roadmap is a tool to show the major product deliverables, when they'll be available based on project conditions, and how the product can grow. A product roadmap also helps you, or the product owner, to secure project funding because it'll show the business value the adaptive project will create. Product roadmaps aren't easy to create, because adaptive projects change frequently; you don't want the product roadmap to be so tight that it doesn't allow changes, but you also don't want it to be so loose that there's little value in the document.

Product roadmaps don't get married to specific project deliverables, but rather embrace goals, visions, and business value. Product roadmaps identify the pain points of an organization, the business value of why the project is being undertaken, and loosely tie the forecasted deliverables to the overall goals and solutions of the project. This enables the project requirements to shift, as expected in an agile project, without conflicting with big promises in the product roadmap.

The product roadmap aims to describe what the project will accomplish more than what the project will create. It can be used to describe when releases from the project will happen, such as "when this business value is realized, a release will go live in the organization." It's tricky business, but it needs to be created to communicate what the project will accomplish and to ensure stakeholders that the project will create value in ratio to the cost and time needed for the project to exist.

Even though product roadmaps are generally associated with adaptive approaches, showing the expected delivery time frames for product features or functions, the roadmap is also a key element in program initiation. In that context, the roadmap is a graphical and chronological representation of major milestones, including when individual program components will deliver outcomes and potential benefits. The key benefit of developing a product roadmap is to show the expected results and potential order in which they will be delivered. A product roadmap can be used internally as well as shared with external customers, vendors, and others.

The project management team will perform the initial planning for an adaptive approach to set expected time frames for new releases or updates to the product. Agile release planning includes high-level release plans and the number of iterations for each release. Together, the product owner and the team can determine what needs they must develop and how long it will take to produce a new product release. These decisions are based on business goals and objectives while considering dependencies and impediments.

You can show these time frames on a product roadmap with an initial identification of the vision of the functionality included at the end of each release time frame. Here you can use the concept of *rolling wave planning*, where you delay the detail (or progressive elaboration of the specifics) closer to the time frame. Rolling wave planning allows you to re-sequence and adapt the product capabilities of individual releases to meet changing priorities and market conditions.

 EXAM TIP "Progressive elaboration" and "rolling wave planning" are PMI terms you should know for the exam.

Because of the changes that need to be supported, the releases identified on the roadmap only include the detail needed to address any project specifics, including size, complexity, and level of risk. Detailed planning for future releases is postponed so time is not wasted planning work that may not be delivered.

As the roadmap is elaborated, the scope of each release may include features, functions, epics, and user stories. This is similar to the decomposition process used in the work breakdown structure (WBS), where work packages are identified and scheduled.

As the project progresses, the roadmap is decomposed into smaller time periods, called iterations. The functionality for the release is then grouped into user stories from the product backlog that apply to that release. These user stories are then placed on a story map, which is a visual representation of the release. The selected user stories then become the release backlog.

The sequencing and prioritization of the user stories on the release backlog help determine the initial scheduled work of individual iterations. The user stories on the release backlog are continually prioritized and refined by the product owner prior to the iteration planning meeting. At that time, the final determination of the work that will be done during an iteration is made by the product owner, in collaboration with the development team. The product owner is responsible for ensuring that the work that is done is aligned with the product vision and that it meets the needs of the users. The development team is responsible for ensuring that the work is feasible and that it can be completed within the timebox.

A product roadmap is essential for any organization developing and launching successful products. It helps to keep everyone on the same page, focus efforts on critical goals and objectives, and ensure that the organization develops the product strategically and efficiently.

In business analysis, a product roadmap has several applications:

- **Communicate the product vision**   A product roadmap effectively communicates the product vision and strategy to all stakeholders, including executives, team members, and customers. It helps to align expectations and ensure everyone is working toward the same goals.

- **Prioritize features and initiatives**   The product roadmap helps the business analyst, product manager, and other stakeholders prioritize features and initiatives based on factors such as business value, customer needs, technical feasibility, and resource availability. By focusing on high-priority items, the team can allocate resources more effectively and make informed decisions about what to build and when.

- **Facilitate collaboration**   A product roadmap encourages collaboration among stakeholders, including product managers, BAs, designers, developers, and customers. It provides a shared understanding of the product's direction and goals, fostering cross-functional teamwork and decision-making.

- **Manage stakeholder expectations**   By clearly outlining the planned product features and milestones, the product roadmap helps manage stakeholder expectations regarding the product's development timeline, scope, and deliverables. This transparency can help prevent miscommunication and scope creep.

- **Track progress and monitor changes**   The product roadmap serves as a tracking tool that helps the team monitor progress toward product milestones and objectives. As market conditions, customer feedback, and other factors change, the roadmap can be updated to reflect these changes and ensure that the product remains aligned with business goals and customer needs.

- **Identify dependencies and risks**   A product roadmap allows the BA and other stakeholders to identify dependencies among features, as well as potential risks and bottlenecks that may impact the product's development timeline. This information can be used to develop risk mitigation strategies and contingency plans.

- **Support marketing and sales efforts**   A well-defined product roadmap can be used to inform marketing and sales teams about upcoming product features and enhancements, helping them create targeted messaging, promotional campaigns, and sales strategies.

PART II

Determine Which Components Go to Which Releases

Task 4, Enabler 2

Determining which components go to which releases is crucial to product development and requires careful consideration and planning. Developing the product roadmap and determining the scope of individual releases is a collaborative effort between the business and the delivery team and is required to arrive at a shared understanding of what is being requested and why. The roadmap provides a high-level timeline showing milestones, significant events, reviews, and decision points.

Before developing the product roadmap, a business case should already be established that identifies the economic feasibility and benefits that will be delivered by the product development effort. The business case, which outlines the reasons why a product is being developed, can affect the order in which features are added to a product roadmap and the expectations for individual releases. These decisions can change over time due to market forces or changes in organizational goals and objectives. It is important that the product roadmap aligns with the organizational strategy and other products.

The product owner and stakeholders can employ several techniques to help identify which components go to which releases on the roadmap. These techniques can include facilitated workshops and story mapping to help identify different solutions. Collaborative games, including product visioning or the development of a product box, can help in visualizing and agreeing upon the direction and features of the product. Finally, a feature model is an adaptive version of a scope model that represents all the solution features in a tree or hierarchical structure. The feature model identifies the features, potential epics, and user stories included in the product backlog. You can document the results of these techniques formally or informally as appropriate.

As more detail regarding the scope of individual releases becomes available, the product owner and stakeholders can create models to address scope boundaries, process sequences, information required for decisions, interfaces to other systems or users, and business rules to be followed. These models can be identified and created at the highest level of the roadmap and then progressively elaborated as additional analysis is required. They help find gaps in understanding and expose where further detail is needed. Finally, you can combine the output of the elicitation techniques with the models into documentation you can use to prioritize backlog items.

The prioritization of both releases on the roadmap and the detailed requirements will continue to change. Change significantly impacts the prioritization of the backlog items for a release. As those changes are identified, it is vital to assess the impact of the change on other areas. This assessment includes identifying the risk associated with the change and the work required for the requested change. It has implications for delivery timeframes and potential costs.

Adaptive approaches often use a less formal approach to analyzing the impact of change, with the emphasis on the value provided by the change. The prioritization of changes within a release is a given, as well as changes in the future release functionality. Regardless, the impact of any change needs to be analyzed not just to the functionality being delivered but also to the dependencies and sequences that might be affected.

If new work is continually added to the backlog, or work currently planned is not completed, the expected results of releases on the roadmap may not be completed as expected and planned. A clear understanding of the definition of done (DoD) is needed not only for individual stories at the iteration level but also for the expectations for the releases within the time frame shown on the roadmap.

Continual improvement of the product and the process used to develop it is essential to meeting the expectations of the product roadmap. This means that product managers and development teams should regularly review the product and the process to identify areas for improvement. This can be done through a variety of methods, such as surveys, interviews, and usability testing.

The DoD is a set of criteria that must be met before a product or feature can be considered complete. It is agreed upon by the delivery team and the product owner (PO). The DoD can be applied to the result of reviews and demos, as well as acceptance criteria.

There is some disagreement about how the DoD applies to burndown charts. A burndown chart is a visual representation of the work that remains to be done in a project. It shows the amount of work that is planned to be done each day, week, or month.

Some people argue that the DoD should not be applied to burndown charts because it is not always possible to know when a feature will be accepted by the PO. They argue that this can lead to inaccurate burndown charts and make it difficult to track progress.

Others argue that the DoD should be applied to burndown charts because it provides a clear definition of what it means for a feature to be complete. This can help to ensure that the team is focused on delivering high-quality work and that the PO is satisfied with the final product.

The best way to apply the DoD to burndown charts is to agree on a process with the PO. This process should include a way to track the progress of features and to communicate with the PO about any issues that may arise.

Here are some steps to help determine which components should be included in each release:

1. *Identify and prioritize components.* Begin by listing all the components or features that are planned for the product. Work with stakeholders to prioritize these items based on factors such as customer needs, business value, resource availability, and technical feasibility.

2. *Evaluate dependencies and constraints.* Assess the dependencies among components, as well as any constraints, such as resource limitations, technical limitations, or regulatory requirements. Understanding these dependencies and constraints will help ensure that components are included in the appropriate release.

3. *Define release goals and objectives.* Establish clear goals and objectives for each release, such as addressing specific customer needs, meeting market demands, or introducing new functionality. These goals and objectives should be aligned with the overall product vision and strategy.

4. *Allocate components to releases.* Based on the prioritized list of components, dependencies, constraints, and release goals, allocate components to specific releases. Consider the following factors when making these decisions:

- Customer needs and feedback
- Business value and ROI
- Technical feasibility and complexity
- Resource availability and capacity
- Regulatory requirements and deadlines
- Market trends and competitive landscape

5. *Balance scope, timeline, and resources.* Ensure that each release has a manageable scope, a realistic timeline, and sufficient resources to achieve its goals. Avoid overloading a release with too many components or overly complex features, as this may result in delays or reduced quality.

6. *Review and adjust as needed.* Regularly review and adjust the allocation of components to releases based on changing circumstances, such as new customer feedback, market developments, or resource constraints. This iterative approach allows for flexibility and ensures that the product remains aligned with business goals and customer needs.

7. *Communicate the release plan.* Once the components have been allocated to releases, communicate the release plan to all relevant stakeholders. This helps to manage expectations, facilitate collaboration, and ensure that everyone is working toward the same goals.

Determine How Project Methodologies Influence Business Analysis Processes

Task 5

Project methodologies can have a significant impact on business analysis processes, as they can help to determine the approach, tools, and techniques used in the analysis phase.

- They can help to define the scope of the project and identify the stakeholders who will be involved. This information can then be used to develop a business analysis plan that will help to ensure that the project meets the needs of the stakeholders.

- Project methodologies can help to structure the business analysis process. This can help to ensure that the process is efficient and effective.

- They can help to track the progress of the business analysis process. This can help to ensure that the process is on track and that any potential problems are identified early on.

- Project methodologies can help to communicate the results of the business analysis process to the stakeholders. This can help to ensure that the stakeholders understand the project's requirements and that they are on board with the project's goals.

Predictive, Plan-Based, and Adaptive Methodologies

As described in Chapters 4 and 5, predictive, plan-based, and adaptive are three popular project methodologies that have different approaches to project management and software development. In predictive and plan-based methodologies, requirements are typically gathered at the beginning of the project. This is followed by a sequential development process, where each stage of development is completed before moving on to the next. This approach can lead to a more structured and formalized business analysis process. However, it can also be less flexible and adaptable to change. Predictive and plan-based methodologies are a sequential approach that follows a linear process, while adaptive is an iterative approach that emphasizes flexibility and collaboration.

The following table compares predictive, plan-based, and adaptive methodologies:

Predictive and Plan-Based	Adaptive
Have a more structured approach with a detailed requirements gathering phase at the beginning of the project.	Focuses on continuous feedback and collaboration between stakeholders and the development team.
May rely more on formal documentation and progress reports.	Emphasizes face-to-face communication and daily meetings.
May have a separate testing phase at the end of the project.	Emphasizes iterative testing and prototyping.
May have more formal review processes and documentation requirements.	Encourages frequent collaboration and feedback from stakeholders.

The choice of project management methodology influences the business analysis process in several ways:

- **Level of formality and structure that is used in the business analysis process** For example, a more formal methodology, such as predictive and plan-based, will require more documentation and planning than a less formal methodology, such as adaptive.

- **How requirements are gathered and documented** For example, a predictive and plan-based methodology will typically involve gathering requirements up front, while an adaptive methodology will allow for requirements to be gathered and refined throughout the project.

- **How risks are managed** For example, a predictive and plan-based methodology will typically involve identifying and mitigating risks up front, while an adaptive methodology will allow for risks to be identified and mitigated throughout the project.

- **How changes are managed** For example, a predictive and plan-based methodology will typically require changes to be approved through a formal change control process, while an adaptive methodology will allow for changes to be made more easily throughout the project.

- **How communication is managed** For example, a predictive and plan-based methodology will typically require more formal communication, such as status reports and meetings, while an adaptive methodology will allow for more informal communication, such as ad hoc conversations and daily meetings.

The choice of project management methodology will have a significant impact on the business analysis process. It is important to select a methodology that is appropriate for the specific project and the organization's culture.

Determine the Role of a Business Analyst in Adaptive and/or Predictive and Plan-Based Approaches

Task 5, Enabler 1

Projects are broken down into phases, releases, or iterations to understand what is required to meet the expected outcomes. The main difference between these groupings is the amount of effort and scope involved in each. Regardless of the approach, the business analyst (BA) helps to understand what is required to meet the expected outcomes.

The BA's role in adaptive and/or predictive and plan-based approaches can vary depending on the specific project and organizational context. However, the BA generally plays a crucial role in both types of approaches. The BA helps to bridge the gap between business stakeholders and technical teams to ensure that the project is completed successfully.

Role of a BA in Predictive and Plan-Based Approaches

The role of the BA is more often recognized when a predictive and plan-based approach is used, because it involves heavy analysis of requirements and determination of the results of the project as part of initial planning efforts. In predictive and plan-based approaches, such as traditional, the role of the BA may be more focused on defining and documenting requirements up front, and then working closely with the project manager to ensure that the project stays on track and meets the planned deliverables. The BA may need to work closely with stakeholders to understand their needs and translate them into clear and specific requirements. The BA may also need to conduct research and analysis to identify risks and dependencies that could impact the project.

BAs may begin their work before a project is officially initiated. This is often done to analyze requirements and develop a business case. The standard information in the business case includes identification of the problem or opportunity, analysis of the current situation and impact to the organization, and recommendations of possible solutions, including expected benefits.

A BA may evaluate alternative options, including analysis of their feasibility based on identified constraints. This feasibility may include review of options based on how well the proposed solution meets the business need (referred to as *operational feasibility*), the technology and compatibility with existing infrastructure (referred to as *technology/system feasibility*), understanding the initial estimate and high-level estimate of costs and value of benefits (referred to as *cost-effective feasibility*), or whether the solution can be delivered within time constraints (referred to as *time feasibility*). These various factors are assessed by the BA working with the appropriate stakeholders to help recommend the most viable option.

As the project scope is further refined, the BA helps elicit, analyze, and document requirements that will become the product scope. These activities require planning and collaboration with the appropriate stakeholders. After the needs are gathered and verified for understanding, the BA uses different models to further understand and analyze the requirements. The choice of these individual models and the detail included is not specific to any approach, though they are utilized more frequently and to a more granular degree within a predictive approach. You can see increased benefits from models when multiple models are created and combined to examine and cross-check requirements from multiple perspectives.

Many predictive and plan-based methodologies specifically identify a business requirement document that includes the details for the requirements that will be approved, managed, controlled, and delivered to meet the project scope baseline. The BA may also review and approve design documents, test plans, and other project artifacts.

Role of a BA in Adaptive Approaches

In adaptive approaches, such as Agile, the role of the BA may be more focused on facilitating collaboration between stakeholders and the development team to ensure that requirements are continuously refined and adjusted throughout the project. The BA may serve as a product owner or work closely with the product owner to define and prioritize product requirements. The product owner knows the "as-is" current way things are done, areas of improvement, as well as expectations of the "to-be" or future outcome.

The product owner often works with a BA to refine the backlog, especially to understand the user stories further. They (product owner and BA) use progressive elaboration to convey the understanding of the prioritized user stories closer to the actual delivery work. The BA may also facilitate requirements workshops and other collaborative sessions with stakeholders to gather feedback and refine requirements.

The BA helps the product owner understand any sequence or dependencies between the stories, specifics on information required for the user story, and business rules that should be implemented. It is important to review your understanding of the acceptance criteria to ensure that the delivered result meets the requirements and expectations.

Even though most requirements are presented as user stories, a BA may help refine the story by describing the additional detail with a use case. The data models used for projects with an information focus, such as business intelligence (BI) or customer relationship management (CRM) solutions, may vary depending on the project's specific needs. For adaptive projects, data models are typically less fully developed and more specific to the feature or function that will be implemented soon.

The discussions between the BA and the product owner allow a deeper understanding of the information the delivery team needs to ensure a complete understanding of the user story. The BA must explain these details to the team during the iteration planning session. The team will then discuss the user stories to help them estimate the effort required and decompose the story further into tasks for inclusion in the iteration. This additional information often documents areas that should be present to meet the definition of ready (DoR). DoR refers to the PO providing all the necessary information to the team regarding the user story—is the user story "ready" to be developed, including a thorough understanding of sequences, information required, and rules that need to be applied? This is most often traditionally provided through a written "use case" with all the sequential steps, information needed, and decisions to be made based on "rules."

Role of a BA in Hybrid Approaches

When using a hybrid approach, the role of the BA is important with respect to the scope or requirements. Regardless of the lead resource for these activities, the BA can provide competencies and techniques to help ensure that the appropriate level of understanding is captured and shared with the delivery team. Possessing this understanding enables the outcomes and results to meet expectations with minimal wasted time and effort.

Regardless of the approach used, the BA is responsible for gathering requirements, defining scope, and communicating with stakeholders. They also work with the development team to ensure that the project meets the needs of the business. The BA works with the development team to ensure that the project meets the requirements and is delivered on time, within budget, and meets the quality standards set by the organization. This includes providing the development team with the requirements, reviewing their work, and testing the project.

Validate Requirements Through Product Delivery

Task 6

Validating requirements throughout the product delivery process is essential to ensure that the product meets the customer's needs and expectations. Here are some key steps that a business analyst (BA) can take to ensure that requirements are validated throughout the product delivery process:

- **Testing and acceptance** The BA works closely with the development team to define test cases and acceptance criteria that will validate each requirement. The BA may also be responsible for reviewing test results to ensure that the requirements are being met and that any defects are identified and addressed.

- **User acceptance testing (UAT)** The BA works closely with end users and stakeholders to define UAT scenarios and test cases. The BA may also be responsible for coordinating UAT activities and reviewing the results to ensure that the product meets the business objectives.

- **Change control** The BA is responsible for managing changes to the requirements throughout the product delivery process. The BA works closely with the project manager and development team to evaluate change requests and ensure that any changes are approved, documented, and communicated to all stakeholders.

- **Post-implementation review** The BA conducts a post-implementation review to evaluate the success of the project and identify any opportunities for improvement. The BA works closely with stakeholders to gather feedback and analyze the results to ensure that the project delivered the expected benefits and that any lessons learned are captured and applied to future projects.

- **Continuous improvement** The BA promotes a culture of continuous improvement, ensuring that the product is regularly reviewed and refined to ensure that it continues to meet the changing needs of the business.

The following are some additional methods and tools to validate requirements throughout the product delivery process:

- **Conduct user research**   Conducting user research throughout the product delivery process can help the BA understand the users' needs, behaviors, and pain points, as well as identify usability issues and opportunities for improvement.

- **Create user stories and acceptance criteria**   User stories and acceptance criteria help to define what the user wants and what is required to meet their needs and help validate that the requirements are being met.

- **Create a scope management traceability matrix**   As previously discussed, an RTM for scope management maps each requirement to its corresponding design, development, testing, and deployment activity to track the progress of each requirement.

- **Conduct usability testing**   Usability testing involves observing users as they use the product and testing its usability to identify any issues and opportunities for improvement.

- **Conduct user acceptance testing (UAT)**   Conducting UAT with the end users ensures that the product meets their needs and requirements and identifies any gaps or issues in the product that must be addressed before release.

- **Perform quality assurance testing**   Quality assurance testing involves testing the product to ensure that it meets the requirements and works as expected to identify any bugs or issues.

- **Collect feedback**   Collecting feedback from users throughout the product delivery process can help validate the requirements and identify opportunities for improvement using surveys, interviews, or feedback forms.

- **Define metrics and key performance indicators (KPIs)**   Defining metrics and KPIs that measure the product's performance against the requirements helps ensure that the product meets the desired quality standards.

In the Real World

I have often found that broader project requirements can be captured and documented as KPIs for determining the success or otherwise of the project, beyond the strict solution requirements of the product. For example, you could have customer satisfaction, health and safety compliance, environmental management requirements, or any other factors set as KPIs of project success, and these factors would be gathered in the requirements documentation.

By validating requirements throughout the product delivery process (see Figure 6-15), the BA can ensure that the product meets the customer's needs and expectations and is of high quality.

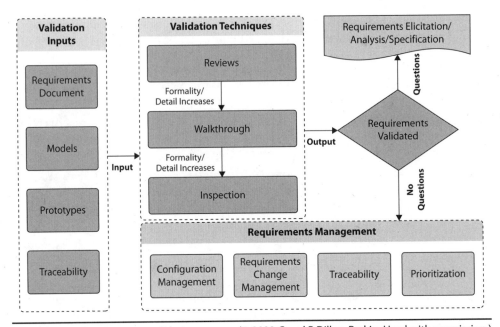

Figure 6-15 Requirements validation process (© 2023 C and P Dillon-Parkin. Used with permission.)

Define Acceptance Criteria

Task 6, Enabler 1

Acceptance criteria are the conditions that must be met for a product, user story, or increment of work to be accepted. They are typically defined by the customer or user and are used to ensure that the product meets their needs and expectations. Acceptance criteria are used to define the parameters and boundaries of a project and to ensure that all parties involved clearly understand the project expectations. You can specify acceptance criteria at varying levels of detail. Depending on the approach used, you can refine these criteria as greater detail is available for the requirement or user story. Regardless, the criteria should express what must be provided to satisfy the requirements. Acceptance criteria are usually developed during the planning phase of a project and can include a wide range of factors such as functionality, performance, usability, security, compatibility, and reliability.

Acceptance criteria are the conditions that must be satisfied for a deliverable to be accepted by the customer or user. They vary based on the project and deliverable, encompassing factors like functionalities, performance benchmarks, user experience, design elements, manufacturing tolerances, and quality standards.

Defining acceptance criteria during project planning aligns stakeholders' expectations with the project team's objectives, avoiding future misunderstandings. Acceptance criteria may be adjusted throughout the project due to new requirements or changes in scope. The business analyst or project manager typically manages these changes and ensures stakeholders are informed.

Defining Acceptance Criteria in Predictive and Plan-Based Projects

The life cycle for a predictive approach includes various checkpoints where validation or acceptance criteria may be specified. At each checkpoint, you may include results of feasibility studies, design, build, and testing activities, and final closure and deployment.

Before you finalize the scope statement, you might conduct a feasibility study to determine whether you can satisfactorily meet the business need. Then, considering both risks and constraints, you can develop high-level acceptance criteria at the end of the feasibility study.

The scope statement includes the requirements for the scope of both the project and the product, along with boundaries and acceptance criteria for identified deliverables. In predictive approaches, acceptance criteria refer to the specific conditions that must be met for a deliverable to be considered complete and acceptable to stakeholders.

Examples of acceptance criteria in a predictive approach include

- The system should allow users to enter up to 50 characters in each input field.
- The system shall be compatible with Microsoft Edge 113+ or above and Chrome 90+.
- The system can handle 10,000 concurrent users without crashing.

Once you identify the requirements to satisfy the scope statement, you can use the requirements traceability matrix to trace progress in completing those requirements. In addition to showing the stages through which a requirement progresses, you can associate the acceptance criteria and validation results from those stages with the requirements on the RTM.

The delivery team works on individual requirements, using the acceptance criteria to develop tests. Using the test-first method, the BA creates a test and then writes the code to satisfy the requirement's acceptance criteria. In addition to verifying the individual requirements, the BA checks the interfaces to other requirements or systems to ensure those acceptance criteria have not been affected by the new requirement introduced.

The final-result validation compares the acceptance criteria to the completed results from a business point of view. It is often the last activity before project deployment. The sponsor, key stakeholder(s), or product owner who initially participated in developing the scope statement take part in this final evaluation.

When stakeholders request changes to the project baseline, the business analyst may work with them to provide the definition and reason for the change and an assessment of the impact of the change. As part of the impact assessment for a requested change, the business analyst (BA) works with stakeholders to establish acceptance criteria. Acceptance criteria are the conditions that must be met in order to determine whether the change has met the expected results. Once the acceptance criteria have been established, the BA can use them to assess the impact of the change and to track the progress of the change implementation.

Defining Acceptance Criteria in Adaptive Projects

In the adaptive approach, the acceptance criteria are defined by the product owner and the delivery team. The product owner is responsible for gathering requirements from the stakeholders and defining the scope of the project. The delivery team is responsible for developing the product or feature and ensuring that it meets the requirements.

The acceptance criteria are written from the perspective of the end user or customer to describe the expected functionality and behavior of the product or feature. The criteria establish a mutual understanding between the product owner, the stakeholders, and the delivery team of what is required and how completion will be measured.

Examples of acceptance criteria for a user story might include

- When users enter their username and password, they should be able to log in to the system within 5 seconds.
- The system shall display a confirmation message when the user submits a form.
- The system should be accessible to visually impaired users and meet WCAG 2.0 accessibility guidelines.

INVEST (independent, negotiable, valuable, estimable, small, and testable) is an acronym usually applied to user stories to help understand and meet expectations. The T for testable requires specifying how to verify the user story to meet the identified acceptance criteria.

Defining Acceptance Criteria in Hybrid Projects

For predictive and adaptive projects, establish all requirements (business, stakeholder, quality, and solution functional and nonfunctional) criteria to understand and deliver the expected results.

Even though adaptive projects refer to user stories as the basis for requirements, often additional detail is needed through development of a use case. Use cases allow you to specify a story's pre- and post-conditions, sequencing, and exceptions. This additional detail allows for a better understanding of what is needed to satisfy the specified user acceptance criteria.

Contracts

Contracts and acceptance criteria are often used together to ensure that both parties are on the same page and that there are no misunderstandings about what is expected. Even though contracts are usually more often found in a predictive or hybrid approach, they can identify both deliverables and acceptance criteria for those deliverables. By clearly defining the scope of work and the acceptance criteria, it is easier to track progress and make sure that the project is on track. Additionally, the terms and conditions of the contract provide additional detail regarding how changes will be handled and the closure provisions for the contract.

Determine If a Project/Product Is Ready for Delivery Based on a Requirements Traceability Matrix/Product Backlog

Task 6, Enabler 2

Determining if a project/product is ready for delivery based on a requirements traceability matrix (RTM) or product backlog involves ensuring that all the requirements have been met and that the highest-priority items have been completed.

In all cases, the project team should review the RTM or product backlog to ensure that they have met all requirements and that the deliverables are high quality. They should also ensure the involvement of all stakeholders in the review process and that there is consensus on the readiness of the project or product for delivery.

However, there are other factors to consider when determining if a project/product is ready for delivery, such as the quality of the code, the stability of the product, and the feedback from stakeholders. Consider testing and quality assurance processes to ensure that the product meets the functional and nonfunctional requirements and is stable and reliable.

Requirements Traceability Matrix

As discussed earlier in the chapter, predictive and plan-based approaches use an RTM for scope management to trace the progression of defined and accepted requirements that are part of the project scope through various stages of development to completion. The RTM document helps ensure that all requirements are met by tracing them from their origin through design, development, testing, and final implementation. The BA determines the amount of detail captured and the effort to maintain this RTM during the project planning activities. The amount of detail is usually based on the project's complexity, criticality, and importance.

Understanding how to prioritize, develop, inspect, verify, and validate individual written requirements in the RTM helps stakeholders and project team members to build a shared understanding of whether the product is ready for delivery.

The RTM is a crucial tool to support the impact assessment of requested changes to requirements that are part of the project baseline. This assessment goes beyond the work needed to satisfy the request, often for a specific shift in currently accepted requirements. It must also consider relationships and dependencies between various requirements. The information on the RTM provides this information.

Verification vs. Validation

It is essential to understand the difference between the verification process and the validation process. Verification entails confirming that the product, service, or result produced complies with agreed specifications or requirements. It is primarily an internal process that the delivery organization performs before submitting the product, service, or result for validation, which also involves the customer. Validation also checks that the product, service, or result meets stakeholder requirements. Verification occurs before validation.

EXAM TIP Validation is performed AFTER verification.

Product Backlog

The product backlog in adaptive projects is a prioritized list of all the features, enhancements, and bug fixes. The product backlog will continue to be refined into a release backlog and iteration backlog when using an adaptive timebox approach. These items translate business requirements to expected delivery of solution requirements.

Initial refinement of the backlog items need to support the DEEP acronym:

- **Detailed appropriately**   Higher-priority items need more detail than those with lower priority.
- **Estimated**   The team feels comfortable with each estimate.
- **Emergent**   The team is able to adapt to changes as additional information, value, and priorities are identified, including removal of items no longer needed.
- **Prioritized**   Prioritization is used to ensure that items are worked on in the order that is most important. Items are continually reviewed and reprioritized from highest to lowest as items are added, removed, or refined.

If a backlog item does not meet all of the INVEST criteria, it may be necessary to decompose it into smaller backlog items that do meet the criteria. This will help to ensure that the backlog items are manageable and that they can be completed within a reasonable time frame.

- **Independent**   The item does not overlap with other items, and you can individually determine the value and size. You can reprioritize the item in any order in the product backlog.
- **Negotiable**   Items should be open to change based on the needs of the customer or user. The stakeholder, product owner, and delivery team can negotiate on details, especially waiting until the latest moment to finalize details. The team and product owner can make trade-offs for cost and function.
- **Valuable**   The item has value to the organization.
- **Estimable**   You can estimate the item's complexity, effort, and sizing.
- **Small**   The item will be worked on and delivered in a single iteration by the delivery team.
- **Testable**   You can evaluate the item for completion and accuracy using the delivery team to assess the requirements, and the stakeholder/product owner assesses the acceptance criteria.

Gradually refine stories on the backlog from inclusion on the initial product backlog to the accepted stories and tasks negotiated by the product owner and team during iteration planning. The product owner and delivery team agree upon acceptance criteria according to the definition of done. Finally, compare actual results to expected results during the demonstration at the end of each iteration.

After the acceptance criteria are met for all the stories in a release, the full release is demonstrated to the end user or customer.

Chapter Summary

Business analysis frameworks can help business analysts systematically analyze and document business requirements and processes, which can help businesses make informed decisions and improve their overall performance.

Business analysts are critical in helping organizations improve their processes, systems, and operations. Their responsibilities include requirements elicitation and analysis, process improvement, stakeholder management, solution evaluation, change management, and documentation. Their work helps organizations make informed decisions and achieve their business objectives. The role of a BA may differ based on whether the methodology being used is an adaptive approach or predictive and plan-based approaches. However, in both approaches, the BA is critical in gathering, documenting, and managing requirements to ensure that the final product meets stakeholder needs and expectations.

Throughout all phases of the project life cycle, the BA role involves ongoing communication and collaboration with stakeholders, the development team, and the project manager to ensure that the project is aligned with the business goals and objectives. This includes identifying and managing risks, conducting impact analysis, and providing guidance and recommendations to ensure that the project is successful.

Identifying stakeholders is a critical step in project management, as it helps to ensure project success, manage expectations, manage risks, build support, and enhance communication. It is important to involve stakeholders throughout the project life cycle to ensure that their needs and expectations are met and to increase the likelihood of project success.

Stakeholder roles related to business analysis have different responsibilities and expectations. Understanding these roles and their unique contributions is necessary to ensure that BAs successfully develop projects and products and meet stakeholder needs. Identifying these roles and responsibilities is essential in stakeholder identification as it facilitates communication, accountability, resource allocation, risk management, and conflict resolution. In addition, it ensures that everyone is working toward the project's objectives and helps the project team succeed.

The primary difference between internal and external roles in business analysis is the scope of the analyst's responsibilities. For example, internal BAs focus on analyzing internal processes and systems, while external BAs provide analysis services to external clients. As a result, both internal and external business analysts require strong analytical skills, communication skills, and an understanding of business operations and objectives. Internal BAs are employed by the organization and focus on long-term objectives, while external BAs are consultants or contractors brought in for specific projects or initiatives, offering a broader perspective and specialized expertise.

Effective communication is essential for a BA to be successful in their role. It helps ensure that all teams are working together toward a common goal and that the final product meets all requirements and specifications.

BAs, just like project managers, spend a lot of time communicating. The most appropriate communication channel/tool depends on various factors, including the audience, content, time constraints, communication frequency, and communication culture. Careful consideration of these factors helps the BA use the most appropriate communication channel/tool to deliver the desired results. Communication is crucial for a BA working with various teams, such as features, requirements, and development teams. Effective communication helps to clarify requirements, promote collaboration and coordination, ensure quality, manage risks and changes, and manage stakeholder expectations. Therefore, it is essential for delivering successful projects that meet business objectives and stakeholder needs.

PART II

Effective stakeholder communication requires careful planning, active listening, and a willingness to adapt and adjust as necessary. This promotes positive stakeholder relationships and increases the likelihood of project success.

While both BA and PM activities play important roles in project management, their focus and responsibilities are different. BA activities are focused on understanding and documenting the business requirements, while PM activities are focused on managing the project to ensure it is completed on time, within budget, and to the required quality standards.

Determining how to gather requirements involves identifying stakeholders, determining the requirements, choosing the gathering techniques, planning the sessions, conducting the sessions, analyzing the requirements, and documenting the results. By following these steps, BAs can ensure that they collect accurate and relevant requirements that align with the organization's objectives. The choice of tools and techniques will depend on the specific requirements of the project and the needs of the stakeholders involved. BAs should consider factors such as the nature and complexity of the requirements, the number and location of stakeholders, and the time and budget available when choosing the appropriate approach.

Requirements gathering and elicitation are important activities for collecting information about stakeholder needs, while requirements engineering is a broader process that involves all the activities needed to ensure that the requirements are well-defined and meet the needs of all stakeholders.

BAs use various tools to track requirements and ensure their completion. Two such tools are a requirements traceability matrix (RTM) and a product backlog. While an RTM tracks the status of requirements and ensures they are properly linked to other artifacts, a product backlog is a prioritized list of requirements yet to be implemented in a project.

A product roadmap is a strategic document that outlines the vision, goals, and priorities for a product over a set period. It helps align stakeholders, prioritize work, manage expectations, identify risks, and track progress. It is an essential tool used by product owners and business analysts to ensure successful product development. It provides a clear and concise way to communicate the product vision, prioritize features, align teams, manage stakeholder expectations, and track progress. The application of a product roadmap in business analysis helps communicate the product vision, prioritize features, facilitate collaboration, manage stakeholder expectations, track progress, identify dependencies and risks, and support marketing and sales efforts.

Project methodologies have a significant impact on the business analysis processes. The choice of methodology will influence the approach, techniques, and tools used in the analysis, as well as stakeholder engagement and requirements management. BAs must understand the chosen methodology and adapt its approach to ensure successful project outcomes.

Regardless of the approach used, the role of the BA is critical to the success of the project. They are responsible for ensuring that the requirements are clearly defined and documented, that the stakeholders' needs are understood and met, and that the development team is delivering high-quality solutions that meet the business objectives.

The BA may also be involved in testing, validation, and post-implementation reviews to ensure that the project delivers the expected benefits and that any lessons learned are captured and applied to future projects.

By defining acceptance criteria, project teams can ensure they meet stakeholder needs and deliver a high-quality product or feature that meets their expectations. The acceptance criteria provide a clear set of guidelines for testing and verification. They can help to reduce misunderstandings and miscommunications between stakeholders and project team members.

The business analyst plays a vital role in ensuring that the requirements are validated throughout the product delivery process. They do this by working closely with the development team, end users, and stakeholders to define test cases and acceptance criteria, manage changes to the requirements, conduct post-implementation reviews, and promote a culture of continuous improvement. By taking these steps, the BA can ensure that the product meets the business objectives and delivers the expected benefits. Deciding which components go to which releases in an adaptive project should be based on carefully analyzing the product vision, goals, and priorities. It should be a collaborative effort involving stakeholders, the development team, and the BA to ensure that the final release plan is aligned with the overall strategic vision and goals of the product. By following these steps, BAs can determine which components should be included in each release, ensuring that product development remains focused on delivering value to customers and meeting business objectives.

Ultimately, you base the decision to deliver a project or product on a combination of factors, including the completion of all requirements, the quality of the deliverables, and stakeholder approval. Using tools such as the RTM and product backlog, the project team can ensure that they deliver a product that meets stakeholder needs and expectations.

Questions

1. What is the main purpose of the requirements traceability matrix?

   A. To hold people accountable for work delivery

   B. To let stakeholders know when the project will be delivered

   C. To map individual requirements back to specific business needs and objectives

   D. To describe the work to be completed in the project

2. Peter is a new BA on the GUY Project for your organization. He needs to use a structured approach to business analysis that can help to improve the quality of requirements and to ensure that they meet the needs of the business. Peter knows this is called a business analysis framework. Which one of the following is not a commonly used business analysis framework?

   A. Business Process Model and Notation

   B. Six Sigma

   C. SWOT analysis

   D. Requirements elicitation

3. Beth is the BA for a large healthcare project. She is working with Allison, the project manager, to define the steps she'll use to perform stakeholder analysis. Which of the following correctly defines the steps for stakeholder analysis?

   A. Identify and document the stakeholder information, create a communications management plan, plan for stakeholder management.

   B. Identify and document the stakeholder information, prioritize and classify the stakeholders, create the communications management plan for stakeholder management.

   C. Identify and document the stakeholder information, prioritize and classify the stakeholders, plan for stakeholder management.

   D. Create a focus group for known stakeholders, identify and document the stakeholder information, prioritize and classify the stakeholders, plan for stakeholder management.

4. Manny is the BA of a large technology project for the Monday Company. Which of the following is not a BA key role or responsibility?

   A. Requirements elicitation

   B. Process improvement

   C. Kanban board organization

   D. Stakeholder management

5. Saleh is the BA of the YUG Project for the Petro Company and is working with the agile project team to understand what work is left to be done in the current sprint. Saleh needs to examine what document?

   A. Project management plan

   B. Kanban board

   C. Sprint backlog

   D. Retrospective

6. Ivan is the BA for the JHG Project and is working with the agile process owner. What is the agile process owner most responsible for?

   A. Updating the Kanban board

   B. Overall performance and effectiveness of the customer support process

   C. Communication with stakeholder management

   D. Reporting on project progress to the sponsor

7. A memo has been sent to Mick, the BA, the project manager, team members, and the project customers. In this instance, who is the sender?

   A. The project sponsor

   B. The project manager

   C. The project team members

   D. The project customers

8. Dorina is the BA for a large construction project and is spending a lot of time working with the project stakeholders. Dorina has not identified the stakeholders and clarified their roles and responsibilities. Which of the following is not one of the reasons it is necessary to identify stakeholders and clarify their roles and responsibilities?

   A. Align expectations and objectives

   B. Effective communication

   C. Project constraints

   D. Facilitate collaboration

9. John is the project sponsor for the FXL Project and needs to decide whether to enlist a BA from his company's business analysis department or hire an external BA for the project. Which of the following is an attribute of an internal BA?

   A. Broad industry knowledge

   B. Long-term focus

   C. Certified professional

   D. Objective viewpoint

10. Donna, a BA, receives a document from the customer containing the new project's requirements. When going through the document, Donna finds it difficult to understand certain requirements, outputs, and, most importantly, the project's goal. What should Donna do?

    A. Ask the customer for clarification.

    B. Reject the new project as it involves a lot of ambiguity.

    C. Start planning the first iteration.

    D. Acquire a team to help analyze the project requirements.

11. What is the role of the product owner in an agile project?

    A. To coordinate the work of the sprint and running the team

    B. To have a vested interest in the project and its outcomes and interface with the stakeholders

    C. To represent the business unit, customer, or end user

    D. To complete the backlog items and sign up for tasks based on established priorities

12. A team of a predictive project discovers that many implemented features are different from the outlined scope in the scope statement. Which of the following documents should April, the BA, refer to for this matter?

    A. WBS

    B. WBS dictionary

    C. Change request log

    D. Project charter

13. Isabella, a BA, is leading a new project. What is the first step she should take in stakeholder communication?

    A. Create a stakeholder register

    B. Complete the project charter

    C. Identify stakeholders

    D. Invite stakeholders to the project kickoff meeting

14. An organization assigned Radhia as a new BA to replace one who recently left the organization. What should Radhia do first?

    A. Consult the issues log and the lessons learned register to check if there is any serious problem.

    B. Consult the project charter to understand the project goals and its business case.

    C. Consult the project management plan to learn about the project baseline.

    D. Consult the stakeholder register to start interacting with the different parties involved in the project.

15. All stakeholders are in a meeting to discuss a new project that is expected to start within one month and to last at least ten iterations. One of the stakeholders mentions that someone should take responsibility for developing and maintaining the product roadmap. Who should have this responsibility?

    A. Product manager

    B. Development team

    C. Scrum master

    D. Product owner

16. Louise is a new BA and needs to determine how best to communicate with the project stakeholder. Which of the following is not a consideration for choosing the communication channel for stakeholders?

    A. Time constraints

    B. Communication frequency

    C. Number of stakeholders

    D. The content

17. Which of the following is not a valid requirement type classification when gathering project requirements for business analysis?

    A. Solution/user requirements

    B. Business requirements

    C. Technical requirements

    D. Transition requirements

18. Jose is a BA working with an agile team to develop user stories. What is the purpose of user stories?

    A. To describe what the user wants to achieve

    B. To describe the project goals

    C. To document stakeholder interactions

    D. To trace requirements to project objectives

19. Grant is a BA for a project and is working on gathering project requirements. Which of the following is not an advantage of using prototypes for requirements gathering?

    A. You get real-time, in-depth user feedback.

    B. Works well in agile environments.

    C. It's the only way to really test how people use physical products.

    D. It can be expensive and time-consuming.

20. What should a BA use to understand the relationship between project requirements and specific test cases?

    A. Requirements checklist

    B. Requirements package

    C. Traceability matrix

    D. Graphical models

Answers

1. C. The main purpose of the requirements traceability matrix is to map individual requirements back to specific business needs and objectives. A is incorrect because the RTM does not hold people accountable for work delivery. B is incorrect because letting stakeholders know when the project will be delivered would be part of your time management plan and communications management plan. D is incorrect because the project scope statement is used to describe the work to be completed in the project.

2. D. Requirements elicitation is not a business analysis framework. A, B, and C are incorrect because all three are common business analysis frameworks.

3. C. Stakeholder analysis starts with Beth identifying and documenting the stakeholders' contact information, knowledge, expectations of the project, and their level of influence over project decisions. Then Beth works with the project manager to prioritize and classify stakeholders based on their power, influence, expectations, and concerns for the project. Finally, Beth should plan for managing the stakeholders based on possible negative or positive scenarios in the project that may affect the stakeholders. A, B, and D are incorrect because these answers do not reflect the correct ordering of steps for stakeholder analysis.

PART II

4. **C.** Kanban board organization is not a key business analyst role or responsibility. A, B, and D are incorrect because they are key business analyst roles or responsibilities.

5. **C.** The sprint backlog defines the work to be done on a specific sprint. A, B, and D are incorrect because they do not provide information on a sprint's activities.

6. **B.** The agile process owner is responsible for overall performance and effectiveness of the customer support process. A, C, and D are incorrect because they are not responsibilities of the agile process owner.

7. **A.** The project sponsor is the sender of the message. B, C, and D are all recipients of the memo, not the sender.

8. **C.** Project constraints is not one of the reasons it is necessary to identify stakeholders and clarify their roles and responsibilities. A, B, and D are incorrect because they are reasons it is necessary to identify stakeholders and clarify their roles and responsibilities.

9. **B.** Long-term focus is an attribute of an internal business analyst because both internal BAs and external BAs may be certified professionals. A and D are incorrect because broad industry knowledge and an objective viewpoint are attributes of an external business analyst. C is not relevant to the question.

10. **A.** In case of ambiguity, the BA should first ask for clarification from the customer before making any further decisions, as the project involves unclear requirements and objectives. B is incorrect because rejecting the project is inappropriate. C and D are incorrect because it's not appropriate to start planning the work or acquire a team without first creating a clear vision of what the project consists of.

11. **C.** The product owner in an agile project represents the business unit, customer, or end user. A is incorrect because the dev team coordinates the work of the sprint and runs the team. B is incorrect because the project sponsor has a vested interest in the project and its outcomes and interfaces with the stakeholders. D is incorrect because this is done by the team.

12. **C.** April, the BA, should refer to the change request log to address the issue of implemented features that are different from the outlined scope in the scope statement. A is incorrect because the WBS is a decomposition of the project scope and does map specific requirements. B is incorrect because the WBS dictionary is used to define the work in detail to help create the product that will be obtained with the execution of the project. D is incorrect because the project charter is a high-level project overview.

13. **C.** Identifying stakeholders is the first step for a BA in stakeholder communication. A is incorrect because the stakeholder register is typically created by the project manager, with input from the project team and key stakeholders., B is incorrect because the project charter is typically completed by the project manager, with input from the project team and key stakeholders. D is incorrect because the project manager typically invites stakeholders to the project kickoff meeting.

14. **B.** First and foremost, as a new BA, Radhia has to understand why the project is being created in the first place, aka its business case. Moreover, Radhia needs to be aware of the project's defined goals. These two elements are found in the project charter. A, C, and D are incorrect as first steps, but Radhia should perform them once she understands the project from consulting the business case.

15. **D.** In agile, the product owner should be in charge of managing the product roadmap since they are responsible for the product's success. The product owner's primary responsibility is to represent the business, which involves the creation and maintenance of the product vision and roadmap, as well as the product backlog. A, B, and C are incorrect because these roles are not responsible for the product roadmap.

16. **D.** The number of stakeholders is not a consideration for choosing the communication channel for stakeholders. A, B, and C are incorrect because they are valid considerations for choosing the communication channel for stakeholders.

17. **C.** Technical requirements is not a valid requirement type classification when gathering project requirements for business analysis. A, B, and D are incorrect because they are valid requirement type classifications.

18. **A.** The purpose of user stories is to describe what the user wants to achieve. B, C, and D are incorrect because they are not related to user stories.

19. **D.** A disadvantage of using prototypes for requirements gathering is that it can be very expensive and time-consuming. A, B, and C are incorrect because they are advantages of using prototypes for requirements gathering.

20. **C.** A requirements traceability matrix is used to understand the relationship between project requirements and specific test cases. A and B are incorrect because they are components of the requirements gathering process. D is incorrect because graphical modes are not valid for understanding the relationship between project requirements and specific test cases.

References

- *Agile Practice Guide* (2017)
- *Business Analysis for Practitioners: A Practice Guide* (2015)
- *CAPM Certified Associate in Project Management Practice Exams* (2019), Haner and McCoy
- *Effective Project Management, Eighth Edition* (2019), Wysocki
- *PMBOK Guide* (2021)
- *Process Groups: A Practice Guide* (2022)
- *PMIstandards+*
- *The PMI Guide to Business Analysis* (2017)

Understanding the Project Management Code of Ethics and Professional Conduct

In this chapter, you will

- Explore the PMI Code of Ethics and Professional Conduct Code
- Learn the structure of the Code
- Serve responsibly
- Uphold the respect value
- Be a fair project manager
- Be an honest project manager

This chapter focuses on the topic of ethics and professional conduct, which describes the way that a professional project manager is expected to act in many different situations.

There are no explicit domain tasks that are reflected in this section. Several years ago there were distinct questions about ethics and professional situations in the CAPM exam. However, these questions have now been incorporated into the main body of questions and may lie hidden within a question that appears to be about interviewing techniques, or risk, or quality, or customer relations, or any other topic. Thus it is very important that you read the question carefully to determine if it is presenting you with a situation that requires you to specify how you would act ethically and professionally.

Although there are no domain tasks for this topic, there is the Code of Ethics and Professional Conduct from the Project Management Institute (PMI). Both mandatory and aspirational standards are captured in the Code. The Code, and the behavior of professional project management practitioners, reflects the values of responsibility, respect, fairness, and honesty.

A breach of this Code can result in an ethics complaint to the Project Management Institute, which has the ability to consider the complaint and take action against anyone found to have breached the Code. The PMI Code is a living document that is regularly updated to ensure that it remains relevant and effective in guiding ethical behavior in project management.

The concepts in the PMI Code are applicable to

- All PMI members
- All PMI non-members who meet one or more of the following criteria:
  - Non-members who hold a PMI certification
  - Non-members who are a part of PMI in a volunteer capacity
  - Non-members who plan to begin a PMI certification process and apply for the same

Your PMI CAPM exam will include these ethical concepts throughout the exam. You'll be tested on ethics as part of your overall project management, not just on a separate section on the Code. After all, ethics are interspersed in your duties as a project manager, so it is appropriate that they be included in your CAPM exam as well. Most of the questions are straightforward. It is important to remember that PMI uses a North American perspective on these topics.

 EXAM TIP To answer project management ethics questions, just remember the most appropriate answer is based on the PMI Code, not personal opinion. Some questions will take information directly from the Code and other questions will have you apply the Code to hypothetical scenarios. The answer is always rooted in the Code. So ask yourself, what would PMI do? Don't worry about what you would do. And don't get bogged down in the details and feel as if you need more context. As human beings, there's always more dynamics to manage than the CAPM exam can present in a few sentences.

Exploring the Code

The project management community should do what's "right and honorable." I'm sure we all want to reflect those values in our conduct and see them in the conduct of other project managers. The PMI Code goes beyond our role as project manager. The Code expects adherence in all areas of our lives: "at work, at home, and in service to our profession." Don't most of us live, eat, and sleep project management, anyway?

The real purpose of the Code is to uphold the reputation of the project management profession. From PMI's point of view, the Code and our agreement to adhere to the Code will raise the perception of the ethical values project managers agree to—and are expected to abide by—as members and participants in PMI programs. The Code is also a motivation to become a better project management practitioner. In theory, establishing a globally accepted Code for our ethics and behavior should raise our credibility, reputation, and collective behavior to new standards.

In the Real World

I have always found that the Code serves as a very valuable reference to guide my own decisions and behaviors in real-world situations where perhaps I might be tempted to act differently. It has also served as a guide to the behaviors I expect of other professional project managers. Keep in mind that sometimes the right course of action isn't the easiest course of action. When considering what is best to do in an ethical situation, one approach is to look at what the impact of a bad decision will do to your professional and personal reputation and credibility. Always make the choice that will enhance your credibility and reputation.

Learning the Structure of the Code

The PMI Code is arranged by chapters and sections. And, as is the case with most documents from PMI, it can sometimes be a dense read. No offense to my pals at PMI—it's a great document. Really. However, in this chapter, I'll break down the document into a slightly less formal, and much less official, approach. I hope you find it helpful.

Chapter 1: Vison and Applicability

Chapter 1 of the PMI Code paints the big picture of what the Code is intended for. The vision of the Code is, no doubt, that the project management community will adopt the Code in their day-to-day operations and lives as representatives of the PMI. The Code is needed because project managers are often in situations where their ethics could be jeopardized. When you consider issues with project labor, unscrupulous vendors, and the temptation of personal gain for project managers, it's a great idea to have a Code of Ethics and Professional Conduct. Let's take a detailed look at this first chapter.

The Code includes four values that are core to the ethics and standards for project managers:

- Responsibility
- Respect
- Fairness
- Honesty

Though these may all seem to be fairly straightforward concepts that you think you both understand and apply consistently, you may not fully understand the implications and expected behaviors. Individually they describe specific behaviors, and collectively they present a unified code by which any professional project manager can guide and assess his or her own actions and the actions of others. Therefore, it is worth taking the time to investigate each one and review the specific actions and behaviors that each demands of a professional project manager.

These four values are the focus of Chapters 2 through 5, respectively, of the Code. Each chapter includes separate aspirational standards and mandatory standards for the corresponding value. Basically, as project managers, we should aspire to some characteristics of these standards, and we must adhere to other facets of these standards. There isn't one set of standards, with both aspirational and mandatory characteristics. Instead, there are separate aspirational standards and mandatory standards.

Violating the mandatory standards subjects the project manager to disciplinary procedures before PMI's Ethics Review Committee, whereas violating the aspirational standards doesn't (unless it's also a violation of a mandatory standard).

Each chapter of the Code also contains one or more comments that provide clarification or examples regarding the preceding section. You'll also find a glossary of terms in the Code. I've made sure to include those terms in the glossary of this book.

 EXAM TIP   Take time when reading an exam question to determine if it is presenting you with a technical situation or an ethical situation. If it is an ethical situation, then answer according to the Code.

Serving Responsibly as a Project Manager

Chapter 2 of the PMI Code centers on responsibility. As project managers, we already have a level of responsibility based on the organizational structure in which we operate (from functional to project-oriented), but we also have ethical responsibilities that apply regardless of the organizational structure.

According to the Code, it is our responsibility, or duty, to take ownership for the decisions we make—or fail to make. It's also our duty to take ownership of our actions—or lack of actions. And finally, it's our duty to take ownership of the results of those decisions and actions. Responsibility is covered under the "stewardship" concept in the *PMBOK Guide*, also.

Aspiring to Responsibility Expectations

Project managers need to aspire to responsibility. Here are the details of the responsibility aspirations for this section of the Code:

- Project managers make decisions that don't adversely affect the best interests of society, public safety, and the environment.

- Project managers accept only assignments that mesh with their background, experience, skills, and qualifications.

- Project managers keep their promises.

- Project managers take ownership of and accountability for their errors and omissions and make quick and accurate corrections. When errors are discovered, project managers communicate them to the proper parties and act to repair those errors immediately.

- Project managers protect proprietary and confidential information. No gossiping or blabbing.
- Project managers uphold the Code and hold others accountable to it as well.

The aspirational standards of responsibility require you to make your decisions and subsequent actions based on the best interests of society, public safety, and the environment and not in your own best interests. The greater good of society, public safety, and the environment must always take precedence over self-interest. This means that if a project you are working on conflicts with or adversely affects society, public safety, or the environment, you should reconsider whether the project is worth doing.

Taking responsibility also means accepting only that project work that is consistent with your background, experience, technical and interpersonal skills, and qualifications. Don't be tempted to exaggerate your own ability; only take on work that you know you are competent to do. After the work is taken on, you must make sure that you fulfill these commitments and see them through to completion.

If you make mistakes, errors, or omissions, you must take responsibility, take ownership, and make corrections as soon as possible. If you discover errors or omissions made by others, you must communicate them to the appropriate body as soon they are discovered. Knowingly acting in error or with information you know is false is considered a breach of this standard.

Finally, taking responsibility means protecting the intellectual property rights, copyright, and confidential information of any person or body. This means that if you are in a situation where you have the opportunity to use intellectual property of a previous client, you should always seek their approval first. Additionally, you should not allow anyone to break any copyright rules, laws, or regulations.

In the Real World

You might be tempted to avoid responsibility, but in my decades of experience I have found that the simple act of taking responsibility not only enhances a project manager's professional reputation and credibility but also contributes to their ongoing leadership development. Great leadership enhances the chances of project success, and being a great leader requires you to take responsibility and lead by example.

Adhering to the Mandatory Standards of Responsibility

Project managers have to deal with regulations, laws, contracts, and other mandatory requirements in their projects. This section acknowledges those requirements. Let's have a look at what the Code calls for:

- Project managers have a mandatory responsibility to adhere to policies, rules, regulatory requirements, and laws.

- Project managers have a mandatory responsibility to report unethical or illegal conduct to management and those affected by the conduct.

- Project managers are required to bring valid, fact-driven violations of the Code of Ethics and Professional Conduct to the PMI for resolution.

- Disciplinary action should commence for an individual who seeks to retaliate against a person raising ethics concerns.

Upholding the Respect Value

Respect in the PMI Code centers not only on the respect we may deserve as project managers but also on the respect that others are due through their work and contributions to our projects. Respect in project management also is aimed toward our respect for the environment we operate within.

Aspiring to Respect

Respect among individuals and toward the environment promotes trust, confidence, and shared ownership of the project work and deliverables. The PMI Code lists four aspirational standards for respect, which I paraphrase as follows:

- Learn about the norms and customs of others, and avoid behavior that others may find disrespectful.

- Listen to others and seek to understand their points of view and opinions.

- Don't avoid people with whom you have conflicts or disagreement. Approach them in an attempt to resolve your differences.

- Conduct yourself professionally, even when those you deal with don't act professionally.

The value of respect means having appropriate regard for yourself and also regard for others personally and professionally. It requires you to negotiate agreements and contracts in good faith and not exercise the power of your expertise or position to influence the decisions or actions of others in order to benefit personally at their expense. This doesn't mean you can't influence people, because that is a key skill in stakeholder management and communications activities. It means that you can't seek to benefit personally by taking advantage of others using your position of power.

As a project manager, you may find yourself working with people from different cultures and countries than your own. You should treat other cultures with respect; just because your culture may differ from that of others doesn't mean your culture is better or worse. When you're working in a country other than your home, you should first educate yourself regarding how to behave in this new environment. You'll want to understand the politics, the culture, and the work ethic to operate better in the environment. And, finally, just because you take the initiative to learn about and respect other cultures doesn't mean they'll do the same for you. Regardless of how you are treated, treat others with respect; you'll win their respect in return.

Culture shock is a feeling of uncertainty and disorientation when you are initially immersed in an unfamiliar way of life in a different culture than your own culture. It can be caused by a variety of cultural differences. These could include, among many others, a different way of greeting (e.g., bowing instead of a handshake), different foods and eating habits, language differences, different modes of transportation, and unfamiliar local customs. Culture shock often causes a sense of frustration, anxiety, and confusion.

Respect also means not acting in an abusive manner toward any other person. Keep in mind that abuse can take many forms, from outright verbal and physical abuse to the more insidious forms of gossip, slander, libel, and passive-aggressive behavior. Complying with this standard means observing the golden rule of treating others as you would like to be treated.

Adhering to the Mandatory Values of Respect

Project managers are to "take the high road" in their dealings with clients and stakeholders. We demand of ourselves and of fellow project managers four things regarding respect. Here's what the Code of Ethics and Professional Conduct details:

- Project managers negotiate in good faith.
- Project managers don't influence decisions for personal gain at the expense of others.
- Project managers are not abusive toward others.
- Project managers respect the property rights of others . . . no ripping off other people's work and no throwing the laptop.

Respect also means that you respect the property rights of others, which ties in nicely with the value of responsibility, in which you must protect the intellectual property rights, copyright, and confidential information of any person or body. This means that you must acknowledge the ownership and copyright that others hold on their work.

Demonstrating respect also means being aware of the norms and customs of others and avoiding engaging in behaviors they might consider disrespectful. This is increasingly important in an ever-more globalized economy, where projects are often done internationally. Also, many stakeholders may have different customs from your own, and effective communication and management of stakeholders requires you to understand their customs and treat them with respect. A key element in effective communications with, and expectation management of, stakeholders is the ability to listen to others' points of view and seek to understand them.

When it comes to resolving conflicts or disagreements, respect means dealing directly and in an open manner with those people with whom you have a conflict or disagreement. Seek to deal with the issue and not let personalities get in the way.

Whatever happens around you and whatever the actions of others, respect also means that you always conduct yourself in a professional manner, even when it is not reciprocated.

These mandatory values of respect have several implications. From the Code: "We cooperate with PMI concerning ethics violations and the collection of related information whether we are a complainant or a respondent. We also abstain from accusing others of ethical misconduct when we do not have all the facts. Further, we pursue disciplinary action against individuals who knowingly make false allegations against others."

> ### In the Real World
> I have always found that having respect for myself and for others is a great personal asset. It improves my ability to build genuine relationships with others and understand their points of view. Keep in mind that people will know, either consciously or subconsciously, if you are faking respect, so make sure that it is always genuine.

Being a Fair Project Manager

Ever hear the phrase, "All's fair in love and war"? Or how about, "Life just isn't fair"? Sure you have. So, what is fairness? Is fairness different from justice? These are the types of questions the PMI Code hopes we will ask others and ourselves.

As defined in the PMI Code, "Fairness is our duty to make decisions and act impartially and objectively. Our conduct must be free from competing self-interest, prejudice, and favoritism." Sounds wonderfully complex, doesn't it?

Aspiring to Fairness

Project managers are to aspire to four things in the realm of fairness:

- Project managers should demonstrate transparency in decision-making.
- Project managers must constantly be impartial and objective and take corrective actions when appropriate.
- Project managers provide equal access to information to those who are authorized to have that information.
- Project managers make opportunities equally available to all qualified candidates.

The value of fairness also extends to favoritism and discrimination. To display fairness, you must avoid both favoritism and discrimination, which means that you neither hire nor fire, neither reward nor punish, and neither award nor deny contracts based on your own personal considerations, bias, or benefit. This means that you should treat everyone equally and fairly, regardless of any preconceived notions you may have. It also means that you must not discriminate against anyone based on gender, race, age, religion, disability, nationality, or sexual orientation.

Adhering to the Mandatory Standards on Fairness

The PMI Code requires project managers to adhere to five values regarding fairness. Two of the mandatory fairness standards apply to conflict-of-interest scenarios, while the remaining three requirements center on favoritism and discrimination. Project managers are to do the following:

- Fully disclose to stakeholders any real or potential conflict of interest.
- Refrain from participating in any decision where a real or potential conflict of interest exists until we, the project managers, have disclosed the situation, have an approved mitigation plan, and have the consent of the project stakeholders to proceed.

- Refrain from hiring or firing, rewarding or punishing, or awarding or denying contracts based on personal considerations such as favoritism, nepotism, or bribery.

- Refrain from discriminating against others on the basis of race, gender, age, religion, disability, nationality, or sexual orientation.

- Always apply the rules of the organization (the organization being your employer, PMI, or other performing organization) without favoritism or prejudice.

To show and prove fairness you must be able to demonstrate transparency and impartiality in your decision-making process and provide equal access to information to those who are authorized to have that information. This is particularly important in legal or contractual matters, because a lack of fairness could be grounds for a legal challenge to your decisions.

I think it's safe to say with regard to these requirements that if we follow the rules of our employers, the laws of our country, and the calling voice of our conscience, we'll be all right.

In the Real World

I recommend that you keep a documented conflict-of-interest register where all employees must disclose and record any real or potential conflict of interest. Often the level of conflict of interest is so small that it can be managed via a simple nondisclosure agreement; at other times it may require those affected to be removed from that particular process or project. Always disclose any real or perceived conflict of interest quickly.

Being an Honest Project Manager

Honesty is being truthful in our conversations and in our actions. This means that we, as project managers, don't overpromise, don't agree to due dates that we know we can't meet, and don't sandbag our budgets and deliverables. We do what we say we'll do, and we say what's truthful. Transparency is one of the key pillars of Scrum, and Disciplined Agile added a fifth point to their manifesto: "Transparency over predictability." Like the other values in the Code, honesty has both aspirational and mandatory standards.

Aspiring to Honesty

According to the Code, project managers should aspire to five traits of honesty:

- Seek the truth.
- Be truthful in communications and conduct.
- Provide accurate and timely information.
- Make commitments and promises in good faith.

- Strive to create an environment where others feel safe to tell the truth. Truth (with a capital "T") is a key Agile concept of empowerment for individuals within a safe environment.

These five aspirations are noble. As project managers, we are often rushed by stakeholders to get the work done. These five aspirations cause us to pause and reflect on what's honest and truthful in our communications to project team members, stakeholders, *and ourselves*.

Honesty seems like one of those self-evident terms. We all know when we are being honest, and if we aren't being honest, then surely we are being dishonest. Or is there some gray area between honesty and dishonesty?

If you want to act in accordance with the value of honesty, there is no gray area; you are either being honest or dishonest. Telling half-truths or omitting key information is dishonest. In order to meet the standards required by this value, you must be 100 percent honest at all times. This means that you, as a professional project manager, will not engage in or condone behavior in others that is designed to deceive anyone. This includes making misleading or false statements, telling half-truths, providing information out of context, or omitting information that, if known, would make your statements misleading or incomplete.

 EXAM TIP As mentioned in an earlier Exam Tip, the most appropriate answer for project management ethics questions is based on the PMI Code and not personal opinion. In addition, you should first abide by the laws of the country in which you're doing business. Second, follow your company's policies. Third, follow the cultural standards of the location where the project is being managed.

Living the Honesty Requirements

There are just two mandatory standards for honesty in the Code:

- Project managers do not engage in or condone behavior that is designed to mislead others. This includes, but isn't limited to, the following:
  - Creating misleading statements
  - Creating false statements
  - Stating half-truths
  - Providing information out of context
  - Withholding information that, if known, would render our statements as false
- Project managers do not engage in dishonest behavior with the intention of personal gain at the expense of others.

Basically, as project managers, we don't lie. We are required, according to the Code, to tell the truth regardless of the impact it may have on us, our project team, or our projects. How many project managers do you know who are living by this requirement?

EXAM TIP   If you are ever presented with a question that asks you what is best to do in a situation where you suspect dishonesty, the answer is always to disclose this, then investigate and rectify the situation with honesty.

The value of honesty also ties in with other values of responsibility, respect, and fairness and demands of us that we do not engage, condone, or participate in dishonest behavior with the intention of personal gain or at the expense of another.

Displaying honesty means being prepared to ensure that the information you are basing your decisions upon or providing to others is accurate, reliable, and timely. Being honest also means being prepared to share bad news even when it may be poorly received.

In the Real World

Being honest will sometimes have repercussions that will test your skill as a relationship builder and influencer. You may even lose some credibility influence in the short term. But over the long term, you will develop a reputation based on honesty, and this will serve you better than a reputation of someone who isn't always honest.

Chapter Summary

CAPMs agree to abide by the PMI Code—it's part of the exam application process. Although no document can force anyone to behave ethically and professionally, this document encourages us to adhere to a standard of ethics, morals, and professionalism. The goal of the PMI Code is to promote ethics in project management as a profession, and you'll be tested on these concepts on the CAPM exam. It will behoove you to read over the actual PMI Code, available for download from the PMI website, and familiarize yourself with the associated concepts, sections, comments, and key terms.

The code includes four values: responsibility, respect, fairness, and honesty. You can apply these four values to all areas of a project—from initiation all the way through closing. As a project manager, you'll likely face some ethical choices, but these four values can help guide you through the correct decisions. These four values also make up the major chapters of the PMI Code. For each of these values, you'll find mandatory standards and aspirational standards: things we're required to do and things we should do.

The key value of responsibility requires a project manager to take personal and professional responsibility for his or her own actions, acting ethically and professionally at all times, and ensuring that others do the same.

The key value of respect requires professional project managers to display respect for themselves and others. It requires that they refrain from abusive behaviors and understand different customs and cultures.

The key value of fairness seeks to avoid either real or potential conflict-of-interest situations and avoid favoritism and discrimination by treating everyone equally and openly.

The key value of honesty requires a project manager to be completely truthful at all times and not engage in half-truths or omission of information.

Questions

1. Rosemary is the project manager of the JKN Project. The project customer has requested that she inflate her cost estimates by 25 percent. The customer reports that his management always reduces the cost of the estimates, so this is the only method to get the monies needed to complete the project. Which of the following is the best response to this situation?

   A. Do as the customer asked to ensure that the project requirements can be met by adding the increase as a contingency reserve.

   B. Do as the customer asked to ensure that the project requirements can be met by adding the increase across each task.

   C. Do as the customer asked by creating an estimate for the customer's management and another for the actual project implementation.

   D. Complete an accurate estimate of the project. In addition, create a risk assessment on why the project budget would be inadequate.

2. Deeti is the project manager for the BNH Project. This project takes place in a different country than where she is from. The project leader from this country presents a team of workers who are all from his family. What should Deeti do?

   A. Reject the team leader's recommendations and assemble her own project team.

   B. Review the résumés and qualifications of the proposed project team before approving the team.

   C. Determine whether the country's traditions include hiring from the immediate family before hiring from outside the family.

   D. Replace the project leader with an impartial project leader.

3. You are the project manager on a new project that is to take place in another country and you are about to begin negotiations. Which of the following should be your guide on what business practices are allowed and discouraged?

   A. The project charter

   B. The project plan

   C. Company policies and procedures

   D. The PMI Code of Ethics and Professional Conduct

4. One of your project team members reports that he sold pieces of equipment because he needed to pay for his daughter's school tuition. He says that he has paid back the money by working overtime without reporting the hours worked so that his theft remains private. What should you do?

   A. Fire the project team member.

   B. Report the team member's actions to his manager.

   C. Suggest that the team member report his actions to human resources.

   D. Tell the team member you're disappointed in what he did and advise him not to do something like this again.

5. You are a part-time project manager on the SUN Project. Your organization is a functional environment, and you do not get along well with the functional manager leading the project. You disagree with the manager on how the project should proceed, the timings of the activities, the suggested schedule, and the expected quality of the work. The manager has requested that you get to work on several of the activities on the critical path even though you and she have not resolved the issues concerning the project. What should you do?

   A. Go to senior management and voice your concerns.

   B. Complete the activities as requested.

   C. Ask to be taken off of the project.

   D. Refuse to begin activities on the project until the issues are resolved.

6. PMI has contacted you regarding a potential ethics violation of a CAPM candidate. The question is in regard to a friend who said he worked as a project manager under your guidance. You know this is not true, but to save a friendship, you avoid talking with the PMI representative. This avoidance is a violation of what?

   A. The Code requirement to cooperate on ethics violations investigations

   B. The Code requirement to report all ethical information

   C. The Code requirement to report any CAPM violations

   D. The universal law concerning ethical practices

7. Richard is the project manager for the Log Cabin Project. One of his vendors is completing a large portion of the project. Richard has heard a rumor that the vendor is losing many of its workers due to labor issues. In light of this information, what should Richard do?

   A. Stop work with the vendor until the labor issues are resolved.

   B. Communicate with the vendor about the rumor.

   C. Look to secure another vendor to replace the current one.

   D. Negotiate with the labor union to secure the workers on his project.

8. Heather is the project manager for the PMH Project. Three vendors have submitted cost estimates for the project. One of the estimates is significantly higher than the others. In this scenario, Heather should do what?

   A. Ask the other two vendors about the higher estimate from the third vendor.

   B. Use the cost estimates from the historical information to check whether the high estimate is consistent.

   C. Take the high cost to the vendor to discuss the discrepancy before reviewing the issue with the other vendors.

   D. Ask the vendor that supplied the high estimate for information on how the estimate was prepared.

9. Ethan is the project manager of the LKH Project. This project must be completed within six months. The project is two months into the schedule and is starting to slip. As of now, the project is one week behind schedule. Based on Ethan's findings, he believes that he can implement some corrective actions to recover the lost time over the next month to get the project back on schedule. Management, however, requires weekly status reports on cost and schedule. What should Ethan do?

A. Report that the project is one week behind schedule but will finish on schedule based on cited corrective actions.

B. Report that the project is on schedule and will finish on schedule.

C. Report that the project is off schedule by a few days but will finish on schedule.

D. Report that the project is running late.

10. As a contracted project manager, Marcus has been assigned a project with a budget of $1.5 million. The project is scheduled to last seven months, but the most recent earned value management (EVM) report shows that the project will finish ahead of schedule by nearly six weeks. If this happens, Marcus will lose $175,000 in billable time. What should Marcus do?

A. Bill for the entire $1.5 million, since this was the approved budget.

B. Bill for the $1.5 million by adding additional work at the end of the project.

C. Report to the customer the project status and completion date.

D. Report to the customer the project status and completion date and ask if they'd like to add any features to account for the monies not spent.

11. Andrew is the project manager of the PMH Project. He has been contracted to design the placement of several pieces of manufacturing equipment. He has completed the project scope and is ready to pass the work over to the installer. The installer begins to schedule Andrew to help with the installation of the manufacturing equipment. Andrew should do what?

A. Help the installer place the equipment according to the design documents.

B. Help the installer place the equipment as the customer sees fit.

C. Refuse to help the installer, since the project scope has been completed.

D. Help the installer place the equipment, but insist that the quality control be governed by his design specifications.

12. Ahmed is the project manager of the 12BA Project. He has completed the project according to the design documents and has met the project scope. The customer agrees that the design document requirements have been met; however, the customer is not pleased with the project deliverables and is demanding additional adjustments be made to complete the project. What is the best way for Ahmed to proceed?

A. Complete the work as the customer has requested.

B. Complete the work at 1.5 times the billable rate.

C. Do nothing. The project scope is completed.

D. Do nothing. Management from the performing organization and the customer's organization will need to determine why the project failed before adding work.

13. Lohshenii is the project manager of the AAA Project. Due to the nature of the project, much of the work will require overtime between Christmas and New Year's Day. Many of the project team members, however, have requested vacations during that week. What is the best way for Lohshenii to proceed?

    A. Refuse all vacation requests and require all team members to work overtime.

    B. Allow vacation requests only for those team members who are not needed during that week.

    C. Divide tasks equally among the team members so each works the same amount of time.

    D. Allow team members to volunteer for the overtime work.

14. Dharam is a project manager for his organization. Dharam's current project is to install several devices for one of his company's clients. The client has requested that he complete a few small tasks that are not in the project scope. To maintain the relationship with the client, Dharam obliges the client's request and completes the work without informing his company. This is an example of _____.

    A. Effective expert judgment

    B. Failure to be honest

    C. Contract change control

    D. Integrated change

15. Jingyi is completing a project for a customer in another country. One of the customs in this country is to honor the project manager of a successful project with a gift. His company, however, does not allow project managers to accept gifts worth more than $50 from any entity. At the completion of the project, the customer presents Jingyi with a new car in a public ceremony. What should Jingyi do?

    A. Accept the car, since it is a custom of the country. To refuse it would be an insult to his hosts.

    B. Refuse to accept the car, since it would result in a conflict with his organization's policy on gifts.

    C. Accept the car and then return it, in private, to the customer.

    D. Accept the car and then donate the car to a charity in the customer's name.

16. A project team member is sabotaging your project because he does not agree with it. What should you do?

    A. Fire the project team member.

    B. Present the problem to management.

    C. Present the problem to management with a solution to remove the team member from the project.

    D. Present the problem to management with a demand to fire the project team member.

17. Noriko is the project manager of a project in Asia. She discovers that the project leader has hired family members for several lucrative contracts on the project. What should Noriko consider first?

   A. Cultural issues

   B. Ethical issues

   C. Organizational issues

   D. Political issues

18. A responsible project manager focuses foremost on which of the following to achieve customer satisfaction?

   A. Completing the project requirements

   B. Maintaining the project cost

   C. Maintaining the project schedule

   D. Completing the project with the defined quality metrics

19. A CAPM has been assigned to manage a project in a foreign country. The disorientation the CAPM will likely experience as he gets acclimated to the country is known as what?

   A. Sapir-Whorf hypothesis

   B. Time dimension

   C. Ethnocentrism

   D. Culture shock

20. Isaac is the project manager for an information technology project. It has come to his attention that a technical problem has stopped the project work. How should Isaac proceed?

   A. Measure the project performance to date and account for the cost of the technical problem.

   B. Rebaseline the project performance to account for the technical problem.

   C. Work with the project team to develop alternative solutions to the technical problem.

   D. Outsource the technical problem to a vendor.

Answers

1. **D.** It would be inappropriate and unethical to bloat the project costs by 25 percent. A risk assessment describing how the project may fail if the budget is not accurate is most appropriate. A, B, and C are incorrect because these choices are ethically wrong. The CAPM should always provide honest estimates of the project work.

2. **C.** Deeti should first confirm what the local practices and customs call for in regard to hiring family members before others. A and D are incorrect because

they do not consider the qualifications of the project team leader and the project team. In addition, they do not take into account local customs. B is incorrect because, although it does ponder the qualifications of the project team, it does not consider the local customs.

3. **C.** The company policies and procedures, based on ethical practices, should guide you and the decisions you make in the foreign country. A and B are incorrect because, although these documents are essential, they usually do not reference allowed business practices. D is incorrect because, although the PMI Code does possess crucial ethics information, the company's policies and procedures are most specific to the project work and requirements as long as the policies and procedures are "generally accepted business practices" in that country.

4. **B.** This situation calls for you to report the project team member's actions to his manager for disciplinary review. A is incorrect because you may not have the authority as project manager to fire the project team member. C and D are incorrect because you are ethically required to take action to bring the situation to management's attention.

5. **B.** As a part-time project manager, you must respect the delegation of the functional manager. A, C, and D are all incorrect because these actions do not complete the assigned work the functional manager has delegated to you as a part-time project manager. The functional manager has not violated the PMI Code in any way that would justify these actions.

6. **A.** By avoiding the conversation with PMI in regard to your friend's ethics violation, you are, yourself, violating the Code requirement to cooperate with PMI. B is incorrect because there is no requirement to report all ethical information. The Code says, "We provide accurate information in a timely manner." C is incorrect because of the Code requirement to report a violation after a determination as to whether a violation has occurred. D is incorrect because there is no universal law about ethics.

7. **B.** The project manager should confront the problem by talking with the vendor about the rumor. A is incorrect because stopping work would delay the project and possibly cause future problems. C is incorrect because replacing the vendor may violate the contract between the buyer and seller. D is incorrect because the agreement is between the performing organization and the vendor, not the labor union, which isn't even mentioned in the scenario.

8. **D.** Most likely, the vendor did not understand the project work to be procured, so the estimate is skewed. A clear statement of work is needed for the vendors to provide accurate estimates. A and C are incorrect because they discuss another vendor's estimate with the competing vendors. B is incorrect because costs may have changed since the historical information was created. In addition, there's no evidence in the question that historical information even exists. This information should be kept confidential between the buyer and seller. In some government projects, you may be required to announce the winning bid.

9. **A.** The project manager should report an honest assessment of the project, with actions on how he plans to correct the problem. B and C are incorrect because they do not provide honest answers to management. D is incorrect because it does not provide a solution to the problem.

10. **C.** An honest and accurate assessment of the project work is always required. A and B are incorrect because these actions do not reflect an honest assessment of the work. D is incorrect because it offers gold plating to the customer and recommends additional changes that were not part of the original project scope. In addition, because this is a contracted relationship, the additional work may not be covered within the original project contract and may result in legal issues.

11. **C.** When the project scope is completed, the contract is fulfilled, and the project is done. Any new work items should not be sent through. In this instance, the contract change control system should be invoked, or a new contract should be created. A, B, and D are incorrect because these choices are outside of the project scope and have not been covered in the contract.

12. **C.** When the project scope has been completed, the project is completed. Any additional work, without a contract change or new contract, would be dishonest and would betray the customer or the project manager's company. This is a good example of a question where none of the choices is a good one, but you must choose the best answer available. Of course, in a real project, you'd have many other choices and options to achieve customer satisfaction. A and B are both incorrect because additional work is not covered in the current contract. D is incorrect because the project did not fail—the deliverables met the requirements of the project scope and the design document.

13. **D.** This is the best choice for this scenario, because it allows the project team to be self-led and is sensitive to the needs of the project team. A, B, and C are incorrect because they are all autocratic responses to the problem, and while the results may seem fair, D is the best choice.

14. **B.** When the project manager completes activities outside of the contract and does not inform the performing organization, it is essentially the same as dishonesty. The CAPM must be held accountable for all the time invested in a project. A is incorrect because this is not an example of expert judgment. C is incorrect because the contract has not been changed or attempted to be changed. D is incorrect because the changes the project manager completed for the customer were not sent through any change control system. Instead, they were completed without documentation or reporting.

15. **B.** This is the best answer. Although this solution may seem extreme, accepting the car in public would give the impression that the project manager has defied company policy. In addition, accepting the car would appear to be a conflict of interest for the project manager. A, C, and D are all incorrect because accepting the car, even with the intention of returning it or donating it to charity, would conflict with the company's policies regarding the acceptance of gifts.

16. **C.** The problem should be presented to management, with a solution to remove the project team member from the project. Remember that whenever the project manager must present a problem to management, the project manager should also present a solution to the problem. A is incorrect because it likely is not the project manager's role to fire the project team member. B is incorrect because it does not address a solution for the problem. D is incorrect because the project manager's focus should be on the success of the project. By recommending that the project team member be removed from the project, the problem is solved from the project manager's point of view. Management, however, may come to the decision on their own accord to dismiss the individual from the company altogether. In addition, a recommendation from the project manager to fire someone may be outside the boundary of human resources' procedure for employee termination.

17. **A.** The project manager should first determine what the country's customs and culture call for when hiring relatives. It may be a preferred practice in the country to work with qualified relatives first before hiring other individuals to complete the project work. B, C, and D are incorrect because they are not the best choices in this scenario. They may be considered after first examining the cultural issues within the country.

18. **A.** The largest factor when it comes to customer satisfaction is the ability to complete the project requirements. B, C, and D are incorrect because achieving each of these factors, while good, is not as complete as achieving the project requirements, which may include the cost, schedule, and quality expectations.

19. **D.** Culture shock is the typical disorientation a person feels when visiting a foreign country. A is incorrect because the Sapir-Whorf hypothesis is a theory that suggests an individual can understand a culture by understanding its language. B is incorrect because time dimension is the local culture's general practice for respecting time and punctuality. C is incorrect because ethnocentrism is a person's belief that their own culture is the best and that all other cultures should be measured against it.

20. **C.** When problems arise that stop project tasks, the project manager should work with the team to uncover viable alternative solutions. A and B are incorrect because they do nothing to find a solution to the problem. D is incorrect because the solution for the problem has not necessarily been addressed. The end result of C, to find an alternative solution, may result in outsourcing the problem to a vendor, D, but should not be the first choice in this scenario.

References

- *Agile Practice Guide* (2017)
- *Business Analysis for Practitioners: A Practice Guide* (2015)
- *CAPM Certified Associate in Project Management Practice Exams* (2019), Haner and McCoy

- *Effective Project Management, Eighth Edition* (2019), Wysocki
- *PMBOK Guide* (2021)
- *Process Groups: A Practice Guide* (2022)
- *PMIstandards+*
- *The PMI Guide to Business Analysis* (2017)
- *The Project Management Answer Book* (2015), Furman

PART III

Appendixes and Glossary

50 Confusing Terms on the CAPM Exam

There are a lot of terms in the CAPM body of knowledge that sound similar but have different meanings, causing a lot of confusion for test takers. This handy reference is intended to help you avoid any confusion regarding these terms. Use this reference as part of your preparation for exam day; it will be your guide on the CAPM exam when you encounter terminology that otherwise might be confusing or unclear. All terms are aligned with the Examination Content Outline (2023 Exam Update), consistent with the books from the Reference List, and alphabetized for easy reference.

1. Accuracy vs. Precision

accuracy: How close a measurement or estimation is to the true or expected value, or how close the actual results of a project are to the planned results. For example, if a project was estimated to cost $80,000 but ended up costing $76,000, the accuracy of the cost estimate is 95 percent because the actual cost is 95 percent of the estimated cost.

precision: The level of consistency or reproducibility of a measurement or estimation. Precision is about how consistent the results of a project are over time. For example, a measurement or estimation that proves to be correct over multiple similar projects, such as the duration of a particular project activity or task.

2. Audit vs. Inspection

audit: A systematic and independent examination of a project or process to determine whether it meets the specified requirements or standards. An audit is usually conducted by an external or internal auditor who reviews the project documentation, interviews team members, and observes the project activities to identify any nonconformances or areas for improvement. The goal of an audit is to provide an unbiased assessment of the project and to ensure that it meets the required standards.

inspection: A detailed examination of a project or product to identify defects or issues that may impact its quality. It is usually conducted by the project team members or stakeholders, who review the project documentation, code, design, or other deliverables to identify any defects, errors, or issues. The goal of an inspection is to identify and fix defects early in the project life cycle to reduce the cost and time of rework.

3. Authority vs. Responsibility

authority: The power or right to make decisions, take actions, or give instructions. Authority is the official power given to a project manager or team member to make decisions or take actions related to the project. Authority can be formal or informal, and it is usually defined by the project charter or organizational policies.

responsibility: The obligation or duty to perform a task or achieve a goal. Responsibility is the expectation that a team member will complete a specific task or achieve a specific goal within the project. Responsibility is usually assigned by the project manager or team lead and is based on the skills, knowledge, and experience of the team member.

4. Baselines: Scope, Schedule, Cost

scope baseline: Includes the project scope statement, the work breakdown structure (WBS), and the WBS dictionary. It defines the scope of the project, the deliverables, and the project objectives. Any changes to the scope must be approved through the project's change control process.

schedule baseline: Includes the project schedule, which is created based on the project scope, and estimates of the time required for each activity. The schedule baseline is used to monitor and control the project timeline and to identify any delays or variances from the planned schedule. Any changes to the schedule must be approved through the project's change control process.

cost baseline: Includes the project budget, which is created based on the project scope, and estimates of the cost of each activity. The cost baseline is used to monitor and control the project costs and to identify any overruns or variances from the planned budget. Any changes to the budget must be approved through the project's change control process.

5. Burndown Chart vs. Burnup Chart

burndown chart: A chart that shows the number of user story points in the product backlog in relation to how many user stories the team can create in each iteration. As more iterations happen and the team completes the user stories, a downward trending line shows fewer and fewer user stories remaining in the backlog, and this reveals a trend for velocity and expectations about when the project can realistically complete all the user stories.

burnup chart: Similar to a burndown chart, a burnup chart also shows the amount of user story points in the product backlog in relation to how many user stories the team is able to create in each iteration. As more iterations happen and the team completes the user stories, an upward trending line shows the accumulation of user stories accomplished and the remaining story points in the backlog. This chart also reveals a trend for velocity and expectations about when the project can realistically complete all of the user stories.

6. Business Analysis vs. Business Analytics

business analysis: Identifying business needs, defining requirements, and recommending solutions to improve business processes, systems, and products. Business analysts use a variety of tools and techniques to gather and analyze data, including interviews, surveys, and data modeling. The goal of business analysis is to help organizations identify and address business problems, improve efficiency, and optimize business operations.

business analytics: Using data and statistical methods to analyze business performance and make data-driven decisions. Business analysts use a variety of analytical tools and techniques to extract insights from data, including data mining, predictive analytics, and machine learning. The goal of business analytics is to help organizations improve decision-making, identify new opportunities, and optimize business performance.

7. Business Case vs. Business Needs

business case: A document that provides a justification for the project by outlining the expected benefits, costs, risks, and timeline. It explains why the project is necessary (business needs), what the expected return on investment (ROI) is, and how the project aligns with the organization's strategic goals. The business case helps to ensure that the project is aligned with the organization's priorities and provides a framework for decision-making throughout the project.

business needs: The specific problems, opportunities, or challenges that the project aims to address. Business needs are the driving force behind the project and help to define the scope and objectives of the project. Business needs are typically identified through a process of analysis and consultation with stakeholders, and they are documented in the business case, project charter, or project plan.

8. Business Needs vs. Business Requirements

business needs: The problems, opportunities, or challenges that the project aims to address. Business needs are typically identified through a process of analysis and consultation with stakeholders. Business needs help to define the scope and objectives of the project and ensure that it is aligned with the organization's strategic goals. It is the "why we are doing this."

business requirements: The specific needs and objectives of the business that must be addressed by a project. Business requirements describe what the system or product must do to support the business processes. They are usually documented in a business requirements document (BRD) or use case document and include functional and nonfunctional requirements. Business requirements are used to ensure that the project meets the business objectives and delivers the expected benefits.

For example: Improve staff morale (business need) vs. eliminate Saturday workdays (business requirement).

9. Business Process Management (BPM) vs. Business Process Model and Notation (BPMN)

business process management (BPM): A holistic approach to managing, optimizing, and improving business processes to achieve organizational goals. It involves identifying, analyzing, designing, implementing, monitoring, and continuously improving business processes. BPM includes various methodologies, techniques, and tools to streamline workflows, increase efficiency, reduce costs, and enhance customer satisfaction. BPM focuses on the end-to-end process and seeks to optimize it from a strategic perspective.

Business Process Model and Notation (BPMN): A graphical notation used to represent and model business processes. It is a standardized language that allows business analysts, process owners, and stakeholders to visually communicate and document business processes. BPMN includes symbols, shapes, and arrows that represent different types of tasks, events, and gateways. It enables users to model complex processes, identify bottlenecks, and visualize the flow of information and resources.

10. Business Rules vs. Business Requirements

business rules: The specific guidelines or constraints that dictate how business processes should be executed. They are usually based on policies, regulations, industry standards, or best practices. Business rules define what is permissible, mandatory, or prohibited within a business process. Business rules are often documented separately from business requirements and are used to ensure compliance with legal, regulatory, or other business constraints.

business requirements: The specific needs and objectives of the business that must be addressed by a project. Business requirements describe what the system or product must do to support the business processes. They are usually documented in a business requirements document (BRD) or use case document and include functional and nonfunctional requirements. Business requirements are used to ensure that the project meets the business objectives and delivers the expected benefits.

11. Change Control vs. Configuration Control

change control: Identifying, documenting, approving or rejecting, and controlling changes to the project baselines (including scope baselines, schedule baselines, and cost baselines). In other words, it is used to control changes to all aspects of an approved project plan.

configuration control: Managing the product (or project's deliverables) and related documents, throughout the life cycle of the product. The determination of what falls under configuration control is part of the project management plan.

Configuration control is applied throughout the life cycle of the product (concept -> design -> develop/manufacture -> service -> dispose), whereas change control is applied during the life cycle of the project after establishing the project baselines.

12. Check Sheets vs. Checklists

check sheets: Also known as tally sheets, used as part of requirements gathering, task execution, quality control, and other aspects of the project to ensure that a task or process is completed accurately. Check sheets are especially useful for gathering data while performing inspections to identify defects.

checklists: Like "to-do" lists—things, actions, or points to be considered, often used as a reminder. They are an effective way to capture lessons learned from similar completed projects. Checklists help in managing the Control Quality activities in a structured manner. This tool can be utilized in quality management, risk identification, and project execution.

13. Closing a Phase vs. Closing a Project

closing a phase: Completing all activities and deliverables associated with a specific phase of a project. This includes verifying that all work packages and activities have been completed, reviewing and validating all project deliverables, and obtaining formal approval from stakeholders for the completion of the phase. Closing a phase is critical to ensure that all work has been completed and that the project is ready to move on to the next phase.

closing a project: Completing all activities and deliverables associated with the entire project and bringing the project to an orderly end. This includes verifying that all project objectives have been met, all deliverables have been completed and accepted, and all project documentation has been archived. Closing a project also involves obtaining final sign-off from stakeholders and formally releasing project resources.

14. Communication Methods vs. Communications Technologies

communication methods: The different ways that project team members, stakeholders, and other relevant parties communicate with each other. These methods can include in-person meetings, conference calls, e-mails, memos, reports, and presentations, among others. Communication methods are selected based on the nature of the message, the intended audience, and the desired outcomes of the communication.

communications technologies: The tools and platforms used to facilitate communication between project team members and stakeholders. These technologies can include e-mail, instant messaging, video conferencing, project management software, and social media platforms, among others. Communications technologies are selected based on the needs of the project team and the stakeholders, as well as the availability and suitability of the technology.

15. Contingency Plan vs. Backup Plan vs. Workaround

contingency plan: (First) A part of the Monitor Risks process and is a plan that outlines an alternative course of action to be taken if a risk or problem occurs during the project. It is a predefined response to an unexpected event that could potentially impact the project's success. The contingency plan is developed during the planning phase of the project, and it is implemented if and when the identified risk occurs.

backup plan (aka fallback plan): (Second) If the initial contingency plan doesn't work; a backup or fallback plan is implemented when the primary response proves to be inadequate. This plan should be reviewed and considered when either a residual or secondary risk occurs. This may be a worst-case scenario plan to enable the organization to "fall back" if a project plan needs to be scrapped because of risks or issues.

workaround: (Third) A solution to an unanticipated problem or issue. Unlike contingency plans and backup plans, which are created prior to project execution to anticipate and address foreseeable issues, workarounds are quick fixes to unforeseen issues that arise during project execution. It's not unusual for the project management

PART III

team to have to devise several workarounds during the course of a project. Because a workaround is designed solely to bypass, not correct, the problem at hand, it should not be expected to survive long past the initial discovery of the problem. This is also the name given to the plan to handle an issue (or when a negative risk occurs and is now considered an issue).

Part of the confusion regarding the terms contingency plan, backup plan, and workaround is that they often are used interchangeably in the real world, but they are not synonyms. In the PMI world, they have three different and distinct meanings. The three are executed sequentially (when all three are needed).

16. Control Quality vs. Validate Scope Processes

The Control Quality and Validate Scope processes are in the Monitoring and Controlling process group.

Control Quality: Measuring and recording results of executing the quality management activities (testing activities) to assess performance and ensure the project outputs/deliverables are complete, correct, and meet customer expectations.

Validate Scope: Formalizing acceptance of the completed project deliverables.

Here are some differences between Control Quality and Validate Scope:

- Control Quality is about ensuring that the deliverables meet the quality requirements defined in the quality management plan. Validate Scope is about formalizing the acceptance of deliverables.

- Control Quality is focused on correctness of the deliverables, whereas Validate Scope is focused on acceptance of deliverables.

- Control Quality is usually done by the project testers and can involve unit, system, integration, and user acceptance testing activities, whereas Validate Scope is done by the customer or sponsor.

Both Control Quality and Validate Scope processes can result in change requests.

In agile projects, the team tests the results before demonstrating to the product owner or stakeholders to gain approval, even if informally. In adaptive projects, validation can be done at the end of an iteration or a release.

17. Cost Baseline vs. Project Budget

cost baseline: A "time-lapse exposure" of when the project monies are to be spent in relation to cumulative values of the work completed in the project. The cost baseline shows the aggregated costs of all the work packages within the work breakdown structure (WBS). The approved cost baseline specifies the authorized budget for the project and provides a basis for comparison of actual costs. Once the cost baseline is established and approved, any changes to the budget or scope of the project must go through formal change control procedures to ensure that the changes are approved and properly managed.

The cost baseline monitors and measures cost performance, includes a budget contingency, and is tailored for each project.

project budget: The amount of money allocated to handle the project work and any unforeseen events (acts of God/force majeure; aka "unknown unknowns"). The project budget includes a management reserve that is outside the project manager's control. Management reserves are corporate "risk money."

18. Cost of Conformance to Quality vs. Cost of Nonconformance to Quality

cost of conformance to quality: The cost associated with the monies spent to attain the expected level of quality. For example, *prevention* costs for training, complying with safety issues, documenting processes, and purchasing the appropriate equipment and materials all contribute to the expected levels of quality. The cost of conformance also includes *appraisal* costs to test the product, complete destructive testing loss, and perform inspections. These are all monies spent to avoid failures.

cost of nonconformance to quality: The cost associated with not satisfying the quality expectations. The cost of nonconformance is evident when the project spends money because of failures within the project. Internal failure costs include rework and scrap (defective products or materials that are discarded and cannot be reworked or corrected.) External failure costs happen when the customer finds defects. External failure costs result in organizational liabilities, warranty claims, and even lost business. The cost of nonconformance to quality is also known as the *cost of poor quality* and the *cost of failure*.

Technically, when it comes to the cost of quality, there are three special terms to know. *Prevention costs* are monies spent to prevent poor quality. *Appraisal costs* are monies spent to test, evaluate, measure, and audit the product, deliverables, or services of the project. *Failure costs* are costs related to nonconformance to quality.

19. Duration vs. Effort

duration: The total amount of time that is required to complete a project activity or task. It is usually measured in days, weeks, or months and is the time from the start of the activity to its completion. The duration is often estimated during the project planning phase and is used to develop the project schedule and timeline.

effort: The amount of work required to complete a project activity or task. It is usually measured in person-hours or person-days and is the amount of time that a person or a team spends working on the activity. The effort required for a task takes into account the skills, experience, and availability of the team members working on the task.

20. Enterprise Environmental Factors (EEFs) vs. Organizational Process Assets (OPAs)

enterprise environmental factors (EEFs): Conditions that the project manager must live with—they are outside the project manager's control. Even if you don't like existing EEFs, there's not much you can do about them; you simply have to deal with them.

PART III

These factors will affect your project, influence your decisions, and even direct how you're allowed to do the project work. EEFs can come from within your organization, such as a policy, standard, or commercial software, or they can come from outside of the organization, such as a law or regulation. EEFs can influence project planning, risk management, and resource allocation.

organizational process assets (OPAs): Factors that are within the control of the organization and the project team and are always internal to the organization. OPAs include anything from within the organization that you can use to manage the current project better, including project management methodologies, templates, policies, procedures, artifacts, organizational knowledge bases, risk data, earned value management outcomes, and even lessons learned from past projects. OPAs are grouped into two categories:

- Processes, policies, and procedures
- Organizational knowledge bases

21. Estimate at Completion (EAC) vs. Estimate to Complete (ETC)

estimate at completion (EAC): An estimate of the total cost of the project when it is completed. EAC is typically based on the actual cost incurred to date, as well as estimates of the remaining work to be completed. EAC is used to forecast the total cost of the project, taking into account any variations from the original project plan.

estimate to complete (ETC): An estimate of the cost required to complete the remaining work on the project. ETC is typically based on the original project plan, as well as the actual cost incurred to date. ETC is used to determine the additional cost required to complete the project, taking into account any variations from the original project plan.

22. Explicit Knowledge vs. Tacit Knowledge

explicit knowledge: Knowledge that can be easily articulated and communicated. It is formal and systematic and can be easily documented, codified, and transferred. Examples of explicit knowledge include project plans, procedures, and manuals.

tacit knowledge: Knowledge that is difficult to articulate and communicate. It is informal and intuitive and is often gained through experience and practice. Tacit knowledge is personal and specific to an individual, and it is difficult to transfer to others. Examples of tacit knowledge include project management skills, insights, and intuition.

23. Fast Tracking vs. Crashing (Schedule Compression)

fast tracking: Overlapping project activities that are normally done sequentially to reduce the overall duration of the project. This technique is achieved by starting an activity before the previous activity is completed. For example, the design phase of a project may begin while the planning phase is still ongoing. This technique may increase project risk since activities are being performed simultaneously, and if one activity is delayed, it may impact the entire project.

crashing: Adding additional resources to an activity or a group of activities to complete the work faster. This technique involves increasing the intensity of work to shorten the duration of the project. For example, adding extra workers or working overtime to complete a project phase earlier. This technique may increase project cost since additional resources may be required to accelerate the project schedule.

24. Focus Group vs. Facilitated Workshop

focus group: A discussion group of typically six to ten participants who share their perceptions, attitudes, and opinions about a specific topic or product. The focus group is led by a moderator who asks open-ended questions and facilitates the discussion. The purpose of a focus group is to gather qualitative data and insights about a specific topic or product from the participants' perspective. Focus groups are often used in market research, user experience testing, and product development.

facilitated workshop: A structured meeting that brings together a group of stakeholders to discuss, analyze, and generate ideas and solutions related to a specific problem or opportunity. A facilitator leads the workshop and uses various tools and techniques to encourage participation, collaboration, and creativity. The purpose of a facilitated workshop is to gather ideas, generate consensus, and make decisions related to a specific problem or opportunity. Facilitated workshops are often used in project planning, risk management, and requirements gathering.

25. Functional vs. Matrix vs. Project-Oriented Organization
Following are characteristics of functional, matrix, and project-oriented organizations.

Functional

- Each department is responsible for carrying out a specific, similar set of activities.
- Several people perform each type of activity.
- Reporting is hierarchical, with individuals reporting to a single manager.
- The project manager's authority is low, relative to the functional manager's authority

Matrix

- The team members may be added from other functional areas.
- The team members report to multiple managers, including the functional manager, their resource manager, and possibly the project manager.
- The structure may be characterized as weak, balanced, or strong, depending on the relative authority of the project manager to the functional manager.

Project-oriented

- The project manager and a core project team operate as a separate organizational unit within the parent organization.
- Core team members are responsible for the work of extended team members in their functional area.

- Team members are often colocated.
- The project manager may report to a program manager with a significant amount of authority and independence.

26. Functional Requirements (FRs) vs. Nonfunctional Requirements (NFRs)

functional requirements (FRs): In IT projects, FRs capture and specify specific intended behavior of the system being developed. They define things such as system calculations, data manipulation and processing, user interface and interaction with the application, and other specific functionalities that show how user requirements are satisfied. The project manager or the requirements analyst assigns a unique ID number to each requirement to ensure that each requirement is uniquely identified and tracked throughout the project life cycle.

nonfunctional requirements (NFRs): Specify criteria that can be used to judge the operation of a system rather than specific behaviors. The system architecture plan includes the plan for implementing NFRs, which is critical to ensuring that the system meets the required level of performance and quality. NFRs are sometimes called "ilities" of the system: quality, maintainability, transportability, and so forth. Simply put, NFRs are constraints imposed on the system. They're used to define the quality attributes that will determine how the system operates. Their main purpose is to make the product (application, software, website, or other) run more efficiently and thus improve the user experience.

Unlike FRs that specify certain functions or behaviors, NFRs set the criteria to evaluate the performance of the system.

27. Gold Plating vs. Scope Creep

gold plating: Providing extra features or functionality over and above the scope baseline. The scope baseline remains unchanged. Gold plating occurs when the project manager, the project sponsor, or even a stakeholder adds in project extras to consume any budget remaining after the scope baseline has been fulfilled. It's essentially adding unneeded features to the product in order to use up all the funds allocated to the project. Though this often happens in the final stages of a project, it can begin during the project cost estimating. Some project teams "do stuff" just to use up the budget. Gold plating delivers more than what's needed and can create new risks and can contribute to a decline in team morale.

For example, a client asks you to develop a hotel application that assists visitors with checking in and out of the property and making requests during their stay. The team completes the app under budget and before the due date, so a senior programmer decides to use the remaining budget and time to add a rating and reviewing system in the app, which wasn't in the original scope.

scope creep: Uncontrolled expansion to the product or project scope without adjustments to time, cost, and resources. The scope baseline is changed. Scope creep is caused by undocumented, unapproved changes that sneak into the project scope and change it, which can adversely affect project time, cost, and resources. Of course, if you're working in an adaptive environment, there is still change control to the product scope and project scope, but change is managed through refinements of the product backlog. Scope creep is handled at the iteration level, with the product owner determining the scope for an individual iteration. Change in a predictive environment is anticipated, but change follows the integrated change control process.

For example, the client wanted a bicycle and you gave them an electric bike.

28. Manage Quality vs. Control Quality Processes

Manage Quality: Developing and implementing a quality management plan for the project. This plan includes defining the quality standards, identifying the quality control and assurance activities, and establishing the quality metrics and criteria for evaluating the project deliverables. The focus of Manage Quality is on preventing quality issues before they occur by proactively planning for quality and continuously monitoring the project to ensure that the quality plan is being followed. Manage Quality, in the Executing process group, is about prevention.

Control Quality: Measuring and correcting the quality of the project deliverables to ensure that they meet the defined quality standards. This process is typically performed throughout the project life cycle and involves activities such as inspecting, testing, and validating the project deliverables to identify and address any defects or issues that may arise. The focus of Control Quality is on identifying and addressing quality issues as they occur and ensuring that the final product or service meets the quality requirements set forth in the project scope statement. Control Quality, in the Monitoring and Controlling process group, is about inspection.

29. Nominal Group Technique vs. Brainstorming

nominal group technique: Small group discussion in which ideas/requirements are ranked/prioritized by all the members of the group after generation of all the ideas/requirements. The nominal group technique prevents domination of a single person over the discussion by allowing the voices of all members to be represented.

This approach builds on brainstorming by adding a vote to each idea to rank the ideas for acceptance, for more brainstorming, or just to prioritize the identified requirements. Here's how it works:

1. The participants silently write down their ideas.
2. The participants share their ideas with the group, and the moderator writes down the ideas on a whiteboard until all of the ideas have been captured.
3. Each idea is discussed for clarity.
4. Individuals vote privately on the ideas, with 1 being the lowest score and 5 being the highest score.

Voting and conversation can take place over many rounds to gain consensus on each item's score and prioritization.

brainstorming: Member(s) are allowed to generate as many ideas/requirements as possible without criticism.

Here are the ground rules:

- Negative responses or criticisms are not allowed.
- Participants are safe to present their own creative ideas even though some ideas may be unrealistic/absurd.
- All generated ideas/requirements are recorded without any assessments.

30. Positional Power vs. Personal Power

positional power: Comes from an individual's formal position or authority within an organization or project. This includes the ability to make decisions, delegate tasks, and assign resources based on their role in the project. Positional power is granted to an individual based on their position within the project hierarchy, such as a project manager or team lead. This type of power can be effective in getting work done, but it can also lead to resistance or resentment from team members if used improperly.

personal power: Comes from an individual's personal attributes, characteristics, and relationships with others. This includes the ability to influence others based on trust, respect, expertise, and social networks. Personal power is not tied to a formal position or authority, but rather to an individual's personal qualities and abilities. This type of power can be effective in building strong relationships, motivating team members, and overcoming resistance or obstacles.

31. Preventive Actions vs. Corrective Actions

preventive actions: Intentional actions taken when the project is likely to trend away from the scope, schedule, cost, or quality plan to ensure the project performance is aligned to the baselines. Preventive actions are proactive actions … to avoid failures. These are actions taken to prevent issues/problems from occurring in the future. Preventive actions are about building a quality product.

corrective actions: Intentional actions that realign project performance with the project management plan. Corrective actions are taken when the project deviates from the scope, schedule, cost, or quality plan in order to bring the project performance back to the baselines. Corrective actions are reactive actions, taken in response to failures. Corrective actions are about fixing the failures found by the project team or failures found by the customer.

32. Product Scope vs. Project Scope vs. Requirements

product scope: Includes the features and functions that characterize a product, service, or result.

project scope: The work that must be performed to deliver a product, service, or result with the specified features and functions.

requirements: Conditions or capabilities that must be present in a product, service, or result to satisfy a business need.

Here's an example to demonstrate the differences of product scope, project scope, and requirements. Let's say you have a plot of land and you want to build a house on it. The house is the product in this case.

- **Product scope example**   The house should have three stories, 3000 sq. ft. of built-up area, four bedrooms with attached baths, two living rooms, a kitchen, a basement, and a garage. The exterior should be white. These are all examples of product scope.

- **Project scope example**   Hiring a building contractor, an architect, and an interior designer; acquiring legal permits; estimating the cost; taking a bank loan; planning for risks such as rain and storms; designing the house; buying construction material; constructing the house; doing the interiors; buying furniture; conducting inspections; conducting regular site visits to track the progress and resolve disputes; making payments and compensations; closing contracts; and moving in are all examples of project scope.

- **Requirements example**   In addition to the product scope, there could be other requirements for the house. Using a certain grade of cement could be a quality requirement. Making the house earthquake proof could be a performance requirement. Getting a weekly progress update from your contractor and making monthly payments could be project management requirements.

33. Progressive Elaboration vs. Rolling Wave Planning

progressive elaboration: Process of gathering details about a project, product, or solution by using deductive reasoning, logic, and a series of information-gathering techniques to identify details about a project, product, or solution.

rolling wave planning: A form of progressive elaboration in which the imminent work is planned in detail, while the work in the future is planned at a high level. As the project progresses and requirements become clearer, more detailed planning is done for the work packages at lower levels of the WBS.

Rolling wave planning is a form of progressive elaboration applicable to work packages, planning packages, and release planning when using an agile or predictive life cycle approach.

34. Project Life Cycle vs. Product Life Cycle

project life cycle: The phases that a project goes through from initiation to closure. The project life cycle typically includes phases such as initiation, planning, execution, monitoring and controlling, and closure. Each phase has specific objectives, deliverables, and activities that must be completed before moving on to the next phase. The project life cycle is focused on the management of the project itself, including the planning, execution, and monitoring of project activities to ensure that the project is completed on time, within budget, and to the satisfaction of stakeholders.

product life cycle: The stages that a product goes through from conception to retirement. The product life cycle typically includes stages such as development, introduction, growth, maturity, and decline. Each stage has specific characteristics, challenges, and opportunities, and the product may require different strategies and tactics at each stage to remain successful. The product life cycle is focused on the management of the product or service itself, including the design, development, marketing, and support of the product or service to ensure that it meets the needs of customers and remains competitive in the market.

35. Project Quality vs. Product Quality

project quality: The degree to which the project management processes are effective in meeting the project objectives. This includes factors such as project planning, execution, monitoring, and controlling, as well as stakeholder engagement and communication. The focus of project quality is on ensuring that the project management processes are effective, efficient, and meet the needs of stakeholders.

product quality: The degree to which the final product or service meets the customer's requirements, needs, and expectations. This includes factors such as product design, features, performance, reliability, and usability. The focus of product quality is on ensuring that the final product or service is of high quality and meets the needs and expectations of customers.

36. Project Schedule vs. Schedule Baseline vs. Gantt Chart

project schedule: A "living" document that is updated as the project is being executed. The project schedule is the "actual," whereas the schedule baseline is "frozen."

schedule baseline: An "approved" version of the project schedule that never changes, but new baselines can be set and created. The schedule baseline is the "plan." A new schedule baseline is created only through the process of an approved change request.

Gantt chart: A bar chart of schedule information that lists activities on the vertical axis, lists dates on the horizontal axis, and depicts activity durations and progress as horizontal bars placed according to start and finish dates. A project schedule does *not* have to be presented as a Gantt chart. Gantt charts are relatively easy to read and are commonly used, especially for predictive projects. (Adaptive projects often use task boards, Kanban boards, etc., to show progress of individual tasks.)

37. Project Statement of Work (SOW) vs. Project Scope Statement

project statement of work (SOW): A description (a written account of a sequence of events) of products, services, or results to be delivered by a project. The SOW is developed from the project scope baseline and defines only that portion of the project scope that is to be included within the related contract. It may also include roles and responsibilities of each party and additional applicable terms and conditions regarding the contract.

project scope statement: The description of the project scope, major deliverables, assumptions, and constraints. The project scope statement is a component of the scope baseline. Even though it is referred to as a "statement," it often spans many three-ring binders.

Remember: The project scope statement is *a component of* the scope baseline, whereas the SOW is *developed from* the project scope baseline.

38. Relative Estimation vs. Absolute Estimation

relative estimation: Estimating the size or complexity of one project or task by comparing it to a similar project or task. It is a quick and easy way to estimate the effort required, and it is often used in agile and scrum methodologies. Relative estimation typically involves using a scale, such as a Fibonacci sequence or T-shirt sizes, to represent the size or complexity of a task or project. For example, a project may be estimated as being twice as large as another project, or a task may be estimated as being similar in size to a medium-sized T-shirt.

absolute estimation: Estimating the actual amount of time or effort required to complete a project or task. Absolute estimation typically involves breaking down a project or task into smaller components and estimating the time or effort required for each component. This can be done using a variety of techniques such as expert judgment, historical data, or statistical modeling. Compared to relative estimation, absolute estimation provides a more accurate estimate of the time or effort required, but it can be more time-consuming and may require more information and analysis.

39. Responsibility Assignment Matrix (RAM) vs. Requirements Traceability Matrix (RTM)

responsibility assignment matrix (RAM): Identifies the various tasks involved in a project and assigns responsibilities to team members for each task. It is also known as a RACI matrix, which stands for responsible, accountable, consulted, and informed. A RAM helps to clarify roles and responsibilities and ensures that everyone on the project team understands what is expected of them.

requirements traceability matrix (RTM): Used to track and manage project requirements. It is a document that links requirements to their origin and traces them throughout the project life cycle. This helps ensure that all requirements are met and that the project team has a clear understanding of what is expected.

While RAM and RTM may seem similar in that they both involve the identification of responsibilities, their focus is different. RAM focuses on identifying who is responsible for each task in the project, while RTM focuses on tracking and managing project requirements.

40. Risk vs. Issue

risk: An uncertain event or condition that could have a positive or negative impact on the project. That's correct—it's possible for a risk to have a positive impact. Risks that have a positive impact are also known as *opportunities*. Technically, risk isn't a bad thing.

PART III

It's the impact of a realized risk that can be painful, costly, or delay the project work. Most project managers look at risk the same way they'd look at leftover shrimp cocktail. Yuck. Some risks, though, are good for the project, and the project manager wants to accept them; other risks aren't so welcome.

issue: A problem or challenge that has already occurred or is currently happening and needs to be addressed to keep the project on track. Issues may arise due to unexpected events, changes in requirements, or other factors that were not anticipated during the planning phase. Issues require a reactive response to address them and minimize their impact on the project. When an issue occurs, the project manager will document the issue in the issue log.

41. Roles vs. Actors

roles: Specific positions or responsibilities that individuals hold within a project team. These roles may include project manager, project sponsor, team leader, business analyst, technical expert, and other specialized positions that are necessary to complete the project successfully.

actors: Individuals who perform tasks or activities within the project but do not necessarily hold any formal project management roles. These individuals may include stakeholders, customers, suppliers, vendors, and other third-party entities that contribute to the project's success.

Roles are specific positions within the project team, while actors are individuals who contribute to the project's success but might not hold any formal project management roles.

42. Strategic Analysis vs. Tactical Analysis vs. Operational Analysis

strategic analysis: A high-level evaluation of the project's overall goals, objectives, and long-term outcomes. This analysis focuses on identifying the project's value proposition, assessing the project's feasibility, and determining the strategic fit of the project within the broader organizational context. Strategic analysis helps project managers to align the project with the organization's overall strategy and make decisions that maximize the project's value.

tactical analysis: A mid-level evaluation of the project's plans, resources, and constraints. This analysis focuses on identifying the specific tactics and actions required to achieve the project's goals and objectives. Tactical analysis helps project managers to develop detailed project plans, allocate resources effectively, and manage project risks.

operational analysis: A low-level evaluation of the project's day-to-day activities, tasks, and processes. This analysis focuses on identifying ways to optimize project performance, improve project efficiency, and reduce costs. Operational analysis helps project managers to identify potential problems and issues that may arise during project execution and to develop effective strategies to address them.

43. Tasks vs. Activities

tasks: The specific work items that must be completed to achieve a project goal or objective. Tasks are typically defined as specific, measurable, achievable, relevant, and time-bound (SMART) activities that must be completed within a given period. Examples of tasks include designing a product, developing a software module, conducting a market research study, or delivering a training session. *Task* is the name used in project management software programs.

activities: The broader set of actions required to complete a task or a group of related tasks. Activities are often nonlinear and may involve multiple steps, dependencies, and interrelationships. Examples of activities include project planning, scheduling, risk management, change control, progress reporting, quality assurance, and stakeholder engagement.

44. Tool vs. Technique

tool: A specific software or hardware system, program, or device that is used to support project management activities. Tools are typically designed to automate or simplify project management tasks and processes, and they may be specific to a particular project management methodology or framework. Some common project management tools include project management software, scheduling software, collaboration tools, and document management systems.

technique: A specific method, procedure, or approach used to perform a project management activity. Techniques are often more general and can be applied across different project management methodologies and frameworks. Some common project management techniques include brainstorming, risk management, quality assurance, and stakeholder analysis.

45. UI vs. UX

UI (user interface): The visual and interactive elements of a software product that users interact with. UI design includes the layout, color scheme, typography, and graphical elements of a software product. The goal of UI design is to create a user-friendly and visually appealing interface that allows users to interact with the product in an intuitive and efficient way.

UX (user experience): The overall experience that users have when interacting with a software product. UX design includes the usability, accessibility, and functionality of a product, as well as the emotional and psychological responses that users have when using the product. The goal of UX design is to create a positive and meaningful user experience that meets the needs and expectations of the target audience.

46. Value Analysis (VA) vs. Value Engineering (VE)

value analysis (VA): Systematic approach to identifying the essential functions and characteristics of a project deliverable and evaluating its cost-effectiveness. The goal of VA is to ensure that the project deliverables meet the required performance standards at the lowest possible cost. VA involves a detailed analysis of the project requirements, functions, and characteristics and identifies areas where cost savings can be achieved without compromising quality.

value engineering (VE): Structured problem-solving approach that involves a team of professionals who work together to optimize the value of a project deliverable. VE involves a detailed analysis of the project requirements, functions, and characteristics and identifies alternative solutions that can provide the required performance at a lower cost. VE also involves a detailed evaluation of the benefits and risks associated with each alternative solution and the selection of the most cost-effective and practical solution.

47. Variability Risks vs. Ambiguity Risks

variability risks: Risks associated with variations in project requirements, scope, resources, or other project parameters. Variability risks arise due to the unpredictable nature of the project environment, changes in project requirements, or changes in the availability or quality of project resources. Variability risks can lead to delays, cost overruns, and quality issues if not managed effectively.

ambiguity risks: Risks associated with unclear or ambiguous project requirements, objectives, or expectations. Ambiguity risks arise when there is a lack of clarity or understanding among project stakeholders about project requirements, objectives, or expectations. Ambiguity risks can lead to confusion, miscommunication, and errors in project execution, which can result in project delays, cost overruns, and quality issues.

48. Velocity vs. Capacity vs. Load

velocity: Measure of the amount of work completed by a team in a given period, usually measured in points or units of work completed. Velocity is used in agile project management to estimate how much work can be completed by the team in a given sprint or iteration based on the team's historical performance.

capacity: Measure of the amount of work that a team can realistically complete in a given period, taking into account factors such as team size, skills, and availability. Capacity is used to plan project activities and allocate resources based on the team's expected performance.

load: Measure of the amount of work assigned to a team or team member, usually measured in hours or days. Load is evaluated to ensure that team members are not overburdened with work and to balance the workload across the team.

49. Verified Deliverable vs. Accepted Deliverable

verified deliverable: Project deliverable that has been checked against the project requirements and validated as complete and accurate. Verification is typically performed by the project team or a designated quality control team to ensure that the deliverable meets the specified requirements and standards. Once a deliverable has been verified, it is considered complete and ready for acceptance.

accepted deliverable: Verified deliverable that has been formally accepted by the project sponsor or customer. Acceptance is typically based on predefined acceptance criteria or acceptance tests that are agreed upon between the project team and the sponsor or customer. Acceptance of a deliverable signifies that it has met the project requirements and standards and is acceptable for use in the project.

50. Work Package vs. Activity

work package: Hierarchical component of a project work breakdown structure (WBS) that defines the smallest unit of work in a project. A work package includes a set of related activities and is often assigned to a specific team or individual for completion. Work packages are used to organize and track project work and to assign responsibility and accountability for completing specific tasks.

activity: Specific task or work item that needs to be completed to achieve a project objective. Activities are often associated with a duration, a set of resources required, and a specific deliverable or outcome. Activities are typically identified during the planning phase of a project and are used to develop the project schedule.

References

- *Agile Practice Guide* (2017)
- *Business Analysis for Practitioners: A Practice Guide* (2015)
- *CAPM Certified Associate in Project Management Practice Exams* (2019), Haner and McCoy
- *Process Groups: A Practice Guide* (2022)
- *PMBOK® Guide* (2021)
- *The PMI Guide to Business Analysis* (2017)

PART III

About the Online Content

This book comes complete with TotalTester Online customizable practice exam software with 300 practice exam questions and other helpful study resources including a downloadable color Memory Card, key term flash cards, word search puzzles, matching exercises, and an Excel score checker to track your performance as you work through the end-of-chapter review questions.

System Requirements

The current and previous major versions of the following desktop browsers are recommended and supported: Chrome, Microsoft Edge, Firefox, and Safari. These browsers update frequently, and sometimes an update may cause compatibility issues with the TotalTester Online or other content hosted on the Training Hub. If you run into a problem using one of these browsers, please try using another until the problem is resolved.

Your Total Seminars Training Hub Account

To get access to the online content you will need to create an account on the Total Seminars Training Hub. Registration is free, and you will be able to track all your online content using your account. You may also opt in if you wish to receive marketing information from McGraw Hill or Total Seminars, but this is not required for you to gain access to the online content.

Privacy Notice

McGraw Hill values your privacy. Please be sure to read the Privacy Notice available during registration to see how the information you have provided will be used. You may view our Corporate Customer Privacy Policy by visiting the McGraw Hill Privacy Center. Visit the **mheducation.com** site and click **Privacy** at the bottom of the page.

Single User License Terms and Conditions

Online access to the digital content included with this book is governed by the McGraw Hill License Agreement outlined next. By using this digital content you agree to the terms of that license.

Access   To register and activate your Total Seminars Training Hub account, simply follow these easy steps.

1. Go to this URL: **hub.totalsem.com/mheclaim**

2. To register and create a new Training Hub account, enter your e-mail address, name, and password on the **Register** tab. No further personal information (such as credit card number) is required to create an account.

    If you already have a Total Seminars Training Hub account, enter your e-mail address and password on the **Log in** tab.

3. Enter your Product Key: `cxgw-wjkb-5054`

4. Click to accept the user license terms.

5. For new users, click the **Register and Claim** button to create your account. For existing users, click the **Log in and Claim** button.

    You will be taken to the Training Hub and have access to the content for this book.

Duration of License   Access to your online content through the Total Seminars Training Hub will expire one year from the date the publisher declares the book out of print.

Your purchase of this McGraw Hill product, including its access code, through a retail store is subject to the refund policy of that store.

The Content is a copyrighted work of McGraw Hill, and McGraw Hill reserves all rights in and to the Content. The Work is © 2024 by McGraw Hill.

Restrictions on Transfer   The user is receiving only a limited right to use the Content for the user's own internal and personal use, dependent on purchase and continued ownership of this book. The user may not reproduce, forward, modify, create derivative works based upon, transmit, distribute, disseminate, sell, publish, or sublicense the Content or in any way commingle the Content with other third-party content without McGraw Hill's consent.

Limited Warranty   The McGraw Hill Content is provided on an "as is" basis. Neither McGraw Hill nor its licensors make any guarantees or warranties of any kind, either express or implied, including, but not limited to, implied warranties of merchantability or fitness for a particular purpose or use as to any McGraw Hill Content or the information therein or any warranties as to the accuracy, completeness, correctness, or results to be obtained from, accessing or using the McGraw Hill Content, or any material referenced in such Content or any information entered into licensee's product by users or other persons and/or any material available on or that can be accessed through the licensee's product (including via any hyperlink or otherwise) or as to non-infringement of third-party rights. Any warranties of any kind, whether express or implied, are disclaimed. Any material or data obtained through use of the McGraw Hill Content is at your own discretion and risk and user understands that it will be solely responsible for any resulting damage to its computer system or loss of data.

Neither McGraw Hill nor its licensors shall be liable to any subscriber or to any user or anyone else for any inaccuracy, delay, interruption in service, error or omission, regardless of cause, or for any damage resulting therefrom.

In no event will McGraw Hill or its licensors be liable for any indirect, special or consequential damages, including but not limited to, lost time, lost money, lost profits or good will, whether in contract, tort, strict liability or otherwise, and whether or not such damages are foreseen or unforeseen with respect to any use of the McGraw Hill Content.

TotalTester Online

TotalTester Online provides you with a simulation of the CAPM exam. Exams can be taken in Practice Mode or Exam Mode. Practice Mode provides an assistance window with references to the book, explanations of the correct and incorrect answers, and the option to check your answer as you take the test. Exam Mode provides a simulation of the actual exam. The number of questions, the types of questions, and the time allowed are intended to be an accurate representation of the exam environment. The option to customize your quiz allows you to create custom exams from selected domains or chapters, and you can further customize the number of questions and time allowed.

To take a test, follow the instructions provided in the previous section to register and activate your Total Seminars Training Hub account. When you register, you will be taken to the Total Seminars Training Hub. From the Training Hub Home page, select your certification from the Study drop-down menu at the top of the page to drill down to the TotalTester for your book. You can also scroll to it from the list on the Your Topics tab of the Home page, and then click the TotalTester link to launch the TotalTester. Once you've launched your TotalTester, you can select the option to customize your quiz and begin testing yourself in Practice Mode or Exam Mode. All exams provide an overall grade and a grade broken down by domain.

Other Book Resources

The following sections detail the downloadable resources available with your book. You can access these items by selecting the Resources tab, or by selecting **CAPM All-in-One Exam Guide** from the Study drop-down menu at the top of the page, or from the list on the Your Topics tab of the Home page. The menu on the right side of the screen outlines all of the available resources.

Memory Card

This full-color PDF is a copy of the trifold memory card included in the physical book and is a helpful resource for portable study. It contains critical information you must know to pass the CAPM exam. It's a great tool for studying on the go.

Flash Cards

These printable flash cards cover every term you learned in the book. All terms are aligned with the books on the CAPM Reference List. Print them out and practice, practice, practice!

Word Search Puzzles

Another great tool for reinforcing memorization of key terms in the book! Print out these puzzles and incorporate them into your study sessions. Start circling now.

Matching Exercises

Matching questions are a powerful tool for learning because they promote active engagement and memory retention. Get ready to compare and contrast.

Excel Scorechecker

Enter your end-of-chapter review scores in this spreadsheet, and you can track which chapters you need more work on and focus your study time accordingly. Maintaining the data about your performance and tracking your progress will help you in knowing the areas of improvement, and working on those areas progressively will enable you to control and ensure steady progress.

Technical Support

For questions regarding the TotalTester or operation of the Training Hub, visit **www.totalsem.com** or e-mail **support@totalsem.com**.

For questions regarding book content, visit **www.mheducation.com/customerservice**.

abusive manner   Treating others with conduct that may result in harm, fear, humiliation, manipulation, or exploitation. For example, berating a project team member in front of the team because they have taken longer than expected to complete a project assignment may be considered humiliation.

acceptance criteria   In business analysis, a set of conditions or criteria that a product or solution must meet to be accepted by the customer or stakeholders. Acceptance criteria are used to define the requirements and expectations for the product or solution and to ensure that it meets the needs of the business and end users.

acceptance test–driven development (ATDD)   Testing approach that considers the perspective of the customers, developers, and testers. The test is written before the coding, and then the developers create code to pass the known test.

active listening   The message receiver restates what's been said to understand fully and confirm the message; this provides an opportunity for the sender to clarify the message if needed.

active problem-solving   The ability to understand the problem, identify a viable solution, and then implement a solution. Active problem-solving begins with problem definition. Problem definition is the ability to discern between the cause and effect of the problem. Root-cause analysis looks beyond the immediate symptoms to the cause of the symptoms, which then affords opportunities for solutions.

actual cost (AC)   For predictive, the actual monies the project has required to date. For agile, the cost of the work actually completed in the iteration.

adaptive leadership   Leadership style of a leader who is able to adjust their approach to match the needs of their environment. Such leaders challenge people, pushing them out of their comfort zones, letting people feel external pressure and conflict in order to effect change.

adaptive project management   An iterative and flexible approach to managing projects that emphasizes the need for continuous adaptation and evolution in response to changing circumstances, customer feedback, and emerging requirements. It is a project management methodology that prioritizes collaboration, communication, and agility, enabling teams to quickly adapt to new challenges and opportunities as they arise.

affiliative leadership   Leadership style of a leader who focuses on building strong relationships and leveraging those relationships to get things done. Affiliative leaders tend to have highly developed social skills and are very good at building networks across the organization.

361

agile earned value An adaptation of the traditional project management practice of measuring actual value of cost, schedule, and scope against a baseline plan using earned value management (EVM) formulas.

agile mindset Prioritizing work on the most important items first and understanding and accepting that change is likely to happen in the project.

agile project management A flexible approach to project management that relies on iterations of project work to create value in product deliverables for the project customers. Agile is change-driven, and work is based on a prioritized product backlog. Agile projects are knowledge work projects, such as software development.

AgilePM Project management framework developed as a subset of the Dynamic Systems Development Method (DSDM) and designed to provide a more focused approach to agile project management. AgilePM is based on the principles of DSDM, but it has been streamlined to provide a more accessible and practical approach to agile project management. AgilePM also provides more specific guidance on project management practices, such as risk management, planning, and governance.

assertive leadership Leadership style of a leader who is active, direct, specific, and honest. Assertive leaders respect themselves, require respect from others, and respect everyone they work with at all levels.

assumption Something that is believed to be true or false but has not yet been proven to be true or false. Assumptions that prove wrong can become risks for the project.

authentic leadership Leadership style of a leader who knows who they are, what they believe in, what their values are, and what their priorities are. Authentic leaders ensure that their words align with their actions in order to build trust.

autocratic leadership Leadership style of a leader who retains most of the authority, gives orders to subordinates, and expects that subordinates should give complete obedience to the orders issued. In this type of leadership, the decisions are taken by the leader without consulting others. Autocratic leadership is characterized by the control of an individual over the decisions that impact a group with little to no input from group members.

backlog *See* iteration backlog, product backlog, *and* sprint backlog.

balanced matrix structure An organizational structure in which organizational resources are pooled into one project team, but the functional managers and the project managers share the project power.

behavior-driven development (BDD) Based on acceptance test–driven development but uses the Five Whys approach to really understand why a feature is to be included in the product. The Five Whys approach asks the question "why?" several times. Each question leads to another question, forming a chain of cause-and-effect that gradually gets closer to the root cause.

benefits management plan   A project management plan that defines how the project will create, maximize, deliver, and sustain the benefits provided by a project or program.

budget at completion (BAC)   Refers to the total estimated cost of a project. It is calculated by adding up the costs of all the individual tasks or activities that need to be completed in order to deliver the project. BAC is used to track the project's budget over time. It can be compared to the actual cost of the project to see if the project is on budget. If the actual cost is more than the BAC, the project is over budget. If the actual cost is less than the BAC, the project is under budget.

burndown chart   A downward-trending chart that shows the number of user story points in the product backlog in relation to how many user stories the team can create in each iteration. As more iterations happen and the team completes the user stories, a downward-trending line shows fewer and fewer user stories remaining in the backlog, and this reveals a trend for velocity and expectations about when the project can realistically complete all the user stories.

burnup chart   An upward-trending chart that shows the number of user story points in the product backlog in relation to how many user stories the team is able to create in each iteration. As more iterations happen and the team completes the user stories, an upward-trending line shows the accumulation of user stories accomplished and the remaining story points in the backlog. This chart also reveals a trend for velocity and expectations about when the project can realistically complete all the user stories.

business analyst (BA)   An individual who works as a liaison among stakeholders to understand the structure, policies, and operations of an organization and to recommend solutions that enable the organization to achieve its goals.

business case   A document that examines the objectives, cost, benefits, strategic goals, constraints, and assumptions of a project and provides justification for an organization to approve the project.

business requirements   The high-level objectives or goals that a business seeks to achieve through a proposed project or initiative. Business requirements are used to define the overall purpose and scope of the project and to establish a clear and measurable set of outcomes for the business.

business rule   A statement that describes a specific aspect of the organization's operations, such as a policy, regulation, or guideline. Business rules are used to guide and govern the behavior of the organization and its employees.

cause-and-effect diagram   A graphical representation of a known and identified effect and the potential causes of the effect. Also called a fishbone or Ishikawa diagram. One of the seven basic quality tools.

change agent leadership   Leadership style of a leader who is able to set a direction for change and lead change. This type of leader is aware of the psychology of people and how to engage stakeholders and staff in order to gain buy-in and overall momentum toward significant change.

charismatic leadership Leadership style of a leader who is motivating, has high energy, and inspires the team through strong convictions about what's possible and what the team can achieve. Positive thinking and a can-do mentality are characteristics of a charismatic leader.

check sheet A standardized list of activities, processes, and steps that need to be completed during quality management activities. One of the seven basic quality tools.

coercive (punitive) power Coercive power is a form of positional power that is based on the threat or use of punishment.

communications management plan A project management subsidiary plan that defines the stakeholders who need specific information, the person who will supply the information, the schedule for the information to be supplied, and the approved modality in which to provide the information.

conflict of interest A situation in which a project manager may have two competing duties of loyalty. For example, purchasing software from a relative may benefit the relative, but it may do harm to the performing organization.

conscientiousness The quality of a project management professional who makes all reasonable efforts to be reliable, thoughtful, prepared, and informed.

consensus leadership Leadership style of a leader who makes a decision only after consulting the group members. A decision is not made final until all the members agree to support the decision.

constraint A restriction or limitation that affects the project's ability to meet its objectives and deliver the desired results. Constraints can be internal or external and can impact the project's scope, schedule, budget, quality, or resources.

continuous flow approach A way of working that emphasizes the continuous and uninterrupted flow of work through the development process. It is a Lean approach that focuses on minimizing waste and maximizing efficiency by eliminating delays and bottlenecks in the workflow.

continuous integration (CI) A software development practice in which team members frequently integrate their work with the main codebase, usually multiple times a day. The goal of CI is to reduce integration problems by detecting and resolving integration issues as soon as possible.

contract A formal agreement, usually in writing, between two or more parties that clearly defines their obligations, roles, and responsibilities.

control chart A graphical representation of data points mapped over time against an expected mean or average; upper and lower control limits. One of the seven basic quality tools.

cost baseline   A "time-lapse exposure" of when the project monies are to be spent in relation to cumulative values of the work completed in the project. The cost baseline shows the aggregated costs of all the work packages within the work breakdown structure (WBS).

cost of conformance to quality   The cost associated with the monies spent to attain the expected level of quality, such as the cost of training, complying with safety issues, and purchasing the appropriate equipment and materials, which all contribute to the expected levels of quality.

cost of nonconformance to quality   The cost associated with not satisfying the quality expectations. The cost of nonconformance to quality is also known as the *cost of poor quality* or the *cost of failure*.

cost performance index (CPI)   Computes the percentage of how costs are over or under budget for work accomplished. The formula is CPI = EV / AC. A value of 1 means the project is exactly on budget. *See also* actual cost (AC) *and* earned value (EV).

cost variance (CV)   The computed variance of actual cost from the cost baseline. The formula is CV = EV – AC. *See also* actual cost (AC) *and* earned value (EV).

cultural norms   The culture and the styles of an organization, such as work ethics, hours, view of authority, and shared values. Cultural norms can affect how the project is managed.

culture shock   A feeling of uncertainty and disorientation when you are initially immersed in an unfamiliar way of life in a different culture than your own culture.

cumulative flow diagram   A stacked chart that shows the total number of items in each phase of the project, such as the backlog, development, testing, and release. This chart can be used to identify too many items in work in progress (WIP) and bottlenecks in the project.

cycle time   In agile, the time it takes to complete a single unit of work, such as a user story or a bug fix. Cycle time is measured from the time the work is started to the time it is completed and delivered. It is a key metric in agile because it can help teams to understand how efficient they are. A shorter cycle time means that the team is able to deliver work more quickly, which can lead to faster time to market and increased customer satisfaction.

daily scrum   A short and focused meeting held by the scrum team every day. The purpose of the daily scrum is to facilitate communication and coordination among team members, ensuring that everyone is aware of the progress made and the challenges faced in achieving the sprint goal.

data model   A visual representation of the data entities, relationships, and attributes that are used to represent a business domain or system. A data model is used to define the structure and format of the data that is stored and processed by an organization or system.

decomposition   The technique of breaking down high-level descriptions into their component parts. When used in the creation of a WBS, decomposition is used down to the work package level.

DEEP   An acronym for detailed, estimable, emergent, and prioritized, a concept used in business analysis to describe the characteristics of a well-defined requirement.

definition of done (DoD)   The qualifications that are needed and defined for a product, user story, or increment of a product to be considered done. It's important to define what constitutes "done" for each item in the product backlog, such as passing a specific test.

definition of ready (DoR)   A set of criteria that a user story or backlog item must meet before it can be considered ready to be worked on by the development team during the upcoming sprint or iteration.

democratic leadership   Leadership style of a leader who encourages each team member to participate in decision-making by sharing their opinions. A democratic leader encourages open conversation, helps their project team members to set goals and evaluate their own performance, and motivates them to grow. Also called shared leadership or participative leadership.

development team   The team that is responsible for sizing the requirements of the product backlog and getting work done in each sprint. The development team is self-organizing, self-led, and its members are called generalizing specialists because they can often do more than one function on the team. An ideal scrum team has no fewer than five people and no more than eleven people.

dignity   The quality of being worthy of respect and esteem as human beings and right bearers in the world.

diligence   The quality of being dedicated, careful, conscientious, and consistently committed to one's best effort in being a professional project manager.

directive leadership   Leadership style of a leader who guides the team's work goals and establishes the path by which they can achieve those goals. Directive leadership sets clearly defined objectives and rules for team members.

Disciplined Agile (DA)   An agile methodology that provides a flexible and pragmatic approach to software development, with a focus on customer value, simplicity, pragmatism, and continuous improvement. It emphasizes a process goal-driven approach, as well as scaling Agile to the enterprise level.

dispersed leadership   Leadership style of an organization in which leadership is embraced by everyone in the organization. Successful leadership in an organization cannot reside solely in the top of the organization. Today's world is a complex, fluid, dynamic environment. Organizations need leaders at every level of the organization from the bottom to the top.

duration The amount of time required to complete a project task or activity. It is an estimate of the elapsed time between the start and end of an activity, excluding non-working time such as weekends, holidays, and planned downtime.

duty of loyalty A project manager's responsibility to be loyal to another person, organization, or vendor with whom the project manager is affiliated. For example, a project manager has a duty of loyalty to promote the best interests of their employer rather than the best interests of a vendor.

Dynamic Systems Development Method (DSDM) One of the predecessors of today's agile project management, relies on a business case to show value and a feasibility study to determine if the development team could create the architecture and requirements the customer identified. DSDM provides more structure than rapid application development (RAD), utilizes iterations, and is a great approach when working with vendors as part of your agile project. DSDM also offers a unique approach as it can be blended with Scrum, PRINCE2, and other project management approaches.

earned value (EV) A technique for measuring project performance and progress. It is a way to measure how much work has been completed against the plan. Earned value is calculated by multiplying the budget for all completed work by the percentage of work that is complete.

earned value analysis (EVA) A technique used in project management to track and evaluate project progress based on the budget and schedule. EVA compares the actual cost and progress of the project against the planned cost and progress to determine whether the project is on track, behind schedule, or over budget.

elicitation The process of gathering and documenting requirements from stakeholders and subject matter experts. Elicitation involves using a variety of techniques and tools to identify, clarify, and document the needs and expectations of stakeholders.

emotional intelligence The ability of a project manager to recognize, understand, and manage their own emotions and the emotions of others in the project team.

enterprise environmental factor (EEF) A condition that affects how the project manager may manage the project. EEFs may be internal to the organization, such as a policy, or may be external to the organization, such as a law or regulation. *See also* external enterprise environmental factors *and* internal enterprise environmental factors.

epic In agile, a large body of work that can be broken down into smaller, more manageable tasks, or user stories. Epics are often used to represent a complex feature or functionality that spans multiple teams or sprints.

estimate at completion (EAC) The expected total cost of completing the project. The formula is EAC = BAC / CPI. *See also* budget at completion (BAC) *and* cost performance index (CPI).

expert power A type of personal power where the project manager has deep skills and experience in a discipline (for example, years of working in IT helps an IT project manager better manage IT projects).

external enterprise environment influences Influences external to the organization that can enhance, constrain, or have a neutral influence on project outcomes. Examples are state of the economy, changes in government policies, etc.

Extreme Programming (XP) Agile project management approach that uses iterations, pair programming, collective code ownership, and an XP coach to complete the user stories of the product backlog. XP also utilizes test-first programming, where tests are created and then the code is written to pass the recently created test.

facilitated workshop A meeting in which a facilitator guides a group of people through a structured process to achieve a specific goal. The facilitator is responsible for keeping the group on track, ensuring that everyone participates, and helping the group to reach consensus.

feasibility study An assessment of the practicality of a project or system to uncover the strengths and weaknesses of an existing business or proposed venture objectively and rationally.

feature/function A distinct capability or behavior of a software system that provides value to the user or customer. A feature or function can be thought of as a specific requirement or piece of functionality that the software system is expected to provide.

feature-driven development (FDD) An iterative approach to software development that bases its progress on the clients' values of features the software will provide. FDD is an agile approach that utilizes a product backlog to complete the project work but follows a more rigid approach to agile project management than other approaches.

fishbowl window Method to engage multiple participants in a focused discussion, while people outside the fishbowl are listeners only.

flowchart A tool for showing in graphical form the steps in a process. One of the seven basic quality tools.

functional requirements Describe what the system or product is expected to do or accomplish. Functional requirements specify the features, functions, and capabilities that are required to meet the needs of the end users and are typically described in terms of inputs, processes, and outputs. Examples are data inputs and outputs, user interface, audit tracking, etc.

functional structure An organization that is divided into functions, where each employee has one clear functional manager. Each department acts independently of the other departments. A project manager in this structure has little to no power and may be called a project coordinator.

governance framework   Describes the rules, policies, and procedures that people within an organization abide by. This framework addresses the organization, but it also addresses portfolios, programs, and projects. Regarding portfolios, programs, and projects, the governance framework addresses alignment with organizational vision, risk management, performance factors, and communications.

histogram   A tool for showing amount or frequency of a variable. Also called a bar chart. Histogram is one of the seven basic quality tools.

hybrid agile approach   Choosing the best parts of several different agile approaches and melding them together into a new homegrown version of Agile that works for the organization. A hybrid agile approach enables an organization to build a customized approach to project management. Hybrid can include traditional methodologies, such as planning in detail up front, and can then implement Scrum, Kanban, Lean, or XP practices thereafter.

hybrid structure   An organization that creates a blend of the functional, matrix, and project-oriented structures.

incremental approach   A software development methodology that breaks down the project into smaller, more manageable increments. Each increment is developed and delivered to the customer as a working product. This allows the customer to get feedback early and often and to make changes as needed.

information power   A type of personal power where the project manager has power and control of the data gathering and distribution of information.

interactional leadership   Leadership style that is a hybrid of transactional, transformational, and charismatic leadership. The interactional leader wants the team to act, is excited and inspired about the project work, yet still holds the team accountable for their results.

internal enterprise environment influences   Influences internal to the organization that can arise from the organization itself, a portfolio, a program, another project, or a combination of these. They include artifacts, practices, and internal knowledge, such as lessons learned and completed artifacts from previous projects.

INVEST   A simple mnemonic to remember an accepted set of criteria to assess the quality of a user story, which should be independent, negotiable, valuable, estimable, small, and testable. These criteria help product owners to properly specify the product backlog requirements (e.g., epics, features, and user stories).

Iron Triangle of Project Management   A theoretical model based on the characteristics of scope, schedule, and cost, which each constitute one side of the triangle. If any side of the Iron Triangle is not in balance with the other sides, the project will suffer. Also known as the Triple Constraints of Project Management, as all projects are constrained by scope, schedule, and cost.

issue   An event that has happened, that reoccurs, or that is going to happen that will likely disrupt the project.

issue log   A document that lists and describes issues that have been identified and the status of those issues.

iteration   *See* sprint/iteration.

iteration backlog   A collection of work items that a team plans to complete during an iteration, which can be a timeboxed period of any length, such as a week, two weeks, or a month. Iteration backlog is a term commonly used in agile approaches such as Kanban, where sprints are not typically used and instead work is planned in iterations. The iteration backlog lists the prioritized work items, which can include features, user stories, bugs, and technical tasks that the team plans to complete during the iteration.

iteration planning   A core practice in agile methodologies that is used to plan and manage the work that will be done during an iteration or sprint. *See also* sprint/iteration.

Kaizen   An organizational approach for managing resources. Kaizen posits that small changes in processes are easier to accept and incorporate than large, sweeping changes for the organization or project.

Kanban   A framework to show the backlog of work items and the flow of the items through columns to the delivery point. Kanban aims to be transparent and to limit the work in progress (WIP), and it is known as a pull system because work is pulled from the left into the workflow on the right.

Kanban board   The primary characteristic of Kanban is the Kanban board, which is where its name comes from; Kanban means visual signal. The Kanban board shows the flow of work through the system so that you can visualize where the team is in the process, how the team delivers work, what work exists, and any limits to the work in progress (WIP). Requirements are written on sticky notes or cards and are moved from the backlog to the different phases of the project to represent where the requirement currently is in the project life cycle.

Kanban method   Visualizes project work on a Kanban board, which enables the team to see the progress of the work and pull the work through the flow. As new work items are needed, they are added to the "to-do" column in the board. Any team member who is available and competent can start a work task, and the task flows through the system and is documented on the Kanban board.

laissez-faire leadership   Leadership style of a leader who takes a hands-off approach to the project. This means the project team makes decisions, takes initiative in the actions, and creates goals. While this approach can provide autonomy, it can make the leader appear absent when it comes to project decisions.

lead time   Negative time that allows two or more activities to overlap where ordinarily these activities would be sequential. In a predictive, plan-based project, lead time is used when scheduling activities. In an agile project, lead time describes the total duration a feature took from the moment it was requested by the customer until the developers created the feature for the customer.

leadership   Aligning, motivating, and inspiring the project team members to do the right thing, build trust, think creatively, and challenge the status quo.

Lean   A project management methodology originally used in manufacturing environments that has been adapted into agile software production environments. IT teams work in a three-phase cycle of building, measuring, and learning. This approach creates a partnership mentality between the development team and the customers to ensure that the work being done is in constant alignment with the business value goals of the customers. Lean aims to reduce waste and boost productivity.

Lean product development (LPD)   A methodology for product development that emphasizes waste reduction, continuous improvement, and customer satisfaction. The goal of LPD is to develop products that meet the needs of the customer while minimizing waste and unnecessary costs.

legitimate power   A form of positional power that is based on the perception that the person who has the power has a right to exercise it.

management   Utilizing positional power to maintain, administrate, control, and focus on getting things done without challenging the status quo of the project and organization.

media selection   Choosing media based on the audience and the message being sent.

meeting management   A form of communication that involves how the meeting is led, managed, and controlled to influence the message being delivered. Agendas, minutes, and order are mandatory for effective communications within a meeting.

milestone   A significant point or event in the project's progress that represents an accomplishment in the project. Projects usually create milestones as the result of completing phases within the project.

milestone list   A list that details the schedule milestones and their attributes. It is used for several areas of project planning but also helps determine how quickly the project may be achieving its objectives. The milestone list is in the WBS dictionary.

minimum business increment (MBI)   The smallest possible deliverable unit that provides some value to the customer and can be independently deployed, tested, and validated. MBIs are often used in agile methodologies to break down larger features or projects into smaller, manageable pieces that can be completed and delivered more efficiently.

minimum viable product (MVP)   A product development strategy used in agile methodologies to deliver a functional product with the minimum set of features required to meet the needs of early adopters or early customers. It is a process that involves creating and releasing a product with basic functionalities to gather feedback and validate assumptions before investing significant resources in further development.

MoSCoW   An approach used in agile methodologies to help teams prioritize requirements and focus on delivering the most critical features first. The acronym MoSCoW stands for:

- **Must have**   These are requirements that are essential for the project's success and must be included in the final product.
- **Should have**   These are important requirements that are not critical but should be included if possible.
- **Could have**   These are nice-to-have requirements that are not critical and can be considered if time and resources allow.
- **Won't have this time**   These are requirements that will not be included in the final product, either because they are not important or because they are not feasible.

nonfunctional requirements   Conditions that do not directly relate to the behavior or functionality of the solution, but rather describe the manner or technical characteristics in which the functional requirements are provided and operate when implemented as capabilities. Examples are speed, security, appearance, taste, etc.

operations   The processes and activities required to maintain and support the project's products or services after the project has been completed. Ongoing operations are the means by which the benefits of the project are sustained over time.

organizational knowledge repository   The databases, files, and historical information that project managers can use to help better plan and manage their projects. This organizational process asset is created internally by an organization through the ongoing work of operations and other projects.

organizational process assets (OPAs)   Organizational processes, policies, procedures, and items from a corporate knowledge base. OPAs are grouped into two categories: processes, policies, and procedures; and organizational knowledge repositories. OPAs are always internal to the organization.

organizational system   A system in which multiple components are used to create things that the individual components could not create if they worked alone. The structure of the organization and the governance framework create constraints that affect how the project manager makes decisions within the project. The organizational system directly affects how the project manager utilizes their power, influence, leadership, and even political capital to get things done in the environment.

outcome   An end result or consequence of a process or project. Outcomes can include outputs and artifacts, but have a broader intent by focusing on the benefits and value that the project was undertaken to deliver.

pair programming   XP approach where developers work in pairs; one person codes while the other checks the code. The pair switches roles periodically. *See also* Extreme Programming (XP).

Pareto diagram   A diagram that illustrates the problems by assigned cause, from largest to smallest. One of the seven basic quality tools.

peer review   A review of a project performed periodically by peers (with similar experience to project personnel), who are independent from the project, to evaluate technical, managerial, cost and scope, and other aspects of the project, as appropriate.

planned value (PV)   The work scheduled and the budget authorized to accomplish that work. PV = percent complete of where the project should be.

PMI member   Anyone, whether certified as a project manager or not, who has joined the Project Management Institute.

PMI Talent Triangle   Defines three areas of PDUs for PMI-certified professionals to maintain their certification: Ways of Working, Power Skills, and Business Acumen. *See also* professional development units (PDUs).

portfolio   Projects, programs, subsidiary portfolios, and operations managed as a group to achieve strategic objectives.

practitioner   In the context of project management, a person who is serving in the capacity of a project manager or contributing to the management of a project, portfolio of projects, or program. For example, a program manager is considered to be a project practitioner under this definition.

predictive, plan-based project management   A traditional project management approach that plans and predicts everything that is to occur within the project. Predictive, plan-based project management is based on a clearly defined project scope and project plan and is resistant to change. Predictive, plan-based is sometimes called *plan-driven* or described as a *traditional (waterfall) approach*.

presentation   In formal presentations, the presenter's oral and body language, visual aids, and handouts, all of which influence the message being delivered.

pressure-based power   The project manager can restrict choices to get the project team to perform the project work. Pressure-based power can be effective in the short term, but it is not sustainable in the long term. This is because people who are pressured into doing something are not likely to be motivated to do it well or to do it again in the future.

process manager   The person who evaluates current business processes and designs, tests, and implements new processes to improve efficiency, profitability, and performance.

process owner   The person who is solely responsible for owning a process, accountable for designing an effective and efficient process, using the right people and financial and technical resources to run the process, and delivering quality outcomes as required within the organization.

product   Anything that can be offered to a market to solve a problem or to satisfy a want or need. Products can be physical, like furniture or clothing, or digital, like an app or a video feature on a website.

product backlog   In Scrum, an agile document that comprises a comprehensive list of all items, features, and user stories the customer wants delivered in the project. The product owner is responsible for maintaining and prioritizing these requirements, ranking them from the most significant to the least significant. The development team then retrieves the prioritized items from the product backlog to incorporate them into their work iteration, known as a sprint. The product owner holds the responsibility of managing the product backlog.

product manager   The person who identifies the customer's need and the larger business objectives that a product or feature will fulfill, articulates what success looks like for a product, and rallies a team to turn that vision into a reality.

product owner   A role on a Scrum team that is responsible for the product's success. The product owner seeks to maximize a product's value by managing and optimizing the product backlog. They are responsible for ensuring that the product meets the needs of the customer and that the development team is working on the right features.

product roadmap   A high-level strategic plan that outlines the vision, direction, priorities, and progress of a product over time. It's a plan of how the project will move from start to finish, with intermittent deliverables to the stakeholders. It answers what conditions must be met to allow the product owner to do a release, what the components of a release are, and the result of the project. It's a plan of action that aligns the organization around short- and long-term goals for the product or project and how they will be achieved. The product roadmap is a big picture of the functionality of deliverables and the product vision. The product roadmap is a way of keeping your team and your stakeholders involved and keeps focus on the project result.

product scope   The characteristics and functions of a product or service. It is a high-level description of what the product will do and how it will work. The product scope is typically defined by the product owner, who is responsible for ensuring that the product meets the needs of the customer.

professional development units (PDUs)   Credit for education and project management–based experiences that are earned after the CAPM to maintain the CAPM certification. CAPMs are required to earn 15 PDUs per three-year certification cycle. Of the 15 PDUs, a minimum of 9 hours must come from educational opportunities with a minimum of 2 PDUs in each skill area of the PMI Talent Triangle.

program   Related projects, subsidiary programs, and program activities that are managed in a coordinated manner to obtain benefits not available from managing them individually.

progressive elaboration   A process of iteratively defining and planning work to be done on a project. The project manager and the project team start very broadly— typically with a project's concepts—and then refine the concepts with details, studies, and discussion until a project scope statement is formed.

project   A temporary endeavor undertaken to create a unique product, service, or result. The temporary nature of projects indicates a beginning and an end to the project work or a phase of the project work. Projects can stand alone or be part of a program or portfolio.

project charter   The foundational document for the project; provides political and financial support for the project. The project charter is like the birth certificate for a project. You need it to prove the project exists and to provide basic but extremely important information about the project. The information it contains is generally quite high level; it is the first document developed in an iterative process, so it won't contain enough information to complete a WBS.

PART III

project initiation   The process of defining the purpose, scope, and objectives of a new project and getting it off the ground. It involves defining the problem or opportunity, conducting a feasibility study, identifying stakeholders, defining the project scope, developing a project charter, and obtaining approval to proceed.

project life cycle   The series of stages that a project passes through from its initiation to its closure. The project life cycle provides a framework for managing a project, including the definition of the project, the planning and execution of project activities, and the monitoring and control of project performance.

project management   The application of knowledge, skills, tools, and techniques to project activities to meet project requirements. Project management refers to guiding the project work to deliver the intended outcomes. Project teams can achieve the outcomes using a broad range of approaches (e.g., predictive, hybrid, and adaptive).

project management office (PMO)   A management structure that standardizes project-related governance processes and facilitates the sharing of resources, tools, methodologies, and techniques. A PMO coordinates the activities of all the project managers by providing improved project management in terms of scope, schedule, cost, quality, risk, and other factors. Its primary goal is to create a uniform approach to how projects operate within the organization.

project manager   The person assigned by the performing organization to lead the project team that is responsible for achieving the project objectives. Project managers perform a variety of functions, such as facilitating the project team work to achieve the outcomes and managing the processes to deliver intended outcomes.

project team   A set of individuals performing the work of the project to achieve its objectives. The team is typically led by a project manager, who is responsible for ensuring that the project is completed on time, within budget, and to the required quality and value standards.

project-oriented structure   An organizational structure that assigns a project team to one project for the duration of the project life cycle. The project manager has high to almost complete project power.

prototyping   A technique of producing an example of the finished product, service, or result to seek feedback from stakeholders.

RACI chart   A type of responsibility assignment matrix (RAM) that identifies team members and activities to be completed and defines whether the team members are responsible, accountable, consulted, or informed. There can be no more than one "A" in each row.

refactoring   The process of improving the design or structure of existing code without changing its external behavior. It is an important practice in agile software development because it helps to improve the quality, maintainability, and scalability of the codebase and to reduce technical debt.

referent power   A type of personal power where the project manager is respected or admired because of the team's past experiences with the project manager. This is about the project manager's credibility in the organization.

release   A version of the software product that is ready to be deployed to users or customers. A release can contain new features, bug fixes, and improvements that have been developed and tested by the development team.

requirements traceability matrix (RTM)   A table that links the origins of individual product requirements to the expected deliverable that meets those requirements so that the project manager can track requirements throughout the project life cycle.

retrospective   *See* sprint retrospective.

reward power   A form of positional power that is based on the ability to give rewards to others. This type of power can be based on tangible rewards, such as money or promotions, or on intangible rewards, such as praise or recognition.

risk register   The central repository for all project risk information. It includes the identified risks, the potential responses, the root causes of risks, and any identified categories of risk. It's updated throughout the project as risk management activities are conducted to reflect the status, progress, and nature of the project risks.

rolling wave planning   A project planning technique that breaks down the project into smaller, more manageable increments. Each increment is planned in detail, but the details of later increments are only planned to a high level. This allows the project team to adapt to changes as the project progresses. Rolling wave planning uses waves of planning, then executing, and is a characteristic of adaptive projects.

Scaled Agile Framework (SAFe) An agile methodology that provides a framework for implementing agile practices at scale in organizations. SAFe is designed to help organizations achieve better alignment, collaboration, and delivery of value across multiple teams, departments, and business units.

scatter diagram A tool for graphically representing the results of two variables. You can use a scatter diagram to help visualize the correlation between the dependent variables, such as the project's budget, against the independent variables, such as errors in the project, changes to the project, and any delays stakeholders may have caused to the project. One of the seven basic quality tools.

schedule baseline An "approved" version of the project schedule that never changes, but new baselines can be set and created. The schedule baseline is the "plan." A new schedule baseline is created only through the process of an approved change request.

schedule performance index (SPI) Computes the percentage of how costs are over or under budget for work planned. The formula is SPI = EV / PV. A value of 1 means the project is exactly on schedule. *See also* earned value (EV) *and* planned value (PV).

schedule variance (SV) The computed variance of actual schedule completion against the schedule baseline. The formula is SV = EV – PV. *See also* earned value (EV) *and* planned value (PV).

scope baseline Includes the project scope statement, the work breakdown structure (WBS), and the WBS dictionary. It defines the scope of the project, the deliverables, and the project objectives. Any changes to the scope must be approved through the project's change control process.

Scrum An agile approach to project management whereby the development team accomplishes prioritized work in defined iterations, called sprints, and then the work is reviewed and demonstrated before moving on to the next sprint. Its goal is to deliver value as quickly as possible to the project customers.

scrum master An individual who serves the team by removing roadblocks, protecting the development team from distractions, ensuring that all members are following the scrum rules, and coaching and educating stakeholders on scrum practices. The scrum master acts as a servant leader to the team by getting the team what they need to be successful. The scrum master facilitates scrum meetings, helps the product owner refine the backlog, and communicates the vision of the project to everyone that's involved.

scrum of scrums A type of meeting in a large project involving several scrum teams in which a representative from each scrum team discusses the project's progress, impediments, and if any work may affect other scrum teams. Rather than having a huge daily scrum, the teams meet separately and then a representative from each team meets in a scrum of scrums to report on each team's progress. The team representatives answer the same questions as in the daily scrum, but for the team rather than individuals. In addition, a fourth question is often posed: Will our team be putting something in another team's way?

PART III

scrum team   A work team that includes the product owner, the scrum master, and the development team. The typical project management activities are divided among these three roles in a scrum project.

sender-receiver model   Model of communication in which multiple avenues exist to complete the flow of communication from sender to receiver, but barriers to effective communication may be present as well.

servant leadership   Leadership style of a leader who puts others first and focuses on the needs of the people they serve. Servant leaders provide opportunity for growth, education, autonomy within the project, and the well-being of others. The primary focus of servant leadership is service to others.

simulation   Imitating the operation of real-world processes or systems with the use of models to represent the key behaviors and characteristics of the selected process or system.

situational leadership   Leadership style that is based on the idea that there is no single leadership style that is effective in all situations and that the best leaders are able to adapt their style to suit the specific needs and development level of the people they are leading.

solution requirements   Specific characteristics that a product must have to meet the needs of the stakeholders and the business itself. Example: The solution must be able to process 1000 transactions per second.

soul-based leadership   Leadership style based on the old concept that every living being on board a ship or a plane is considered a soul rather than an inanimate object. Every soul is important and treated with value. As a leadership style, this requires the incorporation of concepts like inclusiveness, equality, and autonomy. Everyone that works for you is a unique individual with something of value to offer. In the current state of the smart machine age, this also differentiates people from machines.

spike   A timeboxed activity that is used to explore a particular technical or design issue. It is a small experiment or investigation that is conducted by the development team to help them better understand a problem or potential solution before committing to a larger, more complex implementation.

sponsor   The person who provides financial and political support for the project, appoints the project manager, and authorizes the project charter.

sprint backlog   In Scrum, the specific set of user stories, bugs, or features that a development team commits to completing during a sprint. It is a plan for the work that needs to be done in the upcoming sprint and typically includes estimates for each item. The sprint backlog is created during the sprint planning meeting, and it guides the team's daily work throughout the sprint.

PART III

sprint planning meeting   A scrum meeting attended by the product owner, development team, and the scrum master to determine the amount of work that can be accomplished in the sprint based on the prioritized items in the backlog, the duration of the sprint, the complexity of the work, and the size of prioritized requirements. This determination is based on estimates of the items in the product backlog and past sprints. The selected items from the product backlog become the sprint backlog and the goal of the sprint.

sprint planning meeting duration   The sprint planning meeting, at the start of each sprint, should last up to eight hours for a four-week sprint. Shorter sprints will have shorter planning sessions.

sprint retrospective   A meeting held at the end of each sprint to reflect on what went well, what could be improved, and to make plans for the next sprint. It is a core part of the Scrum framework, and it is an opportunity for the team to learn from their experiences and to improve their process. The sprint retrospective is typically held after the sprint review and before the sprint planning meeting for the next sprint. This allows the team to reflect on the work that was done in the sprint and to make plans for the next sprint based on what they learned.

sprint review   A scrum ceremony at the end of the sprint during which the development team demonstrates for the product owner, the scrum master, and other key stakeholders what has been completed in the sprint. This is a four-hour meeting for a four-week sprint. Shorter sprints will have shorter sprint review sessions. Only completed items are demonstrated in the sprint review. This review is an opportunity for the product owner to offer feedback on whether the work has reached the definition of done, specify what, if anything, is missing, and elaborate on corrections or modifications for the increment of work created.

sprint/iteration   A predefined time period for the product owner, scrum master, and development team to complete a cycle of scrum activities, including planning, execution, reviewing, and improvement. The sprint duration is usually two to four weeks, though it can be as little as one week.

stakeholder register   A register of all project stakeholders and information about their interest in the project, the power they have to influence the project, their expectations, and how their expectations will be managed.

stakeholder requirements   A classification of requirements that defines decisions about business needs, goals, and objectives from the perspective of the stakeholders and their role in the business.

story map   A method of arranging user stories to create a more holistic view of how they fit into the overall user experience. It helps teams to understand how users interact with a product or service, from the beginning to the end. Story maps are often used in agile development, but they can be used in any type of project.

story mapping   A technique used to visually organize and prioritize the user stories or features of a software product. It is a collaborative approach that helps teams to build a shared understanding of the product and its requirements and to develop a roadmap for the development process.

story points   In Agile project tracking, story points are used as a relative estimation tool rather than an absolute measurement of time or effort. This allows for greater flexibility and adaptability in the project management process. User story points are assigned to user stories in relation to the size of the user stories. Story points are a subjective measure that considers the complexity, effort, and uncertainty of a task. Story points are a way to estimate the complexity and effort required for individual stories.

story point sizing   A relative approach to sizing user stories based on the complexity of the user story in relation to other user stories in the product backlog. The team may use a variety of factors to estimate the story points, such as the complexity of the story, the amount of research required, and the risk associated with the story.

strong matrix structure   An organizational structure in which organizational resources are pooled into one project team and the functional managers have less project power than the project manager.

supportive leadership   Leadership style of a project manager who does not simply delegate tasks and receive results but instead supports a team member until the task's completion. A major upside to supportive leadership is that the manager will work with the employee until they are empowered and skilled enough to handle tasks with minimal supervision in the future.

technical debt   Sloppy code, shortcuts, and redundancies that need to be cleaned up as the project moves forward. Technical debt can accumulate and cause the project code to become more complex.

test-driven development (TDD)   Development approach that writes acceptance tests before the code is written so the developers know what it takes to pass the acceptance test and can program accordingly.

timeboxed approach   A method of working that limits the amount of time that is allocated to a specific task or activity. The goal of timeboxing is to create a sense of urgency and focus and to ensure that work is completed within a defined period of time.

transactional leadership   Leadership style of a leader who emphasizes the goals of the project and offers rewards and disincentives to the project team. This is sometimes called management by exception because it's the exception that is rewarded or punished.

transformational leadership   Leadership style of a leader who inspires and motivates the project team to achieve the project goals. Transformational leaders aim to empower the project team to act, be innovative in the project work, and accomplish through ambition.

transition requirements   A classification of requirements that facilitate transition from the current state (as is) to the desired future state (to be), but that will not be needed once that transition is complete.

transparency   The practice of sharing information with all stakeholders throughout the project life cycle. This includes sharing information about the project's goals, progress, risks, and challenges. Transparency helps to build trust and confidence among stakeholders, and it can help to identify and resolve problems early on.

transparency, inspection, and adaptation (TIA)   Three principles incorporated into all approaches to agile project management. *Transparency* requires trust, agreement, and open communication throughout the project. *Inspection* is the review of the artifacts, the progress, and the quality of the work. *Adaptation* is needed when issues arise. In other words, if the solution is not going to be acceptable, fix the problem.

Triple Constraints of Project Management   *See* Iron Triangle of Project Management.

user story   Used in Scrum, a story of a role utilizing some functionality to get value from the functionality. User stories follow a formula: "As a <role>, I want <function>, so I can realize <value>." User stories are written from the customer's perspective and describe a feature of the product you're creating. User stories are the items kept in the product backlog, are a small chunk of functionality, and generally take up to 40 hours to create. User stories are prioritized by the product owner.

value   The worth, importance, or usefulness of something. Different stakeholders perceive value in different ways. Customers can define value as the ability to use specific features or functions of a product. Organizations can focus on business value as determined with financial metrics, such as the benefits less the cost of achieving those benefits. Societal value can include the contribution to groups of people, communities, or the environment.

velocity   The number of user story points a development team can complete during a sprint. Velocity helps predict the duration of the project. Velocity may vary widely at first but normalizes after several sprints.

verbal abuse   Language (including that used in online communication) that demeans, humiliates, or insults. Verbal abuse is a type of emotional abuse because it may cause the victim emotional, cultural, or spiritual harm. Given that project managers work with people of many cultures and beliefs, it is important to recognize that personal remarks about appearance, behavior, language, beliefs, religious practices, and so on may be distressing. Behaviors such as sarcasm, teasing, swearing, or threatening are examples of behaviors that may be considered verbal or emotional abuse.

virtual structure   A structure that uses a network to communicate and interact with other groups and departments. A point of contact exists for each department, and that person receives and sends all messages for their respective department.

visionary leadership   Leadership style of a leader who has a clear idea of what they want to do and how they plan to accomplish it, along with the strength to pursue it.

weak matrix structure   An organizational structure in which organizational resources are pooled into one project team and the functional managers have more project power than the project manager.

work breakdown structure (WBS)   A hierarchical decomposition of the project broken down to work package level. This structure should be used to identify all the activities that need to be completed.

work breakdown structure (WBS) dictionary   A document providing additional information about each node in a WBS. The milestone list would be found in your WBS dictionary.

work in progress (WIP)   The current focus of the project team, the tasks that are currently being undertaken. In Kanban environments, WIP is frequently employed to limit the number of work items that can be introduced into the workflow, preventing the team from being overwhelmed or creating impediments. This limit on work items entering the system aims to avoid bottlenecks and maintain a manageable workload for the team.

work package   A unit of work within a project that can be assigned to a single person or team. It is the smallest unit of work that can be estimated, tracked, and controlled in a project. The lowest level of the WBS.

XP   *See* Extreme Programming (XP).

XP coach   XP role that is similar to a project manager; a mentor or a facilitator. The coach coaches people on the project team, helps get things done, and serves as the hub of communications for the project stakeholders.

INDEX